PLAGUES, POISON
AND POTIONS

MANCHESTER
UNIVERSITY PRESS

SOCIAL AND CULTURAL VALUES IN EARLY MODERN EUROPE

Series editor
Paolo L. Rossi
Department of Italian Studies
University of Lancaster

In its exploration of the cultural and social upheavals in early modern Europe, this series crosses traditional disciplinary boundaries. It offers a broad-ranging analysis of the forces which shaped structures of belief and practice at all levels of society, providing original insights into the mentality of early modern Europeans.

The volumes assess the manner in which central as well as peripheral values, institutions and disciplines evolved and, through this identification of metamorphoses, seeks to redefine the mechanics of change and to re-evaluate the meanings of a central or hegemonic culture.

Individual titles address many neglected or emerging subject areas, incorporating the history of the less studied countries of Eastern Europe. In so doing, the contributors examine a vast range of source material, including literary, historical, scientific, philosophical and artistic evidence.

Other titles in the series:

PLAGUES, POISONS AND POTIONS

PLAGUE-SPREADING CONSPIRACIES IN THE WESTERN ALPS
c. 1530–1640

William G. Naphy

Manchester University Press

Manchester and New York

Distributed exclusively in the USA by Palgrave

Copyright © William G. Naphy 2002

The right of William G. Naphy to be identified as the author of this work has been
asserted by him in accordance with the Copyright, Designs and Patents Act 1988.

Published by Manchester University Press
Oxford Road, Manchester M13 9NR, UK
and Room 400, 175 Fifth Avenue, New York, NY 10010, USA
http://www.manchesteruniversitypress.co.uk

Distributed exclusively in the USA by
Palgrave, 175 Fifth Avenue, New York,
NY 10010, USA

Distributed exclusively in Canada by
UBC Press, University of British Columbia, 2029 West Mall,
Vancouver, BC, Canada V6T 1Z2

British Library Cataloguing-in-Publication Data
A catalogue record for this book is available from the British Library

Library of Congress Cataloging-in-Publication Data applied for

ISBN 0 7190 4640 8 *hardback*
      0 7190 4641 6 *paperback*

First published 2002
10 09 08 07 06 05 04 03 02   10 9 8 7 6 5 4 3 2 1

Typeset in Bembo
by Servis Filmsetting Ltd, Manchester

Printed in Great Britain
by Biddles Ltd, Guildford and Kings Lynn

CONTENTS

LIST OF TABLES

SERIES EDITOR'S FOREWORD

The Black Death of 1347, though a calamitous epidemic, was but one of the many outbreaks of plague to hit Europe since the pandemic of the sixth century A.D.[1] Plague struck down its victims without regard to wealth or social status. A bacterial infection caused by the *Yersinia pestis* bacillus, the plague attacked in three forms – bubonic, septicaemic, and pneumonic.[2] It is difficult for us to imagine the fear and panic that must have spread through town and country at the news of a fresh outbreak. Plague originated in the East (where it is still endemic) and can be transmitted by the rat flea (*Xenopsylla cheopis*), and the human flea (*Pulex irritans*). If a person suffering from bubonic plague also develops pneumonic plague then the bacillus can be passed by spittle or mucus. Septicaemic and pneumonic plague are particularly lethal and can cause death within the day.

We have only become aware of the true cause of bubonic plague since the 1890s. Early theories saw causes in: astral conjunctions; the passing of comets; unusual weather conditions; miasmas caused by a great explosion in the East that could affect the humours; noxious exhalations from the corpses on battlefields; person-to-person contact linked to the movement of people such as merchants, travellers and beggars; contact with infected merchandise.[3] Plague was associated with sin, and accepted as a manifestation of divine ire. It was also linked to the poor (the plague was even seen by some as Nature's way of controlling their numbers), and measures were put in place to oversee their movements, and to isolate them in times of pestilence.[4]

Given the mistaken aetiology it is hardly surprising that the precautions taken were not fully effective. At times remedies increased rather than prevented infection. For instance the killing of cats and dogs only allowed the population of rats to increase. The towns of northern Italy, where Public Health Boards were established, led the way in the battle to control the plague. Initially these were set up *ad hoc* in response to particular outbreaks, but eventually, due to the frequent recurrence of plague, they became permanent committees. Measures against the plague included: evacuation of plague sufferers (usually the poor) to huts; the setting up of plague hospitals; the hiring of doctors to cope with the numbers of the sick, and of cleaners for infected houses; disinfection, fumigation, and the burning of infected clothing and bedding; quarantine of those who had come into contact with victims (richer citizens were allowed to remain shut up in their own homes); the restriction of movement at borders, and the hiring of night-watchmen to control incoming goods and travellers; forbidding citizens who had visited places of plague to enter the city under pain of death.[5] People also sought salvation in wondrous medicines such as theriac, and other concoctions which belong to the mystical world of alchemy with such names as *pulvis imperialis, domina medicinarum, manus Dei, oculus Christi, nobilissima medicina, a morte liberans.*[6]

The link between plague and the gods in Homer was echoed in Christian beliefs. These connected plague to Evil, and thereby to the activities of the Devil's followers. The *Malleus Maleficarum* stated that the category of witches that can injure, but not cure, is the most powerful category, and these can cause all the plagues which other witches can only cause in part, 'when the justice of God permits such things'.[7] The mechanism for plague spreading was to make up powders, or an unguent containing an infectious substance(s). Nicolas Rémy wrote in 1545, 'Since it is not convenient for them [witches] to keep this powder ready in their hand to throw, they have also wands imbued with it or smeared with some unguent or other venomous matter.'[8] Rémy makes a distinction between plague spreading by witches which was person specific, and plague spreading by others which was indiscriminate. The ointment did not affect everyone but only those 'whom the witch wishes to injure', whereas others who spread the plague 'strike those whom you least wish to harm'.[9] According to Rémy the witch can only effect her poison due to the 'hidden ministry of the Demon, which does not appear but works in secret'.[10] Rémy makes an important distinction, between demon aided and non-demon aided plague-spreading.[11] Deliberate plague-spreading seems to have been widespread and entered into folk memory. Manzoni, when discussing the plague of Milan in the *Promessi Sposi*, writes of: 'Poisonous arts, diabolical operations, conspiracies of people bent on spreading the plague by contagious venoms or by black magic.'[12] He hints at different categories of plague spreaders using different means to spread the deadly contagion. Other accounts give descriptions of the ingredients used for these powders and unguents; some are composed of natural substances (including some part from an infected corpse), while others are made with the connivance of a demon or the Devil.

It was a desire to clarify the precise nature of the themes listed above, and how they were viewed and tackled in sixteenth-century Geneva, that gave rise to this volume. It is a study, based on a detailed scrutiny of the available archival sources, which in the first part raises fundamental issues about how the authorities of Geneva perceived the plague, and the measures and remedies effected to combat and to mitigate its deadly virulence. The second part focuses on deliberate plague spreading and its relationship to witchcraft. Initially plague spreading in Geneva seems to have been related to conspiracies undertaken for financial gain. Later it was conflated with witchcraft, practised independently, and aimed maliciously at specific individuals. William Naphy unravels the complex interactions of legal, social, political and religious forces that underpinned the accusations and convictions. His sensitive and thorough assessment of these features should act as a warning against arriving at sweeping, general conclusions without evaluating all the evidence.

NOTES

1 There are descriptions of earlier outbreaks. Homer in the opening lines of the *Iliad* was possibly describing bubonic plague as it spread via Apollo's arrows: 'It was Apollo, Son of Zeus and Leto, who started the feud [...] by inflicting a deadly plague on [Agamemnon's] army and destroying his men [...] Day and night innumerable fires consumed the dead. For nine days the god's arrows rained on the camp.' Homer, *The Iliad* (Harmondsworth, 1966), pp. 23–4. For St Sebastian as a plague saint and arrows in the Christian tradition, see C. M. Boeckl, *Images of Plague and Pestilence* (Kirksville, 2000), pp. 46–56. For angels with spears, and demons with arrows, see V. I. J. Flint, *The Rise of Magic in Early Medieval Europe* (Oxford, 1991), pp. 115, 163, 240.

2 For a full discussion of the medical aspects of plague and iconography, see Boeckl, *Images of Plague*, pp. 7–32.

3 'People[...] were more addicted to prophecies and astrological conjunctions, dreams and old wives tales.' D. Defoe, *A Journal of the Plague Year* (Oxford, 1990), p. 21, also pp. 24–7. For Miasmas see C. M. Cipolla, *Miasmas and Disease. Public Health and the Environment in the Pre-Industrial Age* (New Haven, 1992).

4 For attitudes to the poor see C. M. Cipolla, 'The plague and pre-Malthus Malthusians', *Journal of European Economic History*, 3 (1974): 277–84; A. G. Carmichael, *Plague and the Poor in Renaissance Florence* (Cambridge, 1986); B. Pullan, 'Plague and perception of the poor in early modern Italy', in *Epidemics and Ideas. Essays on the Historical Perception of Pestilence,* eds T. Ranger and P. Slack (Cambridge, 1992), pp. 101–23; D. McNeil, 'Plague and social attitudes in Renaissance Florence', in A. Paravicini Bagliani and F. Santi, eds, *The Regulation of Evil. Social and Cultural attitudes to Epidemics in the Late Middle Ages* (Florence, 1998), p. 142.

5 See Carmichael, *Plague and the Poor*, p. 112.

6 C. Crisciani and M. Pereira, 'Black Death and Golden Remedies', in A. Paravicini Bagliani and F. Santi, eds, *The Regulation of Evil*, p. 37.

7 *Malleus Maleficarum*, trans. M. Summers (London, 1967), p. 55.

8 Written in 1545 by Nicolas Rémy, see A. C. Kors and E. Peters, eds, *Witchcraft in Europe 1100–1700. A. Documentary History* (Philadelphia, 1999), p. 241.

9 A. C. Kors and E. Peters, eds, *Witchcraft in Europe 1100–1700*, p. 244.

10 A. C. Kors and E. Peters, eds, *Witchcraft in Europe 1100–1700,* p. 245.

11 In his discussion of plague spreading in Milan and Geneva, Levack does not make this distinction, 'Like other sorcerers, plague spreaders were accused of worshipping the Devil and of acting collectively; thus they became indistinguishable from witches', B. P. Levack, *The Witch Hunt in early Modern Europe* (London, 1995), p. 131

12 A. Manzoni, *The Betrothed*, trans. B. Penman (Harmondsworth, 1987), p. 578.

ACKNOWLEDGEMENTS

It is almost impossible even to begin contemplating the number of persons and organisations to whom this work is indebted. Obviously, the help, assistance and patience of archivists in Annecy, Bourg-en-Bresse, Chambéry, Dijon, Geneva, Lausanne, Lyon, Milan, Neuchâtel and Turin was both welcome and crucial. I was greatly assisted by the comments and support of the Universities of Aberdeen and Manchester as well as the long-suffering editors at Manchester University Press. In various ways I was assisted by the British Academy, the Carnegie Trust for the Universities of Scotland, the Economic and Social Research Council and the Wellcome Trust for the History of Medicine. Other academics, too numerous to name, are owed individual and personal thanks and will, in due course, receive them. However, I take great pleasure in the necessity of acknowledging my great debt to Paolo Rossi for his unstinting work on this text as editor. All errors and infelicities that remain are mine and exist despite his best efforts. Finally, but not least, I take great pleasure in thanking the Antognazza family, who kindly allowed me to stay in their home near Milan while researching in that city.

W.G.N.
Aberdeen

ABBREVIATIONS

ACC   Archives communales de la Côte-d'Or (Dijon)
ACCh   Archives communales Chamonix
ACV   Archives cantonalles de Vaud (Lausanne)
ADA   Archives départmentales de l'Ain (Bourg-en-Bresse)
ADHS   Archives départmentales de la Haute-Savoie (Annecy)
ADR   Archives départmentales du Rhône (Lyon)
ADS   Archives départmentales de Savoie (Chambéry)
AEG   Archives d'État de Genève
AEN   Archives de l'État de Neuchâtel
AJLL   Archives judiciaires de Le Landeron
AJN   Archives judiciaires de Neuchâtel
AMC   Archives municipales de Chambéry
AML   Archives municipales de Lyon
ARG   *Archiv für Reformationsgeschichte*
ASM   Archivio di Stato di Milano
AST   Archivio di Stato di Torino
AVL   Archives de la ville de Lausanne
BB   Série BB (Archives communales antérieures à 1790)
BML   Bibliothèque municipales de Lyon
Boyve   J. Boyve, *Annales historiques du Comté de Neuchâtel et Valangin* (Neuchâtel, 1854–58), five volumes
MDG   *Mémoires et documents publiés par la Société d'histoire et d'archéologie de Genève*
MJLL   Manuels de justice de Le Landeron
MJN   Manuels de justice de Neuchâtel
P&P   *Past & Present*
PC   Procès criminels (series 1 and 2)
PCN   Procédures criminelles de Neuchâtel
PCSS   Procédures criminelles du Senat de Savoie
PH   Pièces Historiques
Processi G. Farinelli and E. Paccagnini, eds, *Processi agli Untori* (Rome, 1988)
PS   Pubblica Sanità
R Const   Registres de Consistoire
RC   Registres du Conseil
Rivoire   E. Rivoire, V. van Berchem *et al.*, eds, *Registres du Conseil de Genève* (Geneva, 1900–40), thirteen volumes
SCJ   *Sixteenth Century Journal*

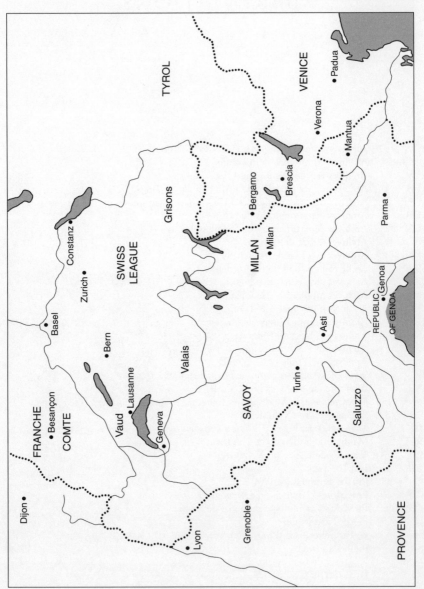

Map of the western Alpine region

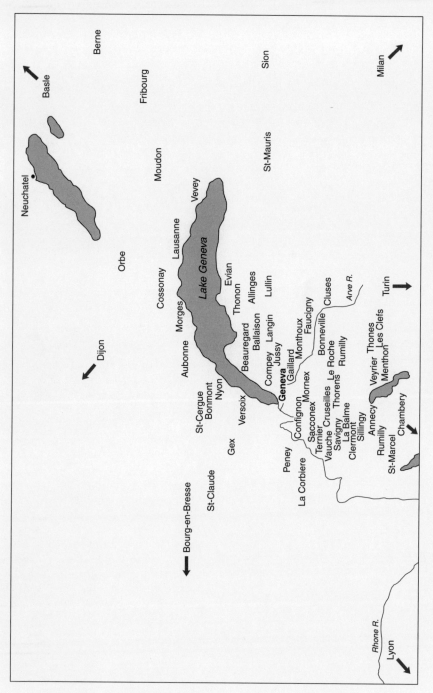

Geneva's locale

INTRODUCTION

There are few aspects of world history between the Roman Empire and the French Revolution that one can assume most people will know. Inevitably, the Black Death probably heads the list. Almost every single person will, at least, have heard about this great epidemic that ravaged Europe in the mid-fourteenth century. Indeed, many will know that the Great Plague of London in the mid-seventeenth century was the same disease. However, few will be aware that this disease struck most urban communities on a regular basis in the intervening three centuries. For the first 150 years the plague returned almost every decade and carried away as much as 20–5 per cent of the population of the towns and cities of Western Europe. In the subsequent 150 years (and more) the pestilence returned every twenty or so years, still killing a fifth to a quarter of the urban crowds. Moreover, this horrific disease was still able to carry away up to 50 per cent of a city's population even as it disappeared from Europe; in 1720 Marseilles lost half its citizenry in a year to the plague.

Thus, plague remains one of the most enduring and best-known realities of the pre-modern world. The Black Death, as the first blast of this pestiferous trumpet, has been raised to iconic status while almost any new and unknown fatal disease is referred to as a plague. Modern societies, beset by vCJD, HIV/Aids, *E. coli*, ebola, BSE, antibiotic-resistant TB and Asian flu, among others, are constantly told that one of them may replicate the devastation of the Black Death. The enduring life of the image of speedy death arises from the immense ability of the disease to kill quickly and in large numbers. In the first half-century after the Black Death, the overall population of Western Europe declined by half. Nor was the disaster confined to the West: the disease ravaged the whole of the eastern hemisphere, carrying off similar proportions of humanity in North Africa, the Middle East and as far afield as China. It is hardly surprising, therefore, that plagues, epidemic diseases and the Black Death remain some of the most fascinating aspects of world history before the French Revolution.

It is just as likely that most people will have heard of the witchcraft trials of late medieval and early modern Europe. Witch hunting, like plague and the Black Death, has become a stock phrase used to describe many modern events. Prosecutions or persecutions that appear to target any individual or group with unseemly enthusiasm and questionable justification are called a 'witch hunt'.

Bizarrely, this past tragedy has survived and become embedded in the modern consciousness while the pogroms and massacres of Jews in the course of the fifteenth century are not especially well known (perhaps having been obliterated by the more horrific manifestations of twentieth-century antisemitism). Regardless of any explanations of why some dramatic events of the past survive into modern memory while others disappear, witchcraft and the persecution of witches have made that transition from past event to folk memory.

Coupled with this common knowledge of witchcraft are various assumptions about how witches were prosecuted. For example, there are constant references to the use of water to discover a witch. The 'urban myth' is that a woman was thrown into a river and deemed guilty if she floated but innocent if she sank (and drowned). The result was a Catch-22 that effectively meant the death of most defendants. Of course, this memory is in part correct but mangled by a complete misunderstanding of trial by ordeal. Indeed, it is skewed on two fronts. First, there is no awareness that the water test was decided quickly and those who sank were pulled from the river by the rope attached to them. Since most people thrown fully dressed into water will sink, one might argue that this test was more likely to result in acquittal. Likewise, modern awareness has preserved this particular example of trial by ordeal while failing to realise that it was but one test among many in a system that, at one point, was very widely used and accepted as a much surer way of deciding guilt or innocence than relying on circumstantial evidence or a single accusation.

One other aspect of late medieval and early modern society that has survived to become a living feature of the modern mind is the Inquisition, especially in its Spanish incarnation. Coupled with awareness of the institution (though with little information beyond the name) is the knowledge that torture was (or so one is led to believe) a major investigative tool used by the Inquisition. The result is that most people have a belief that trials of this period were brutal and inquisitorial. The assumption is that the use of torture meant that once a person fell into the grasp of the inquisitors a torture-induced confession and barbarous execution followed as night follows day. There is almost universal agreement that the prosecution of defendants was unfair, unjust, barbaric and dominated by the enthusiastic use of torture. Moreover, there is a belief that this torture often maimed or killed the defendant and that, in some way, the inquisitors were unconcerned about it. The place and function of judicial torture as well as the methodology of criminal justice and courts – the context of trials – have been stripped away, leaving, in isolation and misunderstanding, a single style of court (inquisitorial) and a single method of investigation (torture).

Finally, almost every person will know that women's lot was not a happy one. Most will assume that witchcraft was a crime almost wholly attached to the fairer sex. Moreover, the general population will know that these poor women, mostly elderly widows, were tortured into making confessions by a harsh, male-dominated justice system and then burnt alive at the stake for their supposed crime. Indeed, witchcraft trials bring together in the mind of the modern person most of the stray folk memories that have survived the previous five centuries. The witches are mostly female and suffer excruciating torture. The judges are relentless inquisitors bent on extracting confessions and then exacting vengeance at the stake. All that is missing from this nexus of folk memories about the late medieval and early modern period is plague and pestilence.

The conspiracies to spread plague that beset Geneva and other cities in the western Alps in the century after 1530 seem to close the circle. Modern historiography accepts that, as Monter has said, 'all of them [were] technically in league with the Devil', although even he adds an important and crucial caveat too often over- looked by those who have relied on his work. He ends the quotation just begun with 'although often lacking most of the ordinary paraphernalia of witchcraft'.[1] His careful study of the various types of witchcraft and varieties of witches that inhabited the Franco-Swiss border in the sixteenth and seventeenth centuries does rely somewhat for its findings about gender, age and marital status on evaluations of the plague-spreading phenomenon in Geneva.[2] However, at critical points in his study he offers comments that make it clear to any careful reader of his work that these same plague spreaders, or *engraisseurs* (greasers), are a group apart. For example, his appendix 'Witch Trials in Geneva, 1527–1681' studiously avoids including those arrested and prosecuted for plague spreading in 1545 and 1571.[3] In addition to this stark and obvious care in handling the *engraisseurs* he also says that it was 'a special type of witchcraft' and produced 'a special sort of panic'.[4] Finally, he is straightforward in asserting that the distinctiveness and peculiarity of plague spreading is not simply a modern historiographical construct: 'dossiers [in 1615] . . . are ambiguous as to whether a person arrested for *sorcellerie* was also an *engraisseur*'. Thus, while there is no doubt that Monter considered plague spread- ing to be a form, albeit bizarre, of witchcraft, he tried to treat this phenomenon as a category apart.[5]

Unfortunately, not all those who have relied on Monter's important work have been as careful in listening to the book's conclusions. For example, one of the leading authorities on witchcraft, Brian Levack, has made extensive use of Monter's figures on Genevan witchcraft, execution rates, gender, age and marital status.[6] While not in itself a problem, it assumes that he continues to differentiate Geneva's peculiar institution of *engraissant* (greasing) from general witchcraft. However, his one extensive comment about the behaviour seems to imply that there is hardly any distinction between a plague spreader and any other witch beyond a sort of special- isation in plague.

In addition to serving as an arena for the practice of sorcery, towns were the only places where plague spreaders [*engraisseurs*] were prosecuted as witches. Plague-spread- ers were persons who allegedly had succeeded in distilling the essence of the plague in the form of an unguent, which they then used to infect various parts of the town. Like other sorcerers, plague-spreaders were accused of worshipping the Devil and of acting collectively; thus they became indistinguishable from witches . . . plague- spreader panics represented a peculiarly urban form of witchcraft persecution.[7]

Moreover, he cites the great witchcraft authority Midelfort when he says that 'these plague spreaders were accused of both magic and devil worship and were prosecuted as witches'.[8]

However, no contemporary Genevan writer, chronicler, council minute or trial record explicitly identified plague spreading with witchcraft. Rather, it was seen as a form of conspiratorial poisoning. Although, as will be shown, there was a conflation of witchcraft and plague spreading (originally quite distinct crimes) the melding was never complete. Thus, one must wonder when the amalgamation of witchcraft and plague spreading became complete in the historiography of the phenomenon. In 1899 Doumergue published his monumental biography of Calvin. He moved from a discussion of plague spreading in Geneva to discussion of witchcraft in the village of Peney with the remark that 'sadly, the affair of the plague spreaders was followed almost immediately by that of the witches. Is there a great deal of difference between them?'[9]

Any evaluation of the plague-spreading phenomenon must, therefore, decide to what extent this behaviour and witchcraft can safely and accurately be amalgamated into a single activity. That is, is plague spreading purely and simply a sub-category of witchcraft or is it, at some fundamental level, a thing apart and different? Moreover, if the two activities have been incorrectly confused and commingled to what extent is this the result of the modern historians' handling of the events and to what extent inherent in the sixteenth and seventeenth-century view of plague spreading? This leaves some crucial questions to be answered. Is plague spreading the urban branch of witchcraft – a behaviour more frequently confined to rural areas? If the plague spreaders had managed to create essence of plague had they done so through their own inventiveness or were they guided by a demonic influence? Was their *graisse* (grease) a natural compound or a product of satanic contact as were the other powders and ointments so often associated with witches? Were plague spreaders actually accused of devil worship? Did they act collectively or individually and did this make a difference? Indeed, did the behaviour remain unchangeably distinguished by certain core features over time? Finally, did the plague spreaders become, as asserted by Levack above, 'indistinguishable from witches'?

Clearly these are important questions and how they are answered would completely alter our understanding of what was actually happening in Geneva when plague spreaders were investigated, arrested, prosecuted and executed. Thus, there is the possibility, at the very outset of this discussion, that the phenomenon under examination may differ entirely from, or at least be more complex than, the received interpretation suggests. Might it be possible to see parallels between the alterations over time in the early modern understanding of plague spreaders as the result of judicial pressure and the *benandanti* of Friuli in the hands of the Inquisition?[10]

It may be possible, though, to avoid any examination of plague spreading, since one may be inclined to question even the possibility of witchcraft. That last can be dismissed with some ease. Whether modern historians believe that witches existed or that anyone considered himself or herself a witch is not as important as the fact that the whole of medieval and early modern society certainly believed in witchcraft. In addition, this society knew what a witch was and how to identify the behaviour. Finally, it stretches credulity to breaking point to accept that the ancient world had individuals who believed themselves capable of good and bad magic as do most other pre-modern societies around the world but that, by some miracle, no one in Western Europe, least of all an elderly widow, would ever have thought themselves capable of magical powers working both good and ill. This would be all the more surprising considering that the entirety of Catholicism and Orthodoxy throughout the Middle Ages and beyond believed that priests, by certain words and rituals, were able to turn bread and wine into the very body and blood of the living Son of God. If men could believe (and presumably some still do) that they had access to such supernatural power it does not require misogyny or a credulous nature to suspect that some women might have thought they too could access powers beyond the normal ken of man (or men). As J. B. Russell said, 'without denying that many of the traits ascribed to witchcraft are physically improbable or that many of the witches condemned were innocent, one is obliged to regard witchcraft as a reality'.[11]

However, the entire process is complicated by the presence of torture in some of the trials. It is the present-day reader's response to this aspect of the criminal trial that complicates the discussion. Most people instinctively take the view that any testimony that appears in a trial that contains even the threat of torture is inherently suspect. There is an almost inherent assumption that judges used torture to force defendants to say what the judges wanted said. In such a scenario the judges would ask leading questions frequently enough for the accused to realise, whether consciously or not, what they were meant to say. Once torture was applied these subliminal hints would pour forth as confessions. While this is certainly possible one must ensure that a fair reading of the criminal records allows of so easy a dismissal of the process and the information it produced. Also, one must be aware that torture does not always, of necessity produce a lie. Were that the case there would be little point in torturing a soldier to gain militarily advantageous information about an enemy. In such a case, leading questions would, by their very nature, be counterproductive.

The context of torture must be grasped before the discussion can progress. In Roman law, as opposed to English common law, the threshold of proof was extremely high. In theory (and, indeed, in practice), guilt required either two eye witnesses or a confession. Circumstantial evidence, no matter how overwhelming, could not convict. In English common law the reliance upon a jury to weigh the validity of circumstantial evidence and to eliminate reasonable doubt made judicial torture unnecessary.[12] In effect, the Roman law system demanded not the elimination of reasonable doubt but the actual presence of irrefutable proof.

The result was that most Continental judiciaries found it difficult to convict anyone. However, the relationship between torture and circumstantial evidence solved many of these problems. Once a person was caught in a lie, or faced an unimpeachable witness (against whom no counter-charge could be made), or sufficient circumstantial evidence was present, the investigating magistrate could ask for permission to torture. Thus, once reasonable doubt had been removed (or the possible innocence of the defendant sufficiently undermined), the court could torture. It was certainly possible that the point at which a Continental judicial panel might impose torture in the early modern period was the same point at which a jury in the English system might convict – and sentence the accused to death. Also, torture was seen to have a special place in conspiracies where guilt was not the issue or the main goal of the investigators. When the court wished to discover the names of fellow conspirators, whether on the Continent or in England, torture was applied.[13] Francis Bacon made the point to James VI of Scotland and I of England that 'in the highest cases of treason, torture was used for discovery, and not for evidence'.[14] Also, *The Body of Liberties* (1641) in Massachusetts allowed the torturing of someone already convicted of a capital crime to uncover other conspirators.[15] Therefore, when examining the trials of the plague spreaders it is essential to understand when and why torture was employed. Was the emphasis on gaining a confession of guilt or on uncovering the extent of any conspiracy?

Any understanding of the plague-spreading conspiracies in the western Alps during the century after 1530 will have to overcome a number of interpretative hurdles. The role and timing of torture will be important. The type and quality of circumstantial and forensic evidence as well as eye-witness testimony will have to be assessed. The place of gender, poverty and xenophobia will have to be addressed to see to what extent, if any, the defendants were being tried less for their activities than for their personal traits of sex, status and nationality.[16] Since this period spans one of the most violent eras of religious conflict in European history, and the western Alps were one of the front lines in this conflict, the place of confessional-isation will need examination. Finally, it will be essential to understand exactly how contemporary judges, defendants, witnesses and the populace more generally understood and interpreted the phenomenon as it happened.

NOTES

1 E. W. Monter, *Witchcraft in France and Switzerland: The Borderlands during the Reform* (Ithaca NY, 1976), p. 47.
2 Monter, *Witchcraft*, pp. 116–19, though crucially he clearly omits the 1571 *engraisseurs* from his statistics.
3 Monter, *Witchcraft*, pp. 208–15. This care, no doubt, derives from Monter's awareness that even early modern contemporaries argued over the conflation of witchcraft and poisoning, with Jean Bodin chastising Johann Weyer for confusing the two in the ancient world, see E. W. Monter, 'Inflation and Witchcraft: the Case of Jean Bodin', in T. K. Rabb and J. E. Seigel, eds, *Action and Conviction in Early Modern Europe* (Princeton NJ, 1969), pp. 371–89, especially 379.
4 Monter, *Witchcraft*, pp. 44, 126.
5 He seemed to have modified his views somewhat when he wrote that 'scores of people were accused of spreading plague with *magical* [emphasis mine] grease', in his *Ritual, Myth and Magic in Early Modern Europe* (Columbus OH, 1983), p. 48.
6 B. P. Levack, *The Witch-Hunt in Early Modern Europe* (London, 1987), pp. 19–20, 132.

See also A. L. Barstow, *Witchcraze: A new History of the European Witch Hunts* (San Francisco, 1994), pp. 6–7, 23, 67–8; J. Klaits, *Servants of Satan: The Age of the Witch Hunts* (Bloomington IN, 1985), p. 143; J. B. Russell, *Witchcraft in the Middle Ages* (London, 1972), p. 240. Although working specifically on England, K. Thomas, in mentioning intentional plague spreading, might have been expected to show some familiarity with this phenomenon. Even though writing before Monter he may have known about the famous events in Milan in the seventeenth century. See his *Religion and the Decline of Magic: Studies in Popular Beliefs in Sixteenth and Seventeenth Century England* (London, 1971). Nor does Monter seem to feature in the more historiographically modern/complex but less Anglocentric D. Purkiss, *The witch in History* (London, 1996). All the more surprising since (as early as 1969) H. Trevor-Roper had identified the western Alps as one of the centres of witch hunting in his *The European Witch Craze of the sixteenth and seventeenth Centuries* (London, 1969), p. 29.

7 Levack, *Witch-Hunt*, p. 122.

8 Levack, *Witch-Hunt*, p. 154, H. C. E. Midelfort, *Witch-Hunting in South Western Germany, 1562–1684: The Social and Intellectual Foundations* (Stanford CA, 1972), pp. 122, 190–1.

9 E. Doumergue, *Jean Calvin* (Geneva, 1899), vol. 6, pp. 46–50 *passim*. Cf. J. Spon, *Histoire de Genève* (Geneva, Fabri & Barrillot, 1730; reprinted Geneva, 1976), vol. 1, pp. 201–3; J. Picot, *Histoire de Genève* (Geneva, 1811), vol. 1, pp. 405–8 (Picot makes no connection between the Peney witches and plague spreading, though he discusses them in close proximity); A. Thourel, *Histoire de Genève* (Geneva, Collin, 1833), vol. 2, pp. 199–200 (he never misses a chance to lambast superstition but confines his criticism to medical ignorance and judicial violence when discussing plague spreading); A. J. P. Pictet de Sergey, *Genève, origine et développement de cette république* (Geneva, 1847), vol. 2, pp. 458–60; J. A. Gautier, *Histoire de Genève* (Geneva, 1896), vol. 3, pp. 235–8. Almost immediately, one begins to see the impact of Doumergue's casual comment, for example, see 'The Plague Plots of Geneva', *British Medical Journal: Nova et Vetera* 2 (July–December 1907): 99–100 ('This mention of locks and dead men's limbs introduces an element of magic into the [plague-spreading] plot, which is in other respects as dull and horrible as possible') as well as Doumergue's impact on O. Pfister, *Das Christentum und die Angst* (Zürich, 1944), pp. 365–8, especially 358 n. 236. For a fuller discussion of this witch hunt see O. Pfister, *Calvins Eingreifen in die Hexer- und Hexenprozesse von Peney 1545 nach seiner Bedeutungen für Geschichte und Gegenwart* (Zürich, 1947).

10 See C. Ginzburg, *Night Battles* (London, 1992).

11 Russell, *Witchcraft*, p. 22.

12 The English jury did not need certain proof, only persuasion. J. H. Langbein, *Torture and the Law of Proof* (Chicago, 1977), p. 80. This is an excellent and highly detailed account of the place of torture in Roman law. See also L. Chevalier, *Recherches sur la réception du droit romain en Savoie* (Annecy, 1953).

13 When Frederick the Great outlawed judicial torture in 1740 he retained it for treason and murder, where 'many culprits are implicated whose involvement has to be discovered'. Langbein, *Torture*, p. 62.

14 Langbein, *Torture*, p. 90.

15 Langbein, *Torture*, p. 151.

16 No minor concern. See P. Desan, 'Nationalism and History in France during the Renaissance', *Rinascimento* 24: 261–88.

CHAPTER ONE

GENEVA, PLAGUE AND THE
FIRST CONSPIRACY

To make themselves rich

Before beginning to discuss the actual events of 1530, the first appearance of the plague-spreading phenomenon, it is perhaps worth while considering Geneva's previous experiences of plague. In this the historian is fortunate, as Geneva possesses extremely good records for the fifteenth and early sixteenth centuries. Prior to the revolution and accompanying religious Reformation of 1535, Geneva's city council minutes were kept in Latin.[1] These minutes were published in a monumental critical edition of thirteen volumes by a team of historians led by Émile Rivoire and Victor van Berchem between 1900 and 1940.[2]

The council minutes begin on 26 February 1409 and are extant thereafter except for significant lacunae for the years 1418–27, 1451–56, 1458, 1463–72 and 1479.[3] That is, for the years 1409–1535 (the date of the revolution), the minutes for ninety-eight years survive while twenty-eight years' are lacking. However, the bulk of the lacunae are before 1473 and after 1479 the minutes are complete. In itself, this represents a significant and important body of records for any examination of official and governmental responses to plague.

There is, however, a second collection of documents which may serve as a useful source for evaluating not only the public responses to plague but also the success of the government's initiatives for preventing, containing and eliminating plague. These are the records of the criminal courts. It is here that citizens and residents may be seen attempting to avoid, thwart or undermine the council's edicts and efforts. An initial survey of the number of trial records surviving would give one cause to expect that this might prove a very rich source indeed. The two series of trial records preserve over 600 cases for the period *c.* 1390–1535. Sadly for the purposes of this study, none of these cases relates to plague until the first conspiracy to spread plague in 1530.

Thus, although the overall number of records is substantial, the council minutes are, in fact, the only significant source available for studying Genevan reactions to plague prior to 1535. Despite the obvious problems posed by this limitation, namely that this gives a very élite bias to the account, one can get some idea of how the city and its citizenry responded to the recurring problem of plague and epidemic disease throughout the fifteenth century.[4] The lacunae make it difficult to speak with certainty of the first three-quarters of the century but for the six decades after 1472 one can speak with increasing confidence.

From the very earliest surviving records it is obvious that the Genevan authorities were concerned with the same issues of sanitation, public health and disease control seen elsewhere in southern Europe. Although these records made no specific references to plague or epidemic disease, there are sufficient comments to allow one to infer that much of the official interest was proceeding from experience of the Black Death and later bouts of plague.[5] Thus, Geneva evidences that the city's magistrates were following the best practices for dealing with the disease being developed in northern Italy.[6] For the purposes of this study, the discussion that follows will highlight two significant factors. First, Geneva's methods and practices for coping with plague are in no way unique. Second, these same methods and practices show a close connection between Geneva and the urban city-states of northern Italy.[7]

In August 1409 the city government implemented controls on animals, markets and refuse. More specifically it commented on the need to prevent the sale of 'infected beasts'.[8] At year's end the city banned Jews from selling meat, although they were permitted to trade in 'whole animals'.[9] It is possible that this may be connected with the growing pan-European pogrom against Jews as plague spreaders.[10] It is, however, just as likely that it is simply an expression of a more general, economically motivated antisemitism. The magistracy followed these edicts with an investigation in 1410 to examine their implementation *vis-à-vis* pigs and refuse.[11]

One may judge the success (or failure) of these efforts by the continual need to re-state edicts and conduct periodic inspections. However, the frequency with which the city returned to these matters also highlights the importance the government put upon good and safe hygiene in the city's production of food, especially meat. Thus, in July 1411, the council again discussed waste disposal. [12] Six years later, the city licensed Mermet Juilliermi to dump refuse at the Water Gate.[13] Also, despite the previous restrictions on Jewish butchers, it is clear that Jews were still present in the city, as the city made a payment to one for services rendered.[14] However, within a decade, the city purchased the 'House of the Jews', which may imply that Jews were much less numerous if not wholly absent from Geneva.[15] A subsequent edict forbidding Jews to be 'dispersed throughout the city' would imply that the Jews were not only present but also becoming too integrated into the community for the comfort of the councillors.[16]

In 1428, the city's records preserve more detailed discussions about food sanitation and a much keener interest in the butchers' trade. In October, the city ordered that a specific area 'outside the walls' in Plainpalais should be designated as a slaughter area.[17] The following month, the city set out four specific ordinances for the regulation of the slaughter ground. First, the meat industry (butchers and merchants) were themselves financially responsible for the maintenance of the buildings. Second, meat could be sold only at set, 'accustomed' times. Third, no refuse from the trade (blood and offal) was to be spilt in the streets (presumably during the transport of the meat from slaughterhouse to shop).[18] Finally, all franchises and rights previously granted to these merchants *within* the city would apply equally *outside* the city in the slaughter area. Clearly these measures were not successful for long, as the next year saw decrees forbidding the gutting of carcasses in the city as well as selling beyond the legal times (i.e. after ten o'clock in the morning).[19]

Decrees were clearly not enough; the government began to impose fines for violations. In addition, the city tried to control not only the presence of animal carcasses and slaughtering in the city, but also the keeping of live animals. In 1430, legislation was passed imposing a three sols fine on anyone allowing pigs to roam the streets; they were to be kept in pens.[20] Indeed, throughout the century, every aspect of animal husbandry was a concern. A few further examples will suffice. In 1458, the city conducted an inspection of butchers' shops and laid special stress on the need to sell meat only from the accustomed shops (i.e. those known and inspected). A stiff fine of forty sols was imposed for any infringements.[21] So concerned was the city that the following year it decreed that the regulations were to be repeated and obeyed 'point by point'.[22] However, the city was also distressed to hear that the meat trade might be the victim of malfeasance. It discovered that the keeper of the Rhône Bridge was hindering the movement of sheep.[23] Despite supporting the meat provisioners on this occasion, the Senate was still forced to reiterate the edicts regulating the trade.[24] Similar attempts were made to regulate the fish trade.[25] Thus, the city took both a proactive and reactive role in controlling and regulating the livestock trade.

In 1460, the city also seems to have decided on a solution to the problem of waste disposal. Most of the Senate's meetings in March and April were dominated by discussions about the problem.[26] By May, the magistrates had began the process of establishing a civic dumping ground in the vicinity of the slaughterhouse.[27] Although the issue of waste disposal had wider implications, it appears that the city was most concerned about the waste generated by the meat trade. Thus, stress was laid on the disposal of ordure, blood, skins and entrails. However, it would be incorrect to conclude that Geneva paid scant regard to hygiene as it related to humans. In fact, as one would expect from a city-state in close contact with northern Italy, Geneva was just as troubled by two sanitation concerns specifically aimed at the populace: clean water and latrines.

In 1410, the Senate ordered the building and repair of the city's latrines as well as forbidding the construction of any 'malodorous edifice'.[28] Clearly the question of finances was raised, as the city was soon forced to concede that the treasury would have to pay for the work on the latrines.[29] More repairs were ordered the following year.[30] The magistrates returned to the problem of latrines in 1429 and also noted that dirty water discharged from houses was causing the city's walls to 'putrefy'.[31] Certainly, this interest in latrines was purely reactive. The government acted when the situation required but seems not to have maintained any systematic approach to repair and maintenance. In 1459 and 1460, the Senate was forced to react to the condition of the latrines, which had 'fallen into ruin'.[32]

Geneva also faced the problem of fresh, safe water with a similar mix of edict, private provision and state funding. For example, in 1442 the city began discussing the relocation of a fountain and the digging of a well before the house of Pierre d'Ambers.[33] Within a month, the Senate returned to the fountain that was to be moved from the Water Gate to Longemale 'so it can be more useful for the common good'.[34] The same fountain, and most certainly the well at d'Ambers', was still a cause of discussion in 1457.[35] The year 1460 saw a more concerted, and expensive, attempt by the magistracy to provide a safe and reliable water supply for the city. Private initiative was still important, however, and saw Claude Boniface digging a well in his property, partially for 'communal use'.[36] Nevertheless, these individual acts were clearly not sufficient. In March, an official from Avignon was consulted about piping water from the lake to the city.[37] Two months later, the city paid a Jew, named 'master Gabriel', the enormous sum of 800 écus to construct twelve fountains and supply them with piped water.[38] Later the same year, the city set aside an additional 100 écus for work on fountains.[39]

There are clearly some constant features in the approach adopted by the state in dealing with issues of sanitation and hygiene. The magistrates were obviously interested in sanitation but in a sporadic and primarily reactive manner. Certainly, there was no creation of permanent (or even temporary) health boards. This is perhaps not surprising, as Geneva was relatively small (no more than 10,000 inhabitants in the fifteenth century and perhaps 12,000 by the middle of the next century). Also, the remit of the Senate hardly ran much beyond the walls of the city and its suburbs. It is arguable, therefore, that the city had little need for a well developed bureaucracy. However, the presence of the Bishop's administration may be a better explanation for the adoption of Italian-style regulations without the creation of the bureaucratic structures which developed in Italy at the same time. The city did not seem to rely on Books of the Dead, medical examinations of sudden deaths, health boards, etc.[40] Of course, the Genevan political structure did not allow for this degree of bureaucratic sophistication. The magistrates might be able to micromanage Geneva's sanitation and hygiene but they were politically unable to make appropriate alterations to the state structure. Geneva, it is important to recall, may well be seen as a merchant-dominated city-state with regard to local matters. However, it was, in fact, a prince-bishopric and the (absentee) Bishop was not inclined radically to overhaul the city's administration or to allow a significant increase in the bureaucratic power of the elected, local magistracy.[41]

This magisterial ability to control local matters is also evident in the provision of a regular, and affordable, supply of bread and wine. As early as 1409, Geneva was controlling wine prices and the circumstances in which wine could be sold.[42] Similar regulations relating to wine were passed consistently in the fifteenth century.[43] Although similar concerns are evident about bread prices (and grain availability) there is also official concern about the quality and type of the bread produced. For example, the city, in 1416, set the price of white bread at 3s 6d and dark bread at 4s 8d.[44] Prices were again fixed during a period of dearth in 1430.[45]

Indeed, grain shortages often spurred the state to act both over bread prices and over bread quality. During a severe grain crisis in 1457, the city imposed licences on bakers and forbade them to make white bread.[46] The magistracy also inspected the weights and prices and insisted that officials should weigh loaves on a regular basis to ensure that customers were not being cheated.[47] Similar official action was noted earlier during times of dearth in 1417 and, again, in 1428 to help the 'miserable people'.[48] Again, one sees a government actively involved in the minutiae of city life but almost entirely in a reactive manner. In other words – and this will be crucial in understanding the state's response to conspiratorial plague spreading after 1530 – Geneva's magistrates responded to problems. They rarely if ever sought them out. One major exception exists to this general observation. The Senate was pro-active and preventative in dealing with the danger of fire; the magistrates made repeated inspections of the city's houses to ensure they were safe.[49] The records also record one notable prosecution of an arsonist.[50]

Finally, it is worth discussing the provision of hospitals in the city. It is hardly surprising that a prince-bishopric had a number of such institutions. Monastic orders most often owned and operated them. More important for the discussion of plague, these buildings were not used in plague outbreaks. Indeed, they would be more accurately viewed as hospices (for orphans, the elderly and the disabled) or hostels (for pilgrims). So, despite their lack of importance in the provision of care during a period of epidemic disease, the hospitals nevertheless were important institutions for the delivery of long-term health care. Geneva certainly appears to have been well supplied, with five mentioned in the minutes before 1460: Pont-du-Rhône, St-Jorius, St-Mary Magdalene, St-Bernard and St-Bolomerius.[51]

What is missing from the previous discussion, however, is any treatment of plague itself. We can infer much from the records about Geneva's increasing adoption of Italian approaches to sanitation, hygiene and animals, yet there is no specific mention of plague. It would, clearly, be an error to assume that Geneva was plague-free before 1459, when the minutes mention the disease. What is more likely is that the occurrence of plague is contemporaneous with the extensive lacunae in the records during this early period.

The reality is that we know little of Geneva's early experiences of plague (*pestis*), as the council minutes preserve no mention of the disease until February 1459. In that year, Jean Triollet and Jean Roguet submitted a report to the Senate relating to various expenses they had incurred, which were being questioned by the government.[52] Part of their response gave the 'plague, which has flourished for many years' as a mitigating factor.[53] This may seem to imply that plague had been a feature of the immediate past, a recurring problem in the past, or was actually present in 1459. However, the second mention of the disease, in July 1459, makes it possible to infer that the disease was probably not actually present in the city but that it had occurred recently, perhaps in the previous year(s). The lack of records for 1458 may therefore be explained by the presence in Geneva of a severe outbreak of plague. The fact that the epidemic is not mentioned in 1457 further supports the conclusion that Geneva suffered an attack of plague in 1458.

In July 1459, the city paid Pierre Lardet and Jean Collomb three florins for part of a lease on a barn held 'during [the] plague time' by Humbert Perodi.[54] In the same month the council seems to have been concerned about the burdens imposed on the city by their overlord, the Duke of Savoy, which the city was incapable of meeting because of the plague.[55] Also, although the city may not have been struck in 1457, it certainly began to prepare for an imminent attack of the disease. In March, prostitutes were herded off the street and into the city's semi-official brothel, where the 'queen' of the harlots could control them. The city, although it disapproved of prostitution in the sense of streetwalking, had little problem with the trade when it operated from a recognised brothel. For example, in 1428, the Prior of St-Victor, the Franciscan monastery, complained about the location of the nearby brothel. The Senate responded that the site had been carefully chosen as it was 'more suitable and less reprehensible' than the alternatives, and there the brothel would remain.[56] However, those who continued to ply their trade on the streets were to be sent to the 'island', the city prison in the Rhône.[57] In May, lepers were forced from the streets as well.[58]

It is essential to introduce a cautionary note at this point. Although these measures are relevant to concern about health and plague, action by the state cannot always be interpreted through medical and sanitary lenses. For example, apothecaries were prohibited from opening their shops on Sundays or during major festivals. This can hardly be seen as a positive move in a city preparing for plague. However, as the move was coupled with identical legislation against moneychangers, it is clear that it had little if anything to do with health concerns.[59] That is, some moves which may have had an impact on health, sanitation, medicine and plague are better understood as deriving from other socio-economic or religious concerns.[60]

That said, the regulations against prostitutes and lepers were much more specifically connected with plague and health, and the connection was made explicit at the time. The year 1459 saw numerous edicts against prostitutes. These were primarily concerned with ensuring that their activities were confined to specific houses. Thus, houses and rooms could not be legally rented to (single) women except in 'the accustomed place'.[61] In addition, prostitutes were ordered to work only in 'accustomed places'.[62] Earlier in the year the city had clearly identified its unholy trinity of social and sanitary undesirables: lepers, mendicants, harlots.[63] Both lepers and beggars found themselves facing the same intrusive levels of social control as the prostitutes. For example, lepers and those suspected of leprosy were to be examined and were ordered 'to separate themselves from those not infected'.[64] In September, the magistracy moved to expel all lepers from the city.[65] This example of health cleansing seems to have failed, as the city decreed the next year that lepers found wandering in the city were to be expelled 'forcefully'.[66]

If the lack of explicit references to plague in the records surviving from 1409 to 1457 is striking, one must also note the frequency of plague outbreaks in the years 1458–1535. As will be discussed in detail in what follows, the city was struck by (or under imminent threat of) the epidemic in 1473–76, 1481–85, 1490–94, 1502–10, 1519–20, 1526 and 1529–30. Thus, if one includes 1457–58, in the (inclusive) period 1457–1535 (approximately eight decades) the city was beset by plague in no fewer than thirty years (37.5 per cent). If one considers only the period 1473–1535 (approximately six decades), the plague was a danger in twenty-eight years (about 44.5 per cent). By 1530, when we have the first appearance of conspiratorial plague spreading, two generations of Genevans had lived with plague on an almost continual basis.

The magistrates of 1530 would have known the constant threat of the disease and the massive disruption that the epidemic could cause to the city's society, culture and economy.[67]

However, before a hasty and breathtaking jump to the events of 1530, it is essential to understand the history of the previous half-century. It was this period, which instilled in Geneva an *ad hoc* yet, of necessity, almost permanent methodology for dealing with plague. Two points must be borne in mind throughout the forthcoming discussion. Geneva never developed a permanent, bureaucratic system of health and sanitation control such as was frequently seen in northern Italian city-states (for all the local reasons discussed above). However, the city did evidence the responses characteristic of these permanent bodies in times of plague. Since plague visited the city so frequently in this period, Geneva *de facto* had a continual though impermanent bureaucracy for preventing, containing and eliminating plague. In addition, the magistrates had extensive experience of functioning as health officials in plague time. Thus, although there was no official bureaucracy for health and sanitation in the city, the magistracy was not inexperienced and, therefore, was unlikely to be prone to hysteria, paranoia or scapegoating during a plague outbreak.

In the immediate aftermath of the attack of the epidemic in the late 1450s, the city made efforts to reinstate the various controls on the economy and society that had been a hallmark of the pre-plague years. Thus one sees that, in 1461, regulations on the sale of foodstuffs are restated, since there had been numerous violations.[68] Bakers were, as before, forbidden from selling bread from any site other than their normal (and licensed) shop.[69] Within months, they were being told what sort of loaves to bake.[70] In addition, 1462 also saw the same sort of controls on wine prices as before.[71] The spring of 1461 also saw repeated attempts to repair damage caused to one of the city's fountains by private building works undertaken by Mermet Buctier and Jean Robert.[72] The concern for the provision of safe water resurfaced in 1462 with attempts to make water more widely available 'in front of houses'.[73] In themselves, these do not so much evidence any specific lessons learned from the recent plague outbreak; rather they seem to be an attempt to return Geneva and its magistracy to some semblance of normality.

However, in one specific area what occurred in 1461 may imply a more lasting effect of the epidemic. As noted above, Geneva had had some problems with its resident Jewish population. It does seem though that these were never very serious and not necessarily connected with plague. The late spring and early summer of 1461 saw a much more dangerous situation for Jews in the city. In May, the government investigated attacks, both verbal and physical, on Jews who it noted had 'been present (presumably peacefully) in the city of Geneva for ten, twenty, thirty [and] forty years'.[74] The magistrates seem not to have been able wholly to quell the situation for the next month the Duke wrote to enquire about the situation, demanding to know what the civic officials were doing to punish the wrongdoers.[75] Is there any reason to suspect that there was a connection between the appearance of violent antisemitism and the plague as seen in the south of France and parts of Germany? The proximity of these events to the plague may, however, have been only coincidental. The records for April make it clear that antisemitic preaching caused the troubles.[76] Of course, one has no way of knowing what was said in the sermon. Perhaps a connection was made between the plague and the Jews. However, it is just as likely that it was in the vein of the antisemitic preaching of Dominicans and Franciscans prevalent in northern Italy at the same time rather than the more visceral and legalistic association of Jews with intentional, conspiratorial plague spreading.[77]

Having enjoyed a decade and a half without plague, Geneva was struck again in 1473. The first appearance of the disease was noted at the end of March.[78] The days and weeks before the start of the epidemic also saw civic officials discussing routine controls on fishmongers and waste disposal.[79] Thus, April began with the trials and traumas associated with preparing the city for the onslaught of the disease. The Senate considered general provisions to be made.[80] Very quickly, however, the minutes began to record specific suggestions needing discussion. On 2 April, the magistrates debated the construction of a plague hospital, including suitable sites.[81] Two days later, the council decreed the erection of a chapel for the afflicted as well as a separate cemetery and 'other necessary things' as part of the buildings accompanying the putative 'hospital pestilential'.[82]

By the middle of April, the city was obviously being forced to confront a very serious outbreak indeed. Moreover, the magistrates were considering a much wider, more dramatic and seemingly permanent range of remedies. The houses of the infected were to be sealed. A single site was to be established for the infected. Gates were to be guarded. Bath houses were closed and games forbidden. All the city's (hospice-like) hospitals were closed, thereby dispersing the poor and infirm. Migrants and indigents were expelled from the city. Finally, the guards were ordered to ensure that no one suffering from the disease was to (re-) enter the city.[83] This vigorous action was aided and accelerated by the offer from Ayme de Versonnex to sell the Hospital of Mary Magdalene and donate the money to the construction of the plague hospital in Plainpalais.[84]

Despite the obvious abundance of positive action, the Senate was forced to accept that these efforts were of little effect when confronted by the almost total lack of trained medical personnel in the city.[85] The city was more than able (and willing) to implement this the most advanced programme of responses to plague yet seen in Geneva, despite lacking most if not all of the personnel to make it work. In May, the problem of trained medical workers was partially solved, as the city was able to hire a barber surgeon, Hugo Fornier. His conditions of service were that he would be paid twelve gros (groats) per month during plague time on the condition that he would visit the sick and avoid all contact with the healthy.[86]

The plight of the citizens could only have been worsened by the dearth of grain that became an increasing problem by the summer. In August, the private sale of grain was forbidden and merchants were restricted to 'normal places and not elsewhere'.[87] During the next month, the magistrates were forced to investigate claims that the bakers were making and selling 'light' loaves.[88] Profiteering became a problem by October, when the Senate was forced to ban the resale of grain and to restrict its purchase to 'personal consumption' because of the 'great increase in price'.[89] Even at the close of the year, the government was confronted by this on-going distraction from dealing with the plague by Guillaume Barre selling imported (and presumably inferior) grain from the Pays de Vaud as local grain.[90] Indeed, the grain crisis and the concern about imported grain may well have stemmed from the controls on access and contact with infected areas imposed by the city in April. In other words, the lack of grain might well have been a direct consequence of plague regulations implemented by the magistrates.

Despite what must have been two all-consuming crises, the magistrates still found time to concern themselves with other problems in the city. For example, in July, two (of the four) syndics were deputed to visiting the lepers of Geneva.[91] October saw official attempts to clear the city of prostitutes, since 'honest women no longer dared to appear in the streets'.[92] Again, it is tempting to view these acts as an integral part of the civic response to plague. However, on closer examination, it is clear that the reality is much more complex. Thus, while the removal of pros-titutes (the morally infected and infectious) often accompanied plague outbreaks, this action by the city was aimed primarily at streetwalkers. That is, Geneva wanted to control, not eliminate, prostitution. Any other interpretation fails to explain the 'ordination' in June (in the midst of the plague and grain crisis) of Clementia of Lausanne as 'queen of the harlots'.[93]

In many instances, the city's actions during 1473 are to be expected and expli-cable as the 'normal' response to plague. However, the detail of information avail-able in the Genevan records forces one to be cautious about associating every state action as a response to plague or about viewing a late medieval, early modern city-state as a place wholly and narrowly consumed with crises. Although the magis-trates were clearly preoccupied with the need to respond to and control these twin crises, there is no sense that the city was in a state of panic. The government and, indeed, the citizenry in general seem to have taken the situation in their stride. When senior magistrates have the time and courage to visit lepers, and merchants can give thought and attention to profiteering in the midst of an epidemic disease, one may well marvel at the resilience and fortitude this evidences rather than look for examples of panic, fear or paranoia.

The beginning of 1474 again saw the city facing the problem of personnel. The *hospitalier* of the (temporary) Plague Hospital in Plainpalais signalled that he wished to resign.[94] It may be thought that this was rather churlish but it is important to remember that plague usually abated or disappeared entirely during winter months.[95] It may well be, therefore, that the *hospitalier* had seen his 'danger money' cut during the winter months. In addition, he may have wanted to leave the city before any possible recurrence of the disease. Subsequent events seem to imply that his decision was economically sound, as it appears that the disease did not return and, thus, the *hospitalier* was surplus to requirements.

In March, the situation was calm enough to allow the city to consider some scheme of compensation for people who had been ejected from their homes because of the 'epidemic disease'.[96] The next few months, which could well have seen new cases, instead were occupied with more mundane civic concerns. Pigs were ordered to be removed from the city.[97] The magistracy again turned its attention to merchants selling their wares in contravention of the city's regulations.[98] Indeed, the disease which most exercised the Senate in 1474 was leprosy rather than the plague of the year before. In June the wife of Guillaume Clement requested state aid, as she was in need as a consequence of her husband's leprosy.[99] It would also appear that discussions in mid-December about building a new hospital related to leprosy, as later in the month it was noted that the *Lazerarium* (leper house or *lazaretto*) in Pessonneria Street was full.[100] Although plague was certainly not a concern in 1474 the city leadership, in the person of the Prince Bishop, had drawn some salutary lessons from the 1473 outbreak. He made it clear to the Senate that the city needed to improve its security at gates and bridges. He was especially concerned that the guards were much too likely to be browbeaten into allowing quarantine violations, since they were 'more afraid of insults than of plague'.[101]

Unfortunately for Geneva, the Bishop was more prescient than the magistracy. In April, the hiring of Pierre Meysin and Pierre Grisod was confirmation that plague had returned. They were made to take an oath on the Holy Gospel 'to visit the sick and to prepare their food and medications'. Their contract was 'month to month'.[102] Two crucial features of the city's relations with its plague workers are evident this year. First, such workers were hired on a temporary basis. In effect, their fairly lucrative positions were wholly dependent on the presence of plague in Geneva. Second, they took an oath to the city before the magistrates. It is absolutely essential to stress the role of oath taking in the process. These workers were more than employees of the hospital; they were bound to Geneva just as were naturalised citizens, permanent residents, guards, judges and all elected magistrates. Breaking this oath was, therefore, not only a breach of contract: it was, most definitely, an act of treason and sedition.[103]

By May, the problem had reached such dangerous proportions that the Senate was forced to remove itself from the council chambers to the more spacious, airier and (presumably) healthier confines of the cathedral cloister.[104] These precautions may have protected the magistrates but they did nothing to alleviate the growing problem of the sick; the Plague Hospital was bursting with patients and near collapse.[105] The officials again considered the idea of a purpose-built site for the plague victims, although it was clear that a much more immediate solution was needed. As a result the city finally sold the Magdalene Hospital and purchased a barn in Plainpalais from Jean Malens for the 'repose of those sick with the plague'.[106] It would seem that his ownership of the barn led to Malens's involvement in the care of the afflicted as well, for late in 1476 he was paid seven florins for working as the *hospitalier* of those 'struck by plague'.[107]

Normally, one might expect a reasonable breathing space before the next outbreak of plague. Such was not to be the case. It is clear that plague was once again threatening (though it may not have been present in) Geneva within five years. In 1481, the government made another attempt to control 'women of bad life' because of plague.[108] There were also moves to maintain an even tighter rein on the city's economic life. For example, Ayme de Versonnex (the enthusiast for the Plague Hospital) was refused permission to export grain; the restriction was explicitly extended to any other would-be exporters.[109] November had seen the most stringent controls to date. Prices were decreed for mutton and beef, with regulations governing the sale of wine, bread and salt.[110] However, the emphasis seems to be on dearth with only a shadowy threat of plague. Even the regulations on prostitutes are not necessarily entirely the result of plague. The city also ruled that prostitutes were an integral part of civic fire prevention; they were required to attend any fire, along with carpenters and domestic servants, to fight the conflagration.[111]

The threatening clouds of plague soon broke on the city. In early February, the Senate dispatched a committee (Nicolas Lingot and Matthieu Scarron) to visit the poor.[112] On 12 February, the city was declared beset by plague and guards were set on the gates.[113] The following month, the magistrates appointed personnel to work in the Plague Hospital; they also sacked the previous *hospitalier*, Grisod.[114] By May, the city was being forced to repair the fabric of the hospital.[115] The summer, which one would expect to have been the height of the plague, brought more severe problems for the government. The Senate noted that bodies were accumulating so quickly that the plague cemetery could not provide sufficient burial space. As a result, the magistracy ordered bodies to be buried in one of the parish graveyards despite 'prejudice to the parish'.[116]

Clearly, the outbreak in 1482 was severe, but of a greater concern to the city was the lingering nature of the attack. Plague was either present or threatening until 1485–86, when the records break off. In 1483, plague deaths were reported in the house of the late Aymon de Lestelly.[117] At the same time, the city ordered all lepers to report for inspection by a committee of magistrates.[118] In the next year, the Senate ordered repairs to the Plague Hospital (usually a reasonably good indication of the disease's presence).[119] The magistrates were also exercised about damage done to city latrines.[120] In 1485 there is clear evidence that plague was in the immediate vicinity of the city; guards were set at the gates as well as in the city's various districts to prevent the entry of the infected.[121] By the following year, the city's concern was again focused on lepers, who were barred, though local lepers were tolerated, as they (and the poor) were assigned special places for begging at the 'church of the preachers'.[122]

It appeared that Geneva was blessed with three years of health in 1487–89. It was in the midst of a major outbreak in 1490, though. This next attack lasted at least until 1494 (with a break in 1491). Before looking at these epidemics in some detail it is worth pausing to consider the possibility that plague had become endemic. Plague, in the last quarter of the fifteenth century, was almost a biennial event. However, in 1502–10, there were plague deaths reported for each year. As we will see, the city did not give in to despair. Instead, the magistracy became even more adept and organised in coping with the disease.

The outbreak of 1490 sparked moves similar to those seen previously. The infected were to be placed in shanties outwith the city and their homes were sealed.[123] The severity of the epidemic forced the cancellation of the collection of the wine *gabelle* (tax).[124] For the first time, though, the city made specific arrange-ments for the care of the souls of the living rather than just the laying to rest of the deceased. In July, it set aside a house for priests to live in for two to three months during which they were to separate themselves from the healthy and concentrate on ministering, especially through sermons, to the sick.[125] Although plague seems not to have struck the following year, by late 1492 the city, again, had to seal the homes of plague victims.[126] In addition, it added yet another requirement, which was that the infected should carry 'signs' indicating that they carried the disease.[127]

As the plague continued into another year the city simply piled yet more regu-lations on to the infection. A barber-surgeon was hired in May; he was required to live, as well as work, in the Plague Hospital.[128] By July, the Senate also had to hire another rector (or chaplain) for the hospital. Pierre Bonfils was instructed 'to visit those struck by plague in a time of great mortality'.[129] In the same month the city moved to restrict the movements of the barber-surgeon's wife.[130] Finally, later in the year, the magistrates closed the Ponte-du-Rhône Hospital (for poor pilgrims) 'to prevent death and greater scandal'.[131] This particular attack of plague (now in its fifth year) finally ended in 1494. The government continued to order the expul-sion of the plague victims.[132] The length of this outbreak also saw the more draco-nian move to prohibit all public gatherings or crowds.[133] In addition, all 'women' (probably prostitutes) were expelled.[134] Treated as a unit, the plague years 1490–94 saw little panic but, instead, a consistent application of previously tried (legislative) remedies as well as the introduction of increasingly innovative and harsh methods. However, one also senses that the magistracy and, by extension in an elective frame-work, the citizenry felt that they had the tools and methods necessary for coping with, and ultimately surviving, the epidemic.

Surely this stoic optimism would not be able to endure the next major outbreak (1502–10)? Nine consecutive years of plague might be expected to destroy both the morale and the effective mechanisms of the city. In fact, the disease seems to have done neither. The first summer of the disease may not have been too severe. The first reaction to the threat of plague was to close the city's gates to the sick.[135] This may imply that the epidemic was not actually present in the city. However, the payment of five groats to Guillaume de Boulo for burning the clothing of the victims suggests otherwise.[136] The one immediate innovation was the decision (perhaps the city recalled the earlier advice of the Bishop) to increase the salary of the gatekeepers.[137] Interestingly, and in keeping with previous practices, the pay rise lasted only as long as the plague.

By the next year, the disease was certainly evident; the minutes recorded that 'plague reigns in the city'.[138] As before, the dead were to be buried at the Plague Hospital.[139] However, in a clear departure from past practice, the Senate decreed that foreigners were to be expelled and, specifically, were not to receive treatment at the hospital.[140] It is likely that this was less a sign of xenophobia than a result of the virulence of the outbreak.[141] The scale of the epidemic becomes more visible the following year. The records note that certain women had been hired to visit the sick at home – the implication being that the hospital may have been filling up.[142]

The city was certainly taking drastic action, as it not only banned sermons but also closed the city's school.[143] Also, for the first time in the records, the Senate ordered religious processions to be held.[144] By September the government had moved to close all churches, schools and baths.[145] In the autumn, the officials instituted two new regulations. First, the magistracy diverted confraternity income to the Plague Hospital.[146] Second, they not only closed the houses of the infected, but also ordered that they should be cleaned 'after eight days'.[147] These two acts show both a certain desperation but also a determined attention to detail and regulation. Finally, the advent of winter saw a ruling that the hospital's barber-surgeon should not enter the city.[148]

The edict about house cleaning highlights the role of the women (and some-times men) hired to clean the homes of the infected. Their task was twofold. First, they were to wash all the linen in the house. Second, they fumigated the rooms with sweet-smelling herbs and woods.[149] In effect, they were disinfecting the house and its contents in anticipation of the eventual return of the occupants, who, in the meantime, had been removed to the Plague Hospital. On 5 May 1505, the Senate approved the employment of 'two good women and one man' to clean the houses.[150] By June, the workers had been found and were inducted into their office. They took an oath 'on the Holy Gospel to clean infected houses' and 'faithfully to exercise their offices'. The people employed for this dangerous task were Nycod Guynet, his wife (Theveneta) and Guigona (widow of Estienne Marchand). They were each to receive 30s per month while the plague lasted, with an extra 2s a day if they actually disinfected a house.[151] Assuming that the plague abated in December and January and that they only cleaned two days each week, this represented approximately forty florins per year. By comparison, the barber-surgeon hired earlier in the year was to receive a guaranteed salary of only twenty-four florins per year, with an unspecified bonus during plague times.[152] The gravedigger for plague victims was paid only two florins.[153] Thus, as the plague outbreak continued, the magistracy increasingly employed both innovative and stricter regulations but also a larger and costlier 'professional' work force.[154] Indeed, the hiring of workers spe-cifically to maintain the machinery for dealing with the sick is one of the most strik-ing features of this outbreak. So determined was the city to provide a more stable and specialised service that, in 1506, it hired Jaques Carrier, a *bourgeois*, as barber-surgeon for the Plague Hospital on a six-year contract.[155]

This raises the question of the lack of any permanent Health Board in the city. In northern Italy such magisterial bodies became a permanent feature of the bureaucratic landscape in most city-states. Perhaps the answer lies in the extensive involvement in the city of its Senate. In effect, the syndics and senators micromana-ged Geneva and, over time, simply added to their other functions that of Health Board. This alone seems to explain the reliance on professional workers (barbers, fumigators, nurses and gravediggers) on more or less permanent contracts without any permanent official oversight. In reality, the (relatively small and tightly knit) Senate, rather than delegating health and sanitation to a sub-committee, dealt with such matters directly.

For the next four years the plague returned without mercy. In 1507, Claude Philippe (a leading citizen) was taken ill with the disease and shut in his house for forty days and forbidden any outside contact even with his family.[156] The use of home quarantine would imply that the disease was so widespread that the Plague Hospital had been overwhelmed. This conclusion is supported by the minute, in October, that plague was 'raging and pulsating' through Geneva.[157] The following year witnessed yet more plague. Early in the year the body of a certain De Vauchon was disinterred for reburial in the Plague Hospital.[158] Presumably, his family had managed to avoid detection and arranged his burial in his local churchyard. The increase of the incidence of the epidemic as spring turned into summer forced the city to return to harsher restrictions. Barber-surgeons who were themselves ill or who worked with the infected were forbidden from entering apothecary shops.[159] More dramatically, the government decreed that anyone violating the regulations would be stripped of his civic status and privileges.[160] The epidemic continued (or recurred) in 1509. Certain parish priests were selected to hear confessions.[161] The baths were closed and more *cabanes* built for the sick.[162] Finally, in what must have been a heart-rending and economically crushing move, the city forbade the passing of the clothes of victims to their heirs.[163] This devastating period of epidemic disease seems finally to have abated in 1510 although plague was perilously close in a number of nearby villages.[164]

Geneva remained unaffected by plague for most of the 1510s. However, in the summer of 1519 the disease struck again. The basic regulations were again implemented; for example, animals were kept from the city and the baths were closed.[165] François de Leamon reported that plague had caused deaths at the Magdalene Hospital and requested that it should be emptied and closed.[166] In addition, the city again turned to the provision of *cureuses* to clean the houses of the infected when the disease continued into 1520.[167] Thus, the employment of 'professional' plague workers was now a regular feature of the city's bureaucratic response to the disease.

Any hope that these two years of plague might signal a lengthier respite was dashed in 1526, when the city experienced yet another outbreak of the epidemic. In August, the city ordered every infected person to vacate the city under pain of the *corde* (the Genevan term for torture or punishment by application of the *strappado*).[168] The city also extended its concern about the possible spread of the disease by health workers when it investigated the accusation that Hugo Fabri, an apothecary, might have been in contact with infected persons, and ordered his shop to be shut should it prove true.[169] Fortunately for the city, the plague of 1526 did not develop into a lengthy outbreak.

However, in 1529 plague appeared yet again. On 5 August, the government received word that a small girl had died at the house of Pierre Maret; she was diagnosed as having had plague.[170] The (by now) traditional action was taken: the Rive monastery and chapel were closed; oil, salt and candles were given to the Plague Hospital; guards were posted at the city's gates.[171] In fact, these responses seem to have become so normal that ordinary citizens began acting on their own; the guards were ordered to remove private *cabanes* (huts) which had been built by the hospital.[172] One pessimistic note appeared in the records, though, in an alteration of terminology – the Hospital Pestilential was referred to as the Hospitale Mortiffero.[173] Geneva's magistracy also began to solicit for professional medical workers. In September, the city hired Hans Frechez (also called Jean Placet or Le Serralion) as barber-surgeon and Pierre de Malodomo as *hospitalier*.[174] Within a few months the Senate discussed the need for an additional barber-surgeon.[175]

Thus, in every sense, the 1529 outbreak – which continued into 1530 – was normal. The government undertook the by now standard responses: regulations were decreed; the *cabanes* set up; the infected segregated; the workers hired; the houses cleaned. And yet 1530 was dramatically different. Despite the years of experience of both plague and plague workers, this epidemic was marred by the exposure of a new, hitherto unknown and inconceivable phenomenon – intentional and conspiratorial plague spreading. In the spring, the city was rocked by the information that its trusted workers were actively sustaining the epidemic through the targeted selection of the homes of key wealthy citizens. Under cover of their proper tasks, the workers were accused of anointing the doors and windows of the homes with a *graisse* made of infected matter. Then, once the inhabitants were ill, they would enter, ostensibly to clean the premises, and pilfer money and other objects of value. Also, since they were paid only during plague time and received bonuses only while actually at work, their activities served to maintain their lucrative employment.

The general outline of the incident can be sketched quite simply. In early April, Michel Caddo was seen in the street dropping a cloth which gave off a noxious smell. He was arrested. At this point, it would seem, the officials were mostly concerned that he might have inadvertently violated decrees meant to contain the disease. That is, he might have been spreading plague unintentionally by carelessness. This was, in itself, an important accusation, as the city had decreed in March that anyone failing to adhere to the containment regulations would be charged as a potential murderer.[176] However, during the course of his trial, the magistrates became convinced that something more sinister was afoot. The council minutes preserve the results of investigations into this potential conspiracy of *engraisseurs*, as the defendants were called.[177] Within days of the initial accusation, Caddo, Placet (the barber-surgeon) and his wife Gonette were dragged through Geneva's streets, beaten before the houses they had (supposedly) infected, beheaded and quartered. Their quarters were exposed in premier locations and their heads at the hospital as a warning to other would-be *engraisseurs*.[178] In May, Claude Ginet (a silk weaver) was arrested and one Jean de Furno (whose case does not survive) was dragged through the streets, pulled with hot irons, beheaded and exposed on the gibbet.[179] In a curious epilogue to these dramatic, if hasty, events, the adolescent son of Jean Placet was also questioned but later released partially for lack of evidence and, in part, on account of his youth.[180]

Thus, in the midst of a major plague outbreak, the magistracy oversaw the arrest, prosecution and execution of its medical workers. Something indeed must have been of great importance to encourage leading senators to come into close contact with and interrogate so many people who had had contact with plague victims. There is no doubt that the government felt the city was in extreme danger. Surprising as this narrative is, the minutes give only the skeleton of the events. For the actual details of what the judges found and what motivated them to such speedy and violent action, one must look to the verbatim accounts of the trials preserved in the criminal records. It is these which must now be considered in some detail, for the information contained there, the pattern observed by the officials and the results of the interrogations are the model against which all subsequent prosecutions must be measured.

Before doing so, some important factors need consideration. In 1530, Geneva was involved in more than just an outbreak of plague. The city was entering the final phase of its revolution against Savoy (and, eventually, the Prince Bishop).[181] There had been a string of crises, often violent, beginning in 1519. The Duke of Savoy had been trying to maintain – indeed, increase – his authority over the city in anticipation of making it his new capital.[182] Moreover, the whole of the region around Geneva was in the throes of religious debate.[183] The Reformation was well under way in the Swiss Confederacy as well as in Germany. In these circumstances, one might expect that the magistrates would have attempted to uncover political or religious motives in any conspiracy. Thus, the interpretation of the motives of the *engraisseurs* by the Genevans is of paramount interest.

On 7 April 1530, Geneva's courts began their interrogation of Michel Caddo, the *citoyen* son of a Genevan *bourgeois*.[184] In time-honoured fashion, he was asked if he knew why he had been arrested. He replied in the negative. Caddo was asked to recount his circumstances and movements in the recent past. He had been in the hospital (as a victim?) six weeks before Christmas (i.e. mid-November). Thereafter, he had resided in Chambéry and elsewhere before returning to Geneva. He lived in the St-Gervais quarter of Geneva with the La Galla household. He was then asked about his activities the previous Tuesday. He recounted his attendance at Mass in St-Pierre (Geneva's cathedral) then lunch with a certain De Corberia at Beguin's house. The afternoon was spent with De Corberia until he went home. He was asked if he had met anyone while returning to St-Gervais; he had chatted to George Plat, tailor. Plat had told him that he had dropped 'vous emplastres' (the infected cloth mentioned above). He then denied, when explicitly questioned, possessing any *papier* (such as would hold medicinal powder) though he did admit to having purchased some 'ointment of white camphor' from François Vulliens, apothecary. This ointment had been carried 'in his tunic at his side'. This minute questioning, which ended the first day's interrogation, was of extreme importance because any variation in the details from subsequent testimony or eye-witness accounts could serve as legal justification for the application of torture (the *corde*).[185]

The following day the interrogation was resumed. The judges now began to question Caddo about the disposition of the cloths. He denied throwing them in a number of places but admitted that one, which had been on his thigh, had been dropped near the *cave* of Guillaume Rey. He still denied possessing any (wrapping) paper. He was questioned about his relations with others in St-Gervais who might want to denounce him. He mentioned that Rey might dislike him but added that he could not imagine any reason why Plat should tell anything but the truth. He also said he did not know why he had been expelled from the Confraternity of St-George. Caddo was also asked if he had been in the hospital any other times (than when he was ill); he had been twice before with Jean Dorbe, a herald. He continued to deny possessing any paper wrappings but Pierre Vuyrier and Claude Coquet, officers of the court, interjected that they had been found on his person. The witnesses against him were now brought in so that he could confront them while their depositions were read out. Caddo was forced to admit that he did have paper wrappers on him but said he had had no evil intentions.

At this point, the investigating magistrate, the city's elected Lieutenant, decided that the alteration in Caddo's testimony was sufficient to allow the application of torture. The defendant was taken to the place of torture and admonished to tell the truth while confronted by the implements of torture. It appears that his confession was spontaneous at this point without the need actually to apply the *corde*. Caddo related that, three weeks before, a small man with a grey cap had approached him on the Rhône Bridge. This man had said that Jean Placet, the barber-surgeon, wished to talk to him 'to his great profit'. Caddo had then met Placet in a barn, where Placet had said, 'If you wish to do something that I will tell you will make you and me better [off]'. Caddo was made to swear not to tell anyone about the discussion. He was then given three packets of wrapping papers and told to secrete them about the city; 'profit' would result.

Caddo next related the householders he had targeted: Pierre Villet, Guillaume Caddo (his brother) and George Plat. The goal, he related, was to spread plague. His motive for selecting these individuals was that Plat and Villet were rich and he was angry with his brother. When asked how he protected himself from infection he replied that he washed his hands and face with vinegar, although this solution was his own, as he had not discussed that matter with Placet. He continued to implicate Placet but said he knew nothing about Placet's wife. Caddo repented of his actions and confirmed that his statement was truthful.[186]

In the following weeks, Caddo was interrogated five more times. He was given the chance to deny or retract his confession; he confirmed his previous comments. He also mentioned that Placet had 'two black powders' in his room. He continued to deny any knowledge of the involvement of Placet's wife or son. Placet's wife and son were then confronted with Caddo. The wife, Gonette, remembered that Caddo had been at the hospital at Christmastide but nothing else. Jean, the son, said that he recalled that Caddo had visited his father twice in the company of Dorbe.[187] The following day, Caddo reconfirmed his testimony though with some prevarication. Torture was threatened and he hastily backtracked. Placet was brought in; Dorbe's involvement was mooted. Caddo then denied everything, saying that he had confessed out of fear of the *corde*.[188] Since Caddo had recanted, the judges were forced to begin the process again. He claimed that he had spoken out of malice and that he did wish his brother ill. This time torture was certainly applied and Caddo admitted that he had recanted because 'he knew full well that he would be hanged to death'. In agony, Caddo returned to his confession. He was asked to implicate someone from the Pays de Vaud and a Pierre 'with a white hat'.[189]

This final statement seems to have satisfied the judges. Caddo was not examined again until ten days later, when he validated his earlier confessions. He was unwilling to denounce Placet's servant, Pierre Bonier (called Bornay or D'Aulbonay, from Thonon). Also, he was unable to implicate any of the *hospitaliers* in Annecy although he had lived there for eighteen days with Claude Morel (called Blanchet).[190] Caddo continued to deny that Pierre Bonier had stayed for the conversation with Placet although he had fetched him from the bridge. The only significant addition to his previous testimony was an immense amount of detail on the oath the conspirators took. They swore 'not to reveal anything about the affair under pain of the damnation of their souls'. Despite the best efforts of the judges, Caddo was unwilling to implicate another possible conspirator, Jeanne Hippolyte. Moreover, it now appeared that Jean Dufour, the priest, was acting (in part) as interpreter, as Jean Placet (also called Hans Frechez) conducted part of the meeting in German. Dufour was certainly the one who actually administered the oath.[191] The denouement of the case followed a week later with a repetition of Caddo's confession on 28 April and the reading out of the sentence against him (for having committed 'an enormous and execrable' crime) on 30 April.[192]

Within days of Caddo's arrest the authorities moved to question Jean Placet, the barber-surgeon and *hospitalier* of the Plague Hospital. On 11 April the interrogation began. Placet informed the judges that he was married, with one son, and a native of Fribourg. He had practised his skill in the care and cure of plague victims four years in Fribourg and ten years at Syon. He had also worked for some time in the Valais, Lausanne and Vevey before coming to Geneva. He assumed that he was under arrest because Ayme Gendarme had spread certain evil rumours in the city about him impugning his relations with 'certain women'; also, the daughter of Jean Martin had said he was 'a sinful man'. He was asked who had told him about Gendarme's accusations and their substance. He replied that the daughter of one Bidalis had told him. The rumours involved him along with Caddo and his behaviour while working with plague victims at Thonon.

The judges then turned their attention to Placet's relationship with Caddo. Placet confirmed that Caddo had been sick in the hospital around Christmas. Placet could give no details of Caddo's character. His only subsequent contact with Caddo had been when he had shown up at the hospital (on his own accord) while Jean Dorbe and Dufour were there. He then denied all the salient charges about the oath and *graisse*, though he noted that he had heard about 'handkerchiefs' and had asked Ami Girard to investigate, as people were anxious. The only other information forthcoming was that he had had no contact with Caddo, had given him no medicine (apart from some powder) and had not told him any preventative cures for plague. For his part, he protected himself by applying vinegar and butter.[193]

On 13 April, Placet was confronted with Caddo. After a number of exchanges, Placet complained that the judges were giving credence to contradictory statements from Caddo and that he was 'a good man as they could prove by [contacting] the magistrates of Fribourg'. Caddo pleaded with Placet to accept the situation and to confess his guilt; Placet remained adamant in asserting his innocence. At this point, Placet was attached to the *corde* but received 'no other torment than being raised a little ways and then lowered [to the floor]'. The torture failed to alter Placet's testimony, so the judges decided on an alternative tack. It was clear that central to Placet's defence was his claim that he did not know Caddo well and had had no contact with him after Christmas. Therefore, the investigation turned to the taking of depositions from witnesses. Moneta, the wife of Pierre Gatens (locksmith) and Thomasse, daughter of La Gignon, were questioned. They both linked Caddo and Placet. Pierre Nycod, a notary, also reported that he (along with Pierre l'Hoste and George Marchand, both prominent Genevans) had seen Caddo and Placet together the previous week. Ayme Gendarme and Jordan Roch both testified that Placet had attempted to suborn their evidence in return for medical attention for Gendarme's wife and son. Presented with these depositions, Placet admitted to more frequent contact with Caddo (and Dufour) but denied it was malicious. He also confessed that he had given Caddo a small book to help him become a better plague worker (although Caddo had previously reported that he could not read). He also said that he, Caddo and Dufour had discussed the plague outbreak at Chambéry; beyond that he denied everything.[194]

The next week saw another attempt to get more details on Caddo and Placet. Aime, the widow of Louis Barbier, could report no more than that Caddo and Placet were often together.[195] The judges were somewhat more successful in their interrogation of Placet's son, also named Jean. Failing to break Placet with more torture, they began to question his son. The younger Placet admitted that some bandages were being left around the city but that his 'father had given them to him to do good', though he implied that he had not fully believed this. He also knew Caddo (who had visited the hospital twice) but knew nothing about medicine except that his father used herbs. When asked about the dinner and oath, young Jean requested a short break. Upon the resumption of questioning, he gave an account that tallied with Caddo's version of the dinner (with bread, wine and apples) and the oath. He also knew his father had some handkerchiefs and had seen some red and green silk flowers.[196]

Although there were numerous other interrogations of both father and son, the crucial session occurred the following day when, under torture, Placet finally confessed.[197] The following interrogations produced little new or interesting, with a few exceptions. Placet admitted to having spread plague in Chambéry.[198] He also gave more detailed information on the oath though in no way differing from the testimony of Caddo.[199] In addition to the information from and about Placet, the records also note that the younger Placet was only fourteen years old. Because of his age (which seems to have saved him) he was given a state-appointed guardian (Pierre Bramet) to advise him during the trial.[200] In the end, his father was executed for devising 'an oath and conspiracy to keep secrets' and for involving others 'in a project to poison and to spread plague in [Geneva]'.[201]

The role of Dufour and the foreignness of Placet are even more noticeable in the documents relating to the interrogation of Pierre Bornier of Thonon. He related that Dufour conducted the oath ceremony in Latin and that '[Placet], his wife and son spoke to one another in German'. Bornier also confessed that they had made their oath on the Gospel (supplied by Dufour) and that the 'master Jean [Dufour] said that it was fitting for us to give this medicine to the people which master Jean [Placet] had made and that we would equally divide the profits among all those who participated in this activity'.[202]

Dufour obviously interested the authorities immensely. He testified that he had been ordained to the priesthood in 1497 as a Franciscan Minor but had left the order in 1521 or 1522. He gives no reason for this although it is unlikely to have been anything related to the Reformation as he specifically stated that he had celebrated Mass recently. During an undated interrogation, he admitted to having known Bonier, Caddo, Placet and Placet's son. He denied everything, including any oath ceremony. He was threatened with torture. Although he now admitted to knowing Bastian Grangier, a barber-surgeon, and his servant, Aymonet Emis, he denied any criminal activity. However, he soon relented and confessed to the crime although torture seems to have been applied. In addition, during subsequent interrogations he mentioned 'other poisons' and implicated Claude Genet. There was another session of questioning on 6 May but Dufour simply repeated his confession. By 14 May, the syndic, Jean Ami Curtet, was able to condemn Dufour for having 'committed many grievous evils worthy of the harshest and most execrable punishment that can be devised'. [203]

The case against Jeanne, wife of Jaques Hippolyte, followed a similar pattern. Her initial interrogation took place on 25 April. It transpired that she had been ill with plague and in the hospital during Christmas, being released four days after Epiphany. She admitted that she had been involved in the purchasing of drugs (for herbal infusions) and bandages.[204] At her next interrogation she strongly denied, despite the threat of torture, that she had been given any 'handkerchiefs or silk flowers'.[205] On 9 May, she faced Dufour but maintained her innocence of the accusations brought by Dufour against her.[206] Within days she was tortured.[207] The interest of the magistrates in these cases is evident in the number of official witnesses to the torture and interrogation; eleven senior magistrates were present in the torture chamber. Not only did Jeanne deny her guilt but also she specifically refuted any contact between herself and Caddo, who she claimed 'wished her ill'. However, once she was hanged from the *corde* and dropped 'moderately' she began to confess. Most important, she named the individuals whom she had targeted, including Jaquemoz Rey (who may or may not have been a relative of Guillaume Rey, a supposed victim of Caddo's).[208] Despite eight subsequent interrogations lasting until her condemnation on 29 October, Jeanne added nothing of interest to the investigation. Apparently she had been able to survive the first wave of executions by claiming that she was pregnant, thus forcing the authorities to delay punishment (but not interrogation and torture) until they were sure she was not with child. She gave no information on an oath (and no other defendant placed her at the ceremony). In the end, like Dufour, she was condemned for trying 'to spread the plague' and participation in 'the conspiracy wishing to poison the city of Geneva and [its] inhabitants'.[209]

The day after Jeanne's trial began, Gonette (or Genette), the wife of Jean Placet (otherwise called Serralion) was arrested and interrogated. It appears that she was interviewed in front of the entire Senate. She admitted that she knew Caddo, Bonier and Hippolyte. She denied, however, that she had ever dined with her family, Caddo, Bonier and Dufour or that any oath had been taken or that she had ever been previously arrested.[210] On 27 April, Gonette was threatened with the *corde*. When she insisted on proclaiming her innocence she was strapped three times; she remained silent.[211] The following day, prior to any torture, Gonette gave details on the oath. Failing to elicit sufficient details, the judges had her tortured; again, they failed. After dinner (lunch) she was questioned once more. She now confessed that they had sworn, under the direction of Dufour, to divide the spoils among themselves. She said her son was not there as he had 'not yet come from Fribourg'. She was asked to explain the motives for their actions and replied that it was for profit though she did not know why the oath was taken. Realising that more could be gained from Gonette, she was attached yet again to the *corde* with a stone to weight her legs. This session produced some very interesting details indeed. The purpose of the plague spreading was clearly financial reward, both in keeping their employment active and in the opportunities for pilfering from homes and corpses. Also, the judges asked whether anyone had actually died from their actions, which may well imply that the councillors were not certain that such behaviour would kill. Gonette affirmed that some people had died, in her view, as a direct result of this nefarious behaviour. She also mentioned that Caddo was keen to kill yet another Rey, this time André Rey. The other titbit of information related to the minutiae of the oath. It had been taken during a meal at which bread, wine and apples had been served.[212] During her final interrogation the next day, Gonette was again quizzed about the motive for her actions. She stressed that the conspirators had been driven by a desire 'to make themselves rich and to divide among themselves the [stolen] property'.[213]

The final trial began on 10 May, that of Claude Genet, silk weaver. Genet related that he was from Rumillier and was a *bourgeois* of Geneva. He assumed he was being questioned because of Dufour. He had known the priest for three years while an apprentice and knew that Dufour had been a Franciscan novice in Avignon because he was a friend of one of Dufour's relatives. They had re-met about five years ago. Dufour did owe him money (for bread he had given him) and Genet had met both Placet and his son while visiting Dufour. In addition, Genet admitted that he had once been imprisoned in Lyon for debt. Genet also knew Caddo but they were not on good terms because of an argument. He had managed as well to strain his relationship with his relative, Hemmoz. He denied that he had ever discussed this personal dispute with Caddo.

As it became increasingly clear to Genet that he was in serious trouble he pleaded with the judges 'to protect his rights and to provide him with an advocate to speak for him since he did not know [how to] maintain or explain his rights'. The judges thought the request of an advocate somewhat suspicious. Genet was confronted with Placet and Dufour and threatened with torture. Genet was then taken from the room declaring that they were lying, that he was an honest merchant and that he needed an advocate.[214] In two subsequent interrogations, Genet related that he had been seriously ill and that his recent contacts with Dufour had begun when the priest had attended his sick bed while Ayme Hemoz (Genet's first cousin) was making his will.[215] The difficulty of this trial led the judges to request legal opinions (which do not survive) from Antoine Suchet and Claude Grossi, doctors of law.[216]

Genet's legal sophistication finally resulted in the appointment of an advocate, Nycod Ruffy. He was now able to produce a string of character witnesses. From his home parish of De Salles, Guillaume Ducats (aged sixty-five years) and Guillaume Charvan (aged seventy years) both testified to his good upbringing, saying that they knew his grandfather and father (who had been a merchant in Holland and had died in Avignon). They admitted that they had not seen him for over thirty years since he had moved to Lyon and Geneva. In addition to these two, a host of Genevan worthies (see Table 1) spoke on behalf of Genet. They said that Genet's wife was concerned about his links with Dufour. It seemed that Dufour had some financial hold over Genet.[217] The court then began to question (over a number of weeks) a large number of witnesses (see Table 2).[218]

The court then deponed Louisa, the daughter of Jean Richard Perrin, the wife of Claude Genet. She was unsure why she was being questioned though she suspected it was related to something Dufour might have said about her husband. The questions produced nothing of substance and much of the remaining records are extracts copied from other trials. Relevant sections concerning Genet had been copied from the interrogations of Bonier, Caddo, Hippolyte, Placet (the elder and younger) and Dufour. Most interestingly, there is also some information (scored out) taken from a case against a prominent apothecary (Pierre Neyrod) who, although he had made some powders for Placet, was, apparently, cleared of involvement at an early stage. The case itself seems to revolve around the accusation that Genet's business dispute with Hemoz had led him to become involved in the plot so that he could kill Hemoz (who had, in fact, died). The legal opinion of Estienne Louis on Genet and Dufour makes it clear that Dufour had indeed poisoned Hemoz but that Genet was not sufficiently implicated to be convicted.[219] Eventually, the court settled on a 'not proven' verdict and banished Genet on pain of death.

Nearly two centuries after the Black Death of the mid-fourteenth century, Geneva had developed a traditional and mechanistic series of responses to plague. Throughout the course of the fifteenth century, the city borrowed and modified ideas originating in the city-states of northern Italy. This pattern of adaptation produced some features worthy of momentary consideration. First, neither the ruled nor the rulers panicked in the face of plague. Second, by the time of Geneva's revolution and Reformation, the government had a fairly standard and bureaucratic manner of dealing with a plague outbreak. That is, when plague threatened or actually appeared in Geneva, the magistrates implemented a set of procedures which

Table 1   Defence witnesses, Genet case, 1530

Name	Details on witness	Details on Genet
Ducats, Guillaume	From De Salles, aged sixty-five	Knew father (Pierre) and grandfather (Martin). Claude was a good person but had moved long ago to Lyon and Geneva
Charvan, Guillaume	From De Salles, aged seventy	Knew Claude from birth but had not seen him for thirty-six years. Knew Pierre had spent time in Holland and died at Avignon
Giglare, Michel	Merchant, *bourgeois*, aged sixty	Knew Claude for seven or eight years
Chaumet, Claude	Merchant, citizen, aged thirty-eight	Knew Claude for five or six years. Claude is a good man although there was a dispute with Hemoz
Bocard, Jean	Cheese-maker, *bourgeois*, aged fifty	Knew Claude for four or five years. Claude is a good man although there was a dispute with Hemoz
Chautemps, Jean	Merchant, citizen, aged forty	Knew Claude for four years. Claude is a good man although there was a dispute with Hemoz and he had visited the hospital frequently around Christmas
Nycollard, Jean	Cobbler, aged thirty	Knew Claude for four or five years. Claude is a good man. Knows nothing about a dispute with Hemoz
Charvet, Jean	Tailor, from Chambéry, *habitant*, aged thirty-eight	Knew Claude for four years. Claude is a good man. Knows nothing about a dispute with Hemoz
Le Vet, Jean	Goldsmith, *bourgeois*, from Villa-en-Michaille, aged thirty-six	Knew Claude for twenty years since he was apprenticed in Lyon. A good man who had been in trouble for debt in Lyon. Comes from a good family.
Dentand, George	Draper, *bourgeois*, aged forty	Claude had had contact with a priest when he was near death from plague.
Bordil, Jaques (called Cardinal)	Tailor, *bourgeois*, aged sixty	Knew Claude for sixty-three years. Claude is a good man, although there was dispute with Hemoz
Vindret, Pierre	Merchant, *bourgeois*, aged fifty	Knew Claude for six or seven years. Claude is a good man

Table 2 Prosecution witnesses, Genet case, 1530

Name	Details on witness	Details on Genet
Clerc, Pierre	Cobbler, *habitant*, aged forty	Knew of dispute with Hemoz
De Muro, Michel	Escoffier, *habitant*, aged twenty-eight	Knew of dispute with Hemoz
Bellevaulx, Jean	Tailor, *bourgeois*, aged fifty	Knew of dispute with Hemoz
Cache, François (or La Cura)	Cobbler, *habitant*, aged thirty-six	Knew of dispute with Hemoz
Favre, Claude	Merchant, aged thirty	Knew of dispute with Hemoz and contacts between Claude and Dufour
Borre, Jaques	Aged twenty-five	Had lived with Genet and Hemoz. Genet thought Hemoz sold his goods too cheap and had frequently insulted him
Michon, François	*Bourgeois*, weaver, aged twenty	Knew of dispute with Hemoz but noted that Genet's wife had wept when Hemoz died

had been tried, tested and proved over the previous decades. Third, Geneva never developed a separate and permanent body of officials in charge of health, sanitation and disease control. In a small city like Geneva, the magistracy was competent to form itself into an *ad hoc* Health Board for the duration of the epidemic. The officials' familiarity with micro-managing the Genevan economy and society as well as their extensive experience with plague meant that they had no need of a specialised, devolved bureaucracy.

Finally, part of the normal governmental response to plague was to hire an entire work force to deal with the disease. Often, these people were foreign, poor or (more often) both. The workers were paid extremely good salaries but their pay and employment were both wholly dependent on the continuation of the epidemic. The extent of senatorial oversight in the control of plague and the management of the epidemic is most obviously available in senators' participation in the trials. As Table 3 shows, in just three trials, over forty magistrates were present at interrogations. More important, each of the syndics attended at least four separate sessions, while two attended six. In effect, the entire magistracy functioned as Health Board and, as in these cases, judicial panels. Geneva's ruling élite showed a constant unwillingness to delegate authority or responsibility to anyone for very long. In a crisis, all magistrates and leading citizens took an active part in the governing of the city.

This brings the discussion to an evaluation of the city's experience with a conspiracy accused of spreading the plague intentionally for profit. It is essential to grasp that the Genevans were more than able to understand this activity in a purely

Table 3   Magistrates' participation in the trials of 1530

Jeanne Hippolyte	Gonette Placet	Claude Genet
Balard, Jean (3)	**Balard, Jean** (2)	**Balard, Jean**
	Baud, Claude	
		Bernard, Claude
		Bordon, Jean
	Bourgeois, Girardin	
	Chapeaurouge, Ami	
	Chapeaurouge, Claude	
	Chapeaurouge, Estienne	
		Chasteauneuf, Claude
Chiccand, Antoine		
Coquet, Jean		
Curtet, Jean Ami (2)	**Curtet, Jean Ami** (2)	**Curtet, Jean Ami**
	De la Rive, Girardin	
	De Savoye, Claude	De Savoye, Claude
	Du Crest, Nicolas	
	Du Mollard, Claude	Du Mollard, Claude
		Du Mollard, Hudriod
Falquet, Petremand	*Falquet, Petremand*	
		Fanson, Bartholome
	Franc, Domaine	Franc, Domaine
	Gervais, Ami	
Girard, Ami		Girard, Ami
Guillet, Michel (2)		Guillet, Michel
Hugo, Guillaume		Hugo, Guillaume
	Le Vet, Jean	Le Vet, Jean
		Lect, Guillaume
		Lullin, Jean
		Mailliard, André
	Malbuisson, Jean	
Malbuisson, Pierre (2)	Malbuisson, Pierre	Malbuisson, Pierre
		Mutiod, Pierre
	Officier, Bon	
		Peter, Boniface
Pecollat, Estienne (3)	Pecollat, Estienne (2)	
		Philippe, Jean
Ramel, Jean Louis (3)		
Richardet, Claude (3)	Richardet, Claude	Richardet, Claude
		Ruffy, Nycod
Sept, Michel (2)	Sept, Michel	Sept, Michel
		Symon, Jean
		(called Picard)
		Tevenin, Pierre
Vandel, Robert (2)	**Vandel, Robert** (2)	
		Vellu, Richard

Table 3 (*cont.*)

Jeanne Hippolyte	Gonette Placet	Claude Genet
Vill[i]et, Pierre (3)	**Vill[i]et, Pierre** (2)	
		Vill[i]et, Jean
15 magistrates	23 magistrates	28 magistrates
	44 magistrates in all	

Notes
The number of sessions attended is given in brackets; if no number is given, the magistrate attended only one session. The syndics are list in **bold**, the Lieutenant is <u>underlined</u> and the steward is in *italics*. In some cases the records note only that some councillors attended. This table presents only those actually named and is therefore the minimum number of magistrates present during the interrogations.

socio-economic schema. Despite being in the final stages of a revolution and surrounded by religious turmoil, the judges made no attempt to analyse the phenomenon through religious or political lenses. They were able to accept that the motivation underlying the conspiracy was purely related to an attack upon the wealthy by the poor for personal gain. Also, although such behaviour was almost unimaginably evil, the officials made no attempt to discover any sinister or demonic component to it. Finally, despite the desire of the authorities to put a stop to this threat, their interest focused on the oath-taking ceremony. To the magistrates, this was a seditious act that fundamentally violated the oath taken by these workers when they were hired. Thus, no matter what else the conspirators were alleged to have done, the very act of taking an oath to commit murder or theft was a violation – and betrayal – of their (Hippocratic-like) oath to care for the city's plague victims. On every level, these workers had conspired to betray Geneva and had done so for the basest of all motives – profit.

NOTES

1 Although court cases and council deliberations were conducted in the local dialect of French from the late fourteenth century, the records were kept in Latin until the revolution. Thereafter, with minor exceptions in the records of some older and more conservative notaries, all Genevan documents were kept in the local dialect. By the end of the sixteenth century, the influx of wealthy, educated religious refugees from France itself meant that records were increasingly kept in a more 'standard' form of French.

2 E. Rivoire, V. van Berchem *et al.*, eds, *Registres du Conseil de Genève* (Geneva, Kündig, 1900–40), 13 volumes (henceforth, Rivoire, volume no., page no., date).

3 The exact dates of the lacunae are 15 December 1417–9 February 1428, 5 February 1451–5 February 1457; 8 February 1458–5 February 1459, 1463–72 and 1479. The Genevan administrative year began in the first week of February, when the city normally

held elections to the various councils. After the upheavals of the 1530 revolution, the constitution was settled to the extent that there was also a round of voting in November when the city elected its investigating magistrate (*Lieutenant*) and his assistants (*auditeurs*) and, by vote of the large council, set the prices of wine and grain. However, these elections were always secondary to the more important elections of February, which saw the inauguration of the new councils as well as the election or confirmation of most other officials. The upper council (the Senate or Petit Conseil) comprised four syndics (the senior magisterial officials), approximately twenty senators, the city treasurer, the secretary and the factor/steward (*saultier*). To this body were added another thirty or so magistrates to form the Conseil des Soixantes which dealt with difficult matters and, in particular, foreign affairs. This combined body was topped up with additional magistrates to form the Conseil des Deux Cents.

4 On the general subject of plague see A. Mack, *In Time of Plague: The History and Social Consequences of Lethal Epidemic Disease* (New York, 1991); P. Slack, *The Impact of Plague on Tudor and Stuart England* (Oxford, 1990); C. M. Cipolla, *Fighting the Plague in Seventeenth Century Italy* (Madison WI, 1981) and his *Faith, Reason, and the Plague: A Tuscan Study of the Seventeenth Century* (Brighton, 1979); D. Herlihy and S. Cohn, *The Black Death and the Transformation of the West* (Cambridge, 1997); C. Platt, *King Death: The Black Death and its Aftermath in Late Medieval England* (London, 1996); and the ever popular P. Ziegler, *The Black Death* (London, 1997). Also see D. R. Hopkins, *Princes and Peasants: Smallpox in History* (Chicago, 1983).

5 The impact of the first few bouts of plague (commonly called the Black Death) was devastating across Europe. Cf. W. M. Bowsky, 'The Impact of the Black Death upon Sienese Government and Society', *Speculum* 39: 1 (1964): 1–34; J. Henderson, 'The Parish and the Poor in Florence at the Time of the Black Death: the Case of S. Frediano', *Continuity and Change* 3: 2 (1988): 247–72; H. Dubois, 'Peste noire et viticulture en Bourgogne et en Chablais', in *Mélanges offerts à Edouard Perroy* (Paris, n.d.), pp. 428–38.

6 Italy remained the centre of medical innovation for much of the late medieval and early modern period. See, for example, W. E. K. Middleton, 'An Unpublished Letter from Marcello Malpighi', *Bulletin of the Society for the History of Medicine* 59 (1985): 105–8.

7 Geneva's ties with Italy were more than political, Piedmontese immigrants formed the basis of the city's élite. For more information on these ties, and Geneva's important geopolitical position, see J. F. Bergier, 'Marchands italiens de Genève au début du XVIe siècle', in *Studi in onore di Armando Sapori* (Milan, 1957), pp. 889–91; A. Gautier, *Familles genevoises d'origine italienne* (Bari, 1893). Also W. G. Naphy, *Calvin and the Consolidation of the Genevan Reformation* (Manchester, 1994), pp. 21–3, and 'The Price of Liberty: Genevan Security and Defence Spending, 1535–1555', *War in History* 5: 4 (1998): 379–99. Also, for an excellent example of the importance and spread of Italian regulations, see P. Basing and D. E. Rhodes, 'English Plague Regulations and Italian Models: Printed and Manuscript Items in the Yelverton Collection', *British Library Journal* 23 (1997): 60–7.

8 Rivoire, vol. 1, pp. 7–8 (August 1409).

9 Rivoire, vol. 1, p. 12 (December 1409).

10 For Jews as medical practitioners see J. Schatzmiller, *Jews, Medicine, and Medieval Society* (Berkeley CA, 1994).

11 Rivoire, vol. 1, p. 25 (November 1410). The committee comprised Girardin de Burdignin, Jean Bovent, Sieur de Orserius, Guichard Balli and Mon. Alamand.

12 Rivoirc, vol. 1, p. 30 (July 1411).

13 Rivoire, vol. 1, p. 90 (November 1417). Juilliermi was an *habitant*. Geneva's citizenry were divided into a number of categories. The premier category was that of *citoyen* (*civis*). This was a native-born child of *citoyen* or *bourgeois* parents. All offices were open to *citoyens*. The next category was that of *bourgeois*, or naturalised *citoyen*. That was a person who had bought or been granted full civic status. However, in the constitutional system operating after 1535, a *bourgeois* (*burgensis*) could not serve as one of the four syndics (Geneva's highest elected post) or as a senator. In all other cases, though, a *bourgeois* was (from the moment the privilege was granted) in full possession of all other civic rights. The lowest status with civic status was that of *habitant*. An *habitant* (*incola*) was a foreigner with the right of (permanent) residence. The *habitants* were bound to the city by oath but had no electoral rights. A final category was the more nebulous *natif*, a person of Geneva and its environs who had no official civic status (and was usually poor).

14 Rivoire, vol. 1, p. 91 (December 1417). This further strengthens the argument that the restrictions on Jewish butchers had more to do with economics and antisemitism than any accusations against Jews as plagues spreaders.

15 Rivoire, vol. 1, p. 96 (June 1528).

16 Rivoire, vol. 1, p. 100 (December 1428).

17 Rivoire, vol. 1, p. 98 (October 1428).

18 On attitudes to trades that produced noxious smells, etc., see K. Stuart, *Defiled Trades and Social Outcasts: Honor and Ritual Pollution in Early Modern Germany* (Cambridge, 1999).

19 Rivoire, vol. 1, pp. 120–1 (October 1428).

20 Rivoire, vol. 1, p. 133 (August 1430).

21 Rivoire, vol. 1, pp. 255–7 (January 1458).

22 Rivoire, vol. 1, p. 309 (July 1459).

23 Rivoire, vol. 1, pp. 283–5 (April 1459).

24 Rivoire, vol. 1, pp. 397 (February 1460), 443 (August 1460).

25 Rivoire, vol. 1, p. 268 (February 1459).

26 Rivoire, vol. 1, pp. 402 (March 1460); 405, 409–11 (April 1460).

27 Rivoire, vol. 1, p. 413 (May 1460).

28 Rivoire, vol. 1, p. 14 (February 1410).

29 Rivoire, vol. 1, pp. 34–5 (January 1412).

30 Rivoire, vol. 1, p. 53 (July 1413).

31 Rivoirc, vol. 1, pp. 117 (August 1429), 106 (February 1429).

32 Rivoire, vol. 1, pp. 312 (July 1459), 326 (August 1459), 360 (December 1459), 413 (May 1460).

33 Rivoire, vol. 1, p. 154 (December 1442).

34 Rivoire, vol. 1, p. 155 (January 1443). On the commonweal see M. S. Kempshall, *The Common Good in late medieval Political Thought* (Oxford, 1999).

35 Rivoire, vol. 1, pp. 223 (August 1457), 227 (September 1457), 242 (November 1457).

36 Rivoire, vol. 1, p. 413 (May 1460).

37 Rivoire, vol. 1, p. 402 (March 1460).

38 Rivoire, vol. 1, p. 430 (June 1460).

39 Rivoire, vol. 1, p. 455 (October 1460).

40 Books of the dead were simply registers compiled by officials (usually a medical

practitioner). In their simplest form they would give a person's name and cause of death. This information might be expanded to include age, address, marital status and other useful demographic information.

41 For a general discussion of urban polities see C. R. Friedrichs, *Urban Politics in Early Modern Europe* (London, 2000).

42 Rivoire, vol. 1, pp. 7 (August 1409), 11 (November 1409).

43 Rivoire, vol. 1, p. 14 (February 1409), 20 (June 1409), 34 (January 1412), 43 (November 1412), 51 (March 1413), 57 (November 1413), 68 (December 1414), 77 (December 1415), 84 (November 1416), 90 (November 1417), 99 (November 1428), 120 (October 1429), 123 (November 1429) and, especially, 470–3 (November 1460).

44 Rivoire, vol. 1, p. 80 (January 1416).

45 Rivoire, vol. 1, p. 134 (November 1430). On the relationship between disease and dearth see A. B. Appleby, 'Epidemics and Famine in the Little Ice Age', *Journal of Interdisciplinary History* 10: 4 (1980): 643–63.

46 Rivoire, vol. 1, p. 195 (May 1457).

47 Grain was to be imported from Lausanne and the Pays de Vaud. Rivoire, vol. 1, pp. 184–6 (April 1457), 192, 194–7 (May 1457), 199 (June 1457), 213 (July 1457), 214 (August 1457), 241 (November 1457), 250 (December 1457).

48 Rivoire, vol. 1, pp. 86 (February 1417), 98 (October 1428).

49 Rivoire, vol. 1, pp. 79–80 (April, June 1416), 142 (May 1442) and, especially, 103–5 (February 1429) which records the inspection of over fifty specific houses.

50 Rivoire, vol. 1, p. 369 (January 1460).

51 Rivoire, vol. 1, pp. 72 (July 1415), 104 (February 1429), 106 (February 1429), 114 (July 1429), 245 (November 1457).

52 Rivoire, vol. 1, pp. 273–4 (February 1459).

53 As this study involved sources in Latin as well as early modern French, German, Spanish and Italian, unless absolutely necessary, all quotations will be given in English. Not only does this make the work more accessible but it also avoids the (word) wasteful practice of quoting the original (in the text or notes) while providing an English translation.

54 Rivoire, vol. 1, p. 310 (July 1549). It is worth noting that the Genevan currency of account (the florin) was comprised of 12s or 144d rather than the more normal 20s or 240d. For more on Genevan money see Naphy, *Calvin*, pp. 113 n. 32 and 142 n. 63; J. F. Bergier, *Genève et l'économie européenne de la Renaissance* (Geneva, 1963); A. Babel, *Histoire économique de Genève des origines au début du XVIe siècle* (Geneva, 1963). It also made use of *écus* (worth about five to six florins) and the *livre tournois* (worth about ten florins and abbreviated by the normal symbol for a pound (£).

55 Rivoire, vol. 1, p. 314 (July 1459). Geneva's pre-revolutionary political situation was very complex indeed. The city's resident and native élite (primarily merchants) stressed the city's position as an imperial free city. Geneva, was also ruled, effectively, by the Bishop of Geneva who held the city from the Dukes of Savoy. In fact, the bishops were normally members of the ducal family. In addition, the bishops possessed extensive lands around Geneva in their own right. Thus, the city was administered by the Bishop's representative (the *vidomne*), the cathedral chapter and the elected merchant magistrates. The Bishop, local citizens, local gentry and Savoyard nobles owned the rural hinterland. Theoretically, this complex structure owed ultimate allegiance to the Dukes of Savoy. In practice, the Bishop, chapter, merchants, nobles, gentry and dukes wove an intricate tapestry of alliances and networks designed to secure optimum power for themselves to the detriment of all the others.

56 Plague regulations were not the only thing to have an impact on prostitutes (or, more generally, the place of women in society), see S. C. Karant-Nunn, 'Continuity and Change: Some Effects of the Reformation on the Women of Zwickau', *SCJ* 13: 2 (1982): 17–41, and U. Rublack, *The Crimes of Women in early modern Germany* (Oxford, 1999).

57 Rivoire, vol. 1, p. 171 (March 1457). Concern about sanitation, in both its physical and its moral sense, began in Italy with the advent of the Black Death. In Florence, during 1348, citizens were told to keep the streets clean, animals were expelled, streets were lit at night, the sale/slaughter of meat was controlled, prostitutes/sodomites were expelled, etc. Cf. A. G. Carmichael, *Plague and the Poor in Renaissance Florence* (Cambridge, 1986). More generally see G. A. Brucker, *Renaissance Florence: Society, Culture, and Religion* (Goldbach, 1994).

58 Rivoire, vol. 1, p. 197 (May 1457).

59 Rivoire, vol. 1, p. 199 (June 1457).

60 For general information on medicine see R. K. French, *Medicine from the Black Death to the French Disease* (Aldershot, 1998); M. Lindemann, *Medicine and Society in early modern Europe* (Cambridge, 1999); L. W. B. Brockliss and C. Jones, *The Medical World of early modern France* (Oxford, 1997); N. G. Siraisi, *Medieval and Renaissance Medicine: An Introduction to Knowledge and Practice* (Chicago, 1990).

61 Rivoire, vol. 1, p. 303 (June 1459).

62 Rivoire, vol. 1, p. 309 (July 1459).

63 Rivoire, vol. 1, p. 269 (February 1459).

64 Rivoire, vol. 1, pp. 277–8 (March 1459). See S. N. Brody, *The Disease of the Soul: Leprosy in Medieval Literature* (Ithaca NY, 1974).

65 Rivoire, vol. 1, p. 330 (September 1459).

66 Rivoire, vol. 1, p. 413 (May 1460).

67 For some brief comments on these disruptions across Europe see D. Steel, 'Plague Writing: From Boccaccio to Camus', *Journal of European Studies* 11 (1981): 88–110.

68 Rivoire, vol. 2, pp. 29–30 (May 1461).

69 Rivoire, vol. 2, p. 63 (September 1461).

70 Rivoire, vol. 2, p. 88 (February 1462).

71 Rivoire, vol. 2, p. 154 (November 1462): wine of Choutagnie, 8*d*; of the Valley 'Submontus', 6*d*; local wine, 4*d*.

72 Rivoire, vol. 2, pp. 12, 14 (March 1461); 33 (May 1461).

73 Rivoire, vol. 2, p. 143 (October 1462).

74 Rivoire, vol. 2, pp. 33–4 (May 1461).

75 Rivoire, vol. 2, p. 39 (June 1461).

76 Rivoire, vol. 2, p. 23 (April 1461).

77 D. O. Hughes, 'Distinguishing Signs: Ear-rings, Jews and Franciscan Rhetoric in the Italian Renaissance City', *P&P* 112 (1986): 3–59.

78 Rivoire, vol. 2, p. 179 (30 March 1473).

79 Rivoire, vol. 2, pp. 174, 176–7 (March 1473). Waste was being disposed of 'contrary to the edicts and to the prejudice of neighbours'.

80 Rivoire, vol. 2, pp. 179–80 (April 1473).

81 Rivoire, vol. 2, p. 181 (2 April 1473). There had been discussions about a plague hospital as early as 1469 but no permanent structure was created until 1482. The city did turn a barn into a provisional hospital in Plainpalais during this outbreak in 1473. Rivoire, vol. 2, p. 361 (December 1473).

82 Rivoire, vol. 2, p. 182 (4 April 1473). A committee of the syndics with three others (Jean d'Orsieres, Aymon de Lestelly, Mermet de Nanto).

83 Rivoire, vol. 2, pp. 184–5 (13 April 1473). This entry also has the first use of *epydemia* as opposed to *pestis*, which had been used heretofore.

84 Rivoire, vol. 2, p. 186 (April 1473); 232, n. 1 (November 1473). The infirm women housed at the Magdalene Hospital were to be relocated to the Hospital of St James. The Hôpital de Madeleine was founded by François de Versonnex on 4 January 1452. For more details on the various hospitals in Geneva see J. J. Chaponnière and L. Sordet, 'Les hôpi-taux de Genève avant la Réformation', *MDG*, 3 (Geneva, 1844): 165–471, especially 264.

85 Rivoire, vol. 2, p. 186 (April 1473).

86 Rivoire, vol. 2, p. 190 (4 May 1473). The coin is not used much after this period.

87 Rivoire, vol. 2, p. 211 (August 1473).

88 Rivoire, vol. 2, p. 222 (September 1473).

89 Rivoire, vol. 2, pp. 228–9 (October 1473).

90 Rivoire, vol. 2, p. 235 (December 1473).

91 Rivoire, vol. 2, p. 203 (July 1473).

92 Rivoire, vol. 2, p. 226 (October 1473). Not only may it have been unsafe but one of the worst insults one could pay a woman was to say, or suggest, that she was a whore. L. Roper, 'Will and Honour: Sex, Words and Power in Augsburg Criminal Trials', *Radical History Review* 43 (1989): 45–71, especially 58.

93 Rivoire, vol. 2, p. 202 (June 1473).

94 Rivoire, vol. 2, p. 253 (February 1473).

95 Cf. the cycle in York. P. J. P. Goldberg, 'Mortality and Economic Change in the Diocese of York, 1390–1514', *Northern History* 29 (1988): 38–55.

96 Rivoire, vol. 2, p. 260 (15 March 1474).

97 Rivoire, vol. 2, p. 269 (April 1474). This seems not to have been a very successful edict, as pigs were again on the agenda in November. Rivoire, vol. 2, p. 321.

98 Rivoire, vol. 2, p. 273 (May 1474).

99 Rivoire, vol. 2, p. 281 (June 1474).

100 Rivoire, vol. 2, pp. 325 (20 December 1474), 334–5 (December 1474).

101 Rivoire, vol. 2, p. 299 (2 September 1474). The pessimistic attitude of people to the ability of the plague structures to protect and heal them is not surprising. As T. D. Murphy observed in his 'The Transformation of Traditional Medical Culture under the Old Regime', *Historical Reflections* 16 (1989): 307–50, 'the brutal reality of medicine's failure before epidemic disease or even before more benign afflictions advised prudence before . . . enthusiasm' (p. 319).

102 Rivoire, vol. 2, p. 361 and n. 1 (27 April 1475).

103 S. Y. Edgerton reminds us that 'disturbing republican order was a violation of natural *and* civic law', in 'Icons of Justice', *P&P* 89 (1980): 23–38.

104 Rivoire, vol. 2, p. 369 (9 May 1475).

105 Rivoire, vol. 2, p. 379 (28 July 1475).

106 Rivoire, vol. 2, p. 383 (12 September 1475).

107 Rivoire, vol. 2, p, 465 (19 November 1476). Despite this payment there seems to have been no plague this year. There are demands that people with grain should convert it into bread and that grain must not be exported, which implies that the cereal shortage had not ended. See Rivoire, vol. 2, pp. 427 (February 1476), 435 (March 1476). There is also a reference to the repair of latrines in Longemale by Pierre Cortager. See Rivoire, vol. 2, p. 436 (April 1476).

108 Rivoire, vol. 3, p. 176 (19 June 1481).

109 Rivoire, vol. 3, p. 191 (December 1481). Cf. stockpiling of grain and other essentials in Nuremberg. W. von Stromer, 'Commercial Policy and Economic Conjuncture in Nuremberg at the Close of the Middle Ages: a Model of Economic Policy', *Journal of European Economic History* 10: 1 (1981): 119–29, especially 123–4.

110 Rivoire, vol. 3, p. 190 (November 1481). Mutton was 5*d* per pound from St Andrew's Day to Ascension Day and 3*d* per pound the rest of the year. Beef was 3*d* per pound all year. Bread had to be sold according to uniform loaf sizes and weights.

111 Rivoire, vol. 3, pp. 191–2 (December 1481).

112 Rivoire, vol. 3, p. 200 (February 1482). For more on caring for the poor see M. K. McIntosh, 'Local Responses to the Poor in late medieval and Tudor England', *Continuity and Change* 3: 2 (1988): 209–45; J. W. Brodman, *Charity and Welfare: Hospitals and the Poor in Medieval Catalonia* (Philadelphia, 1998); M. Pelling, *The Common Lot: Sickness, Medical Occupations and the Urban Poor in Early Modern England* (London, 1998); R. Jütte, *Poverty and Deviance in Early Modern Europe* (Cambridge, 1994).

113 Rivoire, vol. 3, p. 201 (12 February 1482).

114 Rivoire, vol. 3, pp. 203–4 (March 1482). The workers were Pierre Bonfils (*hospitalier*), Thivent Joquet, Pierre Gatiliard, Racemi and Arnollet.

115 Rivoire, vol. 3, p. 215 (May 1482). Clearly, the temporary site had been allowed to deteriorate since the previous epidemic.

116 Rivoire, vol. 3, p. 222 (2 July 1482). For attitudes to death see B. Gordon and P. Marshall, eds, *Place of the Dead: Death and Remembrance in Late Medieval and Early Modern Europe* (Cambridge, 2000); M. J. Dobson, *Contours of Death and Disease in Early Modern England* (Cambridge, 1997).

117 Rivoire, vol. 3, p. 255 (13 March 1483).

118 Rivoire, vol. 3, p. 251 (March 1483): Marquet Boulet, Pierre de Granges, Mon. Joselis.

119 Rivoire, vol. 3, p. 241 (January 1484).

120 Rivoire, vol. 3, p. 304 (January 1484). Nantermet Festi, tutor to the children of Mermet de Vignier, had done building work which had damaged the latrines.

121 Rivoire, vol. 3, pp. 417 (2 August 1485), 432 (18 October 1485).

122 Rivoire, vol. 3, pp. 473 (April 1486), 516 (November 1486).

123 Rivoire, vol. 4, p. 280 (22 June 1490).

124 Rivoire, vol. 4, p. 282 (13 July 1490).

125 Rivoire, vol. 4, pp. 284–5 (23 July 1490).

126 Rivoire, vol. 5, p. 78 (30 November 1492).

127 Rivoire, vol. 5, p. 79 (4 December 1492).

128 Rivoire, vol. 5, p. 117 (24 May 1493).

129 Rivoire, vol. 5, p. 129 (9 July 1493).

130 Rivoire, vol. 5, p. 131 (12 July 1493).

131 Rivoire, vol. 5, pp. 141–2 (1 October 1493).

132 Rivoire, vol. 5, p. 181 (29 March 1494).

133 Rivoire, vol. 5, p. 199 (17 June 1494).

134 Rivoire, vol. 5, p. 211 (2 September 1494).

135 Rivoire, vol. 6, p. 61 (28 July 1502). Amadeus Magraz, guard, was specifically singled out in the decree; he may have been lax in the performance of his duties.

136 Rivoire, vol. 6, p. 64 (22 July 1502). E. Alvarus, *Petit recueil des remedes pour se preserver, guerir, & nettoyer en temps de peste* (Toulouse: R. Colomiez, 1628), p. 35, recommended the burning of any cloth 'that is not of great value'.

137 Rivoire, vol. 6, p. 72 (23 August 1502).

138 Rivoire, vol. 6, p. 98 (10 January 1503).

139 Rivoire, vol. 6, p. 125 (6 June 1503).

140 Rivoire, vol. 6, p. 131 (11 July 1503).

141 Though xenophobia was a potent force and a constant reality in late medieval and early modern societies (probably no more than today). Cf. B. M. Hallman, 'Italian "Natural Superiority" and the Lutheran Question, 1517–46', *ARG* 71 (1980): 134–48.

142 Rivoire, vol. 6, p. 191 (14 May 1504).

143 Rivoire, vol. 6, p. 192 (21 May 1504). A *collège* had been established in 1389; the building was completely rebuilt in 1494. The Senate had only just gained secular control of the institution on 8 April 1502. For more on Geneva's schools see Naphy, 'The Reformation and the Evolution of Geneva's Schools' in B. Kümin, ed., *Reformations Old and New: Essays on the Socio-economic Impact of Religious Change c. 1470–1630* (Aldershot, 1996): pp. 185–202.

144 Rivoire, vol. 6, p. 198 (10 June 1504). Cf. C. Zika, 'Hosts, Processions and Pilgrimages: Controlling the Sacred in Fifteenth Century Germany', *P&P* 118 (1988): 25–64. For a discussion of a truly bizarre response to plague see R. Zguta, 'The One-day Votive Church: A Religious Response to the Black Death in Early Russia', *Slavic Review* 40: 3 (1981): 423–32. Also, compare the Muslim approach as seen in L. I. Conrad, 'Epidemic Disease in Formal and Popular Thought in early Islamic Society', in T. Ranger and P. Slack, eds, *Epidemics and Ideas* (Cambridge, 1992), pp. 77–99; M. W. Dols, *Medieval Islamic Medicine* (London, 1984).

145 Rivoire, vol. 6, p. 214 (24 September 1504).

146 Rivoire, vol. 6, p. 218 (18 October 1504).

147 Rivoire, vol. 6, p. 221 (8 November 1504).

148 Rivoire, vol. 6, p. 227 (3 December 1504).

149 As advised by the best authorities, for example J. Aubert, *Traite contenant les causes, la curation, & preservation de la peste* (Lausanne: J. le Preux, 1571), pp. 43–4.

150 Rivoire, vol. 6, p. 300 (5 May 1505). The name given to these workers was *cureur* or *cureuse*. The character of the cleaners remained crucial, as in E. Gourmelen, *Advertisement et conseil a messieurs de Paris* (Paris: N. Chesneau, 1581, first published in 1567), p. 35: 'For those who undertake to clean those houses already infected, it is necessary, first of all, that they should be honourable people' (*gens de bien*). As late as 1628 magistrates were being advised to hire cleaners who were 'first, those who believed in God, avoiding all thieves; second, those who are sober and learned in keeping from evil; third, those who have the art and industry to clean thoroughly'. Alvarus, *Petit recueil*, p. 33.

151 Rivoire, vol. 6, p. 307 (12 June 1505). For some comparative information on the relative value of these salaries see J. F. Bergier, 'Salaires des pasteurs de Genève au XVIe siècle', in *Mélanges d'histoire du XVIe siècle offerts à Henri Meylan*, Bibliothèque historique vaudoise 43 (Lausanne, 1970).

152 Rivoire, vol. 6, p. 241 (12 March 1505).

153 Rivoire, vol. 6, p. 246 (22 April 1505). The term most often applied to someone doing this task was *marron* or, much less frequently, *croque-mort*.

154 Nor was this the sole financial burden on the city, for Geneva agreed to undertake the expense of providing care for the city's poor as well. Rivoire, vol. 6, p. 256 (20 June 1505).

155 Rivoire, vol. 6, p. 294 (13 March 1506).

156 Rivoire, vol. 6, p. 343 (18 May 1507). The imposition of a strict house quarantine on Philippe should be seen as a clear sign of the city's willingness and ability to impose its medical policy even on the very cream of society. Claude's son, Jean, would later serve as a syndic and military commander-in-chief (*Capitaine Général*) during the revolutionary period in the 1530s, although he was executed after an abortive pro-Bernese *coup* attempt in the 1540s. In addition, his family would provide some of the strongest opposition to Calvin thereafter.

157 Rivoire, vol. 6, p. 361 (12 October 1507).

158 Rivoire, vol. 7, p. 4 (28 January 1508). On burial see C. M. Koslofsky, *The Reformation of the Dead: Death and Ritual in Early Modern Europe, 1450–1700* (Basingstoke, 2000).

159 Rivoire, vol. 7, p. 19 (23 May 1508).

160 Rivoire, vol. 7, p. 24 (16 June 1508). The force of this threat should not be underestimated. Geneva was a very small prince-bishopric and anyone stripped of their status (whether *citoyen*, *bourgeois* or *habitant*) became, in effect, a stateless foreigner.

161 Rivoire, vol. 7, p. 71 (10 April 1509). Two concerns make this of interest. First, these priests would have been segregated as a result of their contact. In effect, the state was maintaining a chaplaincy core to minister (only) to the infected. Secondly, this state intervention serves as a harbinger of the problems the government encountered when trying to get the Protestant ministers to treat the plague victims in the 1540s. See Naphy, *Calvin*, pp. 90–1.

162 Rivoire, vol. 7, p. 73 (20 April 1509).

163 Rivoire, vol. 7, p. 109 (7 December 1509).

164 Rivoire, vol. 7, p. 134 (30 April 1510).

165 Rivoire, vol. 8, pp. 332 (7 June 1519), 390 (29 November 1519).

166 Rivoire, vol. 8, p. 332 (14 June 1519).

167 Rivoire, vol. 8, p. 407 (3 January 1520). Four women were hired.

168 Rivoire, vol. 10, p. 228 (7 August 1526). The normal form of torture employed in Geneva was the use of the *corde*. The defendant's arms were tied behind his back and the *corde* was attached to the ropes at the wrists. The person was then raised from the floor suspended in such as way as to put extreme pressure on the shoulder joints. On some occasions, weights might be added to the feet to increase the pain. In addition, a person could be 'strapped'; this involved allowing the person to fall towards the floor but pulling the rope taut before the feet touched. This gave the shoulder joints a violent jerk, risking dislocation, and caused extreme pain, though it was unlikely to cause either permanent injury or death. This form of torture is commonly known by its Italian designation, the *strappado*. However, for clarity's sake, this work will refer to the *corde* when a person is being suspended and to strapping, when appropriate. As the latter represents a more extreme former of judicial torture and was employed less frequently it is important for the distinction to be maintained.

169 Rivoire, vol. 10, p. 232 (24 August 1526).

170 Rivoire, vol. 11, p. 300 and n. 2 (5 August 1529).

171 Rivoire, vol. 11, pp. 307–9 (20 August 1529).

172 Rivoire, vol. 11, p. 315 (7 September 1529).

173 Rivoire, vol. 11, p. 313 (3 September 1529). The wife of De Tronchant was reported as having been sent thither.

174 Rivoire, vol. 11, pp. 317 and n. 3 (14 September 1529), 321 (27 September 1529).

175 Rivoire, vol. 11, p. 338 (12 November 1529).

176 Rivoire, vol. 11, p. 418 (2 March 1530). The seriousness with which the city took its

regulations is obvious in its treatment of leading citizens: Jaques Emin was quarantined for six weeks with the disease, while Pierre Pechod was shut up for eight days simply for speaking to Emin. Rivoire, vol. 11, p. 461 (12 July 1530).

177 Literally, the accused were those who spread [infected] grease. This remained the normal term for people accused of the activity, though, as will be shown below, they were also called *semeurs de peste* (plague spreaders) and *empoissoneurs* (poisoners). There is, perhaps, a passing reference to plague spreading and grease making in a manuscript tract on *Errores Gazariorum* (Cathars) from *c.* 1450. J. Hansen, *Quellen und Untersuchungen zur Geschichte des Hexenwahns und der Hexenverfolgung im Mittelalter* (Heidelsheim, 1963), pp. 118–22. See also J. H. Langbein, *Prosecuting Crime in the Renaissance* (Cambridge MA, 1974), pp. 277, 281.

178 Rivoire, vol. 11, p. 435 (30 April 1530).

179 Rivoire, vol. 11, pp. 438 and n. 1 (11 May 1530), 439 and n. 1 (14 May 1530).

180 Rivoire, vol. 11, p. 444 and nn. 4–5 (3 June 1530).

181 On its early relations with, and place within, Savoy see E. L. Cox, *The Green Count of Savoy: Amadeus VI and Transalpine Savoy in the Fourteenth Century* (Princeton NJ, 1967).

182 For an early but detailed work see P. Vaucher, *Luttes de Genève contre la Savoie, 1517–30* (Geneva, 1889). Relations between titular overlords and (semi-) independent towns were always problematic. See S. Rowan, 'Imperial Taxes and German Politics in the Fifteenth Century: an Outline', *Central European History* 13: 3 (1980): 203–18, especially 208.

183 One should not forget that some voices were calling for concord and reform rather than conflict and Reformation. See J. M. Headley, 'Gattinara, Erasmus, and the Imperial Configurations of Humanism', *ARG* 71 (1980): 64–98; J. F. D'Amico, 'Beatus Rhenanus, Tertullian and the Reformation: a Humanist's Critique of Scholasticism', *ARG* 71 (1980): 37–63; C. E. Maxcey, 'Why do good? Dietenberger's Reply to Luther', *ARG* 75 (1984): 93–112; M. Hoffman, 'Faith and Piety in Erasmus' Thought', *SCJ* 20: 2 (1989): 241–58; M. Turchetti, 'Religious Concord and Political Tolerance in Sixteenth Century and Seventeenth Century France', *SCJ* 22: 1 (1991): 15–25; M. de Kroon, 'Martin Bucer and the Problem of Tolerance', *SCJ* 19: 2 (1988): 157–68.

184 AEG, PC2: 221 (7–30 April 1530), preserves the trial's records. The document is unpaginated, so precise reference will be made to dates.

185 AEG, PC2: 221 (7 April 1530).

186 AEG, PC2: 221 (8 April 1530).

187 AEG, PC2: 221 (11 April 1530).

188 AEG, PC2: 221 (12 April 1530).

189 AEG, PC2: 221 (13 April 1530). For more on plague and its regulation in the Pays de Vaud see M. Messerli, *Le Médecin vaudois à travers les ages* (Lausanne, 1929), and E. Olivier, *Médecine et santé dans le Pays de Vaud*, in Bibliothèque historique vaudoise 29 (Lausanne, 1962).

190 For more on plague and its regulation in Annecy see G. Letonnelier, 'Mesures prises pour éviter la peste, à Annecy, en 1503', *Revue savoisienne* 52 (1911): 44–8, and J. F. Gonthier, 'La peste à Annecy en 1629–1630', *Revue savoisienne* 37 (1896): 170–2.

191 AEG, PC2: 221 (23 April 1530).

192 AEG, PC2: 221 (28, 30 April 1530). In Geneva, the reading of the summation was the prelude to the execution of a convict.

193 AEG, PC2: 226 (11 April 1530).

194 AEG, PC2: 226 (14 April 1530).

195 AEG, PC2: 226 (17 April 1530).

196 AEG, PC2: 226 (25 April 1530).

197 AEG, PC2: 226 (26 April 1530). In addition to the sessions specifically noted below, Placet was also questioned on 28 and 30 April as well as 12 and 13 May.

198 AEG, PC2: 226 (27 April 1530).

199 AEG, PC2: 226 (29 April 1530).

200 AEG, PC2: 226 (11 May 1530).

201 AEG, PC2: 226 (4 June 1530).

202 AEG, PC2: 222. (These documents are not dated, as they are extracts from other cases inserted into Dufour's dossier for reference purposes by the city secretary, Claude Roset, at the request of the syndics.)

203 AEG, PC2: 222 (6, 14 May 1530). On attitudes to, and treatment of, the condemned see, for example, N. Terpstra, 'Piety and Punishment: The Lay *Conforteria* and Civic Justice in Sixteenth Century Bologna', *SCJ* 22: 4 (1991): 679–94; T. Astarita, *Village Justice: Community, Family and Popular Culture in Early Modern Italy* (Baltimore MD, 1999).

204 AEG, PC2: 223 (25 April 1530).

205 AEG, PC2: 223 (2 May 1530). Silk may not have been an accidental element. Silk workers (a traditionally female-dominated industry) would have been especially hit by the significant break in trade occasioned by an outbreak and therefore likely to seek alternative employment (e.g. in the pest house). M. Wensky, 'Women's Guilds in Cologne in the Later Middle Ages', *Journal of European Economic History* 11: 3 (1982): 631–50, especially 631–2.

206 AEG, PC2: 223 (9 May 1530).

207 AEG, PC2: 223 (12 May 1530).

208 AEG, PC2: 223 (12 May 1530). The magisterial witnesses were the four syndics (Jean Balard, Jean Ami Curtet, Robert Vandel, Pierre Vill[i]et), the Lieutenant, the Senate's factor (or steward, Petremand Falquet), Pierre Malbuisson, Estienne Pecollat, Michel Sept, Jean Louis Ramel and Michel Guillet.

209 The other dates of interrogations were 13, 18, 20 and 21 May; 2 June; 26 September; 22 and 29 October. Torture was certainly applied on 22 October during which it became clear to the judges that Jeanne was not pregnant, as she admitted that it had simply been a ruse to allow her time to escape.

210 AEG, PC2: 224 (26 April 1530).

211 AEG, PC2: 224 (27 April 1530).

212 AEG, PC2: 224 (28 April 1530).

213 AEG, PC2: 224 (29 April 1530).

214 AEG, PC2: 229 (10 May 1530).

215 AEG, PC2: 229 (11, 13 May 1530).

216 AEG, PC2: 229 (13 May 1530).

217 AEG, PC2: 229 (17 May 1530).

218 Depositions were taken on 20 May; 2, 9, 14, 20 and 21 June; 1 and 9 July.

219 AEG, PC2: 225 (1530).

CHAPTER TWO

THE MAGISTRATES AND PLAGUE,
1542–46

Because it has pleased God to chastise us with plague

The question to be examined at this point is when and how the phenomenon was next brought to the state's attention; how the magistrates reacted and what, if any, steps they took to control the situation. Although (as will be shown below) there was an investigation in June 1543 in reality Geneva's magistrates had already been made aware of the threat of yet another plague-spreading conspiracy. On 5 May that year, the magistrates of Lausanne had written to report the arrest of a suspected plague spreader.[1] However, before any serious examination of this new conspiracy can begin it is essential to situate it within the broader context of the events of a particular epidemic. Plague spreading always occurred as a feature of a plague outbreak *in both senses* (conspiratorial and unintentional). Clearly, this behaviour was a serious concern to the magistracy (and the populace) but the reality is that every Genevan was considerably more exercised by the equally pressing threat of dying from plague spread unintentionally. Therefore, the existence of *engraisseurs* can be examined only after a thorough evaluation of the events of the plague outbreak in which they appeared. The period after 1530 had been very traumatic indeed, with both a political revolution and a religious reformation. However, these changes did not force, or allow, the state to slacken its efforts to maintain, preserve and promote the health and welfare of the city.

Just as the 1530 outbreak had taken place against the backdrop of dramatic political and religious change, this next appearance of the disease coincided with the end of an especially traumatic period in the new republic's history. By 1538, the city had already gained effective independence from Savoy. However, it had done so at the cost of heavy reliance on the military assistance of Berne (and, initially, Fribourg). This had placed the government in a very precarious position indeed. In effect, the Bernese clearly desired the establishment of a protectorate over Geneva. Not surprisingly, the Genevans – newly liberated from the Dukes of Savoy and their Prince Bishop – had no desire to place a Bernese yoke on their necks, no matter how light it might be. This forced the ruling élite to contemplate two contradictory approaches to Berne. First, Geneva could submit to Berne's demands in every sense short of an outright protectorate. Second, the city could assert its independence. Neither solution was satisfactory.

In 1538, those politicians favouring compromise were able to gain power and negotiate a truly humiliating treaty with Berne, thereby guaranteeing military protection. In 1540, there was a popular backlash against the treaty (and policy) led by key citizens. They gained power and were then confronted by what may have been an attempted *coup*. The result of these machinations was that in 1541 a sizeable contingent of citizens was forced into exile. In addition, Calvin, who had been expelled as a collateral victim of the 1538 political clash, was recalled to restore order to Geneva's ecclesiastical situation, devastated by the resignations of Ministers appointed by the defeated politicians. Effectively, therefore, the magistracy was bereft of key figures, the Church was forced to hire new ministers, the post-revolutionary constitutional structure needed a complete overhaul, and the newly reformed Church had no set order. In addition, the populace was agitated by political chaos, and, perhaps most dangerously of all, the city had managed to offend Berne so comprehensively as to have lost its military protection. Thus, at every level, Geneva was in a disturbed condition.[2]

In early 1542, therefore, Geneva was hastily attempting to repair the situation. There were regular contacts with Basle, which was then acting as intermediary in the dispute between Geneva, on the one hand, and Berne, along with the exiled Genevans, on the other.[3] In addition, the magistrates were busily settling in a host of new ministers and schoolteachers.[4] Assignments were made to parishes and wages set.[5] In the course of these negotiations and activities, Geneva maintained an extensive and friendly exchange of diplomatic and newsy letters with neighbouring cities whether Catholic or Protestant.[6]

It was in this unsettled environment that plague broke out in September 1542. It may not be coincidental that this unseasonably late appearance of the disease coincided with the passage of 10,000 French troops through Genevan territory in August.[7] Whatever the cause, the outbreak could not have come at a worse time; the hospital's barber-surgeon had been arrested at the start of the month for adultery.[8] Also, in yet another blow to the city's personnel, Jean Martin, the elderly *guydon* (crier/herald) was deemed unfit for his office and had to be replaced by someone able 'to conduct [to the hospital] those infected with plague'.[9] Within days, the Senate

> because it has pleased God to punish us (with just cause) for our sins with his rod – a disabling plague – decided that the Plague Hospital should be set in order. [The Senate also] decided to provide a *hospitalier*, a barber-surgeon, a *guydon*, and a minister to look after those infected with this disease and any other needful matters.

Jean de Cortelles was confirmed as *hospitalier*, Tyvent Furjod as *guydon* and, for a minister, the magistrates decided to ask the Company of Pastors to select one of their number. In addition, the city decreed that 'those who converse in a place suspected [of the infection] should be quarantined in their houses for the space of eight days'.[10] The city's bureaucracy now began to swing into full operation. The hospital's *procureurs* were to construct 'three or four beds' at the Plague Hospital; since the 'general cemetery' had become infected after the burial of some plague victims a new temporary site was to be selected for those who died of anything else.[11] However, Calvin and Castellio supported the more traditional alternative of burying victims of the plague near the hospital.[12]

In a more dramatic move, the magistracy raised its vision beyond the city's walls and ordered spies to be sent to nearby Nyon to watch out for Germans suspected of bringing the epidemic to the city.[13] Internally, the Lieutenant, the militia captains and the *diziniers* (the ward commanders) were to scour the city for plague sufferers.[14] At the suggestion of De Cortelles, the 'city apothecary' (Claude Dupan) was charged with ensuring that the Plague Hospital had a regular supply of the necessary drugs.[15] The magistrates also agreed that De Cortelles would be paid 144 florins per year and Estienne Furjod 72 florins; Claude Pertemps and Jean Chautemps were charged with settling the wages of the other servants, both male and female.[16] Although details are sparse for these other workers, Jean Fiollet (a barber-surgeon and gravedigger) was paid 144 florins per year and some grain on the condition that he lived in the Plague Hospital.[17]

At the end of the following month, the magistracy gratefully accepted the offer of Pierre Blanchet (a minister 'with a large heart') 'of his own free will to go this day into the Plague Hospital to console and solace those poor [folk] infected of plague'.[18] Concern about the consequences of the spreading epidemic led Jaques Bernard, another minister, to ask permission to remove his horse (given to him for his journeys to a rural parish) from the hospital; the city agreed that he could keep it at his mother's house 'to avoid [any] consequences'.[19] However, in a harbinger of things to come, the Senate admonished Nicolas Vandert (minister of the city parish of St-Gervais) for refusing to visit the sick and 'not doing other necessary duties'.[20]

Among the many things the city undertook, it ordered the publication, by the printer Jean Girard, of a work entitled *Remedy against the Plague* after the manuscript had been proof-read by the 'physicians and barber-surgeons of the city'.[21] Edicts were issued ordering anyone suffering from the disease to report to the hospital for confinement.[22] The city was closed to possible sources of the contagion 'under pain of death'; Genevans already ill were subjected to a nine o'clock curfew.[23] Since the corpses were overwhelming the city's gravedigger (Jean Garnier), he was assigned Monet Boccard as an assistant (on 120 florins per year). [24] It would appear that a similar overburdening of work forced the city to seek an assistant for De Cortelles; after passing examination, François de Barberiis was hired.[25] There may, however, have been a much more pragmatic and pressing reason for this appointment. On the evening of 29 October, De Cortelles died of the plague.[26] De Barberiis requested, and received, back pay for expenses already incurred as well as the appointment of two more female workers.[27]

Clearly, the contagion had now reached dangerous proportions. The Senate agreed to find a house for Pierre Compagnion, a barber-surgeon from Lyon, in return for his services.[28] In a more obvious sign of the seriousness of the situation, the magistrates confirmed that the wages owed to the cleaners would, in the event of their death, be paid to their heirs according to 'the ancient custom'.[29] These benefits set the stage for the later accusations of plague spreading both for larcenous profit and for security of employment. This provision guaranteeing wages – a health and life insurance policy – was unique. No other state employees were in a strong enough position to gain or, more accurately, extract this concession.

The work load was obviously increasing, as was the anxiety in the city. De Barberiis recommended that corpses should be buried within an hour 'to keep the air pure'.[30] Other practical concerns also intruded: both De Barberiis and Garnier were facing financial difficulties, no doubt caused by the need to pay for things in anticipation of reimbursement by the state.[31] The stress of the job also began to tell as friction arose between Blanchet and De Barberiis; the latter quit his post very soon thereafter (though apparently on good terms).[32] Other practical concerns about the (unintentional) spreading of the disease by hospital workers arose. For example, the fumigator Angellin Berthier was investigated for chatting with a healthy young lady as early as December 1542.[33] This initial problem was allowed to die away, as the preliminary bout of plague had abated by the end of February 1543 and the workers were sent home.[34]

The councillors also dealt with the much broader picture. Jean Chautemps, senator, was ordered to take a guard and go through the city 'to evict certain [foreign] people'.[35] Although this may have been related to the plague it is perhaps more likely (as on numerous occasions mentioned in the previous chapter) that regulations against foreigners, even in plague time, had other motives. Thus, two months after Chautemps's sweep, the city's officials forbade foreign merchants from trading in Geneva except on Wednesdays, Fridays and Saturdays.[36] Therefore, one might see this commission and related edicts as preparatory measures. Geneva had enough experience of plague to realise that the disease, which seems to have abated in December, was very likely to return with warmer weather.

Immediately before the discussion that saw Chautemps deputed to deal with the foreigners, the Senate gave him orders to see to the proper outfitting of the Plague Hospital. In addition, the workers (minister, barber-surgeon and other servants) at the hospital were given permission to return, temporarily, to their homes.[37] In March, Chautemps was instructed to arrange for the purchase of a 'black shroud' to be used for the transportation of plague corpses to burial.[38] The first few days of April were occupied with a flurry of activity designed to control Geneva's economy. All foreigners were to be stopped and forced to provide documentary evidence for their absence from their native land. If it could not be produced they were to be expelled.[39] Guards were posted at places licensed to house 'strangers'; butchers and bakers were subject to strict edicts, as were taverns and inns.[40] Finally, on 9 April, Chautemps was directed to refurbish the 'rooms, windows and other affairs' of the Plague Hospital.[41] In effect, the city was 'battening down the hatches' in preparation for the epidemic's return.

Jean Fiollet was also rehired to serve in the hospital for (an increased salary of) 240 florins per year and, because of the continuing grain shortage, a grain supplement.[42] On 20 April, the senators were apprised of the news they had feared yet anticipated: '[in the Senate] it was reported that, according to God's good will, the plague has recommenced at the Rose Inn in [the Place] Mollard'.[43] The normal regulations began to swing into operation. Curfews were imposed on plague victims and healthy alike. Bakers were banned from passing through the streets selling their bread outside certain hours. To stress their determination, the government called in eleven bakers personally to hear of the curfew.[44] *Cabanes* were to be allowed only near a certain city wall.[45]

Almost immediately, the plague began to affect the city's administration. Tyvent Furjod, a guard, was suspended from his post (and replaced by Jean Baubre) because his wife was ill and plague was suspected. She was to be examined and he would return to work only if she did not have the disease.[46] Moreover, in addition to setting the hospital 'in order, furnished with whatever will be necessary', the councillors advised the ministers to select one of their own 'to solace and console the poor [folk] infected with plague' in the hospital.[47] Calvin reported that he and Sebastien Castellio, the newly appointed regent of the schools, were willing to serve.[48] Unfortunately, the city was unwilling to risk their lives and asked for another to be selected; the others replied that they 'preferred to go to the devil or to Champel' rather than the Plague Hospital.[49] They were strongly admonished and threatened with dismissal.[50] After consideration, the Senate suspended Castellio's possible appointment and decided that Tallien could console the afflicted until another solution could be found.[51] The crisis was not resolved until 11 May, when Pierre Blanchet agreed to serve.[52]

If these personnel problems were not enough, the officials admitted that Jean Fiollet was not able to be 'alone and to serve' at the hospital.[53] Bernard Tallien (a *habitant* originally from Dijon) was hired, having 'taken the normal oath' for the 'normal salary'. Two female servants were also hired.[54] As in the past, the senators also made provision for more expert workers at the hospital. They discussed trying to obtain the services of Jean Pernet of Neuchâtel, who was 'an expert at helping those inconvenienced by the plague'. They were willing to offer him 240 florins per year and a house. A committee of four officials (Pertemps, Lambert, Chautemps and Louis Bernard) was sent to open negotiations with him.[55] Finally, on 4 May, the *guydon* (or crier) was ordered to identify infected homes and to enlist *cureurs* and *cureuses* (cleaners and fumigators) 'to take the oath dutifully to clean' (see Appendix 1).[56]

With the appointment of the cleaners and other workers there was, in theory, the chance that plague spreading might reappear. Indeed, one might expect that the magistrates, many of whom had served during the trials in 1530, would have been concerned about this potential threat. That they did not is all the more surprising since, on 27 April, François Boulat had been arrested for plague spreading. The officials were sufficiently concerned to strap him seven times and, although he confessed nothing, to imprison him indefinitely.[57] Moreover, even the accusation that servants and cleaners working at the Rose inn (where the 1543 outbreak started) were visiting friends and co-workers in uninfected homes elicited no more than an official investigation.[58] As a result, the city ordered the guards to ensure that cleaners stuck to their tasks and did not mingle with the uninfected.[59] At no point is there any hint that the magistracy expected, anticipated or even suspected that the events of 1530 might be repeated.

At the same time, the magistracy was able to consolidate the personnel situation. Blanchet finally took up his post with an increase in his salary from 240 florins per year to 360 florins per year plus some bread and wine.[60] Another two female servants were hired.[61] Jean Pernet's arrival was set for 15 May; two days later he 'was examined to discover if he was wise enough to console the poor plague victims and to provide them with treatment'.[62] The Senate was more than proud of the result. They were now able to order plague victims – for example, Croset, the butcher in Longemale (whose household was struck down) – to go, along with all others, to the Plague Hospital, where 'at present there is a good provision [both] of a minister and a barber-surgeon'.[63] Moreover, the city was able to augment this fully staffed medical team with treatises on plague remedies written by Louis Beljaquet and François Chappuis.[64] With a clear sense of climax, on 18 May 1543, the Senate swore in Jean Pernet (also called Rojon) from Neuchâtel as the hospital's barber-surgeon and

> [The Senate] made and passed many articles and ordinances on the regime and government of the Plague Hospital, with the declaration of the responsibilities of the minister, the surgeon, the gravediggers, the servants and others along with their [various] wages. These were read in the presence of Master Jean [Pernet], surgeon, and found reasonable. It was ordered that everything should be written down and a duplicate given to those in the hospital so they would know the [regulations].[65]

Obviously, at this point, the city had managed to implement the full range of plague responses it had developed, in particular, over the previous four decades. The magistracy had, once again, taken direct and minute control of the situation. There is certainly no intimation that the city's élite were trying to distance themselves from the crisis. As before, the officials arranged for quarantine, plague shacks and the basic provisions needed at the Plague Hospital. Geneva girded itself for the strict regulation of every aspect of its economy. Also, the requisite personnel were hired to undertake the day-to-day business of caring for the sick and disposing of the dead. There continued to be heavy reliance on foreigners for the provision of daily care. However, despite a revolution in government and religion, there is no suggestion that Geneva's rulers had made any significant changes in their approach to plague prevention or containment. More important, no lessons seem to have been learned from the 1530 trials. One can quite confidently assume that the population and their officials in no way expected the phenomenon to return. In their minds it must have been a violent and bizarre conspiracy completely localised in time and place. Thus, Geneva was taken completely by surprise when the *engraisseurs* returned in 1543.

Initially, however, the return of the plague, although distressing and dangerous, seemed normal enough. Jean Pernet, of Neuchâtel, was hired as a barber-surgeon and, within days, sent to examine a sick girl in Michel Varro's house to see whether she had plague.[66] On the same day, the Senate ordered that he should have everything necessary for the 'recipe of preservatives for avoiding problems'.[67] The city, though not short of medical professionals (see Appendix 2), was certainly not pleased in the midst of a plague to have to prosecute one of its barber-surgeons, Bastien de Nantua, for 'things against God and his profession'.[68] Although this vague wording might imply something very serious, Geneva's judges did no more than banish him, under pain of death, never to return.[69] This case contrasts well with another which serves to highlight the minutiae attracting official attention. On 21 May, Richard Grosse, a baker, was investigated because he – and his dog – had strayed too close to the Plague Hospital.[70]

This minor event may well explain the contemporaneous decision to pay Jean Blanc (*guet*, guard) for every dog and cat he killed.[71] It is, however, more likely that this decision was simply part of the range of rules of 21 May designed to implement, yet again, a copious body of anti-plague regulations. Carpenters in the city were ordered to build thirty-six wooden *cabanes*. Jean Chautemps was given power 'to organise people to clean the infected houses at the expense of those who live in those houses'. The necessities of life were to be arranged for the hospital by its servants and they were to be paid a cash wage. The responsibility for the welfare of those confined in the hospital was given to Chautemps and the workers there. In addition, provision was made for medicines (and the cost thereof) and, the following day, the city apothecary (Claude Dupan) was explicitly ordered to ensure that Pernet, the hospital's barber-surgeon, had the drugs and prescriptions he required. Finally, anyone failing to accept quarantine when required faced a fine of 60s and eight days in jail.[72]

Within days, it became clear that these edicts and provisions were not sufficient. Again the city's leaders were forced to re-examine their rulings and 'fine-tune' them. The cabins they had had built were too close to the Rhône (the city's major water source). The *cureuses* were told to stop washing straw (presumably from bedding) in the river and burn it instead. However, the city set specific hours during which this could be done. The government fined householders who failed to clean the road in front of their houses. Chautemps was given a horse to help him perform his tasks. More timber was to be felled from state forests for additional cabins, and the city noted – and accepted – privately built and equipped cabins.[73] The Senate was even forced to order butchers to keep their animals farther from the plague hospital.[74]

Although these actions evidence some haste, there is certainly no sense of panic. The state (and the city generally) were simply responding in the customary manner to an outbreak of plague. Nothing new, nothing dramatic is apparent. Even the death of the minister Blanchet, on 1 June, and of the barber-surgeon, Pernet, the next day, seems not to have caused undue concern or consternation.[75] Nevertheless, a number of issues were beginning to impinge on the Genevan consciousness. First, personnel was an obvious concern; however, the Ministerial response to Blanchet's death was, once again, to prevaricate in the appointment of a successor when the authorities refused Calvin's nomination.[76] The Senate made it very clear that this Ministerial timidity was more than annoying. The ministers were hauled before the council and informed bluntly that 'their office was to serve God and his Church as much in [times of] prosperity and in [times of] necessity even unto death and that they were required to elect and ordain a replacement for master Pierre Blanchet'. One single exception was made from this rebuke and that was Calvin; he was devoted solely to the Church and was not to serve in the hospital. The response the city received from its foreign ministers must have been depressing and infuriating:

> [the ministers] were admonished [again] that they served not only in times of pros-
> perity but [also] in times of war and plague and other necessity; they were to serve
> the Christian Church and they confessed that this was true and that it was their office
> but that God had not given them the strength and constancy to go to the hospital.

Mathieu Geneston, an (assistant) minister, was chosen (by lot, it would appear) and accepted.[77]

More important, though, in May there was a rumour that fumigators were entering non-infected houses; a report was ordered. At this point the magistrates assigned two guards to watch the workers. A week later the gravediggers, Fiollet and Tallien (both later executed), were dismissed without explanation. In a some-what bizarre twist a barber-surgeon, Bernard Tallien (almost certainly the same gravedigger) was asked to examine the body of Jean Pernet, the hospital's deceased barber-surgeon. Two days later, on 4 June, two young girls were arrested for plague spreading. On 8 June 1543, extra precautions were ordered at the gates after rumours of nocturnal plague spreading.[78] It is worth noting the actually wording of this decree, though. '[Re:] Plague poisoners – as there is a rumour that at night there are poisoners who are spreading plague in the city it is resolved to speak to master Henry, porter at the Tartasse Gate, so he will set a guard [against it]'.[79] The emphasis is on a purely natural, if evil, activity, the possible poisoning of people by the spread of plague.

Despite the problems with the *cureuses* the city seemed much more exercised over its staffing problems. Personnel concerns drove the officials to decree that at least one *médicin* should remain in the city at all times.[80] Chautemps was charged with replacing Pernet. His first nomination was Hans from Zürich. However, when he was interviewed by Henry Aubert and Claude Dupan (both apothecaries) they deemed him unsuitable – he spoke no French, only German. Despite this, he was deputed to work in Geneva's General Hospital.[81] Simon Moreaux and Rene Bellefilles, both from Turenne, were appointed as *hospitalier* and assistant.[82]

Indeed, two related, and perhaps interconnected, events involving the popula-tion in general accompanied the need for workers. Since the defeat of the pro-Bernese party in 1540–41 most of its adherents had been living in Bernese territory. However, in the midst of plague, Geneva began rehabilitating and readmitting leading *Articulants* (as they were called) to the body politic.[83] Seemingly, all Genevans were rushing to the aid of the city and past differences were being put aside in the face of the medical crisis. Just as significantly, the Senate decreed the expulsion, within three days, of all foreigners under pain of the *strappado*.[84] One senses that the city is very much 'circling its wagons'. Although not yet a panic, the situation was reaching a crisis point.

It is hardly surprising, therefore, that the situation in Geneva now took a decided turn for the worse. On 8 June 1543, the city moved to control, yet again, the places where infected linen could be washed. Plague spreaders or, more accurately, 'plague poisoners' were noted on the same day.[85] The city decreed that, because of 'the suspicion that at night there were some poisoners who are spreading plague through the city', the keeper of the Tartasse Gate should ensure an adequate watch to eliminate the danger.[86] It is interesting to note that the city, faced with so serious a threat, decided to remove all corpses from the gibbet. Clearly the Senate was more concerned to defend the public health than to retain the visible deterrence of rotting malefactors.[87] Lest any potential poisoners should draw the wrong conclusion, the government ordered the rebuilding of another gibbet slightly removed from the city.[88] In reality, though, beyond posting a stronger guard, the city did nothing more about the plague spreaders. Among many possible explanations, the best would seem to be that the magistrates took the view that the rumour was no more than the result of popular concern informed by the events of 1530. In effect, their reaction suggests that they simply did not take the matter seriously. Any state used to micro-managing a crisis would have been unlikely to be blasé faced with the possible return of so dangerous an activity unless the government failed to lend the report any credence. In effect, the state was mollifying popular concern, no more.

Subsequent events serve to bear out this interpretation. In July, the Senate ordered that all medical personnel and ministers should read the three books on plague remedies presented by François Chappuis, as they were 'for the profit of the city'.[89] The literary interests of the magistrates continued to be held by Chappuis. He had two books (presumably his own) approved the following day and the Senate ordered a general conference (of all medical personnel?).[90] In addition, Chappuis was given six écus. However, Chappuis returned within less than a month, having failed to convince a publisher that in the current situation the books would sell. The state voted a subvention of ten écus.[91] If this focus on medicinal recipes were not enough to demonstrate the state's indifference to the threat, one need only note that the 1530 events were specifically brought to the Senate's attention on 10 July. Jean Grangier, whose father (it was noted) had died in the Plague Hospital during the 'time of Caddo the poisoner', asked to be admitted as a *barbier* in the general hospital. The city considered the request, stipulating that, in the meantime, he might better serve in some other capacity.[92] Clearly, the city was very sensitive to the power of the popular memory of the 1530 conspiracy and wanted to avoid unduly reminding people of those events. One cannot imagine less likely behaviour if Geneva's élite truly thought the city was being menaced by yet another outbreak of conspiratorial plague spreading.

The minutiae of activities that continued to attract the government's supervision reinforce this view. The city continued to have trouble forcing its infected inhabitants to withdraw to designated locations.[93] Prominent citizens were proving to be especially troublesome. Pierre de Veyrier was allowed to build a cabin in a separate location.[94] Jean Bectier simply refused to leave his house.[95] Etienne de la Maisonneuve, a scion of one of Geneva's premier Protestant families, wanted to withdraw to another (unspecified) location; the magistrates ordered, again, that everyone had to move to cabins.[96] As evidence of the government's increasing frustration, the Senate ordered that the plague regulations should be 'cried' throughout the city once more.[97] This was followed by more controls on the way animals were slaughtered.[98] Finally, Jean Chautemps was given the unenviable task of avoiding confusion in relocating infected people to cabins. Geneva's inhabitants should co-operate since 'it pleases God to batter us with his rod of plague'.[99] It would seem that reminding the goodly Genevans of God's providential care was no more effective an incentive than the constant 'crying' of the plague regulations.

While Geneva was busy trying to enforce its regulations on the citizenry it was also forced to make adequate provision for those who had already suffered for the sake of the city. Jean Blanc was finally relieved as a guard by Tyvent Furjod; the widow of Jean Pernet was given financial assistance, as (eventually) was Blanchet's widow.[100] The problems associated with the loss of (already impoverished) employees may well explain the government's decision to sack those assigned to guard the gates, at a cost of 4s per day, and to replace them with 'the leading householders'.[101] Apparently these Genevan worthies were not overly enthusiastic in responding to the call. The Senate was still discussing the financial problems of employing so many guards three days later.[102]

One might be inclined, viewing all this activity, to infer that the city's relaxed attitude to the rumour of plague spreaders as well as Grangier's appearance were so minor as to elicit a minimalist response. The reality is much more complex. On 13 July, the government again discussed the rumour that grease had appeared on the doors of many houses.[103] Three weeks later, doors were again reported to have been greased 'to spread plague'.[104] In both cases, the response was to set a stronger guard to patrol the streets at night. The fundamental inactivity of the city in response is noticeable. However, the growing concern among the citizenry is clear in the fact that the decision on 8 August was taken, not by the Senate, but by the much larger Conseil des Deux Cents – the largest elected body in the city. There is no reason to assume that the larger council was convoked solely to discuss this matter. It is much more likely that the council was meeting to discuss the great threat posed by the constant passage of Italian troops employed by the King of France to fight the Emperor.[105] The day before the Deux Cents met 5,000 Italians began passing by Geneva and an extra strong watch was posted.[106] Thus, the Senate already had plenty of reason to post numerous guards in the city and to discuss the provision of guards and security (both internal and external) with the city's largest council.

Regardless of the external threat facing the city, it was increasingly clear that people were putting great pressure on the magistracy to do something about the grease. On 10 August, the Senate reported that 'because the turmoil [in the city] is very great the greasing of the door handles to the end that many have gone to God and it is not known if this is because of plague or poison. [It is] resolved to mount a guard.' Unsurprisingly, the government saw no reason to follow the advice of François de Mandallaz, priest, who had written a letter (dated 9 August 1543) blaming the plague on the adoption of Protestantism.[107] Instead, the state took the more practical action of deputing five senior magistrates, including the city's military commandant (the Capitaine Général) and treasurer, to oversee guards assigned to specific sections of the city.[108] The magistrates also became aware that the problems with their plague workers were not confined to the fumigators or, worse, unknown poisoners, and that the very peak of the hospital structure was corrupt. Bernard Tallien, barber-surgeon of the Plague Hospital, was reported for keeping a prostitute among his workers, presumably for his own use. Two syndics were dispatched to help Jean Chautemps, the magistrate in charge, investigate the allegation.[109] The probable outcome of this inquiry became apparent within days when the Senate decided that Tallien should be retained, temporarily, but another barber-surgeon, Guillaume Pernost of Burgundy, who had asked for work should be paid two écus to remain on stand-by.[110] Less than a fortnight later, Tallien was admonished for his behaviour, the girl was fired and the ministers were called in to remonstrate with him 'to desist totally from this abomination [of adultery]'.[111]

One might expect the city to have undertaken a thorough investigation of the situation in the Plague Hospital and among the workers. After all, many of the magistrates had been involved in the 1530 trials. The local populace was increasingly agitated by the reappearance of grease. There was a clear assumption that deaths had been caused by the same grease. From top to bottom, the city was aware that there was corruption and trouble among the plague workers.[112] The situation eventually reached the ludicrous pass that Chautemps reported that Tallien was demanding white instead of red wine and that the minister was not doing his job.[113] Indeed, late September seemed to offer the ideal catalyst for such a move. On 24 September, François Boulat was rearrested. He was charged with possibly spreading the plague and was made to endure repeated applications of torture. However, he refused to confess. Logically, if one believes that a magistracy in the midst of a major social and demographic crisis will seek scapegoats, Boulat should have been accused of spreading grease and, perhaps, reintroducing a conspiracy to spread plague.[114] Instead he was released the same day, and it is clear that the sole charge against him was that he might have unintentionally spread plague by having violated quarantine after burying a plague victim.[115] No attempt at scapegoating is apparent. It is hard to imagine a more likely candidate and yet the magistracy made no attempt to convict Boulat in an effort to appease the people and diffuse the growing panic in the city.

The sheer complacency of the city's rulers is breathtaking. On 12 October, it was reported that the bells had been greased and, ten days later, that the *cureurs* were coming into the city after the curfew. The guards were admonished to keep the gates more secure.[116] On the same day yet more reports were received of (unspecified) 'insolences' at the plague hospital.[117] One can only comprehend the seeming indifference of the magistrates to these troubles by focusing, as they no doubt did, on the greater crisis of mass death. Whole families were disappearing and even the rural parishes were struck.[118] Put simply, the magistrates, although very concerned by the workers' antics, were more concerned that the system should function and, despite its many problems, alleviate the worst effects of the plague. Overwhelming necessity forced the magistrates to accept that troublesome, disobedient workers were better than no workers at all. A Senate preoccupied with a dying city had little time or enthusiasm for investigations or trials, in small rooms, involving defendants who might be highly infectious. The Senate's behaviour is neither irrational nor inexplicable; it stemmed from the logical and perfectly predictable desire to avoid complicating a situation that demanded complete concentration on damage limitation.

It may also be that the city had an eye to the season. Its medical advisers were telling it that the plague was likely to abate with the onset of winter; it would then be able to turn its attention to the system of plague containment. It may be that this important information was contained in François Chappuis's plague treatise published and delivered to the Conseil des Soixantes in November. The larger council advised that the syndics should receive copies and, along with the rest of the Senate, consult the work.[119] The city's ordeal ended on 11 December, when Chautemps reported that 'by God's mercy, the plague has stopped'.[120] However, there was no time for celebration or rest. Chautemps wanted immediate steps taken to clean and refurbish the hospital; he also stressed that its debts should be cleared.[121] The Senate began to settle more than pecuniary debts. Tallien was to be investigated for attempting to kill his wife with poisoned bread.[122] The ministers were called in and told, yet again, to settle on some means of providing the infected with the necessary pastoral care.[123] Unable to get a satisfactory solution from their ministers, they simply ordered the clergy to visit the sick and those in jail.[124] Indeed, the city eventually sharply rebuked the ministers, admonishing them to remember that 'they were employed to serve the Church both in and outwith the city alike in times of prosperity as in necessity be it war, plague or otherwise'.[125]

By mid-January, the magistrates were clearly trying to prepare the city's health system for yet another year of plague. Alexandre Charles applied for work at the General Hospital on 15 January.[126] Supplies were gathered and the wage structure was re-examined. More dramatically, the city finally decided to deal with Tallien. Chautemps reported that his investigation had shown that the barber-surgeon was 'very able at alleviating and controlling a plague but he [was] a great blasphemer, a thief and a fornicator'. Tallien was sacked.[127] At last the Senate seems to have felt secure enough to turn its attention to other concerns. No plague or related medical matters were discussed until mid-March, when the city settled its accounts with Tallien. On the same day, it also allowed Chappuis to conduct an examination of the desiccated body 'of some man or woman' since, as he said, 'the time [was] right' for this 'to the profit and utility of everyone'.[128] Although they were preparing for a possible return of the plague, by March there is clear evidence of growing optimism. In part, it may have been the result of the failure of plague to accompany the advent of spring. More important, the city's long-standing dispute with Berne, which had left Geneva without any military protector, had finally been resolved by Basle's arbitration.[129] In sum, Geneva had every reason to think that a degree of normality and security was returning and, perhaps, that plague might not.

Indeed, the summer was plague-free. Nevertheless, the magistracy put the short respite to good use. In late April, it appointed Jean Fiollet as the new barber-surgeon of the Plague Hospital and ordered another black shroud for use in burying victims.[130] They also instituted discussions in subsequent months about hiring another two barber-surgeons for the Plague Hospital.[131] After examination by other medical workers, Calvin and the other ministers, the city agreed to hire Pierre Valence, but only for three months. Geneva's on-going financial crisis as well as the absence of plague in summer time may have convinced the city's leaders that they could afford to be cautious and economical.[132] Indeed, Geneva's medical personnel, so often in the mind of the rulers, were being put to other uses. For example, on 15 August, four leading apothecaries and 'two doctors of medicine' were asked to carry out an examination of the city's gunpowder supply to ensure its quality.[133]

Within a fortnight, however, the medics, the magistrates and the ministers had a more immediate problem to face. On 29 August, the Senate noted that plague was again raging at Annecy, Nyon, Thonon and other places (i.e. the city was surrounded); the gates were sealed against the infected.[134] The next day, Chautemps reported that a girl had died of plague at the home of one Collomb, a butcher, in Longemale.[135] Porters were again charged with keeping the sick out of Geneva. As if this were not enough, by mid-September, George Malliet related that he had overheard cleaners in his house discussing the spread of the disease. The Lieutenant was to investigate.[136] The Senate had no choice but to accept the inevitable that 'since it pleases God to chastise us with the plague' all normal precautions and regulations should be implemented.[137]

No sooner were these rules reinstated than problems, as ever, appeared. The *cureuses* were reprimanded for bringing infected linen to the Rhône (for washing) in daylight and for dumping other infected items in the river. They were ordered to confine their washing to night time and to throw things only from the Fustier Bridge.[138] Even more distressing was the news that Fiollet was too ill to work; Pierre Compagnion was quickly hired.[139] Even Tyvent Furjod, the guard who had replaced Jean Blanc during the previous outbreak, had to be investigated for violating the quarantine measures when it was alleged that he was overly familiar with the gravedigger.[140] At the same time, Claude Mestral, the hospitalier, asked the city to assist a woman serving in the hospital who was destitute. This highlights one of the obvious practical problems of relying on indigent foreigners to work in the pest house – they could become yet another burden on the already overstretched resources of the city.[141]

Although this plague outbreak had started rather late in the year, its virulence cannot be doubted. By 23 October, Pierre Compagnion was dead.[142] On 30 October, the ministers were asked to provide another minister for the Plague Hospital.[143] The situation was so extreme that Chautemps had to report that the *cureur(e)s* would not obey him. It is not clear whether this means that they were not obeying the quarantine regulations or that they were simply refusing to work. In either case, the Senate ordered the malcontents to be arrested and punished 'according to the edicts'.[144] Once again, one might expect to find the city seeking to apportion blame for yet another outbreak. As with Boulat in 1543, a likely candidate presented himself. In mid-November, Claude Vulliemoz (also called Grangier) was cited as a possible witch. He had been repeatedly told to leave the city but had refused. Eventually, two guards were sent to ensure that he 'abandoned the city and his marriage, as he was not a native, had no visible means of support and was suspected of witchcraft'.[145] Nor was Pierre Roph (called Taborin) singled out although he was guilty of 'extreme violations' of quarantine.[146] Consistently the magistrates show a pragmatic and sensible reaction to the epidemic's appearance. Their moves to prevent, control and eliminate plague are practical and functional. They show no desire to identify scapegoats, nor do they evidence any special violence or antipathy to the (frequent) violators of their regulations. The rulers and, to an amazing degree, the people faced a third year of plague with equanimity and pragmatism. As will be seen, the fourth year was a wholly different affair.

On 27 November 1544, Chautemps was pleased to report that the plague had stopped and to suggest that 'to avoid costs it would be good to discharge master Jean Fiollet and one of the (female) hospital servants'.[147] As before, the magistracy immediately began a post-mortem on the city's effectiveness in dealing with the disease. However, the investigations of that winter were more detailed, as serious accusations had been made by Roph in response to accusations against him.[148] Had the city had time to concentrate on these charges, there might have been major alterations in the regulations and personnel at the Plague Hospital. Even had the investigation produced nothing, there is no doubt that the magistrates would have spent the winter and early spring preparing Geneva for a possible return of pestilence. They had weathered their third year. Although the continual problems of maintaining the quarantine had been clear there is no evidence that anyone in Geneva connected these violations, or even the appearance of grease in 1543, with the events surrounding the 1530 conspiracy. Beset by enemies without and plague within, straining under the constant threat of bankruptcy, and facing the possibility of a fourth year of plague, Geneva and its people focused simply on the task at hand and showed no enthusiasm for seeking explanations for their troubles or identifying scapegoats to blame.

The situation changed on 5 January 1545 when reports came from Thonon. More details, requested by Geneva, arrived on 22 January and Lentille, a plague worker (*marron*), fumigator and barber-surgeon was arrested.[149] Ironically, the arrest coincided with the plague's abatement. Freed from distraction, the magistracy turned to Lentille's case with enthusiasm and wrote for more information. The officials went so far as to send Lentille to Thonon, through Bernese territory, to confront him with his accuser. Three senators and the Senate's secretary escorted him. The whole Senate was present at the subsequent examination and torture of Lentille upon his return. The city decreed that the investigation to uncover accomplices should proceed 'day by day, hour by hour'.[150] They also put 'faithful men' on guard when yet more grease was discovered on doors.[151]

In marked contrast to the attitudes apparent in 1543–44, the senators now explicitly suspected the hospital workers. Tyvent Furjod, a guard at the hospital, was 'suspected because of his great familiarity with the fumigators . . . who are, for the most part, greasing the doors'; he was investigated. The same day, the city ordered all the fumigator to be rounded up in a street and searched bodily for boxes of grease.[152] Lentille's torture proceeded the same day but he was fatally injured on the third application of the *strappado* and, despite the frantic efforts of three barber-surgeons, died. His one statement, noted below, became the basis of all subsequent prosecutions.[153] The prosecutions followed so swiftly that citizens charged with maintaining the hospital complained that, apart from Furjod (who was suspected) and six patients there was no one left at the hospital – they were all in jail. Other citizens took private action. City guards reported vigilante patrols of *anti-engraisseurs*. Vagrants and beggars were herded into the cathedral cloister and searched.[154]

The senators also had external concerns. Neighbouring communities wanted details and sent information which might interest Geneva's authorities. Letters arrived from Lyon on 11 March 1545.[155] Catholic Lyon asked about the Genevan cases and later wrote thanking the city for information and reporting that a careful search of Lyon had failed to uncover any criminals.[156] Another report arrived from Brig (Valais). However, this letter did not request information but provided it. Brig had caught a plague spreader with Genevan connections.[157] Indeed, Petitjean, their prisoner, had confessed, under torture, to trying 'to depopulate' Geneva. Nine accomplices were named, including Louis Papegay, an innkeeper in Geneva, and Louis Danan (probably the Louis Dunant executed for plague spreading).[158] Protestant Geneva replied by rushing off letters to the Bishop of Syon and the Catholic governor of Valais for a copy of the transcript.[159]

Within a week the senators had visited the prisoners numerous times and decided to pass judgement 'as quickly as possible'. For the first time, the senators referred to the phenomenon both as a *conspiracy* and as an *entreprise*. The hasty trials were interrupted by the ferocious return of plague in April. Necessity dictated to the city and the poor – although executing fumigators by the handful the city hired Martinaz, wife of François Dupuis, as a new linen washer. Indeed, by the cruellest twist of fate, the city had to pay two new fumigators to clean the prison where the inmates were dying of plague.[160] Peculiarly, no orders were issued for these new fumigators to be guarded.

The change in the magistrates' approach to plaguespreading from 1543/44 to 1545 could hardly be more dramatic. What can account for such a difference? There is one new element introduced into the situation – conspiracy. Before Lentille's arrest there was a certain complacency about the spreading of grease. Unable to identify even one perpetrator, the magistrates did no more than post guards to stop the offence and to reassure the populace. Once an individual was identified and a conspiracy explicitly apparent the city moved rapidly and ruthlessly to identify and neutralise all conspirators.

This again highlights the reactive nature of the magisterial approach. Rather than launching a strenuous investigation in 1543–44, the city posted guards. Despite questionable behaviour by the fumigators, the authorities only set them watchers. Even the prosecutions have a reactive element. All stemmed from accusations made by other conspirators – the confession at Thonon led the way. In other words, Geneva failed to make any independent identification, arrest or prosecution. Moreover, the city failed to conclude that the plague containment system might be inherently flawed. Once the conspirators were identified and eradicated the city happily returned to the previous methods – the *status quo ante*. There was no conclusion that poor foreign female plague workers were dangerous or suspicious. If there is some form of stereotyping or scapegoating here it is certainly unintentional – indeed, unconscious.

NOTES

1 AEG, PH 1299. They magistrates of Lausanne had arrested Estienne Maliard, one of their officers, as an *engraisseur*, suspected of 'spreading the plague'. The best study of this appearance of the plague-spreading phenomenon is F. M. Burgy, *Les Semeurs de peste : procès d'engraisseurs à Genéve, 1545* (Mémoire de licence, 1982; AEG, Manuscrit historique, 252/241).

2 For more details on these events see Naphy, *Calvin*, pp. 27–52; 'Liberty', 379–87; 'Genevan Diplomacy and Foreign Policy, *c.* 1535–1560: Balancing on the Edge of the Confederacy', in W. Kaiser, C. Sieber-Lehmann and C. Windler, eds, *Eidgenössische «Grenzfälle». Mülhausen und Genf/En marge de la confédération : Mulhouse et Genève* (Basle, 2001): 189–219. See also É. Dunant, *Les Relations politiques de Genève avec Berne et les Suisses* (Geneva, 1894), and A. Roget, *Les Suisses et Genève* (Geneva, 1864), especially vol. 1 (of four), which deals with the period 1474–1532.

3 See, for example, AEG, RC 35, fols 456v (13 January 1542), 465v (23 January 1542), 495 (10 February 1542) 530v (20 February 1542) and 504v (21 February 1542). For more on the role of diplomacy and Basle (in particular) in this period see Naphy, 'Liberty', pp. 379–87.

4 For example, they hired the famous Clémont Marot. On whom see C. A. Mayer, *Clémont Marot* (Paris, 1972).

5 AEG, RC 35, fols 517v (4 March 1542, Henry de la Mare, 240 florins per year), 519v (7 March 1542, Jaques Bernard, 240 florins; Ami Champereau, 240 florins; Jean Calvin, 500 florins; Pierre Viret, 100 florins, and, at the school, Estienne Roph and Pierre Mussard, 84 florins each), 520v (7 March 1542, Nicolas Vandert, 200 florins). For more information on ministerial salaries and wealth see Bergier, 'Salaires', Naphy, *Calvin*, pp. 53–83, and Naphy, 'The Renovation of the Ministry in Calvin's Geneva', in A. Pettegree, ed., *The Reformation of the Parishes: The Ministry and the Reformation in Town and Country* (Manchester, 1993), pp. 113–32.

6 For example, see RC 35, fols 536v (24 March 1542, from Berne re merchandise), 537v (27 March 1542, from Chambéry, re the safe passage of 2,000 Catholic troops, granted the same day), 540 (29 March 1542, from the Bishop of Syon re a debt) and 540v (29 March 1542, from Neuchâtel re the minister Farel).

7 AEG, RC 36, fol. 94v (14 August 1542).

8 AEG, RC 36, fol. 111v (4 September 1542).

9 AEG, RC 36, fol. 123v (18 September 1542).

10 AEG, RC 36, fol. 128 (25 September 1542).

11 AEG, RC 36, fols 129, 130 (26 September 1542).

12 AEG, RC 36, fol. 133v (29 September 1542). On Castellio see M. Derwa, 'L'influence de l'ésprit irénique sur le contenu doctrinal de la pensée de Castellion', *Revue belge de philologie et d'histoire* 58: 2 (1980): 355–81; R. White, 'Castellio against Calvin: the Turk in the Toleration Controversy of the Sixteenth Century', *Bibliothèque d'humanisme et renaissance* 46 (1984): 573–86; G. Remer, 'Rhetoric and the Erasmian Defence of Religious Toleration', *History of Political Thought* 10: 3 (1989): 377–403; M. Turchetti, 'Une question mal posée: Érasme et la tolérance: l'idée de *sygkatabasis*', *Bibliothèque d'humanisme et renaissance* 53 (2001): 379–95.

13 AEG, RC 36, fol. 132v (29 September 1542).

14 AEG, RC 36, fol. 139v (7 October 1542).

15 AEG, RC 36, fol. 140 (7 October 1542).

16 AEG, RC 36, fol. 141 (10 October 1542).

17 AEG, RC 36, fol. 141v (12 October 1542).

18 AEG, RC 36, fols 151v (23 October 1542), 153v (25 October 1542). The attrition rate among clerics as a result of plague could be enormously high. Cf. A. Roberts, 'The Plague in England', *History Today* 30: 29–34, and J. A. H. Moran, 'Clerical Recruitment in the Diocese of York, 1340–1530: Data and Commentary', *Journal of Ecclesiastical History* 34: 1 (1983): 19–54.

19 AEG, RC 36, fol. 176 (24 November 1542).

20 AEG, RC 36, fol. 178 (27 November 1542).

21 AEG, RC 36, fol. 144 (14 October 1542). On the place of the medical practitioner in society see G. Pomata, *Contracting a Cure: Patients, Healers, and the Law in Early Modern Bologna* (Baltimore MD, 1998); D. Gentilcore, *Healers and Healing in Early Modern Italy* (Manchester, 1998); A. Wear, *Healers and Healing in Early Modern England* (Aldershot, 1998).

22 AEG, RC 36, fol. 146 (17 October 1542).

23 AEG, RC 36, fol. 152–152v (23 October 1542).

24 AEG, RC 36, fols 147 (19 October 1542), 151v (23 October 1542).

25 AEG, RC 36, fols 153v (25 October 1542), 154 (26 October 1542), 156 (27 October 1542).

26 AEG, RC 36, fol. 156v (30 October 1542).

27 AEG, RC 36, fol. 158v (31 October 1542). The *cureuses* were given permission to clean cloths and burn straw at the Rive but only on specifically approved nights, RC 36, fol. 159v (3 November 1542).

28 AEG, RC 36, fol. 169 (14 November 1542).

29 AEG, RC 36, fols 128 (25 September 1542), 129–130 (26 September 1542), 132–132v (29 September 1542), 146 (17 October 1547), 159v (3 November 1542), 167 (13 November 1542), 172v (17 November 1542). The decision was confirmed on 20 November 1542 (RC 36, fol. 173v).

30 AEG, RC 36, fol. 175 (21 November 1542).

31 AEG, RC 36, fols 183 (4 December 1542), 184v (5 December 1542).

32 AEG, RC 36, fols 194 (19 December 1542), 206v (5 January 1543).

33 AEG, RC 36, fol. 181v (1 December 1542).

34 AEG, RC 37, fol. 21v (23 February 1543).

35 AEG, RC 36, fol. 190 (12 December 1542).

36 AEG, RC 37, fol. 22 (23 February 1543).

37 AEG, RC 37, fol. 21v (23 February 1543).

38 AEG, RC 37, fol. 30v (12 March 1543). He was paid on 2 April (RC 37, fol. 47v).

39 AEG, RC 37, fol. 47v (2 April 1543).

40 AEG, RC 37, fols 49v (3 April 1543), 53 (6 April 1543). Strangers (or foreigners) troubled most people as seen in the saying 'A stranger abides with you as an enemy, while a kinsman is always your friend' (p. 30). See R. F. E. Weissman, 'Brothers and Strangers: Confraternal Charity in Renaissance Florence', *Historical Reflections* 15: 1 (1988): 27–45.

41 AEG, RC 37, fol. 54v (9 April 1543).

42 AEG, RC 37, fol. 59 (13 April 1543). Fiollet was given one *coppe* of wheat while the ministers were each given four *coppes*. RC 37, fol. 61v (16 April 1543).

43 AEG, RC 37, fol. 66v (20 April 1543). Inns were frequently vectors of plague, as they housed the itinerant journeyman populations. Since journeymen were single, inns were also places frequented by prostitutes. Thus, inns were doubly dangerous. See M. E. Wiesner, 'Wandervogels and Women: Journeymen's Concepts of Masculinity in Early Modern Germany', *Journal of Social History* 24: 4 (1991): 767–82, especially 768, 772; S. Hochstadt, 'Migration in Preindustrial Germany', *Central European History* 16: 3 (1983): 195–224.

44 AEG, RC 37, fols 66v–67 (20 April 1543). The bakers included the widow of Tyvent du Romeney, who lived in St-Gervais and, seemingly, was one of the most prominent bakers in the city.

45 AEG, RC 37, fol. 70 (24 April 1543).

46 AEG, RC 37, fol. 74v (24 April 1543).

47 AEG, RC 37, fols 74v (27 April 1543), 77v (30 April 1543). On attitudes to the poor see B. Pullan, 'Support and Redeem: Charity and Poor Relief in Italian Cities from the Fourteenth to the Seventeenth Century', *Continuity and Change* 3: 2 (1988): 177–208, and his *Poverty and Charity: Europe, Italy and Venice, 1400–1700* (Aldershot, 1994). See also W. C. Innes, *Social Concern in Calvin's Geneva* (Allison Park PA, 1983), and J. E. Olson, *Calvin and Social Welfare: Deacons and the Bourse Française* (Selinsgrove, PA, 1989).

48 For more on Castellio and, especially, his tortured relations with both the city and Calvin see Naphy, 'Calvin's Letters: Reflections on their Usefulness in studying Genevan History', *ARG*, 86 (1995): 78–86.

49 For more on clerical responses to plague see O. P. Grell, 'Plague in Elizabethan and Stuart London: The Dutch Response', *Medical History* 34 (1990): 424–39.

50 AEG, RC 37, fols 80 (1 May 1543), 82 (2 May 1543). Champel was the city's place of execution.

51 AEG, RC 37, fol. 82 (2 May 1543).

52 AEG, RC 37, fol. 89 (11 May 1543).

53 One should not underestimate personnel problems and the effect they might have on current employees. Jean Levrat, a former *hospitalier*, was still trying to collect back pay for 1537–38. RC 37, fol. 87 (7 May 1543). This might well encourage workers to feel that they had to get as much as they could when and where they could during a plague outbreak.

54 AEG, RC 37, fols 77, 79 (30 April 1543).

55 AEG, RC 37, fols 80 (1 May 1543), 81v (2 May 1543). His salary equalled that of the second best paid ministerial posts.

56 AEG, RC 37, 83v (4 May 1543).

57 AEG, RC 37, fol. 75v (27 April 1543).

58 AEG, RC 37, fol. 91v (14 May 1543).

59 AEG, RC 37, 91v (14 May 1543).

60 AEG, RC 37, fols 91v (14 May 1543), 93 (15 May 1543).

61 AEG, RC 37, fol. 91v (14 May 1543).

62 AEG, RC 37, fols 91v (14 May 1543), 96 (17 May 1543).

63 AEG, RC 37, fol. 96 (17 May 1543). Anyone having contact with an infected person was to be quarantined.

64 AEG, RC 37, fol. 96 (17 May 1543). For a detailed study of the numbers of medical practitioners in relation to the number of potential patients see W. G. Hall, 'A Country General Practitioner at work in Somerset, 1686–1706: John Westover of Wedmore', *Local Historian* 20 (1990): 173–86.

65 AEG, RC 37, fols 97v–98 (17 May 1543).

66 AEG, RC 37, fols 98 (18 May 1543), 99v (21 May 1543).

67 AEG, RC 37, fol. 99v (21 May 1543).

68 For medical ambivalence and recalcitrance in the face of disease see O. P. Grell, 'Conflicting Duties: Plague and the Obligations of Early Modern Physicians towards Patients and Commonwealth in England and the Netherlands', *Clio Medica* 24 (1993): 131–52.

69 AEG, RC 37, fols 102 (22 May 1543), 105v (25 May 1543).

70 AEG, RC 37, fol. 100 (21 May 1543).

71 AEG, RC 37, fol. 100 (21 May 1543).

72 AEG, RC 37, fols 100–102v (21, 22 May 1543).

73 Similar private and public huts appeared in Southampton during July 1665. See J. Taylor, 'Plague in the Towns of Hampshire: the Epidemic of 1665–66', *Southern History* 6 (1984): 104–22, especially 112. See also R. Barker, 'The Local Study of Plague', *Local Historian* 14 (1980–81): 332–46.

74 AEG, RC 37, fols 105v–106 (25 May 1543), 108–9 (29 May 1543).

75 AEG, RC 37, fols 110 (1 June 1543), 113v (2 June 1543).

76 AEG, RC 37, fols 112v–113 (1, 2 June 1543).

77 AEG, RC 37, fols 117–117v (5 June 1543).

78 AEG, RC 37, fols 83v (4 May 1543), 91v (14 May 1543), 94v (21 May 1543), 113v (2 June 1543), 114 (4 June 1543). The two servants had been fumigating the Rose inn.

79 AEG, RC 37, fol. 120 (8 June 1543).

80 AEG, RC 37, fol. 115 (4 June 1543). Two physicians, Chappuis and Beljaquet, were given four écus each for services rendered.

81 AEG, RC 37, fols 124 (11 June 1543), 127 (14 June 1543). He was re-examined but rejected yet again, RC 37, fol. 129 (15 June 1543).

82 AEG, RC 37, fol. 118 (6 June 1543).

83 AEG, RC 37, fols 134 (19 June 1543, Claude Chasteauneuf), 135 (22 June 1543, Estienne Chapeaurouge, François Lullin, François Chamois). The Articulants were a political faction who supported extremely close ties with Berne even if it infringed Genevan independence. The treaty (or articles) they negotiated with Berne gave them their name and resulted in their political disgrace. An alleged *coup* attempt (more a riot) saw their leader executed and the faction's most prominent members exiled. See Naphy, *Calvin*, pp. 34–43.

84 AEG, RC 37, fol. 138 (26 June 1543).

85 A. G. Carmichael has made an important point to recall in relation to plague (as a contagion) and poison: 'medieval and Renaissance contagious diseases fit better into explanations of poisoning. It is in the treatises on poisons, in fact, that rabies is usually discussed,' in 'Contagion Theory and Contagion Practice in Fifteenth Century Milan', *Renaissance Quarterly* 64: 2 (1991): 213–56, especially 225 (and n. 20). See also L.

Thorndike, *A History of Magic and Experimental Science* (New York, 1923–58), eight
volumes, especially 3, pp. 525–45; 4, pp. 217.

86 AEG, RC 37, fols 119v–120 (8 June 1543). Gourmelen, *Advertisement*, pp. 9–10, places
great stress on controlling the movement of linens whether infected or not.

87 AEG, RC 37, fol. 121v (9 June 1543).

88 AEG, RC 37, fol. 133 (19 June 1543).

89 AEG, RC 37, fol. 148 (9 July 1543). He may well have been trying to update some ideas
about epidemics as a result of the publication of Hippocrates' *Epidemics* (all seven books
and Galen's commentaries on books 1, 3 and 6) at Rome in 1525 (in Latin) and at Venice
in 1526 (in Greek) and elsewhere thereafter. This rediscovery of the unexpurgated and
unmediated Hippocrates was a significant event in the early modern history of medicine. See N. G. Siraisi, 'Girolamo Cardano and the Art of Medical Narrative', *Journal
of the History of Ideas* 52: 4 (1991): 581–602.

90 AEG, RC 37, fol. 150 (10 July 1543). Larger states were equally reliant upon, and in a
symbiotic relationship with, their medical advisers. See H. J. Cook, 'Policing the Health
of London: The College of Physicians and the Early Stuart Monarchy', *Social History of
Medicine* 2: 1 (1989): 1–34.

91 AEG, RC 37, fol. 169v (3 August 1543). There were some members of the early
modern educated élite (especially those of an empirical bent) who argued strongly that
as much information should be put before the general public as possible. This was part
of the on-going debate within the medical profession between traditional Galenic
medics and Paracelsians. See W. Eamon, 'Science and Popular Culture in Sixteenth
Century Italy: The "Professors of Secrets" and their Books', *SCJ* 16: 4 (1985): 471–85;
H. Dubrow, 'Paracelsian Medicine in *Volpone*', *Durham University Journal* 77: 2 (1985):
175–7; A. G. Debus, *The French Paracelsians* (Cambridge, 1991); H. J. Cook, 'The
Society of Chemical Physicians, the New Philosophy, and the Restoration Court',
Bulletin of the Society for the History of Medicine 61 (1987): 61–77; A. K. Lingo, 'Empirics
and Charlatans in Early Modern France: The Genesis of the Classification of the
"Other" in Medical Practice', *Journal of Social History* 19 (1986): 583–604.

92 AEG, RC 37, fol. 149v (10 July 1543).

93 AEG, RC 37, fols 134 (22 June 1543), 150v (10 July 1543), 155 (16 July 1543).

94 AEG, RC 37, 138 (22 June 1543).

95 AEG, RC 37, 154v (15 July 1543).

96 AEG, RC 37, fol. 159v (19 July 1543).

97 AEG, RC 37, fol. 159 (18 July 1543).

98 AEG, RC 37, fol. 163v (24 July 1543).

99 AEG, RC 37, fol. 165v (30 July 1543).

100 AEG, RC 37, fols 145 (5 July 1543), 147v (9 July 1543), 163 (24 July 1543). In the end,
Françoise Carrey, Pernet's widow, was given a further thirty écus. AEG, RC 37, fol. 169
(3 August 1543).

101 AEG, RC 37, fol. 168 (3 August 1543).

102 AEG, RC 37, fol. 171v (6 August 1543).

103 AEG, RC 37, fol. 154 (13 July 1543).

104 AEG, RC 37, fol. 186v (8 August 1543).

105 Permission for the troops' passage had been sought on 31 July 1543 (AEG, RC 37, fol.
167). The city noted, on 3 August, that they were *en route* to Lyon (AEG, RC 37, fol.
167v). This potential danger, as much as the present danger of plague, probably explains
the re-statement of the order expelling all foreigners.

106 AEG, RC 37, fol. 185 (7 August 1543). The threat of these troops (but not, interestingly, the plague) was so great that the summer Eucharist was cancelled. AEG, RC 37, fol. 209 (31 August 1543). On the threat of these soldiers see also AEG, RC 37, fols 200v–201 (23 August 1543), 209 (31 August 1543), 221 (17 September 1543, the Pope requested permission for 5,000 troops to pass as reinforcements for the French; they were considered very dangerous as they might also be used 'against the Christian religion').

107 He suggested general processions 'of our Holy Mother Church to the glorious Virgin, the precious Body and Blood of our Creator and the other rites of Christianity, for example [private] devotions and the Divine Cult (the Mass)'. AEG, PH 1304.

108 AEG, RC 37, fol. 188 (10 August 1543). The guards were to be paid the handsome salary of 2s per night. AEG, RC 37, fol. 196 (17 August 1543).

109 AEG, RC 37, fol. 194 (15 August 1543). There is no implication, at this point, that the city doubted Chautemp's competence. He was given a bonus payment 'for his good service and expenses' of six écus. AEG, RC 37, fol. 216 (7 September 1543).

110 AEG, RC 37, fol. 195 (17 August 1543).

111 AEG, RC 37, fol. 207v (29 August 1543).

112 In addition, the city was facing a grain dearth and was still seeking to remove foreigners. AEG, RC 37, fols 198 (20 August 1543), 199 (21 August 1543).

113 AEG, RC 37, fol. 238 (8 October 1543). Tallien got his white wine; the minister got a warning. By 11 December, Chautemps was forced to report that the minister, Simon, had abandoned his post (and the hospital) entirely and the ministers were asked to explain his behaviour. AEG, RC 38, fol. 3.

114 AEG, RC 37, fol. 227v (24 September 1543). Boulat, having made his submission, was required to reappear if called. Indeed, some would take an even more extreme position and argue that not only was there stereotyping but, on the other hand, some deviant behaviour by women (witchcraft, possession, prostitution) was a kind of undercover 'proto-feminist' movement. See F. E. Weaver, 'Women and Religion in Early Modern France', *Catholic Historical Review* 67: 1 (1981): 50–9, especially 52; J. Kelly, 'Early Feminist Theory and the *Querelle des Femmes*, 1400–1789', *Signs* 8: 1 (1982): 4–28.

115 AEG, RC 37, fol. 227 (24 September 1543).

116 AEG, RC 37, fols 240 (12 October 1543), 248 (22 October 1543).

117 AEG, RC 37, fol. 248v (22 October 1543).

118 AEG, RC 37, fols 251 (23 October 1543, Antoine Bronges's entire family died and, for lack of heirs, his goods were seized by the hospital; Guillaume Marchand's estate suffered the same fate), 255 (29 October 1543, the dead of Peney were to be buried in the parish's cemetery).

119 AEG, RC 37, fol. 263v (5 November 1543).

120 One sign that Geneva was aware of the impending end of the year's outbreak was the preparation of a list of the workers and the dead inmates (twenty-three named) of the St-Clare Hospital for the period 8 September–23 November 1543 (AEG, PH 1310).

121 AEG, RC 38, fol. 3 (11 December 1543). The declaration of the plague's end may explain Simon's departure from his post (see n. 26 above). Despite the scandal, he was paid six écus for expenses. Where applicable, the estates of plague victims were sold to clear their debts with any excess going to the General Hospital. AEG, RC 38, fols 12v (18 December 1543), 13v (21 December 1543).

122 AEG, RC 38, fol. 6 (14 December 1543).

123 AEG, RC 38, fol. 10v (17 December 1543). Their report, placed before the Senate a month later, recommended that Simon should continue at the hospital, as they were

unwilling to accept him as a fully fledged minister, but perhaps later he might be sent to minister 'in some village'. The city accepted this solution for three months. AEG, RC 38, fol. 30 (14 January 1544).

124 AEG, RC 38, fol. 30v (14 January 1544). There is clear evidence of pique in this order and, previously, of growing tension between the ministers and magistrates. The former had asked for a salary increase (on 24 September 1543) and the Senate had responded with 'strong admonitions of the great expense placed upon the city and that [the ministers] should have a little patience'. AEG, RC 37, fol. 226v. In addition, the wife of Jaques Baud, minister of Celigny, was banished for adultery with Blaise Bornand (who was jailed for seven days and fined ten écus), while Baud himself was removed and sent to work in the General Hospital because 'he [was] not able to announce . . . the Gospel'.

125 AEG, RC 38, fol. 36 (21 January 1544).

126 AEG, RC 38, fol. 32v (15 January 1544). He was still a barber-surgeon there in early April. AEG, RC 38, fol. 155v (8 April 1544).

127 AEG, RC 38, fol. 47 (29 January 1544).

128 AEG, RC 38, fol. 127 (17 March 1544). Despite the host of problems with Tallien, and the presumed problems between him and his wife, the city was not heartless. Tallien's wife was given a sympathetic hearing when she begged that she, her husband and her two children might be allowed to re-enter the city. The Senate replied that he had been expelled and that she and the children should follow him into exile. However, they tempered this harsh ruling by giving the family two florins in alms. See AEG, RC 39, fols 52v (27 November 544), 59 (4 December 1544).

129 AEG, RC 38, fols 128 (18 March 1544)–131v (21 March 1544), *passim*.

130 AEG, RC 38, fols 172v–173v (24 April 1544). Tallien was not 'very suitable'.

131 AEG, RC 38, fols 233v (2 June 1544), 239 (5 June 1544), 275 (4 July 1544). Initially Jaques Cheyserier, a Genevan then living at Presigny, was discussed but, at the suggestion of Alexandre Charles, the city settled on Pierre de Vallence.

132 AEG, RC 38, fols 279v (8 July 1544), 291 (17 July 1544; the short-term nature of the contract was explicitly re-stated).

133 AEG, RC 38, fol. 327 (15 August 1544). Once again, the constant threat of external attack is shown to be a major concern.

134 AEG, RC 38, fol. 344 (29 August 1544).

135 AEG, RC 38, fol. 346 (30 August 1544).

136 AEG, RC 38, fol. 372v (15 September 1544).

137 AEG, RC 38, fol. 377 (18 September 1544). They also began to look for yet another barber-surgeon. AEG, RC 38, fol. 378v (19 September 1544).

138 AEG, RC 38, fol. 398 (6 October 1544).

139 AEG, RC 38, fols 399 (6 October 1544), 401v (7 October 1544, for twenty-five écus per annum).

140 AEG, RC 38, fol. 399v (6 October 1544).

141 AEG, PH 1335 (dated 1 October 1544, received the following day).

142 AEG, RC 39, fol. 17v (23 October 1544).

143 AEG, RC 39, fol. 22 (30 October 1544).

144 AEG, RC 39, fol. 19v (25 October 1544).

145 AEG, RC 39, fols 37 (13 November 1544), 38v (14 November 1544), 44 (17 November 1544).

146 AEG, RC 39, fol. 59 (4 December 1544). The end of the outbreak may have tempered the magistrates' reaction.

147 AEG, RC 39, fol. 52 (27 November 1544). The crippling cost of plague was evident, again, in the use of victims' estates to defray debts. For example, Christophle Furjod's house and other properties left to the city were sold.

148 AEG, RC 39, fols 80v (25 December 1544), 89 (5 January 1545).

149 AEG, RC 39, fols 89v (5 January 1545), 107v (22 January 1545). A *marrone* is an 'infirmier – ou parfois croque-mort – en temps d'épidémie' in the Suisse romande. The word appears in the sixteenth century at Yverdon, Lausanne, the Valais, Vevey, Neuchâtel and Geneva. Cf. W. Pierrehumbert, ed., *Dictionnaire historique du parler Neuchâtelois et Suisse romande* (Neuchâtel, 1926), pp. 352f; J. Ahokas, 'Essai d'un glossaire genevois d'après les registres du conseil de la ville de 1409 à 1536', *Mémoires de la société néophilologique de Helsinki* 22 (1959): 228–41, and L. Favrat, ed., *Glossaire du patois de la Suisse romande* (Lausanne, 1866), pp. 82, 239. Benoit Textor, *De la maniere à preserver de la Pestilance* (Lyon: Tournes & Gazeau, 1551), p. 45, makes a passing reference to 'trop tard apperçu des annes passes des engressuers & empoisonneurs' (with the marginal note: 'Des cureurs ou nettoyeurs, & des empoisonneurs'). On whom see A. Piaget, 'Une lettre de Benoît Tixier aux Quatre Ministraux', *Musée Neuchatelois* (Neuchâtel, 1920): 134–5.

150 AEG, RC 39, fols 108 (22 January 1545), 109v (23 January 1545), 114 (26 January 1545), 115v (27 January 1545: Curtet, DesArts, Dorsière, secr. Beguin), 117v (29 January 1545), 121 (2 February 1545), 125v (6 February 1545).

151 AEG, RC 40, fol. 25v (17 February 1545).

152 AEG, RC 40, fol. 25v-26v (17 February 1545).

153 Gautier, *Histoire*, 3: 237.

154 AEG, RC 40, fols 43–43v (9 March 1545).

155 AEG, RC 40, fol. 44v (11 March 1545).

156 AEG, PH 1347 (7 March 1545): 'poisoniers'.

157 AEG, PH 1345 (March 1545). Letters were also received from the Swiss Diet (PH 1357) and Gex (PH 1358).

158 AEG, PH 1345, fol. 5 (March 1545).

159 AEG, RC 40, fol. 52 (17 March 1545).

160 AEG, RC 40, fols 63–63v (24–5 March 1545), 77v (10 April 1545), 91v (23 April 1545), 93v (24 April 1545: Cholex and Ayme DesArts' servant girl).

CHAPTER THREE

THE CONSPIRATORS OF 1545

They swore to say nothing and thrice to withstand torture

By 1545, the Protestant fathers of Geneva may well have begun to wonder whether God really was on their side. And, if he was, how much more testing the new republic could take. The previous fifteen years had been trying by anyone's standards. There had been a revolution, a religious Reformation, a civil war, invading armies, liberating armies, war with Savoy, near-war with France and Berne, plague in 1530 and, now, the prospect of a fourth year of plague. Little wonder that the magistracy might be on edge. However, for all the turmoil of the previous decade and a half, the magistrates seemed to have maintained control and calm. Despite the accusations of conspiratorial plague spreading in 1530, the city's leaders were certainly not looking for plague spreaders in the city. It is true that there had been rumours and that some arrests had been made since plague had reappeared in September 1542 but these led nowhere. In fact, there is every reason to think that *engraissant* did not always, of necessity, involve *conspiration* – more often than not a plague spreader was an individual who had evaded or violated some aspect of the plague regulations either intentionally or accidentally. Thus, although the magistrates had more than enough to trouble them they seem not to have suspected or even contemplated that they might have another conspiracy to spread plague, *à la* 1530, in their midst.

This all changed on 5 January 1545 when the city received a letter from the judicial magistrates of Thonon, a Bernese-controlled town on the southern shore of Lake Geneva. The letter purported to warn Geneva of a possible link – a conspiracy – between a plague spreader, Bernard Dallinge, whom they were trying and a resident of Geneva, Jean Dunant (alias Lentille). Since Lentille was working as a *marron* (grave-digger and plague worker), a *cureur* (fumigator) and a *barbier* in Geneva, the magistrates had reason to fear that he might indeed be a threat were he actually involved in a conspiracy to spread plague. Just over a fortnight later, on 22 January, Geneva was sent more details which made it clear that the conspiracy had its origin and centre, not in Thonon, but in Geneva. Thonon had merely uncovered one of the tendrils of the group – the vine, though, led straight to the heart of Geneva. Now, with this information from Thonon, Geneva's authorities had *prima facie* proof that Geneva was endangered not by stray individual acts violating their plague containment policies but by an organised effort to poison the city. The dramatic change in the behaviour of the magistrates will be discussed in what follows. For the moment, however, the most important issues to be treated are the very ones that concerned the city. Who was involved? What was the motive for this heinous behaviour? Whom had the conspirators targeted? How long had it been going on? And, most important, how was the city to uncover and root out this poisonous threat to the body politic?

Unsurprisingly, the first thing the authorities did was to arrest Lentille on 22 January. Since his trial, the attendant investigations and his subsequent revelations (under torture) formed much of the core of later prosecutions, it is worth considering them in some detail. Of course, a number of factors need constantly to be borne in mind: some of Lentille's associates were arrested on suspicion of guilt by association and torture was used. Having said that, it is also important to recall that not all information uncovered by the authorities was the result of torture or indeed questioning. In effect, there needs to be a careful examination of the trials of Lentille and the others supposedly leading the conspiracy to see what was discovered by the investigators themselves (e.g. witnesses, 'hard evidence') and the relationship between details confessed before and after torture. Finally, the paramount concern is to remember that torture could be applied only after there had been an accumulation of circumstantial evidence. However, as the trials mounted and confessions under torture proliferated, these forced confessions were able to be amassed in sufficient quantity to qualify as circumstantial evidence on their own and, thus, justify the torture of new suspects. This is not – and this cannot be overstressed – the situation at the start of the trials. In these first few cases, there is not only greater reliance upon, but also actual judicial need for, circumstantial evidence in a more modern sense. This must be examined closely because it is only here that there is any realistic possibility of trying to gain some insight into what may or may not have actually happened. In the later trials, any attempt by contemporary judges or modern historians to uncover the truth is swamped by the driving concern to uncover conspirators and the heavy (-handed) reliance upon torture as the most effective means to a necessary end.

Before examining the trials of Lentille and the others, one must place this alleged conspiracy into context. As is immediately apparent from Appendix 3, the scale of the conspiracy dwarfed the events of 1530. Indeed, it may well be that the almost familial nature of the conspiracy then made the magistrates slow to suspect that, despite the appearance of grease, they were not facing a recurrence of the earlier phenomenon. Likewise, the severity of the plague outbreak in 1542–44 may have left the Senate with little opportunity for, or interest in, uncovering another conspiracy. However, as the details of the trials unfolded before their eyes, it quickly became clear to Geneva's leaders that both the epidemic and the conspiracy of the 1540s were dramatically more dangerous than those of 1530. Whereas the 1530 conspiracy had involved only a handful of perpetrators, the arrest of Lentille eventually led to the prosecution of sixty-five individuals and a series of investigations which did not end until late September 1546 – twenty months after Lentille's arrest. Although the magistrates were convinced they had uncovered an enormous conspiracy, one aspect was almost identical to that of 1530. The earlier trials had involved the active participation of forty-five separate magistrates, while this new conspiracy would require the attendance of forty-six magistrates (see Appendix 4). Seven individuals were witnesses to interrogations in both conspiracies. However, even with an equal number of magistrates in attendance, the scale of the 1545 trials was greater. Over half the 1545 magistrates attended more than twenty interrogations, some well over thirty. These trials riveted the attention of most of Geneva's ruling élite, and the bulk of the Senate's time revolved around the investigations, the details uncovered and, finally, the identification and arrest of every conspirator.

There were three distinct phases in the investigations (see Tables 4–6). Of the sixty-five prosecuted, forty-four (or 68 per cent) were arrested in the period 22 January–31 March 1545. These months saw a continuous wave of arrests. After 31 March, however, there were no arrests until the end of April and then a desultory number thereafter until early July. Laying aside the arrests in August and October (which should probably be included in the second wave), there were no arrests until the third phase that saw a handful of prosecutions in 1546 centred on the period 23 April–28 May. Not only did the trials come in distinct phases, the outcomes of the prosecutions evidence some major differences.

Table 4   Sequence of trials, February–March 1545

Name[a]	Date of trial	No. of interrogations	Sentence
February prosecutions			
Jean Lentille (or Dunant)	22 January – 17 February	20+	Died[b]
Pernette Croysonaz (or Marca)	1 February – 11 March	20+	Executed
Pernon Basseta	1 February – 11 March	?	Executed
Tyvent Furjod	17 February – 23 April	?	Acquitted
Louise Chappuis	24 February – 7 March	6	Executed
Jean Fiollet	25 February – 27 March	11	
Bernarda Monier	25 February – 17 March	9	Suicide
Antoine (or Urbain) Besson	25 February – 10 April	11	Executed
Collette Berchetaz	26 February – 11 March	5	Executed
Pernon Guex	26 February – 11 March	?	Executed
Pernon Mermet	26 February – 11 March	?	Executed
Clauda Mossier (or Peytavin)	27 February – 5 March	5	Executed
Jaquema Mauris	27 February – 5 March	?	
Tibaude Guex (or Bombillier)	27 February – 5 March	?	
Guillauma Coquet	27 February – 5 March	?	
Clauda Depellis (or Curtaz)	27 February – 5 March	7	
Clauda Folliez (or Ville-le-Grand)	27 February – 5 March	?	
Pernon Cherbonia (or Grandclauda)	27 February – 5 March	?	
Martine Gay (or Fresenaz)	27 February – 5 March	?	Executed
Jeanne Collomb (or Cugnier)	27 February – 5 March	?	Executed
Robella Delafontanna (or Pirquaz)	27 February – 5 March	?	Executed
Jean Tissier (or Borbon)	28 February – 28 March	10	

Table 4 *(cont.)*

Name[a]	Date of trial	No. of interrogations	Sentence
Louis Dunant (or Semenaz)	*Circa* 28 February – 10 April	?	Executed
March prosecutions			
Genon[ne] Reviaz (or Bistyn)[c]	March (?) – 4 March 1546	5+	Executed
Rene Bellefille	7 March – 18 April	13	Executed
Antoina Guilloda	7 March – 18 April	5	Executed
Jeanne Fassonet	26 March – 25 May	2	Banished
Christophla Mermilliod	26 March	?	
Mya Bouloz (or Buandiere)	26 March – 7 May	6	Banished[d]
Thassiaz Rey	27 March – 28 April	2	Acquitted
Pernon Bonet	27 March – 28 April	2	Acquitted
Françoise Dars	27 March (?) – 28 April	?	Banished
Guichauda Coquet	27 March (?) – 28 April	1	Acquitted
Georgea Delarpaz	27 March (?) – 28 April	1	Acquitted
Pernon Demugneratz	27 March (?) – 28 April	1	Banished
Daughter of Crespinaz	27 March (?) – 28 April	?	Acquitted
Daughter of Mugniez	27 March (?) – 28 April	?	Acquitted
Bernarda Villard	27 March – 13 May	12	Banished
Thevena Burlat	28–30 March	2	Banished
Thevena Pelloux (or Gervaise)	31 March (?) – 13 April	?	Executed
Rosette Beaufort	31 March (?) – 13 April	?	Executed
Bartholomea Chabbod (or Allemandaz)	31 March (?) – 13 April	?	Executed

Notes
[a] Those in **bold** were tortured.
[b] Despite the best efforts of three doctors, Lentille died as a result of injuries sustained under torture.
[c] The accused claimed she was pregnant, and the magistrates waited until she had been imprisoned for a year before ruling that she was not.
[d] She appealed against her banishment on 4 February 1547 on the grounds that she was a 'good wife and had two good children'. The sentence was lifted. AEG, RC 41, fol. 298.

The first cohort of trials resulted in thirty-two deaths (thirty executions, one suicide and one death from torture). This means that nearly 75 per cent of the defendants died. Another 10 per cent were banished, while slightly over 15 per cent were acquitted.[1] Not only were the consequences of these trials dramatic (and brutal) but over 41 per cent of the accused were definitely tortured and there is every reason to suppose that the use of torture was actually higher.[2]

However, the next fifteen trials (nearly 25 per cent of the total) show a decided move away from the use of torture and an increased likelihood of banishment rather than death as the outcome.[3] Only two trials (13 per cent) definitely involved torture and slightly over 25 per cent of the defendants were executed. That is, the rate of

Table 5   Sequence of trials, April–October 1545

Name[a]	Date of trial	No. of interrogations	Sentence
April prosecutions			
André Chevallier	24 April	?	Banished
May prosecutions			
Jeanne Mutilliod (or Bourgogniaultre)	4–14 May	5	
Genon[ne] Girard (or Molliez)	4–14 May (?)	?	
Pernon Paultra	4–14 May (?)	?	
Henretaz Ormond	13 May	?	Banished
Pierre Roph (or Taborin)	19 March (?) – 16 June	?	Banished
François Boulat	6–16 May[b]	8	Executed
June prosecutions			
Clauda Beguin	11 June	?	Banished
Laurence Galliard	11–15 June	?	Banished
Pernette Bossiez	15 June	?	Banished
Widow of Jean Petitjean[d]	25 June	?	Banished
Widow of Rolet Charrotton	25 June	?	Banished
July prosecution			
Pernette Dorsière	3 July	?	Banished
August prosecution			
Wife of Antoine Dumartheray (or Sept-Diables)	7 August 1545 – 13 September 1546	?	
October prosecution			
Bernard Chappuis	9 October	?	Banished

Notes

[a] Those in **bold** were tortured.

[b] This dossier includes interrogations relating to three previous prosecutions: 12 September 1542 (adultery and, possibly, involvement in infanticide), 4–27 January 1543 (violating quarantine regulations), 7–12 May 1544 (for violating banishment edict and slanderous comments made at Thonon).

[c] She broke her banishment. After being arrested she was also found guilty of theft and was executed on 18 July (see AEG, RC 40, fol. 187).

[d] A fugitive from Genevan justice subsequently apprehended, tried and executed at Catholic Brig for plague spreading.

execution dropped to nearly 33 per cent of that in the first set of trials. Banishment on the other hand increased from approximately 10 per cent in the first set of trials to 66 per cent in the second phase. Despite the increase in banishments over executions, only one person was acquitted outright. The final phase saw seven cases prosecuted in 1546, with torture definitely used in one case (14 per cent). Of these, none resulted in an execution, three (43 per cent) of the defendants were banished

Table 6   Sequence of trials, 1546

Name[a]	Date of trial	No. of interrogations	Sentence
Michele Regnaud	23 April	1	
Jean Palmier (or Mouroz)	19 May – 6 July	2	Acquitted
Antoine Dumartheray	24 May	?	
Jean Berchod	28 May	?	Banished
François Mestral (or Greloz)	26 August – 2 September	?	Acquitted
Pernette l'Hoste	14–20 September	?	Banished

Note
[a] Those in **bold** were tortured.

and another four (57 per cent) were either acquitted or the initial investigations never went to trial.

While one might expect that the discovery of a potentially lethal conspiracy of plague spreaders numbering forty-three in two months would have led to panic, scapegoating and an increasing tide of arrests, with ever greater reliance on torture and harsher punishments, the reality was dramatically different. The last two phases, especially the trials of 1546, seem more an attempt to 'tidy up' the accusations arising from the first wave of investigations. Moreover, it is worth noting that even the trials at the end of the first phase led to milder results: all four banishments and six of the seven acquittals followed investigations begun after 26 March. Subsequently, nevertheless, everyone even remotely connected with the conspiracy or suspected of involvement was questioned and investigated. However, the government seems to have come to the conclusion, as it had in 1530, that it had successfully arrested the conspirators very quickly indeed. Perhaps the state was inclined to limit the panic and trauma associated with the discovery of so great a threat to the body politic by banishing conspirators rather than executing them. While this may well explain the increase in banishments it does not explain the increasing number of acquittals. What seems more likely is that the magistrates genuinely felt that they had successfully apprehended the conspirators. The later investigations served to confirm this assessment; after 25 May no more executions took place.

One other possible explanation must be discussed. It is conceivable that the execution of the conspirators made it impossible to question them about persons subsequently arrested. However, three conspirators (Villard, Bouloz and Fassonet) were not executed until after the arrests of early May – indeed, Fassonet lived until 25 May. It is important, despite the foregoing caveat, to note that only Fassonet survived past the execution of Mya Bouloz on 13 May and that no one arrested after that date was executed. Thus, it is conceivable that the lack of conspirators after mid-May made it almost impossible to amass sufficient circumstantial evidence to allow torture. (Of those arrested after 14 May only Jean Palmier was definitely tortured.) The haste and zeal of the government to identify and crush the conspiracy may have hampered later prosecutions and saved many of the defendants in the second and third phase from torture and death.

Fascinating as one may or may not find statistics and this general analysis of the cases, the real focus of the discussion at this point must be the evidence revealed in the interrogations themselves. Not only does the mass of surviving documentation demand particular attention but the fact that the magistrates spent almost every single day in February–March 1545 questioning and torturing defendants requires a similar interest to be evident in the contemporary reader. The magistrates, all amateur jurists with no legal training, indulged themselves in the amateur's voyeuristic interest in detail.[4] Even after a defendant's guilt was proved, the judges often repeatedly tried to learn more. For the purposes of this investigation, the magisterial focus on specific details is of less interest than the consuming fixation on one particular aspect of the early trials – the identification of a motive. Although the judges could, and did, identify guilt they were extremely unwilling to end a trial with an execution until they had been able to understand why those involved had engaged in an activity so incomprehensibly evil.

On 22 January 1545, the Senate received a letter from Thonon informing them that Bernard Dallinge had 'spontaneously' confessed that during May 1544 while living in Geneva he had been enticed by a certain Jean Lentille, a hospital worker (*marron*), with the promise that he could 'earn lots of money'. Together they went to Champel (the location of the gibbet), removed a foot from someone hanging there and took it back to a cabin near the Plague Hospital.[5] The foot was then rendered to get the fat and this, while liquefied, was mixed with pus from the buboes of a dead plague victim. Once cool, the greasy concoction was smeared on to the doors of two butchers, *petit* Gonin and Pierre. Both butchers subsequently died, as did Pierre's children. Lentille had also 'greased' a number of other homes whose residents then died. The Bailiff of Chablais, George Wingarten, reported that the confession had been made the day before and advised that Geneva should be 'on guard' against this threat.[6] Geneva's Lieutenant immediately arrested Lentille and his interrogation began the same day.

In addition to the Lieutenant's judicial investigation, Chautemps, as the magistrate in charge of the Plague Hospital, was also ordered to investigate aspects of the case. First, he was asked to ascertain whether it was true that plague had reappeared. He was able to announce that the suspicious death was not plague-related. Chautemps also said that Louise Chappuis (then a plague worker and later an executed conspirator) had reported that there were only two sick persons in the hospital; however, money was desperately needed to cover the debts accumulated during the epidemic's peak. Two specific requests were put to the hospital *procureur* (steward/factor) relating to Lentille. First, he was told to visit the gibbet to see whether there was indeed a one-footed corpse there. Second, he was asked to ensure that the examination of Lentille would not endanger public (or magisterial) health.[7]

The Lieutenant's investigation was hampered by the lack of detail from Thonon. On 23 January, the Senate wrote requesting more information.[8] Also, there was a careful enquiry into 'the regime of the Plague Hospital' where 'maystre Regne [Bellefille], his wife [Antoina Guilloda], the servant Loyse [Chappuis] and also maystre Jeha[n] Fiollet' were in charge. The Senate ordered the workers and the situation at the hospital to be examined further. Thus, for the first time, there is a proactive response from the magistrates, which suggests that they were beginning to suspect that they might have a major crisis on their hands.[9] Within days, the Senate had taken the momentous decision to send Lentille, under magisterial escort, to Thonon to face his accuser. However, as this required passage through Bernese-controlled Ternier, the city wrote to request permission for this unusual action.[10] The magistracy seemed determined to witness Lentille's actual response to the charges against him. Chautemps, for his part, began to behave as one might expect of a senior and seasoned politician. He blamed René Bellefille, the barber-surgeon, for any and all problems at the hospital and demanded his removal. The Senate decreed that no hasty decisions would be taken on personnel.[11] Perhaps they were worried that precipitous action might bring the entire system to a halt. Certainly the next day they were forced to imprison one *cureuse*, Martina Gay, for refusing to clean and fumigate an infected house.[12] The greatest problem facing the authorities was the lack of evidence against Lentille and, therefore, they had no idea of the scale of the conspiracy headed by Lentille and Dallinge.

While the Senate awaited permission from Ternier, they appointed a high-powered committee to accompany Lentille to Thonon: Jean-Ami Curtet (syndic), Jaques Desarts (syndic), Pierre Dorsière and François Beguin (the Senate's secretary).[13] The presence of two of the four syndics is evidence of Geneva's concern. Also, it is worth noting that Curtet had witnessed all the trials of 1530. Two days later, a Bernese herald arrived with permission from Ternier to pass through the *mandement* of Gailliard. Lentille's previous testimony (in response to the charges in Wingarten's letter) were re-read by the Senate, which decided that he should not be tortured until after the trip to Thonon.[14] Lentille's case returned to the Senate on 2 February, by which time he had already been to, and returned from, Thonon, where he had denied every charge while confronted with Dallinge. The government decided that the *corde* (with weights) should now be employed; however, he should not be questioned under torture, only raised, then lowered and, later, exhorted to tell the truth.[15] By 6 January the Senate decided that the case was so important that 'day by day and hour by hour one ought to proceed with the prosecution of this case'.[16] The magistracy had every reason for haste. Within a fortnight, it had become clear that despite 'having some prisoners detained for having spread the plague and greasing door handles nevertheless the greasing has not stopped'. The six 'captains of the city' were augmented with extra 'faithful men' and told to make a more careful watch throughout the city.[17]

Lentille's early interrogations give some idea of the confusion facing the Senate. A single accused was unlikely to provide them with the personal or circumstantial evidence necessary for a conviction. In addition, the case against Lentille was itself complicated by the absence of Dallinge. Nevertheless, the authorities began their interrogations on the day of Lentille's arrest. The first two questions were those traditionally used to open all prosecutions. He was asked when and why he had been arrested. He replied that, for some unknown reason, he had been arrested that day. He then denied that he knew anyone named Bernard Dallinge from Cervan. He confessed that he had tended some vines near Champel but denied any contact with exposed feet, plague excretions or grease. He was then asked if he knew a *cureur* who had cleaned the house of Gonin, the butcher. He said he had but did not know that the owner's name was Dallinge. He had only heard of a trial at Thonon involving someone named François. He continued to deny any conspiracy with Dallinge and would admit only to having worked with him in the house in Plainpalais. The session closed with the note that Lentille 'was asked about nothing else'.[18]

The importance of this first day's questioning was twofold. First, Lentille had denied any knowledge of Dallinge but then had admitted that he had worked beside him. The judges were less than convinced that he had not known his co-worker's name. Second, he had worked with Dallinge in Plainpalais. This piece of testimony agreed with Dallinge's accusation (still unknown to Lentille) that they had met and worked together in Plainpalais in a butcher's house and that it was there that the conspiracy had been concocted. Equally important, but also unknown to Lentille, was the report by Pierre Malbuisson (controller), Claude Michallet (guard) and Jean Granjean (executioner) that the oldest corpse on the gibbet was missing its right leg below the knee.[19]

Later that same day, the questioning resumed. At least thirteen magistrates were present on this occasion. Lentille 'specifically denied [making the grease] and [said] he'd never done anything [like that]'. He still asserted the scant contact he had had with Dallinge. When pressed about his conversations with Dallinge he, at first, said they were confined to 'Good day', 'Good evening'. Then he admitted that he had told 'the said Bernard and others that they could earn more by cleaning than [some]one not cleaning'. However, he denied that he had promised or given money to anyone. The Lieutenant then changed tack and began to ask about the medicines Lentille used in his work (to protect himself from plague). Lentille said he usually chewed three leaves of *serve* (sage) picked in the morning, which he had heard, and found, beneficial. Why not four or eight instead of three? He had no idea. His meetings with Dallinge were again queried. Lentille then admitted that they had met ten to twelve times, though not since they had worked together, and that they had met in places other than Plainpalais. He was also asked about his relationship with Genon Girard but denied knowing the woman, though, when she was described to him, he said he knew where she lived and had seen her a few times.[20]

When the case resumed two days later, the magistrates employed a frequent strategy: for no apparent reason they changed the direction of the questions. Lentille was asked whether he had taken an oath 'to clean well'. He had, twice, before the syndics Antoine Gervais and Jean Coquet. He denied that he had ever been forbidden from cleaning and maintained his denial even after a confrontation with the guard Estienne (Thivent) Furjod, who said he had banned him from working. He admitted that he had heard of the grease's appearance, but then, so had everyone else. Also, he had heard that a large man, dressed in black, was suspected of the activity. He was then surprisingly asked why Chautemps had banned him from cleaning. He said there had been a dispute because he had not wanted to clean Claude du Pont's house. Furjod interjected that both he and Chautemps had banned Lentille primarily because he did not want to have to open the Tartasse Gate at all hours of the night to let Lentille come and go. The personal nature of this exchange became even clearer when Furjod said that Lentille had responded to him that 'he might have the keys to the Tartasse Gate but he didn't have the keys to Paradise'. Finally, when asked why he had denied knowing Dallinge, he replied that he knew lots of people and was not sure if one of them was named Dallinge. Again, Lentille was forced to alter (or vary) his testimony. In legal terms, variations or contradictions were one basis for the use of torture 'to discover the truth'.[21]

Some of the questions may seem bizarre. However, the authorities were using subsequent details garnered from Dallinge's interrogations to form the basis of their current investigation. They had received a copy of Dallinge's testimony from Thonon on 24 January. From this information they had learned that Dallinge had lived in Geneva for about six weeks. He and Lentille had worked together and Lentille had told him that 'they could earn a lot while cleaning'. They had gone to the gibbet and removed a foot (from just below the knee), but not the thigh, from an extremely decayed corpse. As he did not know the names of many people in the city he could not say which houses had been 'greased'. He did know an old widow named Pernon whom Lentille also knew. Finally, Dallinge said that they 'had promised one another to reveal nothing and to say nothing' about their actions.[22]

Two days later, Lentille's interrogation resumed. At first the questions concentrated on identifying all the houses in which he had cleaned. It quickly became clear that Lentille was a very popular cleaner indeed. Also, in what was technically a violation of the ordinances, he was being privately paid for his work. Theoretically, the state was paying for the *cureur*. In addition, the judges discovered that he was dispensing herbal remedies to the sick and employing various greases and powders that he had obtained from diverse apothecaries. However, they failed to identify the ingredients, as Lentille did not know how, or of what, the medicaments were made. The magistrates then began to ask a series of general questions. Lentille confirmed that he was not a native Genevan, being from Greyssier-en-les-Bournes, although he had lived in Geneva's St-Leger suburb for over three decades. He said he had settled there because he liked the area and property prices were reasonable. He also said he was a widower, as his wife had died soon after the suburb had been demolished (in the early 1530s). Three of his four children had already died. He had been married in the church of Notre-Dame-le-Neuve by (father) Jean Franquet. Although he had lived and worked in Geneva primarily he had, at times, worked in Annecy. Having moved the questions to his employment, the court again asked about his co-workers. He said he had worked with many people but did not know their names. As before, once the questions turned to the specifics of Lentille's relationship with Dallinge, contact with the gibbet or any other criminal activities, the accused denied everything.[23]

The short interrogation on 27 January failed to elicit any additional information. It is interesting to note that he was asked again about plague spreaders but, instead of mentioning the recent attacks (as he had previously), Lentille referred to the 1530 trials. He had witnessed the executions but said that he had no idea what the conspirators of 1530 had used or how. However, the Lieutenant did request the court to authorise the use of judicial torture because of the many variations in Lentille's testimony. The judges agreed but decided not to proceed immediately to torture. The next day, Lentille was questioned as before except that he was now asked about his work in the village of Bessiez. Also, he was asked about some suspicious views about Satan that he had been heard to express, as well as a locket he wore around his neck. Apparently, the court was trying every possible avenue of interrogation in an effort to discover what might have led Lentille to act as he did. Their questions seem designed to identify (or eliminate) the possibility that he was a heretic, a witch, or overly superstitious (and, therefore, perhaps a Catholic). As these lines of investigation failed to advance the case and, as Lentille continued to deny the charges, the state now authorised the use of torture so that he would 'speak and confess the truth with his own mouth'.[24]

The results of the torture were apparent in the answers given by Lentille the following day. He now gave details of his conversations. Lentille had said that those who cleaned 'gained paradise or they gained hell'. Rather, Lentille had suggested, they should aim at more material reward and had noted that 'they [could] gain more by [cleaning] the houses than the hospitals'. He also related that he had worked with Dallinge in other places, including Morges and Thonon.[25] More important, Lentille confessed that he had stolen cloth from places he had cleaned. He also affirmed that he and Dallinge had been together in a cabin and, in connection with this meeting, he named Pernon Basseta and Pernon Marca. Genon Girard had come to the door (without entering) to fetch him. She needed help cleaning the house of Estienne de la Maisonneuve, one of Geneva's leading citizens. In addition, Lentille confessed that he had fornicated with Marca. He also related that while passing a number of rich houses he had said to her, 'I wish that the plague would strike there so we could profit a lot.'[26]

Two days later, on 31 January, Lentille was confronted with Dallinge in Thonon. The latter testified that he had known Lentille for five years, having first met him in the village of Bessiez, where they had both been working in the house of Claude Pertemps from Messon. This confirmed information already uncovered in Geneva. However, although Lentille had freely admitted to working for Pertemps, it was not until he was tortured that he confessed that Dallinge was there as well. They had met again in Geneva, where they were both working as *cureurs*, and had begun to discuss old times. Dallinge then re-stated the details already relayed to Geneva about the acquisition of the foot from the gibbet and the plague pus. However, he also said that Genon Girard had helped them in collecting the plague excretions from a dead woman. The three had then 'greased' a number of houses, targeting the rich so they could gain access to their goods while cleaning. Dallinge repeatedly mentioned both poison and venom when discussing the grease rather than plague. He then broke off his testimony and addressed Lentille directly, begging him to save himself from further torture, throw himself on the mercy of God and the court and confess. Lentille hotly rejected his appeal and denied his accusations, saying Dallinge was a liar. Lentille seems then to have thrown himself not on the mercy of the court but upon Dallinge's neck; the two had to be physically separated.[27] These details further confirmed depositions made on 29 January in Geneva, where witnesses had said that Dallinge and Lentille had been seen in each other's company behaving as close friends. The witnesses also said Girard had been seen with the two and that her cabin was next to Dallinge's abode.[28]

Taken together, the trials of Dallinge and Lentille, even without further arrests and interrogations, provided the authorities with some convincing circumstantial evidence. Both men had separately confirmed details of their relationship. Lentille had clearly tried to hide his history with Dallinge. A corpse on the gibbet was missing part of a leg. Eye witnesses were able to place Girard, Lentille and Dallinge together and confirm their close association, even friendship. The judges might not be sure of many things but they were certain that Lentille had lied about Dallinge from the very beginning of the trial. There was every reason to continue the investigation by questioning their other associates. The course of action seemed even more necessary as Lentille's final exhortation as he was being tortured (to death, as it happened) was to look to the plague workers.[29]

The investigation had already expanded to include Pernon (or Pernette) Marca and Pernon Basseta.[30] These two women would be the only defendants questioned before Lentille's death on 16 February. However, although they were not officially being investigated, Lentille's trial had also thrown up the names of Jean Fiollet, Clauda Folliez, Bernarda Monier, Collette Berchetaz, Clauda Depellis, Louise Chappuis, Pernon Cherbonier and Guillauma Coquet, who were called on numerous occasions to face accusations against them. Thus, the authorities acted very quickly after the confrontation in Thonon to arrest those others named in these two cases. In addition, they seem to have cast their net wide enough to gather in all the known associates of Lentille, Marca and Basseta. After Lentille's death, which denied the state a valuable source of further information, the Senate moved to control the workers. Although many were already in custody, grease was still appearing on doors. A strict guard was to be mounted but this time it was to be composed, not of hired servants, but of 'faithful men' under the direct command of the city's militia captains. Tyvent Furjod was arrested because he was 'suspected of [having] a great familiarity with the *cureurs* who cleaned the infected houses [and] who are, for the most part, suspected of greasing the doors'.[31] Finally, all *cureurs* were to be rounded up by the new guards and brought to a single street where they could be physically searched for boxes of grease. To underline their resolve, the Senate ordered Lentille's body to be dragged through the street and then burned 'until entirely consumed' in Plainpalais 'where the grease was made'.[32]

Marca's case, which opened on 2 February after her arrest the previous day, is interesting because she was eventually convicted of two separate crimes. Her summation makes clear that she was arrested for activities associated with the conspiracy ('the crime of spreading the plague, making the poison and greasing the door handles'). In addition she was also tried for 'the crime of heresy', which, as often, meant witchcraft.[33] However, despite this second charge, the initial list of questions makes it clear that the court was primarily interested in the former charge. The prosecutor laid out his line of interrogation. How was the grease made? When was it done? Who gave her a box of grease? Where is the box? What was in the box (i.e. what did the grease look like and of what was it composed)? What oath was taken? As will be shown, witchcraft was later added to the charge sheet as a result of information revealed in the interrogations.[34]

At her first interrogation, Marca said that she knew Lentille but not Dallinge. She denied having received 'a box full of poison'. When asked, she said that she was crying because 'Jean Lentille had accused her without cause'. She also testified that Lentille had tried to seduce her but that she had realised that 'that one was a dog'. All further questions about grease, oaths and corpses were met with complete denials. However, Marca was forced to confess that she had tried to hang herself but had failed from a lack of rope. Although an attempt at suicide would almost certainly have given the Lieutenant sufficient grounds to request torture, he did not.[35]

On the very next day, Marca was examined in the morning and later after lunch. She was asked if she had 'any box full of poisonous grease'. She denied it and said that she had no means to make such a thing. This was a crucial denial, since Lentille and Dallinge had implied that she was the source of the mortar and pestle used in making the grease. Marchand, the prosecutor, asked if she had had such an implement. She said she had, about two years before, but it had been for culinary purposes, as her master at the time (Heustance Vincent) was a 'great glutton'.[36] After lunch, Marca's defence collapsed spectacularly and she began to confess. She admitted she had had a box but said she had burned it. She had realised that 'it was evilly made' and that 'Lentille had said it was good for applying to handkerchiefs and door handles' and that is was made 'of material for becoming very rich'. However, she denied she had done anything with the grease beyond hiding it and then burning it. She confessed to repeated fornication with Lentille. The box had been given to her in May 1544. She had lied because she had forgotten all about it. Although vague, she confirmed the basic outline of events given by Lentille and Dallinge: all three had been together in a cabin where the grease was first made. Not only had she thus provided the authorities with sufficient material to convict but also, along with Lentille's mention of the 1530 executions, her mention of 'handkerchiefs' strongly connected the behaviour of 1545 with 1530.

Although there was now enough evidence to convict Marca, the court returned to the question of motive. Marca said that 'Lentille said that [the grease] was for us to make profit by money, saying if we could spread it in some houses of the very rich we would gain much money'. They had agreed 'to declare nothing and to keep [things] secretly'. Lentille implied she would go to the devil if she 'exposed us'. After confirming the details of the transfer of the box, the magistrates returned to the question of the oath. Marca repeated that they had been asked to 'declare nothing but to hold things in secret'. When questioned she was able to give no clear information on the composition of the grease except to say that some of it was green and that arsenic was included.[37] After more information on the possible ways of applying the grease, the Lieutenant asked for permission to apply torture. The court agreed but ordered that she should be raised no more than a foot off the ground. When raised, Marca cried out for mercy and agreed to confess everything. She was lowered and then reiterated all she had confessed while asserting that she had not been present when the leg was removed from the gibbet. Again, the latter fact agreed with the testimony of Lentille and Dallinge that placed her at the collection of plague secretions but not the foot. It is crucial to realise that after the second day of interrogation the court had more than sufficient evidence to convict and execute Marca. However, it did not. Clearly, the state was determined to identify more details (which could be used in other trials), the names of conspirators (whose testimony could be checked against Marca's) and, very important, details of who had been targeted by the conspirators.[38]

The following morning, Marca was asked to identify the houses greased. She confessed to specific attacks against sixteen homes, businesses and even the city baths. There seems to have been no other requirement for being greased than that the occupants of the residence were rich. After dinner, she added a further three homes. She also said that Lentille had specifically suggested targeting the ministers (while cleaning Geneston's house) because 'the preachers are too fat'. Despite the wealth of detail, she confined her testimony to implicating herself, Lentille and Dallinge. However, she frequently mentioned Girard and, less often, Fiollet.[39] The next day saw the prosecutor seeking more details of her relationship with Lentille. She again confessed to fornication. She then abruptly began to retract her confessions. The judges sent her out and called in Lentille (though no details survive) and Marca was recalled. She again confessed to everything, including the fornication. When asked how they intended to protect themselves from the plague she mentioned that Lentille advised that they should urinate on their hands. The interrogations were adjourned.[40] The trial, when resumed the next day, failed to add any more detail. Marca was able to identify neither the source of the behaviour nor the exact date when the greasing began.[41] It would seem that the judges felt they had gained all they would from Marca, as the trial was adjourned until 16 February. There is little reason to doubt that she was being kept alive purely to serve as a source of information, accusation and counter-accusation in the other trials.

Two days before suspending Marca's trial, the Senate had begun questioning Pernon Basseta. The most the court was able to uncover was that Basseta knew Lentille, Dallinge and Marca. More important, she confirmed that she had worked with them in cleaning the house of Claude Malbuisson, a leading magistrate. This coincided with the information obtained from Lentille and Marca. However, Basseta said that her conversation with them had been limited to 'Good day', 'Good evening'.[42] She denied any knowledge of grease or any acts of fornication with a certain François, the Italian, though she admitted that she knew him well. When asked, she specifically denied taking any oath 'to give herself to the devil or some other sort of behaviour'. Marca was then brought in to face Basseta. She confirmed that they had sworn 'to give themselves to the devil and to endure three applications of the cord before confessing'; she also listed the homes they had greased.[43] Basseta denied everything. Since she was being denounced by Marca (the day after being tortured) and had admitted to her presence at places where greasing, oath taking and conspiracy planning had been admitted by Dallinge, Lentille and Marca, the Lieutenant had sufficient evidence to request the application of torture. However, despite being raised and strapped, Basseta refused to confess anything.[44] Again, the magistrates took a break from the process of interrogation to focus on investigation and the arrest of other suspected conspirators and known associates; Basseta's trial was adjourned until 21 February.

Two features of these trials need some careful examination. First, exactly what did the oath entail and what can be inferred from it? Or rather, what did the magistrates think the alleged conspirators had sworn to do? Second, what is the role of judicial torture and is it necessary to assume that all testimony acquired after the application of torture is, by definition, untrue? These two sets of questions are crucial for any understanding of the phenomenon of conspiratorial plague spreading. If the emphasis in the oath is on the giving of oneself to the devil the entire conspiracy is a bizarre form of witchcraft. If one is to assume that the mere threat of torture, let alone its application, completely and irredeemably invalidates the information revealed in the interrogations, these trials represent no conspiracy at all. Rather they are the result of a magisterially driven form of scapegoating arising from overwhelming paranoia and fear. With the rapid increase in the number of defendants questions will need to be addressed repeatedly. However, two points must be raised before attempting to answer the questions. Except for Marca, no one was executed as a witch and the judges made no attempt to uncover any demonic practices (e.g. Sabbath attendance) when questioning the defendants. Second, if the magistrates were using torture to extract false confessions, their interest in and, finally, acceptance of a motive based purely on social and economic gain lacking any supernatural or confessional aspects seems strange. That is, if the magistrates, driven by their own fears, wanted to force confessions that would justify their own suspicions, prejudices and brutality then one might expect them to insist on uncovering a more 'frightening' and self-justifying motivation than simple, base greed.

The Lieutenant reopened the case against Marca on 16 February. Part of the explanation for the hiatus is that the ten-day period coincided with Geneva's magisterial elections (8–12 February).[45] Once the new Senate and judiciary were elected, the trial resumed. This first session and the second (on 18 February) focused on details about the oath. Marca repeated a number of versions of the oath that she said was taken 'on the hands of the said Lentille'. On 16 February, she said that the conspirators had promised 'not to reveal one another'. During her next interrogation she related two additional versions. According to the first, they had sworn 'not to reveal [one another] on pain of enduring being attached three times to the cord'. She later said that in Plainpalais they had sword 'to give [their] body and soul to the devil for not revealing this on pain of having the cord three times'. In addition, although she admitted knowing Basseta, and that Basseta had fornicated with Lentille, she would not directly implicate her. This testimony presented the judges with some interesting features. Despite her earlier accusations, Marca now refused to implicate Basseta or anyone else. However, she freely admitted that she had fornicated with Lentille and that she had maintained a friendly working relationship with both Lentille and Basseta while knowing that they had had sex as well. If nothing else, this casual attitude to immorality would have shocked the court. More important, when asked again about her attempted suicide, Marca mentioned that she had seen the devil although she had not spoken to him. This admission and the continuing partial retractions and variations allowed the Lieutenant to use torture yet again. This time Marca was strapped, but without result.[46]

One might expect an admission of a demonic vision so early in these trials to have led the judges to seek Satan in other trials. Surely they would focus on this aspect of Marca's trial if nothing else. However, neither happened. On the next day, Marca was again questioned. She was asked about the houses targeted and any accomplices. Only then did the prosecutor, Jean Balard, turn to the issue of Satanism. She now confessed the stereotypical behaviour of a witch. While grieving over the loss of a florin one night, Satan had appeared to her as a small man. He asked if she would give herself to him and, when asked who he was, had said he was the devil. He offered to take her to the synagogue, where she could dance and kiss his face. He also touched her and gave her his mark. His touch was cold and, he said, his name was Satan. She said she had not gone to the Sabbath and had never spoken to the Devil thereafter. Indeed, she was roused from her vision when her husband called to her and woke her by his touch. Subsequent questioning produced the confession that her resistance had finally been overcome and she had indeed gone to a Sabbath. In addition to the normal celebrations at the witches' meeting, she received some ashes, which could kill men and beasts, as well as a blue stick, which would take her to him, if she said, 'White stick, black stick.'[47] There had been two other women and two men there as well, though she did not recognise them. The powders (ashes) in the box had been used to kill at least one young boy. She no longer knew where the Devil's box or staff was but the box of grease was, she thought, at the hospital. She was sent off with two magistrates (Lambert and Chautemps) to find it. What is clear from this is that the magistrates immediately realised that her confessions were relating two distinct activities. She was clear that she had had two boxes, one containing powder given to her by Satan at the Sabbath and another received from Lentille full of grease which she had seen being made.[48] The first box was supernatural in origin while the latter was most certainly of this world.

The four subsequent interrogations of Marca focused, not on the Sabbath, but rather on the plague-spreading conspiracy. Indeed, the judges returned to the same main points: the houses targeted, the details of the oath, the motive and the names of other conspirators. The final three are of most interest for the present discussion. In the fullest account of the oath-taking ceremony, Marca confessed that 'Bernard [Tallien] held a small book on which every woman swore to give themselves body and soul to all the demons and that they would not reveal [anything] until they had thrice endured the cord'. As for motive, she averred that 'they had undertaken to kill many in Geneva to improve their lives and [gain] lots of money'. While this added little to the information already revealed by the investigation, Marca did greatly expand the scope of the case by naming a substantial body of co-conspirators. She implicated Louise Chappuis, Jean Fiollet, Guillauma Coquet, Pernon Basseta, Jean Lentille, Bernard Tallien, Bernard Dallinge, Urbain Besson, Jean Tissier, Collette Berchetaz, Bartholomea Chabbod, Genon Reviaz, Louis Dunant, Clauda Mossier, Jeanne Mutilliod and 'the Serralion' (probably Jaquema Mauris).[49]

On 21 February, the court had reconvened Basseta's trial. Her time in jail had obviously served to loosen her tongue. She now confessed to fornication with Lentille. She also reported that a number of women had mentioned that Lentille had a way of getting rich. She was exhorted to make a full confession. Although she had no idea who had been implicated in Marca's trial she now 'spontaneously confessed' to attending an oath with Tallien, Dallinge and Lentille. She outlined an oath with the same features as those mentioned by Marca: 'they would be given to the Devil not to reveal not declare and also to endure three straps before revealing one another'.[50] Subsequent interrogations centred wholly on the identification of other conspirators. Independently of Marca, Basseta named Chappuis (Tallien's servant), Fiollet, Chabbod, Clauda Borreaud, Clauda Depellis, Bernarda Monier, Martina Gay, Dunant, Tallien, Guillauma Coquet, Mossier, Lentille, Dallinge, Tissier, Berchetaz, Reviaz, Mya Bouloz and Rene Bellefille.[51] She also denounced a certain Françoise who had moved with her husband to Lyon.[52]

By late February, the Genevan magistrates had sufficient separate denunciations from Lentille, Marca and Basseta to move against a substantial number of the hospital workers.[53] This they proceeded to do. They also had a rough idea of the substance of the oath and the motives behind it. All workers had sworn an oath faithfully to serve the city in return for very generous pay. They had now violated that oath with a subsequent oath to injure the city in return for even greater gain. Marca's involvement with witchcraft was never confused with the appearance of the Devil in the oath or other contemporary witchcraft persecutions (see Appendix 5). It would seem that the authorities accepted the oath for what it was, a forfeit oath.[54] If anyone were to fail to fulfil the oath and name any other conspirators before enduring three straps their body and soul would be lost to the Devil (or the demons). So, when the right hands of the executed were eventually removed and nailed to the gibbet, it was evidence of the state's fury at the oath as an example of treason and diabolical (in the sense of evil, rather than satanic) activity.[55] Secondly, although torture had been used in all three cases, the details and names independently elicited were consistent. It may indeed be true that torture had forced the three to confess to details already given to them in earlier interrogations and they may well have simply named all their associates as accomplices. Nevertheless, these three trials provide the interested observer with the same thing they gave the prosecutor of the day – disturbing and potentially damning circumstantial evidence.

In addition to the evidence internal to these three trials there was also the information gained from Dallinge. However, that was not all. The mention of Lyon in Basseta's case obviously convinced Geneva's Senate of the need to seek further information. Lyon's magistracy, in a letter dated 7 March, wrote requesting more information. Obviously, they had been alerted to Basseta's confession. On 24 April they wrote thanking the Protestant Senate for its letter of 18 April and relating, with some relief, that Catholic Lyon had found no plague spreaders.[56] Crucial confirmation was received on 10 March from Catholic Brig in the lands of the Bishop of Syon. Jean Petit, also called Sermet, had been arrested as a plague spreader there. He confessed, during a trial in which torture was employed, details relating to corpses, grease and poison. He also said that the conspirators were numerous and 'wanted to depopulate the city of Geneva'. He also named certain accomplices: Jean, a barber-surgeon (probably Fiollet), Louis Dunant, Clauda Depellis, Clauda Folliez, Christophla (Mermilliod?), Laurent (Galliard?) and Jeanne Montillier (probably Mutilliod). This information had been sent 'in great haste'.[57] All the details relating to the production of grease and its application tallied with information already uncovered in Geneva and Thonon. The magistrates had little reason to doubt that they were facing a very grave threat.[58]

In the four days after 24 February, no fewer than eighteen additional trials were opened of plague workers. The comprehensive body of (circumstantial) evidence was crucial to the speedy prosecution of these cases. The material gleaned, and forced, from Dallinge (in Thonon), Lentille, Marca, Basseta and Petitjean (in Brig) allowed the authorities to apply torture immediately if they felt the defendant was stalling. Louise Chappuis, for example, was tortured at her first interrogation.[59] This was after she had denied any knowledge of, or involvement with, the conspiracy. All she did confirm was that she was paid four florins per month plus her keep. Just as interesting is her confrontation with Guillauma Coquet although the latter's trial had not yet 'officially' opened. The implication of this is that the magistrates were gathering information from individual plague workers outwith the context of formal interrogations. In effect, the host of workers were 'helping the authorities with their enquiries'.[60] Once she was raised and strapped, Chappuis immediately implicated Chabbod, Guilloda, Tallien, Marca, Basseta, Lentille, Coquet and Fiollet.[61] As in the other trials, the same names appeared. Yet again, though, one must wonder if this simply represents a person under the force of torture identifying friends and co-workers. However, she was also accused by three witnesses[62] who had heard her boasting about two years before that she had 'killed many people' and had 'gained some good money'.[63] In later sessions, where torture again featured, she confirmed the oath, the process of grease production and motive.[64] Her testimony also clarified a major feature of the dynamics of the conspiracy. Previous testimony had implied that only the women took the oath. From Chappuis it is clear that, regardless of who swore, the behaviour was generally under the direction of men (Dallinge, Lentille, Tallien, Fiollet and Besson) but, in particular, of trained barber-surgeons (Tallien and Fiollet).[65] On the final day of her trial she provided the interesting fact that Louis Dunant, in addition to being the bastard son of François Bonivard, the former Prior of St-Victor and hero of the revolution, was also the cousin of Petitjean (arrested and executed in Brig).[66]

Jean Fiollet, a barber-surgeon living in St-Gervais (one of Geneva's neighbourhoods), originally from Usenens, was the next defendant. The contemporary folder for the trial preserves the chilling drawing of a gallows with a hand nailed to it and (red–hot) pincers. The secretary has also kept a tally of the accused. The title of the case makes it clear that Fiollet was arrested 'following the accusations of Basseta, Coquet, Marca and Chappuis'. He testified that he worked with the plague victims at the hospital and helped dispose of bodies as he had for three years. His co-workers were 'master René [Bellefille], his wife [Antoina Guilloda], Bartholomea [Chabbod], one named Louise [Chappuis] and Guillauma Coquet'. After these general questions he was asked specifically about any other oaths he might have taken. His quick reply was that 'if some of the prisoners had accused him or said anything about him it was not true because he was innocent of it'. He continued to maintain his innocence despite confrontations with Marca, Basseta, Coquet and eventually Chappuis. Unsurprisingly, considering his work, he admitted reasonably close relations with them as well as the acquaintance of Lentille and Dallinge. Faced with an impasse, the judges adjourned for lunch.[67]

As soon as the trial resumed, the Lieutenant asked for torture. After being raised and strapped once, Fiollet agreed to confess. He implicated the same basic group of people, confirmed the details of the oath and said that it had been Lentille's idea 'to make a good profit'. However, he admitted that he had added arsenic to the concoction. His recipe for the grease was the most detailed to date, 'the flesh of a hanged person, the grease of the dead, cow's blood, pig blood, arsenic and white arsenic'.[68] On 12 March, he explained that Dallinge had gone to Thonon, think-ing he could make more money there. Also, he confessed that Lentille 'had pre-served this practice since the reign of Master Jean the *hospitalier* who was executed [in 1530]'. This provided confirmation of the actual link with the earlier trials implied in Lentille's testimony. Fiollet also said that poisonous powders had been made and that samples both of the grease and of the powder were hidden in his boutique. Claude du Pain (the city's apothecary), Louise Bernard and Roz Monet returned during the session with boxes of grease and of powder in a paper wrap-ping which they had found as Fiollet had described.[69] Once again, the evidence of the oath, the motive and the grease was accumulating. Also, the list of accomplices was beginning to solidify as the same people were named time and again. The recovery of boxes of grease and powder would have simply given the judges more circumstantial evidence. Armed with this, they were free to apply torture to acquire what they most desired – the names of any additional conspirators.

Monier's trial ended disappointingly for the magistrates when she killed herself on the evening of 16 March. Her trial is interesting for a number of reasons. First she said that she had been a *cureuse* since the early 1530s.[70] There is no reason to assume that she had been directly involved in the earlier cases, as she was a native of Lausanne and may have started her career there. She was also subjected to an extreme number of torture sessions, especially before confessing anything. She was tortured, in total, three times before confessing (if she had taken the oath, she had fulfilled it).[71] She endured two more applications of torture[72] before hanging herself with a cloth the gaoler had provided (as a poultice or winding) for her stomach.[73] Her health was an important feature of the crime, since she had tried to avoid torture by claiming, first, to be pregnant (proved false after she was examined by midwives)[74] and, second, to being seriously ill. The latter was believed to the extent that her trial was temporarily adjourned from 3 March to 12 March and she received the means of her own death.[75] Her testimony also revealed that she had been advised to wash her hands in her own urine and, if at all possible, to avoid handling the grease, using a wooden spoon to apply it.[76]

The official summary of the case against Antoine Besson is revealing. It says that he was 'of the number and of the adherents [who] had conspired and endeavoured to make some poison composed in the form of grease and also powder for use on people to make them die and, also, [among those who had] together made an execrable oath to reveal nothing'. The importance placed on the oath as an act, rather than its actual content, is clear here as in Monier's case. Her hand was removed and, with the others, exposed near the place in Plainpalais where the oath was taken. Besson's summary immediately reinforces this by saying that

> it was true that notwithstanding [that] the said Antoine Besson was in the service of [the state] in the Plague Hospital and had taken the oath loyally to exercise his office to clean for the profit of the community and to avoid damage and to reveal everything which might be prejudicial to the city he had not done this. Rather, in place of this as though inspired by the Devil and a very evil will, one day, during the summer time about two years before, he found himself in Plainpalais [where he and the others took their evil oath].[77]

Much to the fury of the judges, he would not confess. This despite being strapped and, eventually, tormented with hot irons. In all, he was tortured six times.[78]

The cases of Louis Dunant and Jean Tissier, the other two men usually placed at the head of the conspiracy, add little more to the details noted above. Nothing survives of Dunant's trial except the summary and the sentence. However, these do connect Lentille's knowledge of plague spreading with the 1530 trials.[79] Tissier admitted (before being tortured) to knowing most of the accused conspirators, though this was to be expected. However, he also added that he had seen Fiollet and Tallien, in the presence of Besson, making some ointment (or grease) but he knew nothing more about the matter.[80] He was tortured at the end of his first interrogation and subsequently on 2 and 5 March. Although he confessed nothing then, he began confessing at the start of his interrogation on 6 March.[81] He placed Tallien and Fiollet at the head of the conspiracy and identified the small book upon which some had taken the oath as a New Testament. Despite this detailed knowledge, he could say only that the grease contained some poisons. He also implied that his original intention had been to take the grease and use it at home in Burgundy. Finally, when asked about his box of grease, he said that his mother-in-law had thrown it in the river.[82] Considering Lentille's liaisons with Marca and Basseta, as well as Dunant's relationship with Petitjean, it is worth noting that Tissier admitted to fornicating with Genon Reviaz.[83]

In the midst of the trials of Dunant and Tissier, the state opened investigations against Rene Bellefille and his wife Antoina Guilloda.[84] Two factors are worth considering at this point. First, although many more women were eventually arrested and prosecuted for the crime than men, at this stage in the prosecutions nearly half the accused were male. Also, many of these men had medical training and, the greatest shock to the state, Bellefille was the barber-surgeon with overall responsibility for the medical care of the plague victims. If the government was not already reeling from the trials' revelations then the alleged involvement of Rene must surely have pushed them over the edge.

The first interrogation with numerous confrontations produced only two interesting pieces of information. Bellefille and his wife were accused of possessing two boxes of grease. Moreover, Guilloda was accused of having asserted to one of the women that the grease had been made by the barber-surgeons. This last piece of detail, along with the involvement of the male medical practitioners, again stresses the role of poison in the grease production. The grease was not being produced with the expectations that it would work by means supernatural or demonic. Instead, trained medical men were mixing a 'medicine' which they believed would kill persons who came into contact with it either by giving them plague or by poisoning them. The male ringleaders were using their specialist knowledge – and position of social and intellectual primacy over their female co-workers and servants – to produce and propagate a poisonous and disease-bearing substance. They had every reason to believe (and the magistrates ever reason to fear) that the grease would work, since they were employing the very best and latest medical and pharmacological principles and ingredients in its production.

Bellefille confessed that he had taken an oath to the Senate 'to rule and govern well the afflicted'.[85] Earlier, Fiollet had accused Rene of having spoken well of the Mass.[86] This latter charge was never pursued although it might have allowed the judges to pursue a confessional motivation for the attempt to kill so many leading (Protestant) citizens. On 31 March, Bellefille was tortured (by being strapped) for the first time. He stood firm, saying that he could be 'taken to the gibbet and there killed [but] that he had never done anything evil'.[87] Despite torture and numerous interrogations, Bellefille continued to deny everything evil, although he did eventually admit that he had had boxes full of grease and that they had come from Lentille and Fiollet, but he said he had been assured that the grease was a medication which would help plague victims.[88] On 7 April, however, he confessed to receiving poisonous powders from Tallien (for use in soup) and having heard Tallien bragging about poison. Further he connected Tallien with Thonon (and, by extension, with Dallinge). He also gave a version of the oath in which he had sworn 'rather to die than to reveal the [conspiracy]'.[89]

At a later session, he said that the ointment was green and called *appostoloix* and that Fiollet had said it was a purgative which was used to clean the heart.[90] It was not until 16 April that he finally confessed that he had made some grease out of plague excretions. Despite this evidence, the magistrates rejected the request by the Lieutenant for more torture to be applied.[91] In the official summation of the case it was reported that Bellefille had tried to justify his actions by saying that, although he had hoped personally to profit, he was also working

[87]

for the profit of the republic [since] he only intended to kill useless people such as women who would not obey their husbands, children who were rebellious to their fathers and mothers, servants who disobeyed their masters and mistresses, as well as others not inclined to obey God or the magistracy.

This appeal to utilitarian patriotism was entirely lost upon the judges, who scored the defence out of the summation. The magistrates preferred that any public recitation of the details of the trial should omit this alleged motivation in favour of the more banal assertion that the accused 'held certain villainous views'.[92]

Although the dossier purports to include the trials of both Bellefille and his wife, the bulk of the surviving material relates to the husband. We learn from a report of 31 March that Guilloda tried to commit suicide by throwing herself out of a prison window. Her explanation for the attempt was that she feared further torture. Having been tortured earlier that day, she knew what to expect.[93] She appears not to have been questioned again for over a week, as the next surviving session dates from 9 April. On that day she said that she had begged her husband to burn the box of white grease that Tallien had given them upon his return from Morges. When asked why she had done this she said it was because 'the said Bernard [Tallien] was an evil man'.[94]

On the next day, Guilloda 'spontaneously confessed'.[95] She had seen the grease being made and had taken an oath but only in the presence of her husband and Tallien. However, she had never used the grease, preferring instead the 'reddish powder' that caused people to 'vomit before they died'. She specifically denied that she had given, or sworn to give, herself to the Devil. Her motivation was to get rich.[96] The summation adds that she had 'fallen away from God and joined herself to the Devil'. It goes on to connect this judgement not with the oath but with her attempted suicide, which showed she had lost 'confidence in the mercy of the Lord and also in His justice'.[97] The most shocking aspect of these two intertwined trials was the use of the poisons, powders and greases to kill plague victims placed in their charge. The judges' fury and horror at this probably explain why Bellefille and Guilloda were condemned to be drawn by hot irons and quartered instead of the normal punishment of hanging.[98]

The remaining prosecutions in the first wave of trials ended in sentences of banishment, though one, against Christophla Mermilliod, may have seen a harsher verdict. The implication of the sentence for 'many enormous and execrable evils worthy of punishment' is that she was executed. Only the partial sentence and a summation survive. The latter is interesting for preserving her confession that the male conspirators were paid eight écus while the females received only five. A separate hand has added to her summation that eight years previously (c. 1537) she had fled her native village (Ponchy-en-Faucigny) when her own mother had accused her of witchcraft.[99] Four other cases, against women (Jeanne Fassonet, Mya Bouloz, Bernarda Villard and Thevena Burlat) were relatively brief and ended in two banishments and two executions.[100] Fassonet and Burlat received only brief trials and appear to have been suspects by association. However, the number of accusations against them was sufficient to lead to their execution. Bouloz's trial is more inter-esting because she was tortured at least three times but never wavered in, or varied, her testimony despite the accusations made to her face by Fiollet. Indeed, so suc-cessful was she that her sentence was quashed on appeal on 4 February 1547, when she asked to be allowed to return to Geneva because she was a 'good wife and had two good children'.[101]

Villard's case was considerably more complex. She was tortured at least six times.[102] She had been implicated by Fiollet as well as Berchetaz and had worked alongside Dallinge. However, she steadfastly denied any part in the plot and any conversation with Dallinge except about 'wholly good matters'.[103] It would seem that her association with the confessed (and largely executed) conspirators was suffi-cient to allow the application of judicial torture. Her background also seems to have worked against her. At her first interrogation she was asked how and why her father had died. She admitted that he had been burnt at Nyon for having sex with a cow.[104] This question strongly implied that the judges had already been in contact with sources in Nyon to gain information about Villard. Indeed, the day after she was first tortured, 29 April, she was asked first about her past and not about the conspiracy. At this point the court finally got her to admit to the information she had obviously been withholding. She admitted that she had also been a fornicator with three bastard children in addition to her father's penchant for nature's crea-tures. She defended herself by saying that all these sins had been committed before the 'reformation of the Gospel', i.e. while she was still a Catholic.[105]

With her past, and her full confession under torture, one might expect that she would have been executed forthwith. The detail she gave was similar to that in other trials and she, too, confirmed a lower rate of pay for female conspirators (six écus) than for the men (nine écus).[106] Nevertheless, the judges seem not to have been content with some aspect of her confession. Perhaps it was because she imme-diately retracted her confession on 30 April after a second application of torture.[107] On the next day, she was asked why she had confessed in the first place. She avowed it was because of the pain inflicted during the initial round of torture. She was then tortured again and held to her retraction.[108] Despite repeated applications of torture the prosecutor was led to accept her retractions on 12 May.[109] However, she was sufficiently suspect to be banished the following day.[110]

The first wave of trials also included a clutch of perfunctory examinations (Françoise Dars, Guichauda Coquet, George[a] Delarpaz, Pernon Mugneratz, Thassiaz Rey, Pernon Bonet, the daughter of Crespinaz and the daughter of Simon Mugniez). It seems clear from the surviving documents that these women were arrested because they were *cureuses*. Only two cases, against Rey and Bonet, involved more than one interrogation and only one, Rey, the use of torture. Although the women had been held since the end of March, they were not examined until a month later. By that point, many of their potential accusers had already been exe-cuted and the judges seem to have felt that the crisis had passed. One conclusion is that they had been arrested in the general round-up of all the plague workers on the offchance that they might be implicated in the on-going interrogations of the ringleaders. When no evidence or accusations arose they were brought in, questioned and then, depending on the suspicions of the judges, either acquitted outright or banished. Two (Dars and Mugneratz) were banished; the other six (including the tortured Rey) were freed.[111]

The importance placed on accusations cannot be overstated. Only one other case, that of Bartholomea Chabbod, remains to be discussed. On 13 April, the prosecutor summed up the evidence against her. What is clear is that she consistently denied any involvement in the conspiracy. Nevertheless, she was executed. The court seemed confident in this verdict because of the number of separate accusations made against her by convicted conspirators. It is perhaps useful to dwell upon this point as one leaves the examination of the first wave of prosecutions. Torture was not used against Chabbod. It would seem that she did not vary her testimony. With the number of accusations against her one would expect that torture would still have been applied. However, with a large number of accusations the court seems to have felt that there was no need. In other words, sufficient evidence was supplied in the confessions and confrontations of others to allow the court to convict her outright. In effect, the accusations served as eye-witness accounts.

One can conclude from this that acquittal would result: if there were few (if any) accusations against the defendant, if the defendant was able to maintain his or her defence without variation; obfuscation or perjury; and if torture failed to produce a consistent and coherent confession. If there was a weakness in any one of these areas the result was likely to be banishment. If, on the other hand, the defendant failed in all three areas, death was the normal consequence. Although not compatible with a modern understanding of trial procedure one must remember that the judges were amateurs and that the prosecutor was also a magistrate. It is also worth noting that for all its failings the judges seem to have been quite sensible and discriminating in the use of their system of investigation and prosecution.

The seeming aplomb of the magistrates in the face of this alleged conspiracy is even more amazing when one recalls that they were also trying to hold Geneva together during its fourth successive year of plague. The arrest, detention, prosecution and execution of many of the city's plague workers placed an immediate burden on the state. Replacements had to be found and the system shored up. On 14 April 1545, the city heard (and granted) a request from Calvin that a special lodging should be built for the minister assigned to the Plague Hospital near the structure in Plainpalais to make his task easier (and to keep him effectively quarantined).[112] Two days later, the city hired Villiez Frans from Zealand as a barber-surgeon for the pest house on a wage of six écus per month (about 360 florins per annum). He was also provided with a house at the city's expense.[113] These burdens were undoubtedly aided by the bequest, on 27 April, of 100 écus (500 florins) from the wife of Henry Aubert, one of the four recently elected syndics.[114]

In the second set of trials, two deserve some close examination: those of François Boulat and Jeanne Mutilliod. Both trials survive in some detail and Boulat is the last male executed for plague spreading and one of the last prosecuted. He is also interesting because he was accused of a number of crimes: witchcraft, plague spreading, breaking the city's plague quarantine (for which he had been previously banished) and arson.[115] Indeed, his case required the collection of previous dossiers relating to crimes committed in 1542 (adultery and infanticide), 1543 (violating plague regulations while grave-digging) and 1544 (slander and violating his exile).[116] Mutilliod also cut a fascinating figure. She was closely connected with Boulat and also accused of witchcraft, plague spreading and arson. One should note that the only other two cases ending in executions after the first wave (those of Girard and Paultra) are grouped in the same dossier with Mutilliod.[117] Thus, the cases of Boulat and Mutilliod (and, by extension, of Girard and Paultra) seem to form an interconnected whole. If one excludes these four, then all the subsequent prosecutions ended in banishment or acquittal. Hence, these trials, in the minds of the judges, marked the end of the conspiracy.

Mutilliod became associated with the other defendants while staying in the Plague Hospital with her child, who was ill with plague. A number of the workers had discussed their pay and conditions with her but she denied any knowledge of an oath or grease. She stated that she had been offered the chance to earn six sols but she would not, or could not, specify for what. She freely admitted this without even the threat of torture. The prosecutor then read out the places in another dossier where she had been accused, giving exact references: Marca (fol. 28), Folliez (fol. 3r–3v), Paultra (2 May), Guex (fol. 1), 'Serralion' (fol. 3 or, perhaps, the 3rd of a month).[118] With this wealth of accusations and her partial confession of involvement in the details of the conspiracy the court was able to agree to torture her, although without result.

The very next day the very threat of torture produced a confession. She now implicated both Paultra (Pernon Dorsier) and Boulat (who, she said, was the source of her grease). The details she now related tallied with those from other trials: for example, the use of plague pus and a limb from the gibbet. She further confessed that an additional motive had been revenge: Boulat wanted to punish some magistrates who had used torture. Presumably, this related to one (or more) of his previous trials before the Genevan magistracy.[119] On 6 May, she continued to confess and placed special emphasis upon Boulat's desire for revenge. She also said that she had gunpowder (as well as the poisonous powder and grease) which was to start fires in the houses of their victims. Besson had administered the oath to her. Finally, she admitted that the previous Christmas Satan had appeared to her while she was grieving for her dead children. She later attended a Sabbath along with Berchetaz, Chappuis, Folliez, Depellis and Marca.[120] At her next session she recanted her witchcraft. She continued to confess to plague spreading and possessing grease and powders combustible or poisonous. However, she denied she had ever tried to fire any house, only that she had the means and Boulat the motive.[121] At her final interrogation she maintained this qualified confession and the Lieutenant accepted it as the truth. That is, although witchcraft had entered the discussion, the magistrates eventually accepted that Mutilliod was not, in fact, a confessed witch. She was executed for attempted murder by spreading plague and poison. All three women,

Mutilliod, Girard and Paultra, gave a completely natural explanation for their murderous activities: they were trying to gain extra money by cleaning more homes and creating the opportunities for pilfering.[122]

By the spring of 1545, the magistrates seem to have exhausted their investigation and suspicions. In any case, there were few remaining workers to interrogate or execute. The increase in the number of plague victims increasingly occupied the attention of the state. The General Hospital transferred ten écus to the Plague Hospital on 30 April 1545.[123] The guard or herald, Thivent Batista, resigned from his post at the pest house because he was no longer able to do the work; Jean Saubre replaced him.[124] Chautemps was again busy with the minutiae of the unfolding epidemic as well as with the aftermath of the previous year's outbreak.[125] The magistrates also reissued the decrees on quarantine – violators faced six months' banishment – and the mandatory cleaning of streets by householders every Saturday – a fine of 3s was to be imposed on delinquents.[126]

The cases against the accused plague spreaders were not, however, forgotten. Sentences of death were passed by the Senate on 'La Freneysan' (Martine Gay) and 'La Pricqua' (Robelle de la Fontanna) on 30 April 1545 for 'having made the oath to spread the plague and for having used poisoned grease and powder'.[127] Their sentence was confirmed along with that of Jeanne Collomb on 5 May. The Senate noted that Collomb (called Cugnier) had not actually taken the oath but had spread the grease.[128] Despite the severity of the situation, the magistrates were able to be somewhat lenient; Mya Buandiere and her family who had been implicated by two (executed) conspirators were 'perpetually banished' because of 'her good name and reputation'.[129] Banishment, despite evidence, was the result in a few other cases. Henrietta Ormond was banished because she had refused to confess even after torture although grease had been found in her room and she had tried to get some of her fellow workers to take an oath to one another. Likewise, Bernarde Villars, who had been accused both by Fiollet and by Basseta, was banished. She had been tortured and confessed but then later retracted her confession and maintained the retraction despite subsequent interrogation (and probably torture).[130]

However, leniency was not the normative feature of the Senate's reaction to the accused plague spreaders. Its minutes are full of the notification of final decisions on suspected conspirators. Jeanne Mutilliod, Pernon Dorsier and Genon Girard were sentenced to death on 13 May.[131] The Senate also, at last, ended the torment of François Boulat.[132] The number of condemned probably explains the order to give a large two-handed sword to Jehan Granjean, the public executioner.[133] The magistrates also had to deal with those implicated in a few cases but against whom no additional information existed. Clauda Beguinaz, who had only been accused by Clauda Folliez, was perpetually banished.[134] A single accusation existed against Laurence Galliard but despite attempts to uncover additional evidence the case collapsed; she, too, was perpetually banished.[135] The same circumstances resulted in an identical fate for Pernette Bossiez.[136] There were also banishments decreed against some women 'guilty by association'. For example, the wives of Petitjean (executed at Brig) and Rollet Charrocton were expelled from the city solely on the suspicion of being involved in the conspiracy. The denouement of the entire conspiracy came on 15 May, when the Grand Council (the eligible voters of the city) ordered the burning of the poisonous powders and grease found in the possession of the executed plague spreaders.[137]

Although banishment was preferable to death, it was a serious punishment. In effect, the person was left stateless and unprotected. Such a person was left an outlaw and unlikely to find sympathy or assistance anywhere in the vicinity of Geneva. Some idea of how detrimental it was to their social and economic well-being is evident in the number of people willing to risk death or beating by violating their banishment and returning to Geneva. The enormous cost paid by François Boulat has already been noted. Other, lesser, criminals also tried to slip back into the city. Jeanne Fassonet, mentioned above, was arrested on 25 May for breaking her banishment. She was told to leave and stay away or she would suffer the fate of the conspirators with whom she had been accused of having contact and knowledge.[138] Laurence Galliard was caught in the city stealing on 18 July and hanged as much for violating the sentence against her as for any thefts.[139] Accused plague spreaders were not the only ones tempted to return from exile. Katherine, the wife of Antoine du Fossal, who had been banished because of her 'very evil reputation as a witch and sorceress', was flogged in public and banished again.[140] Another suspected witch, Rolette (the widow of Pierre Pilliciez) was also re-banished.[141]

The return of accused witches should remind the reader that the city also faced other types of 'diabolical' activity. Although any detailed study of such witches is beyond the scope of this volume, there were a number of witchcraft trials in the autumn of 1545 centring on the villages of Peney and Satigny. In a few cases, as already noted, plague spreaders were also accused and convicted of witchcraft. An example from this later date, after the effective end of the plague-spreading trials, is the mention in the Senate's minutes of Pernette Dorse, who was perpetually banished for poisoning, 'greasing' and witchcraft.[142] The important clutch of witch trials was first brought to the attention of the Senate on 9 October 1545 when the chatelaine of Peney, Donzel, announced the arrest of six suspected witches.[143] The fact that the better part of the summer months of 1545 separates the last executions for plague spreading and the start of this 'witch hunt' is yet another reason to suspect that any attempt to conflate the two activities – the one natural (plague spreading for profit), the other supernatural (witchcraft and Sabbath-going) – would be difficult.[144]

Donzel was certainly overwhelmed by the number of witches he was uncovering. Two leading magistrates, Pierre Tissot and Henry Aubert (a syndic), were sent to help him in his investigations.[145] He eventually reported an extensive list of suspected witches: Louis Verchiere (from Satigny), Andrea (widow of Pierre Juget), Claude Malliez (from Satigny), Amyed Darnex, Henry du Gerdil, Leonarda (widow of Claude Donne), Thevena Paris.[146] Calvin and the minister in the rural area, Jaques Bernard, went to the Senate to demand that 'this race be extirpated from the land'.[147] The only case that seems to have caused any serious problem for the courts was that of Amyed Darnex. He had confessed to being a witch (sorcerer, warlock) for six years and to having paid homage to the Devil. However, the legal opinions solicited in his case could not agree on the death penalty. Even after being tortured by 'heating his feet' he would confess nothing more than that he had renounced God and paid homage to the Devil. In the end, he was perpetually banished.[148] His wife was daring enough to suggest that they should not have to pay the cost of the trial, since his life had been spared.[149]

This brief digression into the realm of the supernatural must end with an abrupt return to the very natural reality of a city beset by yet another summer of plague. By 11 May, Chautemps was forced to report that there were forty inmates in the pest house and that both its barber and its minister had the plague.[150] In addition, there was only one cask of wine left and no money. The Senate rushed to shore up the city's defences for yet another siege by the pestilence.[151] Two days later, the magistrates were informed of the death of the barber, Guillaume le Planien. His worldly goods, amounting to four écus in his purse, were distributed in part to his servants and the rest to the Plague Hospital.[152] Effran Legier, who offered to take up the post in the pest house, was deemed 'incapable and someone else ought to be found'.[153] The next day, the Senate hired François Pantray. He was given two écus to send to his wife (presumably still in Beauregard, whence he came) and told that 'as long as he works he will get paid'.[154] The Senate noted the severity of the outbreak on 25 May and was gratified to know that Michel Varro (former factor of the General Hospital) and the current factor (Pierre Bonna) would transfer funds to the pest house.[155] The city also noted that the pestilence was being worsened by violations of the quarantine regulations and decreed that every suspected case had to leave the city either for the Plague Hospital or for the cabins near it in Plainpalais.[156]

The manifold difficulties facing Chautemps, the magistrate responsible for overseeing the city's response to the epidemic, were exacerbated by the suggestion that had he done his job well the conspiracy would not have happened. He complained to the Senate that 'he had borne a lot of expense and in recompense he was blamed, demanding that, if he were guilty, he wished to have a trial and, if innocent, his good [reputation] should be defended'. The city decided that Pierre Roph (called Taborin) should be investigated, since Chautemps said he had, in particular, been slandering Chautemps.[157] Roph had accused Chautemps of 'participating in the activity to spread the plague'. After a lengthy examination Roph was flogged and perpetually banished.[158] He went to live near the Arve Bridge and continued to accuse Chautemps to anyone who would listen. The Senate was forced to ask the (Bernese) bailiff of Ternier to do something.[159] A similar case erupted the following year when François Mestral outraged the staff of the pest house by saying they were all 'greasers'.[160]

Eventually, the advent of winter's cold saw the decline of the epidemic. Chautemps reported that Claude Choudens, commissary of the pest house, had died of the disease but that the drop in new infections meant that people were asking to be allowed to go home. Also, he complained that Claude Moche was not doing his job. The Senate gave Chautemps ten écus to replace Moche and said he could release inmates in the pest house at his discretion.[161] Despite Chautemps's complaints, Moche was reinstated in December.[162] There was certainly a recurrence of the plague in 1546 but it was clearly not virulent and confined to a few cases only. On 12 March 1546, Chautemps reported that a woman had died of plague and that something should be done to clear Geneva of indigent foreigners. Louis Bernard, a senator, was deputed to deal with the foreigners.[163] Three houses were classified as infected on 30 March and Chautemps wanted permission to allow Jean Saubre, the guard, to open the city's gate (facing the pest house) at night so that the ill could safely retire to the Plague Hospital. The Senate agreed to the request as long as a strong guard was kept while the gates were open.[164] On 26 July, the house of one of the ministers (Ferron) was sealed because a Frenchman had died there and plague was suspected. Doctors were sent to examine the corpse.[165] Chautemps complained that the quarantine rules were still being flouted and the magistrates reissued them[166] The mildness of this outbreak is best exemplified (in addition to the paucity of references to plague in the records) by Moche's report that he thought most of the deaths were more likely to have been the result of poison than of plague and that he and the minister of the pest house had enough time on their hands to argue about living arrangements in their accommodation at the hospital.[167]

Moche's comments about poisoning serve to remind us that plague spreading, or the threat of it, had not completely disappeared from the minds of the citizens of Geneva with the last executions in May 1545. Although no new conspiracy was uncovered, the Genevans were certainly 'sensitised' to the problem. They were not quite at the point of finding 'greasers' under every bed (or sticking to every door) but they were certainly willing to act quickly to investigate any possible return of the phenomenon. Indeed, the city responded quickly to any accusations of poisoning. On 17 November 1545, as the plague waned, the Senate was told that Petremand Bourgeois and Claude Margat (from Martigny) had been trying to buy arsenic. They immediately wrote to the chatelaine and judges in Martigny to see if they could uncover any explanation for the men's actions. By 11 December, the state was able to conclude that they had wanted to poison Petreman's father, Jean, and his mistress. They were sentenced to be burned – the same sentence given to the plague spreaders except that their right hands were not amputated. The latter omission perhaps supports the conclusion that the display of the hands of the conspirators, and the ferocity of the city's response to them, was in part a reaction to their conspiratorial oath.

This isolated, but illuminating, trial for poisoning was not the only case to recall the events of early 1545. In 1546, the city again arrested some suspected plague spreaders: Jean Palmier, Pernette l'Hoste, Antoine du Martheray (see Table 6), Jean Berchod and Michel Regneaud. Jean Palmier was examined on a number of occasions but eventually released (acquitted without punishment) because of lack of evidence.[168] Berchod's case is mostly unknown except that he had been banished as a suspected plague spreader but was allowed to appeal against his conviction on 28

May; no result was noted.[169] Regnaud was interrogated for being found in the main plaza of the city (Bourg-de-Four) and refusing to empty his pockets when confronted by the city secretary, François Beguin. He had then removed some grease wrapped in paper and eaten it. He said 'it was two pieces of chicken and to remove any suspicion that he was up to no good he had eaten them'. He also had some root vegetables in his possession. He admitted that he had been arrested before in Geneva for stealing some grapes. In Avignon he had had his tongue as well as his copy of the New Testament burned. He denied that he had practised any form of medicine or that he had given any medicines to a certain Du Gerdil, the wife of Claude du Buchet, only two eggs. He was eventually released after being admonished by the court for his rebellious attitude to the magistrates and citizens who had approached him the night of his arrest.[170]

The cases of Pernette l'Hoste and Antoine du Martheray are interconnected, as they were married to one another.[171] More interestingly, the arrest of Antoine again links the accusation of plague spreading with male medical practitioners, as he was an apothecary. It seems that Pernette was actually suspected. She had worked as a *cureuse* while her husband had been ill with the plague. In fact, she was also working as an unofficial medical practitioner, bringing medications from her husband (and their shop) to sick people. She was eventually banished (for a year and a day) though she was able to have the sentence remitted on an appeal to the Council of Two Hundred.[172] Her husband was not punished and was able to get the Senate to return the keys to his shop but only after the syndic Dupan (himself an apothecary) had carefully examined the contents of a box found there.[173] The cases seem to have amounted to little in the end and may have been motivated by on-going disputes between Pernette (nicknamed Sept-Diables) and her neighbours, who provided the information against her.[174]

These few cases as well as the generally desultory nature of the 1546 outbreak would lead one to believe that the epidemic was not great enough to cause a panic of any sort. However, the few investigations of suspected plague spreaders demonstrate that even a few plague cases could make the city suspicious. The speed of the arrests even when the cases eventually went nowhere is in marked contrast to the attitude of the government prior to the discovery of the conspiracy. In 1542–44, the presence of a virulent outbreak of plague even with the appearance of grease did not lead the state to suspect a conspiracy *à la* 1530. However, after January–May 1545, the magistrates were more willing to believe and investigate such accusations. This suspiciousness (or watchfulness), coupled with the mildness of the outbreak, afforded the courts time for a number of extremely bizarre investigations. On 29 June 1546, the Senate began to investigate Charles de Soye, a surgeon, from Bonne.[175] They had heard reports that he had been invited into the city by Jaques Symon to use 'diabolical arts for divination'. In addition, the wife of Jean Pasteur from the village of Vandoeuvres was found practising the 'art of stones' (apparently another form of divination) in the house where she was employed as a servant; the house happened to belong to the Protestant minister of the parish.[176] Her case languished in obscurity but we know that Soye had been invited by Symon to go into the house of Laurent Symon (while he was not there), Jaques's brother, 'to use some enchantments to learn about some stolen money'. Other members of the household were involved in the event. Eventually, Soye was admonished and freed; the interventions of his wife seem not to have helped his case.[177]

A few salient points about the conspiracies of 1530 and 1545 need to be kept in mind. For some reason, the magistrates of the 1540s did not immediately suspect that the appearance of grease during a plague outbreak signalled a possible conspiracy. For the most part, they treated the initial charges of using grease to spread plague as individual acts. They seem considerably more concerned with the constant violation of quarantine regulations. Even the general populace was not overly concerned. Complaints were made but there was no sense of threat or panic. However, the information obtained from Thonon radically and quickly altered this situation.

Once the authorities began to suspect that their foreign plague workers (barber-surgeons, grave-diggers, fumigators, cleaners and general servants) might be involved in an organised conspiracy to profit from plague spreading, they moved speedily to control the problem. There can be no doubt that they believed that this conspiracy actually existed. Citizens who came to the Senate complaining about the grease on their houses and doors were also convinced that the activity was real in a natural sense. There is also a substantial amount of circumstantial evidence in these trials. Boxes and pots of grease and powder were found. The barber-surgeons had access to any number of poisonous drugs, such as arsenic, that were regularly used in the treatment of plague. The evidence in the trials, especially before the application of torture, suggests that at least some of the workers were conspiring together. Moreover, the testimony from Dallinge in Thonon and Petitjean in Brig independently confirmed many of the details uncovered by the Genevan investigations.

The information contained in these dossiers differs dramatically from that associated with witchcraft trials. In the latter, most of the 'crimes' are impossible to corroborate and stereotypical. Witches flying to Sabbaths, animal familiars, consorting with Satan, killing by curses, etc. (by their very nature) enter into a trial only when they have been 'confessed'. The role of torture in eliciting these stereotypical responses is also an important feature of witchcraft trials. Although torture is used extensively in the trials of the plague spreaders it is not integral to the gathering of circumstantial information. Rather, it serves a fundamentally different purpose in the minds of the judges. Torture was used to gather more names to ensure that the entire conspiratorial 'cell' had been uncovered. In later cases, the courts was more than willing to dispense with torture when there was not enough circumstantial evidence or testimony from other trials to warrant its use. Acquittals and 'not proven' verdicts are rare in witchcraft trials, especially after the use of torture, but they do occur regularly in the plague-spreading trials. Torture was the only means available to gather evidence in witchcraft trials (short of an outright voluntary confession) but was used in the plague-spreading trials for a different purpose (the acquisition of information *additional* to, or *confirmatory* of, what was needed to convict).

The most important aspect of the trials is the motivation assigned to the behaviour by the courts, the citizenry and, even, by most of the accused. The supernatural did not enter into the cases as a part of the crime of plague spreading. A few individuals were accused of the additional charge of witchcraft. The magistrates believed that they were facing a very real and natural conspiracy to poison (by using arsenic and plague secretions) for personal financial gain. The conspirators were under the direction of men (barber-surgeons) fully qualified to commit such a crime. Grease and powders said to contain arsenic as well as plague secretions were found and impounded by the investigators. People said there was grease on their doors and their neighbours and magisterial committees confirmed this. Trials independent of, and external to, Geneva corroborated crucial details uncovered in the city. There was certainly every reason for the judges to think that the activities were real, not imagined. Spreading plague, they knew, was an almost inconceivably evil activity; the rationale for it – profit – was no less base.

Finally, the predominance of women among the accused cannot be seen as an example of the targeting of women by some panicked patriarchy. The women were seen as the tools of the men for the distribution and application of the poison as well as (often) their sexual playthings. Also, on a practical level, women predominated as plague workers. They were being used, and it would seem that the court even recognised this – those acquitted were women. Finally, the state saw the oath not as a sign of consorting with Satan but as a conspiratorial oath against the city, which broke the oath taken before the magistrates to protect and serve Geneva. The oath was a seditious (not demonic) pact. No clearer evidence of the 'natural' interpretation given to plague spreading can be advanced than that, when some of the women confessed to witchcraft, there was no attempt to fit the rest of the defendants into the stereotypical mould of witches. Considering the availability of torture, it would not have been difficult for the judges to prosecute these people, mostly women, as witches. Had they suspected that the oath, the use of poisonous grease and powder or the malevolence of the behaviour itself was evidence of satanic direction they would have certainly pursued that line of enquiry. They did not.

NOTES

1 It is essential to realise that banishment was normally the punishment inflicted after a 'not proven' verdict. When the investigation failed to produce either two eye witnesses or a confession there might still be sufficient circumstantial evidence to question a defendant's innocence. In that case, the magistracy often banished the person on the grounds that, while guilt had not been proved, innocence had been sufficiently undermined to allow the courts to 'do something'. In the three cases where no punishment is noted, the assumption is that the case lapsed for lack of evidence, i.e. was an acquittal. As Monter noted, even in witchcraft, which had torture to get confessions, Geneva preferred banishment to execution. 'Witchcraft in Geneva, 1537–1662', *Journal of Modern History* 43: 2 (1971): 179–204, especially 186–8. In Venice, only about 18 per

cent of witchcraft trials ended in *any* verdict. See R. Martin, *Witchcraft and the Inquisition in Venice, 1550–1650* (Oxford, 1989). More generally on Venice, see J. E. Law, *Venice and the Veneto in the Early Renaissance* (Aldershot, 1994).

2 In some multiple trials is it not always clear how many defendants were questioned, or tortured, in any given session. The designation of tortured defendants is, therefore, the most conservative result available. If one were to assume that in all multiple trials in which one defendant was tortured they were all tortured the figure would be over 70 per cent.

3 Banishment was, in fact, the most frequent punishment in Geneva. B. Lescaze, 'Crimes et criminels à Genève en 1572', in *Pour une histoire qualitative : études offertes à Sven Stelling-Michaud* (Geneva, 1975): 45–71, especially pp. 63–9, 69 n 1.

4 For more on the amateur nature of early modern bureaucracies (even in sophisticated Florence) see G. Brucker, 'Bureaucracy and Social Welfare in the Renaissance: a Florentine Case Study', *Journal of Modern History* 55: 1 (1983): 1–21, especially 2.

5 For the use of body parts in magical potions and as talismans see L. Roper, *Oedipus and the Devil: Witchcraft, Sexuality and Religion in Early Modern Europe* (London, 1994), pp. 181, 189. More generally, D. Hillman and C. Mazzio, eds, *The Body in Parts: Fantasies of Corporeality in early modern Europe* (New York, 1997).

6 AEG, PC1: 388 (22 January 1545). Although the depositions are arranged chronologically, the dossiers are unpaginated. Therefore, the notation will be to the dossier and the specific date of the interrogation. See also AEG, RC 39, fol. 107v (22 January 1545), where the Senate discussed the letter and ordered Lentille's arrest.

7 AEG, RC 39, fol. 108 (22 January 1545).

8 AEG, RC 39, fol. 109v (23 January 1545).

9 AEG, RC 39, fol. 111 (23 January 1545).

10 AEG, RC 39, fol. 114 (26 January 1545). For more on crime and, especially, witchcraft in Ternier see C. Duval, 'Procès de sorciers à Viry, bailliage de Ternier de 1534–1548', *Bulletin de l'Institut national genevois* 24 (1882): 297–515.

11 AEG, RC 39, fol. 114v (27 January 1545).

12 AEG, RC 39, fol. 115v (27 January 1545).

13 AEG, RC 39, fol. 115v (27 January 1545).

14 AEG, RC 39, fols 116–117v (29 January 1545). The details of the confrontation are preserved in PC1: 388 (31 January 1545).

15 AEG, RC 39, fol. 121 (2 February 1545).

16 AEG, RC 39, fol. 125v (6 February 1545).

17 AEG, RC 40, fol. 25v (17 February 1545). They were promised recompense beyond their normal wage.

18 AEG, PC1: 388 (22 January 1545).

19 AEG, PC1: 388 (22 January 1545). The corpse had been there about eighteen months. Jean Granjean the executioner gave an individual report on 24 January affirming that when (the day before) he had gone to bury all the bodies exposed on the gibbet there was indeed one with its right leg missing below the knee. The Lieutenant had actually been ordered to inspect the gibbet but it appears that he had delegated the duty to Granjean. AEG, RC 39, fol. 108 (22 January 1545).

20 Since her name had arisen in Lentille's case, the magistrate in charge of the pest house (Jean Chautemps) was asked to locate her. A rumour had arisen, which he doubted, that she had died of plague. AEG, RC 39, fol. 108 (22 January 1545).

21 AEG, PC1: 388 (24 January 1545).

22 AEG, PC1: 388 (24 January 1545). Separate sheet from Thonon.

23 AEG, PC1: 388 (26 January 1545).

24 AEG, PC1: 388 (27, 28 January 1545).

25 On Morges in this period see E. Küpfer, *Morges dans le passé: la periode bernoise* (Lausanne, 1944).

26 AEG, PC1: 388 (29 January 1545).

27 AEG, PC1: 388 (31 January 1545).

28 AEG, PC1: 388 (29 January 1545).

29 AEG, PC1: 388 (16 January 1545). See also AEG, RC 40, fol. 26 (17 February 1545). On the third application of the strap, Lentille's shoulders had dislocated and he had begun to bleed from under his arms. He was immediately removed from the cord and given over to the ministrations of three barber-surgeons (Guillaume Villars, Alexandre Charles and Claude Combert). He died three hours later.

30 Their cases are contained in a single dossier: AEG, PC1: 389. Marca's case, in its entirety, comes first.

31 He was suspected and questioned for a considerable time. See AEG, RC 40, fols 118v (18 May 1545). His wife, Humberte Viennesin, contracted plague on 21 May (AEG, RC 40, fol. 122v).

32 AEG, RC 40, fols 25–26v (17 February 1545).

33 See AEG, RC 40, fol. 39v (7 March 1545), where the sentence against her is also recorded. Marca 'had taken the oath with her accomplices to spread the plague and to apply the poisonous grease', in addition she 'was also a heretic (witch) and had paid homage to the Devil and [had done] many other evils [things]'.

34 AEG, PC1: 389 (1 February 1545). It is essential to recall the long and close connection of poisoning with witchcraft. Charlemagne decreed that witches should be treated the same as murderers, poisoners and thieves and the Sixth Council of Paris (829) declared that 'there are other very dangerous evils which are certainly legacies of paganism, such as magic, astrology, incantations and spells, poisoning, divination, enchantment and the interpretation of dreams'. J. C. Baroja, 'Witchcraft amongst the German and Slavonic Peoples', in M. Marwick, ed., *Witchcraft and Sorcery* (London, 1982), pp. 98–100.

35 AEG, PC1: 389 (2 February 1545).

36 AEG, PC1: 389 (3 February 1545), before dinner (the midday meal). The evening meal in Geneva was supper.

37 The use of this dangerous poison was approved by physicians. Alvarus, *Petit recueil*, p. 23. Although bizarre, this recipe was no less peculiar (or potentially dangerous) than the use of butter, goose grease, hen's fat or a whole egg to lubricate the birth process. B. M. W. Dobbie, 'An Attempt to estimate the True Rate of Maternal Mortality, Sixteenth to Eighteenth Centuries', *Medical History* 26 (1982): 79–90. The very use of poison as a cure was at times compared to magic: 'for as physicians use poisons as antidotes, so magic serves to avert evils, destroy witchcraft, cure diseases, drive away delusions'. M. H. Keefer, 'Agrippa's Dilemma: Hermetic "Rebirth" and the Ambivalence of *De Vanitate* and *De Occulta Philosophia*', *Renaissance Quarterly* 41 (1988): 614–53, especially 643.

38 AEG, PC1: 389 (3 February 1545), after dinner.

39 AEG, PC1: 389 (4 February 1545).

40 AEG, PC1: 389 (5 February 1545).

41 AEG, PC1: 389 (6 February 1545).

42 Note that Lentille initially said the same of his conversations with Dallinge.

43 It may be recalled that most judges assumed that women were better able to withstand torture. R. Briggs, 'Women as Victims? Witches, Judges and the Community', *French History* 5: 4 (1991): 438–50, especially 438.

44 AEG, PC1: 389 (4 February 1545).

45 AEG, RC 40, fols 1–22 *passim*.

46 AEG, PC1: 389 (16, 18 February 1545).

47 Cf. the place of the staff (and ointments) in the general misogyny of attitudes to witch-craft. L. C. Hults, 'Baldung and the Witches of Freiburg: The Evidence of Images', *Journal of Interdisciplinary History* 18: 2 (1987): 249–76, especially 253–8, and 'Baldung's *Bewitched Groom* Revisited: Artistic Temperament, Fantasy and the "Dream of Reason"', *SCJ* 15: 3 (1984): 259–79; S. Clark, 'The "Gendering" of Witchcraft in French Demonology: Misogyny or Polarity?' *French History* 5: 4 (1991): 426–37.

48 AEG, PC1: 389 (19 February 1545).

49 AEG, PC1: 389 (20, 25 February; 7, 9 March 1545). Her execution was decreed on 7 March (AEG, RC 40, fol. 39v) along with that of Louise Chappuis. A single dossier, AEG, PC1: 396 (27 February–5 May 1545) contains interrogations from the trials of Clauda Mossier and Jaquema Mauris (mentioned here) as well as Thibaude Guez, Guillauma Coquet, Clauda de Pellis, Clauda Folliez, Pernon Cherbonier (Grand Clauda), Martine Gay, Jeanne Collomb and Robelle de la Fontana (Pricqua). There is also a dossier dated 23 February 1546 (AEG, PC2: 685, case 2) containing an additional deposition by Jean Saubre (hired as a guard at the pest house on 4 May 1545, AEG, RC 40, fol. 103) against Guillauma Coquet.

50 AEG, PC1: 389 (21 February 1545).

51 See AEG, RC 40, fol. 41 (9 March 1545), where the detainees are given as Louise Chappuis, Rene Bellefille, Antoina Guilloda, Martine Gay, Mutilliod and others.

52 AEG, PC1: 389 (22, 24, 27, 28 February; 4, 7, 10 March 1545). She was executed, along with Colette Berchetaz and Pernon Guex, on 11 March (AEG, RC 40, fol. 45). The mention of a fugitive in Lyon may explain the request for more information from Lyon received on 11 March (AEG, RC 40, fol. 44v).

53 AEG, PC1: 396 (27 February–5 May 1545) contains the trials begun against ten separate workers: Clauda Mossier (daughter of Pierre, a shoemaker called Peytavin, the widow of Jean François Grangast, the city's 'master of works'), Jaquemaz Mauris (daughter of Claude, widow of Gaspard, a locksmith and *habitant*; she is probably the one nicknamed Le Serralion), Thibaude Guez (daughter of Claude, wife of Jean Garseney, called Bombrule), Guillaume Coquet (daughter of Pierre from Artas), Claude de Pellis (called La Curta, daughter of Jaques, a labourer and *habitant*), Claudaz Folliez (daughter of Humbert from Ville-le-Grand), Pernon Cherbonier (called Grand-Clauda, daughter of Gonin, widow of Jean Dunant, an *habitant* from Messeriez), Martine Gay (called Freneysan, daughter of Jean, wife of Jaques Bechod, a merchant and *habitant*), Jeanne Collomb (daughter of Pierre, a labourer from Seyssel known as Cugnier), Robelle de la Fontana (called Pricqua, daughter of Jean).

54 The Senate recorded a very precise version when they sentenced Berchetaz. The oath was 'on pain of enduring three straps and giving the body and souls to the Devil not to declare [anything]'. AEG, RC 40, fol. 45 (11 March 1545).

55 AEG, RC 40, fol. 42v (9 March 1545).

56 AEG, PH 1347. They had found no 'poisoners or plague spreaders'.

57 AEG, PH 1345.

58 This, as much as the presence of the plague, probably explains the magistrates' reitera-
tion of the decree to clear the city of unemployed foreigners and the need for a licence
to rent to any foreigner. In addition, they ordered a visitation to find all resident foreigners. AEG, RC 40, fol. 54v (18 March 1545). Less than a fortnight later they mandated
a fine of ten écus (an enormous sum) for illegally letting to foreigners. AEG, RC 40,
fol. 66v.

59 She worked as a servant to Tallien.

60 AEG, PC1: 391 (24 February 1545).

61 AEG, PC1: 391 (24 February 1545). The next day she implicated Berchetaz, Reviaz,
Mossier, Besson, Tissier and Dunant.

62 Antoina, wife of Jean Goullaz; Genon, a female servant of Laurent Meigret (an
extremely important French refugee); and Collette, daughter of Jean Rudet.

63 AEG, PC1: 391 (24 February 1545). Second interrogation of the day.

64 AEG, PC1: 391 (29 February 1545).

65 AEG, PC1: 391 (4 March 1545).

66 AEG, PC1: 391 (7 March 1545). See also RC 40, fol. 39v (7 March 1545), for her sentence. On his father's 'colourful' antics see R. M. Kingdon, 'The First Calvinist
Divorce', in R. A. Mentzer, ed., *Sin and the Calvinists: Morals, Control and the Consistory
in the Reformed Tradition* (Kirksville MO, 1994): 1–14, especially 7. Still, Bonivard was a
patriot and hero, cf., P. Blickle, 'Communal Reformation and Peasant Piety: The
Peasant Reformation and its Late Medieval Origins', *Central European History* 20 (1987):
216–28, especially 226–7.

67 AEG, PC1: 392 (25 February 1545). He had been detained on 24 February.

68 AEG, PC1: 392 (26 February 1545). Arsenic was also used as a talisman in sachets,
amulets and lockets. M. E. Alvarus, *Sommaire des remedes tant preservatifs que curatifs de la
peste* (Toulouse: widow of I. Colomiez, 1628), pp. 23, 26. Aubert, *Traite*, p. 19, recommends the use of hellebore. See also M. R. Baldwin, 'Toads and Plague: Amulet Theory
in Seventeenth-Century Medicine', *Bulletin of the Society for the History of Medicine* 67:
2 (1993): 227–47. On the use of poisonous substances and magic in other non-Western
cultures see I. Schapera, 'Sorcery and Witchcraft in Bechuanaland [Botswana]', in M.
Marwick, ed., *Witchcraft and Sorcery* (London, 1982), pp. 108–18, and, in the same work
(pp. 102–7) R. F. Fortune, 'Sorcerers of Dobu'.

69 AEG, PC1: 392 (12 March 1545). Subsequent sessions produced no more information.
It is worth nothing, however, that Petitjean's testimony was copied into the end of the
dossier. There is also additional information, including a summary and sentence relating to Fiollet and Tissier, in PC2: 628 (28 March 1545).

70 AEG, PC1: 393 (26 February 1545).

71 AEG, PC1: 393 (26 February; 2, 12 March 1545).

72 AEG, PC1: 393 (13, 14 March 1545).

73 AEG, PC1: 393 (16 March 1545). For just such a recipe for stomach unguent see N.
Hovel, *Traicte de la Peste* (Paris: G. de Pré, 1573), p. 34, and C. Fabri, *Les contrepoissons
et experiences certaines contre la Peste* (Paris: N. Chesneau, 1580), fol. 41v.

74 She was examined by Rolette, widow of Thomas de la Ravoye, and Andrea, widow of
Gonin Genod.

75 AEG, PC1: 393 (3 March 1545).

76 AEG. PC1: 393 (13 March 1545). Boaistuau in his *Histoires prodigieuses* (1560) – though
probably without any empirical evidence – said that a hand washed in urine can be
safely dipped in molten lead. See K. Park and L. J. Daston, 'Unnatural Conceptions:

The Study of Monsters in Sixteenth and Seventeenth Century France and England', *P&P* 92 (1981): 20–54, especially 36.

77 AEG, PC1: 394 (undated).

78 AEG, PC1: 394 (27 February; 3, 9, 10, 12, 18 March 1545). See also AEG, PC2: 646 (24 June 1545), which includes a piece relating to Besson dated 24 February 1545 as well as an unrelated document from Claude Michael, officer of the chatelaine of Coppet (dated 1 June 1546).

79 AEG, PC1: 398 (10 April 1545).

80 AEG, PC1: 397 (28 February 1545).

81 He was not tortured again in the six later interrogations and consistently confirmed his confession.

82 AEG, PC1: 397 (6 March 1545), after dinner.

83 AEG, PC1: 397 (9 March 1545). The case against Reviaz was postponed for ten months because she had claimed to be pregnant. She had said she was one month pregnant, and after eleven months the magistrates were inclined to doubt her. She was examined (more as a formality) by Rollet, widow of Thomas de la Ravoye, who said she was not pregnant. AEG, PC2: 679 (28 December 1545–4 March 1546). It also appears that the trial was postponed because she was nursing another child and no wet nurse could be found. AEG, RC 40, fol. 323 (11 December 1545). See also AEG, RC 41, fols 31v (27 February 1546), 35v (4 March 1546).

84 AEG, PC1: 403 (7 March–18 April 1545).

85 AEG, PC1: 403 (30 March 1545).

86 AEG, PC1: 403 (27 March 1545).

87 AEG, PC1: 403 (31 March 1545).

88 AEG, PC1: 403 (3, 6, April 1545).

89 AEG, PC1: 403 (7 April 1545). He repeated these details of the oath the next day, as well. On 9 April, he expanded the detail to: 'not to declare [anything] under pain of death and to endure three straps of the corde'.

90 AEG, PC1: 403 (10 April 1545). Three days later, AEG, PC1: 631 (13 April 1545) preserves the brief cases against Bartholome Chabbod (called Rosetz, daughter of Ayme, from Beaufort, wife of Jean Pillitier, an *habitant* from Jussy) and Thivene Pelloux (called Gervais, daughter of Gonin, from Contamine, wife of Gervais Galliene, from Faucigny).

91 AEG, PC1: 403 (16 April 1545). It would appear that there was a vote and from the document that it went against torture by a margin of seven to three.

92 AEG, PC1: 403 (undated but immediately after the session dated 18 April 1545).

93 AEG, PC1: 403 (31 March 1545).

94 AEG, PC1: 403 (9 April 1545).

95 AEG, PC1: 403 (10 April 1545). The court used this phrase to refer to information gained without the immediate application, or threat, of torture even when torture had been previously applied.

96 AEG, PC1: 403 (10 April 1545).

97 AEG, PC1: 403 (undated but immediately after the session dated 19 April 1545).

98 AEG, PC1: 403 (18 April 1545). Despite this exemplary punishment, their right hands were to be added to the macabre display in Plainpalais.

99 AEG, PC2: 627 (26 March 1545). For more information on plague, its regulation and crime in Faucigny (a village frequently associated with plague spreaders, see below) compare J. M. Lavorel, *Cluses et le Faucigny* (Annecy, 1888).

100 AEG, PC2: 626 (26 March 1545, Jeanne, widow of Humbert Fassonet, from Bernex); PC1: 400 (26 March–7 May 1545, Mya Bouloz, widow of Pierre Gradel); PC1: 402 (27 March–13 May 1545, Bernarde, daughter of Jaques Villard from Nyon, wife of Humbert Guillat); PC2: 629 (28–30 March 1545, Thevenaz, daughter of Claude Burlat, from Entremont, *habitant* of Longerey).

101 AEG, RC 41, fol. 298.

102 AEG, PC1: 402 (28, 29, 30 April; 1, 8, 11 May 1545).

103 AEG, PC1: 402 (16 April 1545).

104 AEG, PC1: 402 (27 March 1545).

105 AEG, PC1: 402 (29 April 1545).

106 Although women were normally seen as inferior to men (and therefore paid less) this view was not universal, see J. Murray, 'Agnolo Firenzuola on Female Sexuality and Women's Equality', *SCJ* 22: 2 (1991): 199–213; for a more traditional (if somewhat extreme) view see M. P. Fleischer, '"Are Women Human?" The Debate of 1595 between Valens Acidalius and Simon Gediccus', *SCJ* 12: 2 (1981): 107–20.

107 AEG, PC1: 402 (30 April 1545).

108 AEG, PC1: 402 (1 May 1545).

109 AEG, PC1: 402 (12 May 1545).

110 AEG, PC1: 402 (13 May 1545).

111 All these trials are contained in AEG, PC1: 401 (28–9 April 1545).

112 AEG, RC 40, fol. 82.

113 AEG, RC 40, fol. 83v (16 April 1545). To compare, Calvin was paid 500 florins per annum, with some additional payments of wine and grain in kind. The other city ministers received 250 florins per annum.

114 He had been elected on 8 February 1545 (AEG, RC 40, fol. 2–2v). Her bequest was from her personal wealth which she had had settled on her at her marriage and by a subsequent bequest made to her by Claude de Compois. AEG, RC 40, fol. 96v.

115 AEG, PC1: 408 (6–16 May 1545).

116 The number of previous prosecutions as well as his banishment (which he was violating) meant that he was (legally) already under sentence of death. This explains the willingness of the magistrates to employ extreme forms of torture. On 9 May 1545, the Senate decided that, since he would not confess, he should be 'strapped' (given the *strappado*) and, if that failed, he could be pulled with pincers 'until the truth comes out of his mouth'. AEG, RC 40, fol. 109v. By 13 May, he had been strapped nine times and drawn four. Still he would not confess. The Senate asked the ministers to speak to him and admonish him to confess. If that failed he was to be drawn two more times by hot pincers and, regardless of the result, to be executed. AEG, RC 40, fol. 112–112v.

117 AEG, PC1: 407 (4–11 May 1545).

118 AEG, PC1: 407 (4 May 1545). The interrogations of Paultra do not survive; Serralion is probably Jaquemaz Mauris, daughter of Claude, widow of Gaspard, a locksmith and *habitant*.

119 AEG, PC1: 407 (5 May 1545).

120 AEG, PC1: 407 (11 May 1545). These women were already dead by this point and these additional accusations were, therefore, meaningless.

121 AEG, PC1: 407 (14 May 1545).

122 AEG, PC1: 407 (the undated summations at the end of the dossier).

123 AEG, RC 40, fol. 97v.

124 AEG, RC 40, fols 98 (30 April 1545), 103 (4 May 1545).

125 AEG, RC 40, fol. 99 (30 April 1545). He was told to sort out some compensation for the widow of Pierre Compagnon, although nothing had been done by 8 May, when Chautemps and Roz Monet went to talk to her (AEG, RC 40, fol. 107). Also, on 1 May 1545 (AEG, RC 40, fol. 100v) he was ordered to ensure that the remaining (or newly hired) fumigators and cleaners would wash infected linen only in the assigned place ('dempuys Longemale en bas') and to not to let any animals pass near the pest house *en route* to slaughter.

126 AEG, RC 40, fol. 101 (1 May 1545). His arrest was officially reported to the Senate on 7 May 1545 (AEG, RC 40, fol. 105v) and they decreed that the case should be investigated 'day in, day out, hour by hour'.

127 AEG, RC 40, fol. 98.

128 AEG, RC 40, fol. 104v.

129 AEG, RC 40, 103 (4 May 1545). The Senate was not unmoved by the plight of her children and ordered them to be given some aims. AEG, RC 40, fol. 107–107v (8 May 1545).

130 AEG, RC 40, fol. 112 (13 May 1545). Both had fathers named Jaques. Villars came from Nyon and was the wife of Humbert Garliat.

131 AEG, RC 40, fols 112v, 114v. Jeanne (daughter of Guillaume Mutilliod from Tournon in Dauphiné, widow of Raymond Verna, *habitat* and baker), Pernon (called Paultra, daughter of Tyvent Dorsier, *habitant*), Genon (called Cugnier, daughter of Jean Girard from Compesiere).

132 AEG, RC 40, fols 116v (15 May 1545, before the Grand Council of all voters), 117 (16 May 1545). He had been strapped at least seven times and pulled with red-hot pincers at least six times. In addition to the other charges against him, he was accused of arson.

133 He was to keep it well guarded and return it to the Senate whenever asked. AEG, RC 40, fol. 117 (18 May 1545). He was later prosecuted because his demeanour was not to the liking of the magistracy, as he was 'very insolent and disobedient', although nothing was actually done to him beyond a verbal warning. See AEG, RC 40, fol. 159v (23 June 1545), 161v (25 June 1545).

134 AEG, RC 40, fol. 145v (11 June 1545).

135 AEG, RC 40, fols 145v (11 June 1545), 148v (15 June 1545). She was the daughter of François Galliard from Sonnes near La Roche, on which see A. Vaullet, *Histoire de la ville De la Roche* (Annecy, 1874).

136 AEG, RC 40, fol. 151v (16 June 1545). Her father was Pierre Bossiez from the county of Consignion. The courts had tried to uncover additional incriminating evidence but had failed.

137 AEG, RC 40, fol. 116.

138 AEG, RC 40, fol. 126 (25 May 1545).

139 AEG, RC 40, fol. 187.

140 AEG, RC 40, fol. 147v (13 June 1545).

141 AEG, RC 40, fol. 153 (17 June 1545).

142 AEG, RC 40, fol. 171 (3 July 1545). She was the daughter of Monet Dorse from Pratiez and widow of François du Nant.

143 AEG, RC 40, fol. 255v.

144 One of the best studies about the witch hunt remains Levack, *Witch-Hunt*.

145 AEG, RC 40, fol. 261v (15 October 1545).

146 For full details see: AEG, RC 40, fols 270, 271 (23 October 1545), 271v–272 (26 October 1545), 279 (2 November 1545), 284v (6 November 1545), 286 (10 November

1545), 288 (12 November 1545), 294–294v (17 November 1545), 308 (1 December 1545).

147 AEG, RC 40, fol. 295v (19 November 1545).

148 AEG, RC 40, fols 294 (17 November 1545), 297v (20 November 1545), 299 (23 November 1545), 317v (8 December 1545).

149 AEG, RC 40, 328v (17 December 1545).

150 The minister, Malisier, survived and was rewarded for his service to the city. He was compensated for medicines he had bought out of his own pocket. Also, when the plague abated with the approach of winter, he was transferred to the rural parish of Bossey and was given a 'bed fully kitted out and some other furniture' because of his 'good courage'. See AEG, RC 40, fol. 216v (17 August 1545), 260 (13 October 1545), 268v (20 October 1545).

151 AEG, RC 40, fol. 110.

152 AGE, RC 40, fol. 114v.

153 AGE, RC 40, fol. 122 (21 May 1545).

154 AEG, RC 40, fol. 124 (22 May 1545). Another, unnamed surgeon (from Challon in Burgundy) was hired on 7 August 1545. AEG, RC 40, fol. 208v.

155 AGE, RC 40, fol. 127 (25 May 1545). More money was sought on 4 August. AEG, RC 40, fol. 205.

156 AGE, RC 40, fols 127v, 129v (25 May 1545).

157 AEG, RC 40, fol. 117v (18 May 1545).

158 AEG, RC 40, fols 120v (19 May 1545), 127v (25 May 1545), 144v (11 June 1545), 151 (16 June 1545), 152v (17 June 1545).

159 AEG, RC 40, fol. (14 July 1545). A few days later, the city received a letter from the meeting of the Swiss Confederacy telling it (among other things) that fugitives ('people of low quality') who might have been involved in the conspiracy had not been found in their cities. PH 1357 (17 July 1545). On 13 July, they had received a letter from Ambroise Imhoff, bailiff of (Bernese) Gex, about a suspected plague spreader, Jean (son of Jean Baptiste from St-Pierre), arrested there. PH 1358.

160 AEG, RC 41, fols 183 (26 August 1546), 188v (31 August 1546), 190 (2 September 1546).

161 AEG, RC 40, fol. 286 (10 November 1545).

162 He was to get 50 florins per annum as a base salary with an extra five florins during months when there was plague. During non-plague months, he was to work in the General Hospital. AEG, RC 40, fols 338 (29 December 1545), 338(a)v (31 December 1545). He later got permission to go to the village of St-Claude for four days to look after his personal affairs there. AEG, RC 41, fol. 13 (12 February 1545). The 'danger pay' was given to him on 17 January 1547 after 'the danger of the plague during nine and a half months'. AEG, RC 41, fol. 270v.

163 AEG, RC 41, fol. 47v.

164 AEG, RC 41, fol. 61v.

165 AEG, RC 41, fol. 153v. Arriving at a correct diagnosis was severely handicapped by the lack of information about human anatomy as a result of social anxiety about dissection. See R. L. Martensen, '"Habit of Reason": Anatomy and Anglicanism in Restoration England', Bulletin of the Society for the History of Medicine 66: 4 (1992): 511–35, for a late-seventeenth and early eighteenth-century contrast.

166 AEG, RC 41, fol. 208 (28 September 1546).

167 AEG, RC 41, fols 195v (9 September 1546), 210v (30 September 1546).

168 AEG, RC 41, fols 95 (19 May 1546), 136v (2 July 1546), 138 (5 July 1546), 140 (8 July 1546), and AEG, PC2: 709 (6 July 1546).

169 AEG, RC 41, fol. 101v.

170 AEG, PC2: 703 *bis* (23 April 1546). He was the son of Henry Regnaud and was the domestic servant of Robert Vandel, factor (?) of Marie Demeraud.

171 AEG, RC 41, fols 97v (24 May 1546), 197v (13 September 1546), PC2: 720 (14–20 September 1546). See Appendix 2.

172 AEG, RC 41, fols 234 (4 November 1546), 239 (12 November 1546).

173 AEG, RC 41, fol. 202 (18 September 1546).

174 I am extremely grateful to Dr Thomas Lambert for the following references relating to consistorial appearances by the couple and their neighbours. Not only did Pernette frequently fight with her neighbours but the couple were quarrelsome at home as well. On one memorable occasion (18 August 1547) the minister Raymond Chauvet suggested to the Consistory that the two should be allowed to fight it out until bloodied. AEG, R Const 3, p. 119. See also R. Const. 2, fols 46v (1 April 1546), 56 (6 May 1546), 78 (31 August 1546), 98 (16 December 1546); 3, pp. 117 (11 August 1547); 4, fol. 19 (29 March 1548); RC 42, fol. 221 (19 August 1547); 43, fol. 61v (29 March 1548).

175 AEG, RC 41, fol. 134v.

176 AEG, RC 41, fol. 136v (2 July 1546).

177 AEG, RC 41, fol. 136v (2 July 1546), 138 (5 July 1546), 140 (8 July 1546).

CHAPTER FOUR

THE MAGISTRATES AND PLAGUE, 1567–72

The people and leaders of this city are all plague spreaders

The next period of plague, 1567–72, was the worst to afflict the city. However, disease was not the only calamity facing Geneva. The republic was confronted by the possibility that the Duke of Savoy, with imperial help, might attempt to reassert over Geneva the sovereignty he had lost in the revolution of the early 1530s.[1] Added to the danger of war and plague was a third threat: witchcraft.[2] Nevertheless, no specific precautions were taken to prevent a recurrence of plague spreading, no link was made between the witches and possible *engraisseurs*, and no efforts to contain the disease were initiated – no fumigators were hired. It may well be that this lackadaisical attitude was the result of the suddenness of plague's arrival, the abruptness of its departure and the mildness of the attack.[3] However, the respite was short-lived; the plague returned in May 1568.[4]

The magistrates were not wholly idle, however. Before the outbreak of plague they had been making attempts to control the supply of foodstuffs to the city. They focused their attention on the supply of fish and the role of seasonal fishmongers in the trade. The Senate ordered that action should be taken to limit the trade to natives only.[5] This concern may have had a number of motivating factors. Clearly, the Senate wanted to protect local merchants. In addition, it was concerned about 'good and false merchandise', that is, it was determined that the fish supply should be fresh and, thus, healthy. Finally, facing a possible military attack and blockade, the lake was likely to supply much of the sustenance needed by the population. The Senate's control of the fish trade, therefore, highlights its focus on health, and the economic and politico–military threats facing the city. Similar concerns are apparent in the actions of the *procureur* for the General Hospital on 25 July. He suggested that a detailed survey be made of all the drugs and medicaments present in the shops of Geneva's medical practitioners and that a new city apothecary should be appointed.[6] This move had the twin advantages of allowing the rapid and effective deployment of medicines against the plague as well as ensuring that the authorities knew the location (and quantity) of all dangerous substances.[7]

The connection between the control of foodstuffs and the impact of the plague was made explicit in August. The Senate noted that grain sellers from Morges and Coppet had plague and that their access to the city should be curtailed.[8] Despite the presence of plague in Geneva and its immediate environs, the city was more concerned about the fish trade.[9] Indeed, it would appear that the outbreak in 1567 was very minor. François Chappuis, a doctor, asked for and was granted permission to move his practice to Neuchâtel and Pierre Prevost, surgeon, was the sole medical worker receiving any payments from the city.[10] Had the outbreak been severe the city would have hired more medical workers at premium wages rather than allowing local doctors to relocate to another city. The only sign that this outbreak even produced fatalities was a single reference to sorting out payments to the gravediggers who had been responsible for disposing of plague victims.[11]

Moreover, it is important to note that Geneva had not been wholly idle in the period from the last plague outbreak in the 1540s and 1567. Indeed, the 1567 outbreak would not have come as a complete surprise, as there were threats of plague and discussions about it with neighbouring states from 1564 onwards. September and October 1564 saw a flurry of correspondence between Geneva and the authorities in Savoy, Annecy and the County of Geneva (controlled by Savoy). Geneva was told what sort of passports would be issued to avoid counterfeiting. Promises were made that Genevan health certificates would continue to be accepted.[12] However, physical conferences proved difficult because of quarantine regulations in the various areas.[13] Similar letters in 1565 and 1566 notified Geneva's magistrates of the presence of plague in Gex and Lausanne.[14]

Perhaps more worrying, though of little apparent long-term impact, were the letters exchanged with neighbours in the same period relating to conspiracies to spread plague. Even worse, these letters accused Geneva and its rulers of being explicitly involved in the plots. The correspondence relates, in the first case, to accusations made by Jaques de Savoie (Duc de Nemours, Comte de Genevois, the governor of the Dauphiné and Lyonnais, etc.) about a plot to kill him by spreading plague under the direction of a ringleader named Pierre Filliet. He charged that he had been told that the grease was made in Geneva under the instructions of the magistracy and that it would have also been used to kill the Cardinal de Lorraine. Clearly, these charges were part and parcel of the distrust and polemic associated with the religiously charged environment in France and echo the interpretation of the phenomenon advanced in Lyon (see Chapter six).[15] Savoy expanded the charge to a wider plot (involving 120 *engraisseurs*) to kill Savoyard Catholics. They related that Pierre Signac from Amboise (a bakery worker for Mon. d'Anjou) while in Seissel with three others was attacked by a crowd of local villagers crying that 'they are some of those grease spreaders from Geneva' and that 'Messieurs [Geneva's magistrates] had delegated 120 men to poison all of Savoy'. Pierre and his friends (also denounced as 'evangelicals from Geneva'), after being arrested, questioned and publicly humiliated, were eventually released.[16] In both cases, the Duke and the Savoyard authorities seem not to have taken the accusations seriously. Rather, they involved the Genevans in the investigation. Everyone clearly accepted the existence of plague-spreading conspiracies but what the Catholics rejected was a religious motivation for the plot(s).

Although the events of 1564–66 and the minor epidemic of 1567 set the stage for the plague that would return in 1568, initially the great drama of 1568 was the discovery and prosecution of a large number of witches in the city. Geneva's authorities were especially concerned to recoup, via the confiscation and sale of the witches' property, the great cost of the investigations and trials.[17] It took Michel du Puys until April to render a full account of the expenses and costs recovered. The magistracy was pleased to learn that the total cost of the witch cases was Fl. 265 8s, while the confiscated goods had produced Fl. 940-7s-6d resulting in a 'profit' of Fl. 674 11s 6d.[18] Although fixated on this series of spectacular trials, the government did not ignore the city's health situation. The minor outbreak of 1567 had waned and, seemingly, was not inclined to recur with the advent of spring. In March, the Senate noted that only the wife and children of Claude Martiere were in the Plague Hospital.[19] Within days, the magistrates concluded that the pest house was overstaffed, too costly and in need of 'downsizing'.[20] Thereafter, the only reference to any other afflicted occurred in early April, when Jean Prodhomme was given permission to visit his son, who was confined suspected of leprosy.[21]

Thus, although 1568 had begun on a worrying and frightening note because of the witch trials, from the point of view of plague the city had every reason to feel optimistic by May. Had the minor outbreak of 1567 been a true harbinger of a greater epidemic to come, the plague might have been expected to reappear earlier, in March or even April. However, the city's hopes were dashed in mid-May, when the Senate was forced to note that a number of homes had been afflicted simultaneously and that, in effect, the plague was breaking out across the city. Immediate efforts were made to hire doctors and surgeons to treat the poor.[22] Within days, Geneva's medical practitioners and clergy were called into conference with the magistrates to discuss the best means to curtail the impact of the epidemic.[23] The second year of plague had begun in earnest.

Senator Chasteauneuf asked to be relieved of his position as the hospital's apothecary 'because of his infirmity' and Jean Prevost was given the charge instead. The doctors were asked 'voluntarily' to provide the Plague Hospital with two medics who were to be paid the stupendous sum of five écus per day for the contractual period of four months. In addition, they were to be assured that, in the event of their death, their wives and children would be made wards of the state. A surgeon was to be hired for ten écus per month for three months.[24]

The lateness of the advent of the plague seems only to have increased its virulence. The day after deciding whom they should hire, the Senate learned that the hospital's apothecary was besieged by the infected.[25] The magistracy responded with a flurry of activity. The infected were barred from church services, including baptisms. The healthy, however, were enjoined to frequent the churches and to beg for God's mercy on Geneva. A collection was ordered for the poor plague victims in the churches. This focus on religious responses to the plague coincided (as in the 1540s) with the unwillingness and inability of the clergy to supply the Plague Hospital with a chaplain. The doctors and apothecaries working at the hospital were to be quarantined for a full ten days after contact with an infected person, while midwives were sequestered for twenty days.[26] Finally, the Senate decreed that a barber-surgeon should be sought at Neuchâtel.[27]

One new feature is evident in this outbreak that distinguishes it from the previous epidemics of the 1530s and 1540s. It is clear that the citizenry were much more inclined to flee to the countryside than before. The Senate responded, not with prohibitions, but by declaring that any child born outwith the city in the next three months would still be deemed a *citoyen* as though born in Geneva itself. The order was confirmed a month later.[28] The wholly positive tone struck by this discussion would imply that families were not fleeing in their entirety. Rather, it would appear that Geneva's citizens were dispatching their pregnant relatives (and perhaps more generally their womenfolk) to the comparative safety of the countryside.[29] The implication of this is that social reactions to the plague had altered slightly in the previous quarter-century. Although citizens may have fled in early outbreaks the scale was such that the issue of civic status seems not to have arisen. One can infer from these new rulings that the exodus of (female) citizens was such that the city had to act to safeguard the civil rights of (prominent) citizens. Moreover, it may have been in recognition of the large number of naturalised citizens (mostly French religious refugees) who had been granted citizenship in the 1550s. While the children of native-born Genevans born in rural refuges in the 1530s and 1540s never had their status questioned, the first-generation children of immigrants may have been less secure in their position. Hence, the city moved to ensure that no legal cloud could be cast over them in future as the first generation of these families legally able to hold the office of syndic or senator.

Early June saw the city in a stronger position. The Senate ordered the bathhouses to be closed and stray dogs and cats to be eliminated. More important, Nicolas, the son of Claude Bollu from Granges, was hired as a barber-surgeon in the pest house for forty florins (about eight écus) plus some wine and grain.[30] Within days of the advent of seeming stability, the first mention of intentional plague spreading arose. The government decreed that no one was to be in the streets after nine o'clock without a lantern and that patrols were to be established to discover 'some poisoners who were spreading this plague'.[31] The next night, because 'someone had *greased* three different houses in the city', the captains of the city's (twelve) sectors were each to chose two volunteers 'to guard this night diligently, and tomorrow more advice will be given'.[32]

In the event, no report was given or decision taken the next day. The records note the hiring of another barber-surgeon, Abraam [Guidoct] from Grandson and that while the victims were resorting to cabins they were still bereft of a chaplain.[33] Not until 8 June did the Senate return to the matter of plague spreading and, interestingly, to the cleaners and fumigators as well. The plague workers were to be controlled during the night and both their movement and their activities curtailed. However, the extra patrols were deemed a failure because they 'overtaxed the watch without any success'. Instead, the magistracy ordered the employment of an additional twelve guards on pay to patrol the city and placed their regulation and pay in the hands of the captains (*diziniers*).[34]

The same day saw definitive proof, if any were needed, that the city was beset by plague. A report was presented to the Senate about a girl who had been examined in the Plague Hospital and found to have 'a swelling under [her] arm'.[35] Swift deliberation resulted in the imposition of a forty day quarantine.[36] The declaration of a 'state of plague' strained (economic) relations with Annecy and Chambéry.[37] The Senate continued to lament, vainly, the lack of a chaplain or deacons to work with the plague sufferers.[38] This internal concern contrasted greatly with the optimistic assessment of the city's health situation expressed on the same day to Bochet, governor of Savoy, that the economic blockade should be lifted as there had been no new cases in eight days.[39] As the number of the infected increased, the city's health system came under increased pressure. The captains asked for the guards' wages to be increased, the pest house was unable to find sufficient supplies of fresh meat, a decision was needed about the clothing of the infected, no agreement could be reached over controlling and paying for the disinfecting of houses.[40] In addition, the quarantine system had to be reannounced – with the clear implication that it was not being observed.[41]

The only optimistic aspect to June was the apparent disappearance of plague spreading. The patrols had reported that no one had been caught and that no sign of the activity (grease on houses) could be found. In a move that was surely designed to save money, the Senate reduced the patrols from nightly to bi-weekly. As in 1543–44, the minute the government thought the activity had stopped the patrols were cut back. Once again, one gets no sense that the Senate was keen to uncover any possible conspiracy. One might expect that, after the experiences of the two previous plague outbreaks (both within living memory), the state and, indeed, society would have been more enthusiastic in their investigation even of the hint of plague spreading. Moreover, despite the moves to control the cleaners and fumigators, there is no evidence that the magistracy necessarily suspected them of being complicit in the few isolated cases of greasing that had been reported. The error of this desultory approach to the problem was revealed within a fortnight of the decision to reduce the patrols. Grease reappeared and the Senate decreed the re-establishment of nightly patrols.[42]

It would appear that the state had learned its lesson both from the events of June 1568 and from those of the 1540s outbreak. The patrol seems to have continued for the rest of the year with success, as there is no further mention of plague spreading or grease. Nevertheless, one cannot assume that the plague was so easily controlled. The epidemic, both in and around Geneva, continued to exercise the concern of the Senate. Information on conditions in Savoy and the Dauphiné, both afflicted, were sought from Annecy just as words of comfort and encouragement arrived from Geneva's close ally, Berne.[43] The city's water supply, straining to supply the cabins and pest house, was barely adequate for the emergency.[44]

More workers were also needed to help with the crisis, which had increased to the point that the infected had to be housed in the General Hospital.[45] Jehan, son of Henry Prevost, from Nancy (in Lorraine), was hired as an additional barber-surgeon, again for forty florins per month with board. Four more gravediggers were also employed.[46] The plague ordinances were ordered to be read through the streets yet again in attempt to enforce them.[47] As the infection intensified both within and outwith Geneva the city was increasingly isolated.[48] However, the reality was that the regulations were simply not being obeyed.[49]

Moreover, the cleaners and fumigators became a cause of greater concern the worse the epidemic became. With more victims, they were obliged to disinfect more and more houses, goods and linen. This meant they were increasingly in the streets with infected items coming from infected houses. Eventually, the Senate had no choice but to accede to popular demands and limit the work of the cleaners to the hours from nine o'clock at night to three in the morning.[50] The city also faced problems with its other plague workers. The need for medical practitioners forced the Senate to consider hiring a German doctor despite language problems.[51] Worse still, Jehan Prevost announced that he wanted to return home to Lorraine because 'he was not well pleased in the hospital'.[52] It is hardly surprising that the city granted another barber-surgeon, Abraam Guidoct, *bourgeois* status in an effort to keep him at his post.[53] All these moves to control and maintain an adequate cadre of workers occurred against a backdrop of failed quarantine legislation and financial disputes relating to pay and the disposal of the goods of the dead.[54]

To control the situation, the Senate reissued and fine-tuned the quarantine regulations. Infected houses were to be sealed for a full thirty days and then disinfected. Anyone having had contact with an infected person or goods faced a thirty-day quarantine. Domestic servants, depending on their proximity to the infected, might have the quarantine reduced to twenty days. Anyone who was even suspected of contact faced a ten-day quarantine. The health workers themselves were to be sequestered for fifteen days, with the exception of *sages-femmes* (midwives), who were confined for twenty days.[55] Anyone who broke these regulations was to face perpetual banishment from Geneva.[56]

Fortunately for the city, just as the situation reached the point of collapse (with serious disorder reported in the pest house) the plague began to abate.[57] Letters exchanged with rural areas convinced the authorities that the epidemic was lessening both in and around the city.[58] This hopeful news allowed the city to release a barber-surgeon and two gravediggers.[59] Within a fortnight more barbers were sacked.[60] With the danger withdrawing, the citizenry turned their attention to complaining about the 'mopping up' activities of the cleaners, whose work would have increased dramatically as the magistracy ordered a general cleaning of the city to prevent a recurrence of the plague in 1569.[61] The city did as it had ever done: it braced itself for the possible return of the disease, it endeavoured to prevent a recurrence and it sacked as many health workers as possible to save money. Only Abraam Guidoct, now a *bourgeois* legally bound to the service of his adopted homeland, was retained.[62]

Having survived two years of plague, the city had as much reason to fear that the epidemic might return as to hope that it would not. Both in 1567 and 1568, there had been suspicions (and more) that plague spreading might be occurring. However, the threat of this activity, even when confirmed by the discovery of grease, did not panic either the population or their leaders. As in the 1540s, the city instituted a patrol, which seems to have been designed to ward off both plague spreading and popular anxiety.[63] What is certainly not evident is any real desire to identify and prosecute the culprits, let alone to begin any 'witch hunt' aimed at the group identified as conspirators in the 1540s, the plague workers. There was no assumption that a conspiracy was afoot. There was no panic. There was no scapegoating. Indeed, the situation on the eve of 1569 was almost identical to that at the end of 1544. It remained to be seen whether another unexpected event, such as the arrival of the letter from Thonon in 1545, would spark another mass prosecution for conspiratorial plague spreading.

The new year of 1569 began with the Senate occupied with two major concerns. First, the previous year of plague and its consequences had to be resolved. For example, a committee was appointed to consider how best to ensure that plague victims were able to make (and enforce) final testaments.[64] Also, the disinfecting of the few remaining houses touched by plague gave the city freedom to introduce the novel idea of removing all the furnishings of the houses outside the city's wall for cleaning.[65] Normally, the goods would have been cleaned in the house, the street or at the lakefront, depending on size and ease of transport.

Sadly, the second concern, avoiding the return of plague, proved to have failed by the beginning of April.[66] While the late arrival of plague in 1568 had given the city cause for hope, 1569 was not a year for any optimism. The Senate quickly decided that quarantine measures would need immediate implementation and, when a cursory investigation showed the parlous condition of the city's medical supplies, that the city's health defences needed rebuilding.[67] A committee of two leading senators, Henry Aubert and Ami de Chasteauneuf, along with Geneva's doctors, barber-surgeons and apothecaries, was deputed to guarantee an adequate, safe and comprehensive supply of medical drugs and materials.[68] The committee 'On the Reform of Medicine' reported within the week that a general conference of magistrates and interested professionals was essential.[69] A few days later 'the Senate expressly assembled, with all the physicians, surgeons and apothecaries of the city present, [and] read out the articles devised by them for the Reform of Medicine'.[70] A week later 'the Ordinances on Medicine, Pharmacy and Surgery, having been returned by the *chambre des comptes* and considered article by article, were passed and [ordered to be] decreed' throughout Geneva.[71]

There is little doubt that the Genevan authorities intended to control the situation from the start. In 1569, there is evidence of a much more proactive and less reactive approach to plague. However, their best intentions and most strenuous efforts were in vain: five days after the conference the Senate's minutes recorded that five houses were infected and that 'God was visiting the city with plague'.[72] Indeed, the problem of non-compliance with the regulations surfaced almost immediately.[73] Although serious in itself, the violation of quarantine legislation was not the only problem facing the city at the outset of its third year of plague. The water supply continued to be a source of concern and the physicians were agitating about their professional privileges. In particular, the doctors insisted that the customs of 'all other cities and, in particular, the imperial laws' exempted them from the obligation to serve on the city's watch.[74] Worse, although the ministers (in the person of Beza and Colladon) were able to advise the government on the spiritual impact of the epidemic, they were still unable (or unwilling) to provide one of their own to serve as chaplain in the pest house.[75]

Indeed, there is reason to suggest that the third year of plague was beginning to cause the city's health system to collapse. The water supply was increasingly corrupted by the increase of the disease.[76] By midsummer, the authorities were given some hope that the epidemic might be on the wane. Alas, it was no more than wishful thinking. The physician Bauhin and the surgeon Montillion declared a body found in the house of one of the schoolteachers a plague victim. The ten additional practitioners consulted at the Senate's request concurred.[77] However, a young girl presumed dead of plague was deemed after being examined by four physicians and two surgeons to have died of quinsy.[78] This confusion about whether or not plague was actually present arose, in part (as Senator Pierre Dance explained), because some doctors were not reporting plague deaths accurately. The magistracy called the practitioners together and remonstrated with them, admonishing them to perform their tasks according to the regulations.[79]

Despite these disputes, confusions and problems the greatest difficulty faced by Geneva related to quarantine. On two fronts the magistrates faced disaster. Internally, the ordinances were not being obeyed and the situation was not being contained. Those in contact with the infected were not carrying 'white wands' when abroad in the street. Houses were not being effectively sealed. The cleaners were dumping infected straw (bedding) along the bank of the Rhône. The gates were not sufficiently controlled at night. Bodies were accumulating at a dangerous rate and the gravediggers were not obeying their instructions. Worse, cats and dogs that 'can carry the contagion from one house to another' were still roaming the streets and had to be killed.[80]

The mounting chaos in the city was only compounded by the economic disruption being caused by the blockade of the city imposed by neighbouring localities, principally at the behest of the Duke of Savoy. Geneva's authorities were probably right in suspecting that the quarantine imposed on their trade had more to do with the Duke's religious and political dislike for his former possession than concern to contain the disease. After all, the plague existed on both sides of the economic barrier. Annecy had closed itself to Genevans in May, while Gex and other baileys had done so by mid-July.[81] The success of the blockade was mirrored by the failure of the magistracy even to arrange a meeting with the Duke's representatives to argue the case for relaxation.[82]

At the end of August, the Senate's minutes sadly noted that 'the plague is everlasting'.[83] This doleful situation would not have been helped by the suggestion from Jean Trembley, one of the ministers, that he should attempt to console the afflicted from his window rather than actually 'moving among them'.[84] The corpses of those beyond consolation continued to pile up and Senator Dance asked that a new large cemetery should be opened.[85] Moreover, not only were the quarantine rules still being violated but even the physicians advised the government that their sequestration made it impossible for them to do their job properly.[86] The Senate accepted their argument and relaxed the rules 'to permit them to move about the city'. Attempts to reconcile public fear of the cleaners with their necessary activity also failed, as did efforts to eradicate the city's stray cats and dogs (even when Geneva's executioner was offered 3s per head).[87] Exasperated, the Senate met to review its regulations 'because they are not being obeyed' but eventually decided that no other options were available and that 'they ought to be observed and so that no one could plead ignorance they should be publicly announced again'.[88]

There seems little doubt that the failure of the plague to wane in October gave rise to serious alarm among the city's élite. Senator Dance reported in the second week of November that the plague was still raging and that the afflicted continued to be removed to the cabins near the pest house. He was told to maintain his efforts to contain the situation.[89] By mid-November the Senate was grasping at straws when it agreed to investigate the claims of a Piedmontese surgeon that he had a cure.[90] Three days later the secretary noted in the minutes, no doubt with great relief and joy, that 'the plague was lessening'.[91] Exactly a month later a committee of magistrates (Pierre Choudet, Claude de la Maisonneuve alias Baudichon, Ami de Chasteauneuf and Pierre Dance) met the physicians to discuss ways of cleaning the city to prevent the return of the disease.[92] A general conference of senators, physicians, surgeons, apothecaries and (for the first time) midwives as well as nurses met to review the regulations.[93] The cleaning and disinfecting of the city were intensified during the winter. Cleaners were to get 6s per day along with room and board if necessary. Everyone was to stay away from his or her home until given permission to return. The estates of the dead were not to be inventoried or sold until three months after being disinfected.[94]

The minutes for the year closed with two important notices. First, all the regulations were to remain in force and, in particular, all corpses were to be examined for signs of plague.[95] The activity in December suggests that the authorities had already resigned themselves to another year of plague. At the end of 1568 they seem to have thought that a thorough cleansing of the city would prevent a recurrence of the epidemic. Now, rather than awaiting its return, they were moving in the direction of a permanent state of health crisis. The second notice closing the minutes of 1569 was the listing, by name, of the apothecaries, physicians and surgeons who had been sworn to the city's service on 26 May 1569.[96] The contracts as originally understood were set to run for three or six months. Clearly, the city was renewing these contracts in advance of the return of pestilence. In all previous outbreaks, including just twelve scant months before, the normal practice had been to release as many health workers as possible from their contracts in an effort to save money. Genevan behaviour had changed. The Senate intended to begin 1570, and perhaps a fourth year of plague, with a fully functioning and competently staffed health and regulatory system already in place.

The precautionary and proactive policies adopted by the magistrates at the end of 1569 were continued into the next year even though the Senate was advised in mid-January 1570 that the Plague Hospital was 'empty and in order'.[97] A month later, in addition to setting a regular patrol on the walls and gates, the Senate reissued the plague regulations and renegotiated the cleaners' contracts.[98] The ministers were called into the council chamber to discuss how best to meet the spiritual needs of the community should the plague return.[99] A similar conference was held with the medical practitioners, and the needs of the poor were specifically addressed.[100] At the end of March, a meeting was held with representatives of Gex to arrange for co-ordinated action against the disease and to discuss their request for the extradition of 'a prisoner charged with poisoning and plague spreading in the lands of His Highness [the Duke of Savoy]' currently held by the chatelaine in Celigny.[101] These meetings and rulings took place despite the absence of plague since early December. Indeed, on 3 April the Senate noted with joy that 'the plague, thanks be to God, does not rage about'.[102]

By this point in the story of Geneva's experience of plague, readers will not be surprised to learn that any jubilation was premature and short-lived. Within a fort-night the importance of the plague regulations, especially quarantine, was being stressed in the Senate and in early May the minutes note briefly that 'the plague continues'.[103] Almost immediately, the Senate reconvened its senior spiritual and medical advisers for consultations on the best way to proceed.[104] As has been seen in previous outbreaks, a major concern at the onset of any new epidemic was early and correct diagnosis of the infected. The magistrates encouraged their medical practitioners to be sure of their diagnoses, noting, for example, that needless worry had been caused when Pierre Alliod, a senator, was declared dead of plague rather than, as was correct, of dropsy.[105]

Through the late spring and early summer, the records reveal a city coping sur-prisingly well with its fourth consecutive year of plague. The system that had been maintained throughout winter's respite was working, if not without some prob-lems. Individuals continued to circumvent or ignore pieces of regulatory legisla-tion. For example, too many bodies were being buried without the correct medical certification.[106] Some medics, such as Jean Bauhin, while performing their duties, risked spreading the disease through casual and professional contact with suffer-ers.[107] The cleaners remained a cause of concern to the state because of the situa-tion and to the people by their existence.[108] The plague physician, Philippe Rustici, appealed for assistance. He wanted colleagues to help confirm his diagnoses.[109] He also asked for practical support in the form of money and a horse for visiting sus-pected plague victims outside the city walls.[110] Despite these multifaceted com-plaints and difficulties there was no scramble, as in previous outbreaks, to hire workers, implement rules, ready facilities or acquire drugs. The city was prepared for this year's epidemic.

This proactive approach to the pestilence of 1570 proved to be prescient if not life-saving. The plague was particularly bad. The pest house and the cabins were overflowing with the afflicted and, as in 1569, the General Hospital (in the city) had to be pressed into service.[111] Indeed, so bad was the outbreak that the government began to relax its own regulations. While still insisting that those who had had contact with the infected should carry white wands in the street, they conceded that home confinement was making the situation worse. The Senate agreed to allow people to leave for rural accommodation.[112] A week later, this change in policy bore dramatic fruit. The magistrates noted that because 'there are few ministers and few people in the city, it was agreed that sermons should cease for a while at the Madeleine [Church] on Sundays and Wednesdays, likewise the morning services on Sundays and Wednesdays at [the] St. Gervais [Church]'.[113] As the plague continued to rage into the autumn, the few remaining citizens found themselves increasingly at the mercy of their rapacious cleaners, who were demanding ever higher wages for their services.[114] Senator Jean Colland 'assembled all the cleaners, reading their names and addresses from the list and prohibited them from exacting more for their disinfecting'. They were to be content with the fifteen florins per month approved and provided by the state.[115]

Although more serious than any of the outbreaks in the previous three years, even the 1570 epidemic came to an end without destroying the city. In early October, the Senate's secretary was able to note that the plague was abating. Jean Flamand, the surgeon hired in June to help in the care of the sufferers being housed in the General Hospital, could (with his charges) be relocated to the pest house and the plague cabins.[116] The actions taken by Geneva's rulers in the winter of 1569–70 had proved their value. By maintaining their health bureaucracy and plague staff they had been better prepared than ever before for the recurrence of plague.

Having learned the wisdom of preparation, Geneva began (even while the plague was continuing) to conduct a post-mortem on the events and lessons of 1570. Goods associated with the afflicted and the dead were not to be sold.[117] A general conference was held with medical and spiritual advisers to discuss the provision of sermons, regulations, practitioners and drugs 'to solve the confusions and disorders that one saw daily with regard to the plague . . . [and] to avoid the great cost and expenses [incurred]'.[118] The ministers were especially vociferous in their complaints about the system of house confinement and sequestration of those who were trying to help plague victims.[119] The greatest concern, however, for everyone was the dreadful state of the city's poor. The Senate eventually decided 'to review the ordinances made about the pestilence and to remedy many of the inconveniences which appeared because of their overly rigorous application with regard to the poor [plague] victims . . . after long deliberation it was finally resolved to give some assistance to the poor sufferers'. The assistance was to allow the poor to disinfect their homes themselves, and so avoid the need to pay a professional cleaner. Other possible aids and subventions for the poor were remitted to a later session of the Senate.[120]

By the end of November, the situation in Geneva was beginning to return to some semblance of normality. The full schedule of sermons was restored, as 'the greater part of the people have returned'.[121] In discussions with Gex about the health of the wider locality, Geneva was able to report that 'whether in the hospital or the city there were not more than a couple of sick people'.[122] The new year, 1571, began with the even more joyous news that 'it has been reported that, thanks to God, there are no more sick people'.[123]

Much to the shock of the city's magistrates, the plague not only returned in 1571 but also did so in wintertime. The relocation of the gravediggers and the Plague Hospital's surgeon from the pest house into the city because of 'a great tumult' proved premature.[124] On 20 February, the Senate noted that 'the plague is still continuing and is especially severe for the time'.[125] The reports of infected houses, dead citizens and, even, a young girl who had escaped from the pest house and 'raged through the city' began to pour into the Senate.[126] The magistrates convened a hasty conference with the physicians and apothecaries.[127] More cleaners were needed to cope with the scale of this fifth year of plague.[128] The magistracy appointed a new committee to consider the (re-)drafting of the plague regulations.[129] On 23 April, the ordinances (in seventeen articles) were published.[130]

While Geneva was as prepared in January 1571 as a year before, the proactive approach simply failed to cope with the scale of this epidemic. The secretary noted on 7 May that 'the plague continues and is worsening'.[131] The next day, the dogs were again ordered to be destroyed for making 'an evil and great tumult at night'.[132] Massacring dogs failed, as 'the plague continued harshly'.[133] In May–June, for the first time in two years, at the height of the epidemic the spectre of plague spreaders re-emerged.[134] As the next chapter will show, June marked the period of most intense activity against supposed conspiratorial plague spreaders. More important for the present discussion, this single comment is the only reference to the phenomenon in the midst of a major period of investigation and prosecution.

Clearly, the highest level of Geneva's government, unlike in the 1530s and 1540s, was more concerned about the actual management of the epidemic than the minutiae of the plague-spreading cases. The gravediggers were overcharging (up to 30s per funeral) and the ministers were, again, failing to supply a chaplain to console the afflicted.[135] The surgeons were not performing their duties properly and the hospital was overflowing and woefully understaffed.[136] In sum, the magistrates found themselves recording the old familiar refrain: 'No one is obeying the plague regulations.'[137]

With a palpable sense of despair the Senate decided that the ministers should 'exhort the people more strongly . . . to repentance . . . to give the people, who are in such anxiety, courage'.[138] Unfortunately, the situation only worsened. At the end of August, the ministers confessed to the Senate that they were overwhelmed by the disaster.[139] A week later, the surgeons lodged a similar report with the magistracy.[140] Money was running out at the pest house.[141] The Genevan plague control system (and society more generally), after five years of stress, was collapsing under the strain. The Senate asked its ministers what could be done to appease a God who had 'greatly increased His chastisement of the city'.[142]

The pestilence of 1571 had struck early and, fortunately for Geneva, it began to wane in late October just as the city teetered on the abyss. The secretary noted that we 'have good hope', as only thireen houses were infected (containing seventeen sufferers) with a further fifteen in the pest house.[143] 'God having almost withdrawn His chastisement', the Senate ordered the emptying and disinfecting of the General Hospital.[144] The aftermath of the outbreak was dealt with quickly and efficiently, with only a few discussions being brought before the Senate: places to disinfect were listed, infected goods were banned from sale, corpses still had to be certified plague-free.[145] Finally, after five continuous years of plague and two of strict plague regulations the magistracy took the somewhat surprising (if undoubtedly necessary) step of relaxing the plague ordinances.[146]

The *dénouement* of this outbreak that had begun in late 1567 finally came in 1572.[147] On 25 March, the Senate noted that 'the plague has returned in a number of places'.[148] The infected were to be identified and quarantined.[149] A month later, the magistrates ordered a general inquiry into the possibility that some plague spreaders were again at work.[150] After having started later than the outbreak of the previous year, the epidemic showed signs, in May, of being just as severe as the plague not only continued but worsened.[151] As ever, the quarantine regulations were a failure and Geneva was beset by 'a great disorder throughout the city because of the infected, as well as the surgeons, going everywhere indifferently mingling with the healthy'.[152] Moreover, the other problems with the system were equally evident: gravediggers were overcharging and the pest house spilled over into the General Hospital.[153] Although the state seemed determined to maintain a more normal atmosphere by retaining the sermons, the people took a leaf out of the previous two years' regulations and abandoned the services. The local captains (*diziniers*) were told to exhort people to attend the sermons lest God increase His punishment of the city.[154]

However, the epidemic of 1572 broke in mid-August, much to the surprise and relief of all Geneva: 'it has been reported that, thanks to God, the plague has ceased and no one else has been infected'. The Senate immediately chose to take advantage of what might prove to be only a brief respite by ordering the cleaning of the General Hospital and the relocation of the few remaining patients to the pest house.[155] Their action proved prescient though unnecessary, for the few additional cases that appeared a fortnight later were simply a final and weak encore.[156] The last mention of the plague and the sad parting reference to its victims was the order that the few remaining bodies should be taken out of Geneva 'in the morning by the Great Gate during the sermon'.[157] Six years of plague had, at long last, come to an end.

On the surface, the magistrates' behaviour in this lengthy outbreak was identical to that of the 1530s and 1540s. The reactive predominated. There was a slight drift towards preventative and preparatory action both relating to plague generally and plague spreading specifically. However, the change was minimal and applied only to 1570–71. In one major area there was a difference. In reality, this outbreak saw the greatest number of prosecutions (115) and executions (forty-four) for plague spreading. Some may well wonder why little mention has been made of this previously. It is because I have been confining my remarks throughout this chapter to the magistrates' behaviour and views as apparent from the Senate's deliberations. In both earlier outbreaks the magistrates were so concerned with the phenomenon that they took personal responsibility for the examination, torture and sentencing of the accused, and this involvement was explicit in the discussions minuted by the

Senate's secretary. There was no necessary institutional reason for their direct involvement. They were concerned – indeed, afraid – and took complete control. By 1567–72 the Senate seemed confident enough of the handling of the situation to allow the courts and prosecutorial bureaucracy to deal with the issue. Indeed, reading the Senate's debates one would almost be unaware that any greasing had happened. For example, the secretary did not even note the receipt of a letter warning of a plague spreader apprehended at Lausanne who had confessed to crimes in Geneva.[158]

There is no reason to conclude from this that the senators were uninterested or uninvolved in the trials of the accused plague spreaders. Rather, when they were involved it was in their individual capacity as judges. The Senate, as a body, did not discuss the phenomenon or the accompanying trials and executions. In part, this may be a sign, as just mentioned, of mature confidence in their own legal structures. Likewise, it could be that familiarity, if not having bred contempt, had at least made plague spreading a less uncommon topic of senatorial debate. There is also the possibility, as will be examined more closely in the next chapter, that Geneva's magistrates and society had come to understand the phenomenon in a way that made it more familiar and less fascinating (if no less threatening). Only a close examination of what the magistrates actually did in the trials is likely to explain why, in the course of two decades, they went from being mesmerised by plague spreading to rather *blasé*.

NOTES

1 AEG, RC 62 (1567), is full of comments relating to troop movements and other preparations for war.
2 AEG, RC 62, fol. 158 [155, actually] (6 February 1567); RC 67, fols 7 (18 February 1568), 17v–18v (11 March 1568).
3 AEG, RC 62, fol. 52 (2 May 1567): 'la peste commencer a pulluler de la ville'.
4 AEG, RC 63, fols 24v (18 March 1568), 49 (17 May 1568).
5 AEG, RC 62, fols 11 (21 February 1567), 23 (13 March 1567).
6 A similar inventory had been taken in September 1556 (PH 1873 bis). There is some debate about the correct date of this document (with April 1569 being suggested) but the apothecaries mentioned (Pierre Scarron, Philippe Cene, Pierre Frojon, Christofle Berthollet, Merlin, Leonard de Bougier, François Vulliens, Thomas de la Rive, Amied Andrion, Amied Varoz, Guillaume Beney, Jean Lucian) supports the earlier date.
7 AEG, RC 62, fol. 87v (25 July 1567). Cf. L. Joubert, *Popular Errors*, trans. G. D. de Rocher (London, 1989), p. 96, on the potential threat posed by apothecaries.
8 AEG RC 62, fol. 94 (7 August 1567).
9 Further discussions took place on 14 August 1567 (AEG, RC 62, fol. 97v).
10 AEG, RC 62, fol. 116v (10 October 1567), in kind.
11 AEG, RC 62, fol. 145 (1 January 1568).
12 AEG, PH 1767 (12 September, 7 October 1564).
13 AEG, PH 1768 (2 October 1564).
14 AEG, PH 1793 (9 November 1565), PH 1811 (27 February 1566).

15 AEG, PH 1780 (14, 21 December 1564; 20 July 1566), PH 1781 (4, 13 January 1564; 18, 20, 25 January 1565).

16 AEG, PH 1767 (23 September 1564); PH 1768 (24 September 1564); PH 1769 (25 September 1564).

17 AEG, RC 62, fol. 155 (6 February 1568), RC 63, fol. 7 (18 February 1568).

18 For the many detailed references to the goods and costs of individual witches see AEG, RC 63, fols 17v–18v (11 March 1568), 31 (8 April 1568), 39 (22 April 1568).

19 AEG, RC 63, fol. 22v (15 March 1568).

20 AEG, RC 63, fol. 24v (18 March 1568).

21 AEG, RC 63, fol. 32 (9 April 1568).

22 AEG, RC 63, fol. 49 (17 May 1568). On poor relief see M. Pelling, 'Healing the Sick Poor: Social Policy and Disability in Norwich, 1550–1640', *Medical History* 29 (1985): 115–37.

23 AEG, RC 63, fols 50v (20 May 1568), 52v (24 May 1568). Such meetings were problematic if for no other reason than the professional jealousy among medical practitioners; see J. Hardin, 'Johann Christoph Ettner: Physician, Novelist, and Alchemist', *Daphnis* 19: 1 (1990): 135–59, on relations between a physician and apothecaries (especially 141) and Murphy, 'Transformation', 323.

24 AEG, RC 63, fol. 56 (27 May 1568). Assuming only two doctors and one surgeon, this represented an expenditure on salaries alone of nearly 500 écus.

25 AEG, RC 63, fol. 57 (28 May 1568)

26 AEG, RC 63, fols 57–57v (31 May 1568).

27 AEG, RC 63, fol. 58 (1 June 1568).

28 AEG, RC 63, fols 58 (1 June 1568), 74 (5 July 1568). For example, Sieur de Grilliet, Lord Ville-le-Grand, informed the Senate that he was retiring to his rural estates until the plague abated. PH 1861 (16 October, 1 December 1568).

29 Cf. G. Clark, 'London's First Evacuees: A Population Study of Nursing Children', *Local Historian* 19 (1989): 100–6.

30 AEG, RC 63, fol. 58v (1 June 1568). The original order would have been to pay him 50 florins (ten écus) per month and nothing in kind.

31 AEG, RC 63, fol. 59 (3 June 1568).

32 AEG, RC 63, fol. 60 (4 June 1568).

33 AEG, RC 63, fols 60v–61 (4, 7 June 1568).

34 AEG, RC 63, fol. 61v (8 June 1568).

35 AEG, RC 63, fol. 62 (8 June 1568).

36 AEG, RC 63, fols 62v, 63 (10, 11 June 1568).

37 AEG, RC 63, fol. 64 (18 June 1568). The syndics of Annecy and the Council of [the county of] Genevois kept up a constant contact with Geneva, expressing 'our great sorrow that the pest is raging furiously in your city' and noting with alarm 'this dangerous plague'. PH 1850 (29 May, 14 June, 1 July, 14 October 1568).

38 AEG, RC 63, fol. 65 (18 June 1568).

39 AEG, PH 1852 (18 June 1568). The magistracy's alarm at the effects of restrictions on the movement of goods and people did not hinder them from imposing similar restrictions on the nearby villages of La Roche, Bonne and Cruseille. PH 1853 (18–30 June 1568). For its part, the Gex blockade was, no doubt, the logical culmination of the increasing concern expressed by the Comte de Montmajeur, governor and judge of Gex, in numerous letters. PH 1845 (17 September; 1, 8, 13, 27 October 1568). The count announced a renewal of the blockade on 4 March 1572 because he was unhappy

with the guarantees offered by Geneva. PH 1921. On plague, religious conflict and economic growth see C. J. Mathers, 'Family Partnerships and International Trade in early modern Europe: Merchants from Burgos in England and France, 1470–1575', *Business History Review* 62 (1988): 367–97, especially 371; J. P. Cuvillier, 'Economic Change, Taxation and Social Mobility in German Towns in the late Middle Ages', *Journal of European Economic History* 15: 3 (1986): 535–48.

40 AEG, RC 63, fols 69–72 (22 June–1 July 1568).
41 AEG, RC 63, fol. 71v (29 June 1568).
42 AEG, RC 63, fol. 70 (28 June 1568).
43 AEG, PH 1843 (3, 16 July 1568). The presence (or rumour) of plague in the city continued to complicate its relations with Savoy even after the last case for the year had ended. PH 1844 (10 December 1568).
44 AEG, RC 63, fols 73, 74v (3–6 July 1568).
45 AEG, RC 63, fol. 76 (7 July 1568).
46 AEG, RC 63, fol. 75 (6 July 1568). The gravediggers were Didier, son of Bartholome, from Champagne; Jean, son of Matthieu de Mas, from Auvergne; Pierre, son of Pierre Robert, a *bourgeois*; and Albert, son of Antoine de Niquez from Lombardy.
47 AEG, RC 63, fols 76v–77v (9 July 1568). In addition, a list of registered cleaners was to be drawn up. AEG, PH 1765 (9 July 1568).
48 AEG, RC 63, fol. 83v, 84v, 85–85v (26, 27, 28 July 1568). Rural Gex was badly afflicted.
49 AEG, RC 63, fol. 79 (15 July 1568).
50 AEG, RC 63, fols 85v (30 July 1568), 89v (10 August 1568).
51 AEG, RC 63, fol. 91v (13 August 1568).
52 AEG, RC 63, fol. 91v (13 August 1568).
53 AEG, RC 63, fol. 92v (16 August 1568).
54 AEG, RC 63, fols 93, 94v (16, 17 August 1568).
55 AGE, RC 63, fols 97–97v (30 August 1568). Houses were to remain vacant for thirty days after being disinfected. AEG, PH 1765 (30 August 1568). On midwives see W. Perkins, *Midwifery and Medicine in Early Modern France: Louise Bourgeois* (Exeter, 1996); B. H. Traister, '"Matrix and the Pain Thereof": A Sixteenth Century Gynaecological Essay', *Medical History* 35 (1991): 436–51.
56 AEG, RC 63, fol. 111 (30 September 1568).
57 AEG, RC 63, fol. 99v (2 September 1568).
58 AEG, RC 63, fols 112v, 113v, 114v (4, 5, 11 October 1568). Geneva was especially interested in the situation in Gex.
59 AEG, RC 63, fol. 122 (27 October 1568).
60 AEG, RC 63, fol. 128 (9 November 1568).
61 AEG, RC 63, fols 129, 130 (12, 16 November 1568).
62 AEG, RC 63, fol. 134v (29 November 1568). His fixed-term contract was extended for six months and his wage left unchanged at ten écus per month.
63 The power of anxiety in similar societies (albeit in the context of religion and apocalypticism) can be seen in D. Crouzet, *Les Guerriers de Dieu* (Champ Vallon, 1990), two volumes.
64 AEG, RC 64, fol. 13 (20 January 1569).
65 AEG, RC 64, fol. 30 (18 February 1569).
66 AEG, RC 64, fol. 55 (5 April 1569).
67 AEG, RC 64, fol. 58 (11 April 1569).
68 AEG, RC 64, fol. 64 (22 April 1569).

69 AEG, RC 64, fol. 67 (29 April 1569).

70 AEG, RC 64, fol. 67 (2 May 1569).

71 AEG, RC 64, fol. 71 (11 May 1569).

72 AEG, RC 64, fol. 73 (16 May 1569).

73 AEG, RC 64, fol. 75v (19 May 1569).

74 AEG, RC 64, fol. 77v (24 May 1569). The critical need for another surgeon was also a problem. AEG, RC 64, fol. 82 (2 June 1569). Grillier, Lord Ville-le-Grand (see n. 22 above) reported that the lock on one of his houses (on his rural estates?) had been found greased. PH 1871 (25 May 1569).

75 AEG, RC 64, fol. 81v (2 June 1569). By the end of the month the Senate was still discussing problems being caused by the ministers, poor foreigners and quarantine breakers. AEG, RC 64, fol. 91 (20 June 1569).

76 AEG, RC 64, fol. 89v (16 June 1569). The Senate decided to seek advice from specialists about how best to maintain a supply of fresh water.

77 AEG, RC 64, fol. 98 (1 July 1569).

78 AEG, RC 64, fol. 106v (12 July 1569). The severe inflammation of the throat may have looked rather like the swelling of lymph glands.

79 AEG, RC 64, fol. 108 (15 July 1569).

80 AEG, RC 64, fols 108v (18 July 1569), 119 (8 August 1569), 121v (15 August 1569), 124 (22 August 1569), 125 (25 August 1569), 126 (27 August 1569), 127v (29 August 1569). For more on cats and dogs see Gournelen, *Advertisement*, p. 8, and Textor, *Pestilance*, p. 40.

81 AEG, RC 64, fols 79 (26 May 1569), 108v (18 July 1569). A vain attempt was made to convince Savoy that the plague had ended in the city on 21 July (PH 1877).

82 AEG, RC 64, fols 109v–110 (21 July 1569).

83 AEG, RC 64, fol. 128 (30 August 1569).

84 AEG, RC 64, fols 128 (30 August 1569), 129v (2 September 1569). The Senate was not happy with the suggestion, or Trembley's adoption of it, and called upon Beza and Chauvet (leading ministers) to speak to him.

85 AEG, RC 64, fol. 128v (31 August 1569).

86 AEG, RC 64, fols 129 (1 September 1569), 132v (12 September 1569).

87 AEG, RC 64, fol. 129v (2 September 1569), 147 (24 October 1569).

88 AEG, RC 64, fol. 148v (27 October 1569).

89 AEG, RC 64, fol. 155 (11 November 1569).

90 AEG, RC 64, fol. 156 (15 November 1569). Though no effective cure actually existed many did recover and even more thought there were cures for plague and other devastating diseases such as syphilis (the 'French pox'). See P. Barolsky, 'Cellini, Vasari and the Marvels of Malady', *SCJ* 24: 1 (1993): 41–5, and J. Arrizabalaga, J. Henderson and R. K. French, *The Great Pox: The French Disease in Renaissance Europe* (New Haven CT, 1997). Most bizarrely of all, tobacco was seen as a panacea. D. Harlay, 'The Beginnings of the Tobacco Controversy: Puritanism, James I, and the Royal Physicians', *Bulletin of Medical History* 67 (1993): 28–50. On syphilis see P. A. Russell, 'Syphilis, God's Scourge or Nature's Vengeance?' *ARG* 80 (1989): 286–306.

91 AEG, RC 64, fol. 158 (18 November 1569).

92 AEG, RC 64, fol. 175 (18 December 1569).

93 AEG, RC 64, fol. 176v (22 December 1569). Alvarus, *Petit recueil*, emphasises the fourfold nature of the structure of plague prevention personnel: 'physicians, pharmacists, surgeons, cleaners', p. 6. For more on the interaction of medical practitioners from

every level of society and both genders see R. S. Gottfried, 'English Medical Practitioners, 1340–1530', *Bulletin of Medical History* 58 (1984): 164–82.

94 AEG, RC 64, fol. 177 (23 December 1569).

95 AEG, RC 64, fol. 180 (30 December 1569).

96 AEG, RC 64, [181 (30 December 1569)]. Physicians: Jehan Chesolme (or Lescossais, i.e. John Chisolm), François Chappuis, Philibert Sarasin, Mondon Fauchier, Jehan Bauhin, Adam Maupeau, Philiberte Rustici, Jaques Pons, George Carrat; surgeon: Pierre Tissot; apothecaries: Jehan Mollet, Claude Mollet, Perrin Mus, Valeran Donrez, Pierre Accaurrat, Jaques Preudhome, Boniface Morine. Another surgeon, Banissard de Georgis, was hired on 12 January 1570 (AEG, RC 65, fol. 7).

97 AEG, RC 65, fol. 10 (16 January 1569).

98 AEG, RC 65, fols 26v–28 (17 February 1570). The heavy guard may have had more to do with the threat of a Savoyard attack than pestilence.

99 AEG, RC 65, fols 28–28v (13 [20] February 1570), 30v (23 February 1570). The community, whether a locale or a group, was of great importance. See K. B. Neuschel, *Word of Honor: Interpreting Noble Culture in Sixteenth Century France* (London, 1989).

100 AEG, RC 65, fols 34–34v (28 February 1570). As the century progressed, the care of the poor became increasingly important to early modern civic governments. See W. J. Wright, 'A Closer Look at House Poor Relief through the Common Chest and Indigence in Sixteenth Century Hesse', *ARG* 70 (1979): 225–37, especially 232–3, and P. Rushton, 'Lunatics and Idiots: Mental Disability, the Community, and the Poor Law in North-east England, 1600–1800', *Medical History* 32 (1988): 34–50.

101 AEG, RC 65, fol. 45 (20 March 1570); PH 1864 (26 March 1569). Geneva, in turn, wanted information on Renier Bastard. PH 1864 (9 April 1569).

102 AEG, RC 65, fol. 54v (27 April 157).

103 AEG, RC 65, fols 68 (27 April 1570), 72 (2 May 1570).

104 AEG, RC 65, fols 73–73v (4 May 1570).

105 AEG, RC 65, fol. 76v (8 May 1570). It is also possible that the change to Alliod's death certificate was meant to protect his family and estate from the effects of quarantine.

106 AEG, RC 65, fols 77v (9 May 1570), 80v (12 May 1570).

107 AEG, RC 65, fol. 80 (12 May 1569).

108 AEG, RC 65, fol. 80v (12 May 1570).

109 AEG, RC 65, fol. 96v (2 June 1570). Claude Mutillier and 'the Scot' (John Chisolm) were hired to assist him.

110 AEG, RC 65, fol. 103 (13 June 1570).

111 AEG, RC 65, fols 108v (24 June 1570), 116 (8 July 1570). Beza supported the use of the location within the city's walls as a necessary, if risky, expedient, fol. 117 (10 July 1570).

112 AEG, RC 65, fols 119v (13 July 1570), 122v (20 July 1570).

113 AEG, RC 65, fol. 126v (28 July 1570).

114 AEG, PH 1864 (16 August 1569). They also faced the effects of economic disruption of trade to neighbouring areas such as Gex. PH 1864 (16 August 1569).

115 AEG, RC 65, fols 148v (28 September 1570), 149v (2 October 1570).

116 AEG, RC 65, fol. 151v (5 October 1570).

117 AEG, RC 65, fol. 152 (9 October 1570).

118 AEG, RC 65, fols 154v–155 (14 October 1570).

119 AEG, RC 65, fols 156v–157 ([17] October 1570).

120 AEG, RC 65, fol. 162v (1 November 1570).

121 AEG, RC 65, fol. 172v (20 November 1570).

122 AEG, RC 65, fol. 184v (19 December 1570).

123 AEG, RC 65, fol. 192v (2 January 1571).

124 AEG, RC 66, fol. 31 (12 February 1571). Three weeks later the guard complained that the location of the gravediggers conflicted with their task as body collectors and the city's plague regulations, fol. 39v (1 March 1571).

125 AEG, RC 66, fol. 35 (20 February 1571).

126 AEG, RC 66, fols 37v (26 February 1571, six houses infected), 44v (15 March 1571, François Bonivard, hero of the revolution, died), 50v (29 March 1571). Bonivard's estate was valued at Fl. 209 5s 1d (fol. 68v, 11 May 1571).

127 AEG, RC 66, fol. 50v (29 March 1571).

128 AEG, RC 66, fol. 55v (12 April 1571). Two days later Beza briefly commented on the plague spreaders in a letter (no. 64) to J. Corrasio, a senator in Toulouse ('ea nos certè totum sexennium valde exercuit'). *Epistularum theologicarum Theodori Bezae* (Geneva: Eustathium Vignon, 1575). I am grateful to Dr S. Manetsch for this reference.

129 AEG, RC 66, fol. 59 (19 April 1571); two senators, Ami de Chasteauneuf and Pierre Dance, and a syndic, Pierre Chappuis.

130 AEG, RC 66, fol. 60v (23 April 1571).

131 AEG, RC 66, fol. 67 (7 May 1571).

132 AEG, RC 66, fol. 67v (8 May 1571).

133 AEG, RC 66, fol. 68v (11 May 1571).

134 AEG, RC 66, fol. 79 (7 June 1571).

135 AEG, RC 66, fols 92v (19 July 1571), 93 (20 July 1571).

136 AEG, RC 66, fols 98 (6 August 1571), 99v (9 August 1571).

137 AEG, RC 66, fol. 101v (17 August 1571).

138 AEG, RC 66, fol. 102 (20 August 1571).

139 AEG, RC 66, fol. 104v (27 August 1571).

140 AEG, RC 66, fols 107 (4 September 1571), 122 (1 October 1571): Flamand, Abraam Guidoct and Joseph Destanaz said they could not meet the demands made of them. The transfer of Flamand to his post at St-Gervais on 21 August had not ameliorated the problem (fol. 102v).

141 AEG, RC 66, fols 117–117v (24, 25 September 1571).

142 AEG, RC 66, fol. 112v (12 September 1571).

143 AEG, RC 66, fol. 132v (29 October 1571).

144 AEG, RC 66, fol. 141v (15 November 1571).

145 AEG, RC 66, fols 149v (3 December 1571), 153v (13 December 1571), 156–156v (20 December 1571); RC 67, fol. 23 (12 February 1572).

146 AEG, RC 66, fol. 164 (4 January 1572).

147 It also saw the publication of J. A. Sarrasin, *De peste commentarius* (Lyon: L. Cloquemin, 1572). Sarrasin was a Genevan physician and must have written the work during the events of this outbreak (see, especially, pp. 103–5).

148 AEG, RC 67, fol. 46 (25 March 1572).

149 AEG, RC 67, fol. 46v (28 March 1567).

150 AEG, RC 67, fol. (22 April 1572).

151 AEG, RC 67, fol. 74 (9 May 1572).

152 AEG, RC 67, fol. 78v (20 May 1572).

153 AEG, RC 67, fols 86 (2 June 1572), 96v–97 (19 June 1572), 101v (26 June 1572), 102 (30 June 1572), 104v (3 July 1572).

154 AEG, RC 67, fol. 123 (4 August 1572).
155 AEG, RC 67, fol. 128v (15 August 1572).
156 AEG, RC 67, fol. 134v (29 August 1572).
157 AEG, RC 67, fol. 148 (13 September 1572).
158 PH 1907 (27 June 1571).

CHAPTER FIVE

THE CONSPIRATORS OF 1571

Burnt alive in a raging fire until reduced to ashes

As the previous chapters mentioned, plague spreading was not in any sense a phenomenon unknown to Geneva's leaders or citizens. Most would have had personal knowledge of the events of the 1540s and, some, of those in the 1530s. Moreover, the period before the return of plague in 1567 witnessed the discussions with the Duc de Nemours and Savoy about plague-spreading conspiracies putatively involving Geneva's Protestant magistracy. Plague spreading and conspiracies to poison were intimately connected with the Genevan experience of plague. The question that arises is to what extent any lessons had been learned from the previous examples of the phenomenon and how far the people and politicians of Geneva would 'anticipate' a conspiracy simply because plague was present. In addition, it remains to be seen whether the mere rumour of plague spreading or even the appearance of *graisse* was sufficient to provoke a mass investigation by the authorities or whether, as in the previous outbreaks, the magistracy continued to be uninterested in uncovering conspiracies. Finally, since Monter's work focused so explicitly on the plague spreaders of the 1570s as witches, it will be important to see whether the trials dossiers bear out his view that the plague spreaders were simply a 'bizarre form of witchcraft lacking most of the normal paraphernalia' of witchcraft.

Having been alerted to the presence of plague spreaders in 1564–66 by their neighbours, and undoubtedly keen to prove that they were not at all involved in such a nefarious behaviour, one might expect the magistrates to have rushed to find their own *engraisseurs* the moment plague reappeared. In fact, there were no prosecutions in 1567, though two cases opened in January 1568 and must relate to events during the 1567 outbreak. Thus, from the very first year of this lengthy series of epidemics, plague spreaders were being discovered.

On 20 January, the trial began of Antoine (also known as Bauliez), son of Jaquemoz Moudon, who was a native of Geneva aged twenty-five.[1] His initial interrogation provided the judges with their ideal: variation and perjury. He denied that he was married though admitting he had been married five years before. He could not explain this apparent contradiction. Also, he began by giving his name as Antoine Patterie (of Geneva). Under questioning he admitted he was really Antoine, son of Jaquemoz Bauliez. Such employment as he had had was mostly as a fumigator and cleaner (a *cureur*); he had worked in Grand-Sacconex, Fonnex, Gingin, and Ornex. At first, he denied having any preservative against the plague but eventually confessed that he drank his own urine every morning as a prophylactic and ate a burnt nut. He could not explain why he was using an assumed name and begged to be freed 'since he had committed no crime'.[2]

During his second interrogation, the state moved quickly to torture him – a move legally allowed because of his previous lies and variations. He accused a number of people and admitted to possessing (in a box in his wife's chest in Ornex) a *graisse* made from plague secretions, poison and rotten pigs' fats.[3] He accused Claude Guenand of using a 'grey and violet' grease made from the blood coming from buboes against whose harm he protected himself by drinking a glass and a half of urine a day. He also implicated Jean de Geneve and admitted that although he was born in Geneva his parents were from Gingin. He was specifically asked about Satan and said that the Devil 'had never appeared to him'. His testimony told they had clasped hands and taken an oath that 'I promise you, on the damnation of my soul, that I will never accuse you and that if I accuse you I [thereby] renounce God and [my] baptism and take the Devil as my master'.[4] His motivation was twofold: to steal from homes he disinfected after greasing them and 'so that they could disinfect [i.e. work] more'.[5]

Despite querying him about contact with Satan, the official sentence made no mention of anything supernatural or diabolical. He was a thief and brigand who had poisoned people and taken 'a damnable oath' while working 'under the pretence of helping' poor plague victims. He was condemned to be burned alive.[6] The detailed summation of the investigation listed his criminal career in detail. He had been a highwayman about seven to eight years before and, as such, he had robbed and murdered (including a poor merchant near Nyon). Four years before he had begun his career as a *cureur*. He quickly conspired with others 'to grease and poison some places to maintain and continue the plague'. To this end, 'he received from the aforementioned accomplice a box full of grease promising never to accuse or denounce one another on pain of death'. When the conspirators had moved from Grand-Sacconex to Fonnex the forfeit was varied to 'the damnation of their soul and the renunciation of God and [their] baptism and taking the Devil as their master'.

The second trial surviving from this period was of Michee Maillard (daughter of Jean), the widow of Claude Guenand who was denounced by Moudon and appears to have been executed at some point during her trial.[7] Beyond mentioning some poisonous powder, her trial adds nothing to Moudon's. Indeed, the evidence confirms the information he confessed. There is no evidence that Maillard was tortured. The investigating magistrate summed up his investigation saying she had been arrested as a poisoner. About four to five years before she had been employed at Grand-Sacconex to clean and fumigate (*nettoyer et curer*) along with husband. He had been tried and executed during the course of her trial for the same crime for which she would soon be 'burnt alive in a raging fire until reduced to ashes': they 'conspired to poison and grease [*engraisser*] through the village to sustain and cause the plague to rage more fiercely there'. Also, 'to better sustain themselves in this evil plot [*complot*] and activity [*entreprinse*] they mutually promised one another by oath made hand in hand [*sur les mains les ungs et aultres*] not to accuse [*accuser*] or denounce [*deceler*] one another'.[8]

In the summer of 1568 a further three cases were prosecuted. In June, Antoine de Bassat, a carpenter, was arrested and ultimately banished.[9] His dossier opens with a number of depositions about him (alias 'Fiddler' for the instrument he carried). Albert de Migne and Jehan Bonne (a citizen) accused him of being a witch. They all said that he was associated with two other women and that all three had dropped pieces of bread at various places in Geneva.[10] When the interrogations began the questions proceeded along two lines of enquiry. First, the inquisitors wanted to know about his background (and possible grease spreading) in Ornex. Second, they sought more information about the bread that he had dropped. Their fixation with Ornex probably arises from the close connection of the two cases earlier in the year (bearing in mind that the case against Michee Maillard was still being prosecuted) with the village. Louis, son of Ayme Sesiez, accused him of killing chickens and dogs at Gex as well as grease spreading at Ornex. The accused remained steady in his denials.[11]

His defence was that he had left Berne (where he had lived five years) for Gex-la-ville and Geneva *en route* to Germany. He passed through Orbe at some point.[12] Because of a broken arm five to six years before, he had been left unemployable (as a carpenter). The bread had been his daily allotment from the General Hospital (in effect, the dole) and he admitted he might have dropped some while walking along.[13] He denied ever attending a *sabbat* and said that although it might be possible that demons existed he did not know this for certain.[14] He was given a *petite estrapade*.[15] He was tortured again on 16 June though without confessing anything. During his interrogation on 21 June he asked 'that he be killed rather than being made to suffer any more'. The final session on 23 June produced no further information or a confession. He was banished, since the state had been unable to gain conclusive evidence that he had committed any crime.

The dossier then moves to consider Louis Sesiez, who had given evidence against Bassat. He admitted at his first interrogation, without any torture (and two days before Bassat was first tortured), that he was a witch.[16] He also admitted that he had greased houses in various local villages.[17] Although there is no clear evidence of how the trial ended one can safely infer that he was executed.

The third trial of that summer was of Jaquema Porrier, who had been implicated by Antoine Moudon (Bauliez).[18] The delay in her trial was because she was not actually in Geneva. The magistrates had had to find her (in Grand-Sacconex) and have her arrested and brought to the city. She was confronted with Michee Maillard as well as the information contained in Moudon's dossier but denied everything, admitting only that she had been a widow (for twelve years) and had worked as a *cureuse* in Grand-Sacconex.[19] Interrogations on 11 and 16 August produced nothing, but the accusations raised by Moudon and Maillard were sufficient to allow the court to apply torture on 17 August. She was strapped twice and now confessed to her work with Moudon and Maillard (though she studiously avoided implicating anyone else). She said she had spread grease to gain money and also admitted that 'they had given themselves, body and soul, to the Devil'. She confirmed Moudon's testimony that they drank their own urine as a preservative against plague.[20]

Her account of her meeting with Satan was formulaic and tallied not at all with the information garnered from Moudon or Maillard. She had met the Devil (a big black man) during the daytime in the countryside. She had renounced God and promised to give her new master a chicken each year. He gave her fourteen florins that she subsequently gave to Nicolas Molet ('of this city'). She also received a box of green grease. She went to Sabbaths riding a white staff (*baston blanc*).[21] An incantation ('white staff, black staff, carry me where you will by the Devil') activated the transport. There had been a wonderful feast at the first Sabbath with lots of meat and she had kissed Satan's backside, which was very cold.[22]

The interrogation on 28 August produced some interesting variations in that some related to Satan and Sabbaths while other parts confirmed in detail the oath-taking ceremony described by Moudon. However, this latter oath was entirely separate from any demonic activity, as it took place only in the presence of Moudon and Maillard. Porrier placed her hands between those of Maillard and swore the forfeit oath described by Moudon. Satan was not present and the events and circumstances related were wholly natural, albeit terrific in intent. She then returned to the Sabbath events and insisted that the fourteen florins she had been given were good (i.e. they had not turned to leaves upon Satan's departure). When she used the grease she chanted, 'I touch you that you die in three days.' She had not spread any grease in Geneva and Satan had promised that she would not go to Hell.[23]

Subsequent interrogations produced nothing additional and the magistrates seem to have been content, as they did not apply torture again. She consistently kept the circumstances and individuals associated with the oath-taking ceremony distinct from those of the Sabbath.[24] More important, the summation made the same distinction, saying she had been arrested 'for the crimes [plural] of witchcraft and poisoning'. The sentence makes the distinction less clear, describing her crimes as witchcraft and *actes diaboliques*, which one may understand either as a sub-category of the first charge or as a comment on the horrific nature of the plague spreading.[25] Although some distinction is being made by both the accused and the judges it is also clear that the two activities of witchcraft and plague spreading were becoming more closely intertwined than ever before.

This mingling of crimes continued in the clutch of cases prosecuted at the end of 1568. As in 1545, there seems to have been some relation between the waning of plague and the authorities' enthusiasm to prosecute plague workers as plague spreaders. As Table 7 shows, the numbers were not yet dramatic, nevertheless they introduce a crucial element into this discussion. There was an organic connection between the events of 1545 and 1568.[26] As the reader may recall, in 1545 some of the accused conspirators had been implicated in the 1530 trials, thus creating a link

Table 7   Sequence of trials, 1568

Arrested	Name[a]	Sentence
January	<u>Antoine</u>, son of Jaquemoz Moudon (alias Bauliez), Genevan native, aged twenty-five	Executed
	Michee, daughter of Jean Maillard from Annecy, widow of Claude Guenand from Petit Sacconex	Executed
June	<u>Antoine</u>, son of Jean de Bassat, from Cussiez, carpenter *Louis*, son of Ayme Sesiez from Gex	Banished
August	*Jaquema*, daughter of Claude Fol from Logras, widow of Claude Porrier from Miez	Executed
November	***Claudine***, daughter of Pierre l'Hoste, citizen, wife of Claude Nicolas (alias Grimaud)	
	<u>Claude Nicolas</u>, lace maker, raised at the General Hospital after being abandoned[b]	Executed
	<u>Elizabeth</u>, daughter of Estienne Bousier, widow of (1) Antoine Liquet, (2) Michel Noblet, native Genevan[c]	
	Gonine, daughter of Louis Lengard from Collogny, widow of Jacques Rinit, shoemaker	
	Pernette, daughter of Claude Bioley from Vandoeuvres	
	<u>Mya</u>, daughter of Claude Vellu from Lucinge, labourer, *habitant*	
	<u>André</u>, daughter of Michel Picte, widow of Pierre Marguet	
	Pernon, daughter of Louis Racouz from Perlier, widow of Bernard Cloye from Burgundy[d]	Executed

Notes

[a] Those named in **bold** were involved in the 1545 conspiracy; those in *italics* were convicted of witchcraft, those <u>underlined</u> were tortured.

[b] The nineteenth or twentieth-century folder gives a summation listing witchcraft but the sixteenth-century material gives no supporting evidence for the charge.

[c] Although there is nothing in this case to suggest an association with witchcraft, her trial in 1571 (PC1: 1649) says she had been banished for witchcraft and poisoning.

[d] While it is not clear what befell the previous five, Pernon was executed. Colladon recommended banishment.

between the two. These cases from 1568 now form an unbroken chain of personal, individual contact with the earlier supposed conspiracies. Nevertheless, as we shall see, subtle alterations were being made in the understanding of the behaviour and the interplay between accused and accusers.

The first substantial number of surviving cases comes from the end of 1568. These cases, at first glance, appear to have more in common with those of 1530 and 1545 in that they come in a period when the plague had abated. The earlier cases in 1568 occurred during plague when the magistracy was, for very good reasons, distracted. By November and December, the state was able to turn its full attention and investigatory energy to prosecuting accused plague spreaders. Indeed, the affinity between these trials and those of 1545 leaps to one's attention in the very first case: the prosecution of Claudine (alias Grimauda), daughter of Pierre l'Hoste (a citizen), the wife of Claude Nicolas, for the twin crimes of sorcery and plague spreading.[27]

The case against Grimauda opened with seventeen depositions. Two witnesses said they knew her only as a *femme de bien*.[28] Most simply said that they had heard various rumours that she was not a particularly pleasant person.[29] Some of those giving testimony associated her specifically with minor crimes: theft, violating plague regulations and fornication/adultery.[30] Jehanne (widow of Jaques de la Rue) linked her with Ayme Biolley, a surgeon at the pest house. This immediately suggests the possibility of a conspiracy run by barber-surgeons *à la mode* of 1530 and 1545. Marguerite, the widow of Etienne Chasteauneuf (a former senator and syndic) accused her of theft while Grimauda was a cleaner during the 1545 outbreak.[31] More damagingly, Andrée (the wife of Jaques Paguet) named her as an associate of Jean Lentille, the accused and executed leader of the 1545 conspiracy.

Françoise, the wife of Claude Servand (a baker), who was quarantined in the pest house, made the most devastating accusation. She had been told by another Françoise Vassel (the wife of Dominique Parpille) who was working there that she had found two basins of grease in the straw of a bed that abutted Servand's bed. Vassel asked Servand what she had done with the grease and was told that she had burned it. Vassel did say that she had acted impulsively and regretted that she had not taken the bowls to the magistrates. She told Servand that she was sure the grease belonged to Grimauda and that the accused was an evil woman and a witch.[32]

At her first interrogation, Grimauda admitted that she knew Claude Blanc, another cleaner, and Jaques Bastian, a gravedigger, as well as Martin another gravedigger. She denied that she had said that 'the plague will last until Christmas'.[33] There was no attempt to deny that she had cleaned and disinfected during the 1545 outbreak. When asked about her relationship with Aime Biollet, the surgeon, she was somewhat evasive. Finally, Grimauda knew that Servand had mentioned the two basins of grease but she had said they belonged to Vassel. Colladon gave an initial legal opinion on the case strongly suggesting that the investigation should be prosecuted enthusiastically.[34]

Two depositions taken on 17 November added dramatic new information to the case. Michel Grangier (a *bourgeois*) and his daughter Elisabeth reported that her younger brothers had seen Claude Nicolas (Grimauda's husband) messing around their windows. He had caught the young boys and beaten them, ordering them to say nothing to their father, Michel. The next day, this line of investigation was continued. Rolette (wife of Jean Canard, citizen), Louise (wife of François Paquet), Jeanne (another daughter of Michel Grangier) and witnesses deponed on 22 November; they added nothing more than vague rumour and hearsay.[35] While this generalisation about their testimony is broadly accurate, three witnesses added some crucial new information. Vassel confirmed that she had found two wooden bowls full of grease and a wooden spoon with one of them. She said she had burned the bowls, spoon and bed straw. The smoke 'was very stinky'.[36] Both Genon (daughter of Antoine Griffort, from Faucigny) and Hugine (widow of Orme Deroches, an *habitant*) confirmed the existence of the grease, though under questioning it became clear that they were simply repeating what Vassel had told them.[37] Finally, Martin Leschiere (a carpenter) reported that Grimauda had tried to pimp her daughter to him while he was in the pest house.[38]

The case continued with a fruitless interrogation on 24 and 27 November and confrontations on 3 December. More depositions were taken on 4 December but other than some comments about her penchant for keeping black dogs and vague references to a 'black man' the most interesting testimony came from Claude Miure, an *habitant*. He said that he had overheard Grimauda saying to her husband that 'he would be very rich and [that] this is the time to earn well and [that] she would earn enough for [both of] them'.[39] A further interrogation, with confrontations, occurred on 6 December but resulted in no new information.[40]

After a month, the court finally resorted to the threat of torture.[41] Grimauda then accused Jean Chautemps (in charge of the city's plague containment exercise in 1545) with offering her food in exchange for sexual favours during the earlier outbreak. She was raised and strapped. However, she would say only that 'she had [not] done anything bad other than thieving and fornicating'. She said she had stolen from Jean Chapeaurouge but on the question of the grease she said that 'she is innocent of all that'.[42] An additional 'small strap' brought no further revelations. Two straps the next day did no more than produce repeated accusations against Chautemps. Eventually, she implicated Ayme Biolley (a surgeon at the pest house) and said he gave her the grease. She said that she had not bought any drugs nor seen any 'except those that the Devil gave them near the hospital'. Supposedly, a child died when she applied the grease to it. Grimauda's testimony also linked her with Bartholome and Guilloda from the 1545 outbreak, since she said that she been one of their co-conspirators. She also implicated Mya, Guillaumera, Pernon Bernard, Hudriod and her husband, Claude Nicolas.[43]

The one question the judges put to her about the Devil related to his temperature. She said that 'he was cold like ice, completely black and very big and tall'.[44] Interrogations (without torture) on 11 and 12 December only served to confirm the confessions extracted under torture. The official report of the investigation's results states that she admitted her involvement in the 1545 conspiracy as well as adultery. She had 'continued to grease with the said grease and moreover [*en oultre*] she had immersed herself on the side of Satan who had appeared to her at the [Plague] Hospital when she [worked] there and she gave her faith and homage [to him]'. Satan had given more grease to her and 'her other accomplices (named in her dossier) who also cleaned in the infected houses' and the grease was 'to make the plague continue for ever, telling them that they [*elles*] would be well recompensed'.[45] The association of the (additional) grease with Satan is not as explicit in the official sentence read out before her execution. She had 'made and compounded the grease and poison along with a close accomplice to spread and maintain the plague continually' in 1545, while in the latest outbreak 'she had received the Devil and paid him homage, renouncing God, the Creator'.[46]

November and December saw the case against Grimauda expand to include seven other accused conspirators. The most important was her husband, Claude Nicolas (a lace maker who had been raised at the city's General Hospital after being abandoned by his parents).[47] The summation of the case and the official sentence both mention his (tenuous) involvement with the events of 1545 as well as his supposed plague spreading with his wife. She is, again, named as a witch but he is not accused of contacts with Satan.[48] After torture he admitted to using green grease and having some poisonous (yellow and green) powders.[49]

Elisabeth Noblet confessed under torture that Claude Blene (or Bleve) gave her a box of grease and that Mya Vellu gave her some powder in an envelope.[50] She had destroyed both.[51] She confessed to greasing and taking an oath 'not to say anything under pain of being beaten and battered (and burned)'.[52] She tried to retract her confession but Senator Guillaume Chiccand returned with a box of green grease that he had found where she had said it was hidden.[53] Gonine Lengard maintained her innocence throughout her trial and various confrontations. She went to sermons 'a little' and placed her hope in the death and passion of Christ.[54] Beyond confessing that she did use an ointment (grease) that she had bought from an apothecary three years before, Pernette Bioley's trial passed without incident.[55] The cases against André[e] Pictet and Mya Vellu were intertwined.[56] Although extensive torture was used, the lawyer Colladon pointed out in his legal advice that the boxes of grease were not found where they were supposed to be. He seems to assume that their confessions were torture-induced and untrustworthy. Hence he recommends only banishment.[57] Just as interestingly, none of these six cases mentioned any connection with the 1545 conspiracy or Satan.

The final case of late 1568 saw Pernon Racouz (alias Bernarda) accused of both.[58] The summation of the investigation said she was involved in the 1545 events (about twenty-four years before) and greasing (poisoning). She did not appear to have renounced God and paid homage to Satan until about 1564. She had attended a Sabbath (synagogue) and been involved in a plot to spread plague in the Valais and at Thonon. She said Grimauda and Mya had given her the grease she had been using recently in Geneva. The sentence mentioned her 'long service to the Devil' and that she had 'greased and poisoned in the city and elsewhere' with the 'intention of spreading the plague'.[59] Members of three leading families gave depositions saying that they had known her for about twenty years and that she had the reputation of being 'an evil woman and a greaser' and 'an accomplice of Jehan Lentille' as well as 'given to wine and dissolute'.[60] The actual details of her trial add nothing to the information garnered elsewhere except on two counts. First, she admits that she had been banished around 1553.[61] Finally, she implicates a number of people not mentioned in other cases: Mya du Burdel, Maurice, Prudence (wife of a serge maker), Thevena (from Thonex), Françoise, Thyvent Guenda (from Pont d'Arve), Penon (wife of a shepherd from St-Jean-de-Gonville), and Louise.[62]

There are only five relatively disparate cases surviving from 1569 (Table 8). The case against Dumont revolved around his having been seen near the house of Joachim de la Mer very soon before grease was discovered.[63] De la Mer found the grease, called his neighbours to bear witness to its presence and then burned it.[64]

Table 8   Sequence of trials, 1569

Arrested	Name[a]	Sentence
January	<u>Claude</u>, son of Jean Dumont from Mure-en-Bornes, a mendicant	Banished
February	Martin Leschiere	
August	Mermette, daughter of Gonin Tagan from Neydens	Banished
October	Albert, son of Antoine de Nicque from Ferrars, *habitant*, gravedigger	Executed
December	Jaques, son of Hugues Garnier, baker, from Dauphiné	Banished

Note
[a] Those named in **bold** were involved in the 1545 conspiracy, those in *italics* were convicted of witchcraft, those <u>underlined</u> were tortured.

All torture could get out of him was that he had been begging near the house and that the door (on which the grease was found) was open. It appears that he was perhaps trying to break in with the intent of robbing the house. A minor investigation of Martin Leschiere at the same time produced nothing on a charge that he had infected an infant.[65]

Mermette Tagan's trial focused on a box of green grease found in her presence that she claimed had been given her by Claude [Moutellier], a surgeon and *bourgeois*.[66] Both Michel Barrillier (a citizen) and Moutellier said that they did use green ointment for treating buboes. Moutellier said it was called *appostoloix*. However, when they examined Tagan's box of grease they said it was not the same kind but was 'much greener' in colour.[67] The association with legitimate, medically prescribed ointments seems to have led the authorities to decide that the case could not be proved and she was banished.

The final two cases of the year involved plague workers but not as plague-spreading conspirators. Albert de Nicque was executed for insolence, theft and the abuse of a ten-year-old girl (although he was married). He had also committed adultery with an adolescent girl.[68] Jaques Garnier was banished for doing a bad job disinfecting homes and property – he had left much linen 'dirty and soiled'. He had also wandered about the city and mingled with healthy people after being in contact with infected goods.[69] Indeed, these two cases stand as exemplars of all those in 1569. Plague spreading in any organised, conspiratorial sense was not prosecuted. One can infer from this that the magistrates were of the opinion that the prosecutions of 1568 had been successful in breaking any possible conspiracy.

The handful of cases from 1570 (see Table 9) is similar to the disparate prosecutions conducted in 1569. Abel le Fert was arrested on 8 March for being a bad *cureur* and a thief.[70] He admitted a number of thefts and confessed that he had cut corners while disinfecting houses. He had used cleansers allocated for one room to clean two.[71] He had left unwashed 'a barrel of linen' which (according to the sentence)

Table 9   Plague spreaders in 1570

Arrested	Name	Sentence
March	Abel, son of Claude le Fert, taffeta maker and *habitant*	Executed
	Noel de Bert (from Tours), velvet maker, *habitant*	Banished
	Sebastien, son of Renauld Hardiet, shoemaker (from Burgundy), *habitant*	Executed
	Jaquema Justin (from Larpa)	
May	Catherine	
July	Christofle Mothey	
	Jeanne Valoire	Jailed[a]
August	Pernette	
	Wife of Jean Clemensin	
September	Jaques Bastian	
December	Tevena (alias Jappa or Moutouniere), daughter of Claude Rey, widow of Girard Bonivard[b]	Executed

Notes

[a] For three days on bread and water.

[b] The case began in late December (the 22nd) and it is clear from PC2: 1331 (a list of those prosecuted in 1571) that she is seen as connected with the cases of the next year, not those of 1570. Although grease appears in her trial, plague spreading is not specifically mentioned.

could 'bring on a new infection'.[72] Both the court and Colladon (in his legal opinion) make it clear that his 'great salary' and oath 'to clean faithfully' should have been enough to ensure loyal and conscientious effort. Colladon suggested, and the court accepted, a death sentence.[73] Noel de Bert was prosecuted for the same crimes but was only beaten and banished. Although he too should have been content with his 'great salary' (of as much as nine écus per house), he had only 11*s* from one house and had left some linen uncleaned. His crimes were not as great, so his punishment was less – he was publicly beaten and banished in perpetuity.[74]

Indeed, the cumulative effect of multiple crimes is most evident in the trial of Sebastien Hardiet. He eventually admitted (without torture) to adultery with a married woman, fornication with an unmarried woman, singing dissolute songs, and theft. In addition, he had 'abandoned his service leaving the said rooms full of filth and very smelly and the largest part of the [linen and furniture] sitting in Plainpalais'. Although he was asked about any possible contact with witches and plague spreaders, he steadfastly maintained his innocence of these crimes and the matter was not pursued. In the end, the collective punishment for his many crimes was death.[75]

The remaining welter of cases involving cleaners and their work reveal little except that the state was certainly not attempting to uncover more conspirators or conspiracies. Christofle Mothey was suspected of witchcraft and accused of

Table 10   Sequence of trials, January–March 1571

Arrested	Name[a]	Sentence
January	_Martine_, daughter of Pierre de Grandchamp, wife of Jean Croset (an _habitant_)	Executed
March	_Mathieu_, son of Pierre Roy (from Mure, labourer, _habitant_), aged eighty[b]	Banished
May	_Christofle_, daughter of Claude Mothey (from Arve), wife of Michel Bonivard (from Levre, _habitant_)	Executed
	Mya, daughter of Tomas Bouloz (from Grave), widow of Pierre Gradel (native of Geneva)	Executed
	Prudence, daughter of Jaques Vesin, widow of Jean Destone (_habitant_)	Executed
	Françoise (alias Miranda), daughter of Antoine Favre (from Marsilly), wife of Mama Chappuis (_bourgeois_)[b]	Executed
	Genon (alias Faguesa), daughter of Rollet de Coing (from Faucigny), wife of Jehan Faguey (seamster, citizen)	Executed
	Petremande, daughter of François Boquet (from Pellonez), wife of Pierre Conte (from Cursillez)[c]	Banished
	Claude (alias Borsiere, native of Geneva), daughter of Jean des Bois (from Bonna), widow of Jaques Blanc (from Contamine)[c]	Executed
	Jaquema (alias la Serralion), daughter of Jaques Cartier (from Vernier), widow of Ayme du Bouloz (locksmith, _bourgeois_)[b, c]	Banished
	Clauda, daughter of Pierre Bosson (from Vuache), widow of François du Cloz (smithy, _bourgeois_), aged forty[c]	Banished
	Ayme (alias Papaz), daughter of Bernard Baud (from Langin), wife of Jean Janin (alias Papa, from Collogny)[c]	Banished
	Janne, daughter of Guillaume Novel (from St-Cerges), aged thirty[c]	Banished
	Henriette (alias Trompillore), daughter of Collet Fais, wife of Claude Dentant, widow of Jehan Favre (butcher, citizen)[c]	Executed
	Marie (alias Lievre), daughter of Claude Renyn (packman)[c]	Executed
	Georgea, (illegitimate) daughter of François de Langin, widow of François Perrisod (from Faucigny)[b]	Executed
	Pernon (alias Chontagne), daughter of Mama Roch (packman), widow of Jehan de la Planche (mason, _habitant_)[d]	Executed
	Guillauma, daughter of Claude Tissot (from Clermont-en-Genevois), wife of Jehan Conte (mason)[b, c]	Banished
	Elizabeth, daughter of Estienne Bousier, widow (1) of Antoine Liquet, (2) of Michel Noblet (fisherman)[e]	Executed
	Ayma (alias Grenoulliere), daughter of Claude Rollet, widow of Antoine Besson[c]	Executed
	Françoise, daughter of Vincent Guaydon (from Faucigny), aged thirty[b]	Banished
	Serma (spinster, alias Revenderessa or Provencale), daughter of Gabriel Cousturier (from Faucigny), aged seventy[b, c]	Banished

Table 10 (*cont.*)

Arrested	Name[a]	Sentence
	Pernette (alias Motardia), daughter of Pierre Curt (from Puplinge), wife of Jaques Donzel (citizen)	Executed
	Mamade (alias Foissode), daughter of Levet Chappuis, widow (1) of Gonet Bene (labourer, *habitant*), (2) of Jean Tabuis[b]	Executed
	Clauda (alias Gernon), daughter of Bertod Voula (from Faucigny), widow of Pierre de la Rue (labourer, *habitant*)[b]	Executed
	Jehan, son of Jehan de Laon (from Montpellier), lace maker, *habitant*	Executed
	Laurence, daughter of Jean Esperon, wife of Perceval Volland [f] (labourer, *bourgeois*), aged fifty[b, c]	Banished
	Guillaume, daughter of Claude Cusin (Prisilliez), widow of Pierre Magnin (from La Mure)[b, c]	Banished
	Louise, daughter of Philippe Farquet (from Faucigny), widow of Jaques Pampigny[b]	Executed
	Claude, son of Thivent de Meyriez, citizen, needle maker	Executed
	Vincente, daughter of Michel Rogier (from Gex), wife of Colin Gervais (from Petit-Sacconex)[b, c]	Executed

Notes

[a] Those named in **bold** were involved in the 1545 conspiracy; those in *italics* were accused of witchcraft, those underlined were tortured.

[b] Accused of using grease to commit evil (and to kill) but not explicitly to spread plague or not accused of contact with any grease.

[c] Mentioned in the sixteenth-century 'roll of witches and plague spreaders' preserved in AEG, PC2: 1331 [1571].

[d] See AEG, PC1: 394 [1545] for the execution of her husband.

[e] She had already been banished (1568) perpetually, suspected of sorcery and poisoning. This is the third time she had returned to the city. See AEG, PC2: 1307 [1569] and PC1: 1516 [1569].

[f] Executed earlier for an unrelated crime.

becoming engaged to Michel Bonivard while she had plague.[76] Jeanne Valoire was given three days on bread and water for becoming a *cureuse* without her husband's permission.[77] Jaquema Justin, Jaques Bastian, Catherine and Pernette were all investigated for possessing suspect powders and greases. Grease was certainly present on various objects associated with them and their work but in the end the magistracy did not pursue these four cases.[78] Indeed, the cases never went beyond a single interrogation. The case of the anonymous wife of Jean Clemensin further reinforces the belief that the authorities were not very interested in finding conspiracies. Information was taken about a possible link between the unnamed *cureuse* and infected linen from Michel Grangier's house. Since Grangier had been a target of the mini-conspiracy uncovered in 1568 one might have thought his return to the courts would spark another hunt.

However, the few people investigated in 1569 and 1570 did not produce another clutch of conspirators and did not lead the state to scapegoat anyone for its third and fourth year of plague. In fact, the unwillingness of the courts and Senate to be

Table 11 Sequence of trials, June–December 1571

Arrested	Name[a]	Sentence
June	*Thivent* (carpenter, *habitant*), son of Claude Commona	Banished
	Jaquema, daughter of Claude Longenoz (alias Grangier, from Lonnay), wife of Thivent Commona[b]	Banished
	Pernon, daughter of Monet Calabri (from Corsinge), widow of Michel Rocher (from Vandoeuvres)	Executed
	Janne, daughter of Gabriel Curlat (citizen, alias Du Sel), widow of (1) of Jean Pelagra, (2) Pierre Berthod[c]	Banished
	Jehanne, daughter of Pierre Richard, wife of Tyvent Berthod (labourer)[b, c]	Banished
	Jehanne (alias Nerota), daughter of Pierre Jaquemoz (from Logra), wife of Humbert Tardif (labourer, *habitant*, from Russin)[b, c]	Banished
	Humbert, son of Pierre Tardif[c]	Banished
	Pierre, son of Voulthiez Berchod (labourer, from Bornes)[b, c]	
	Wife of Pierre Berchod[c]	
	Ayme, daughter of Louis d'Aynault (from Champagne), widow of Claude Lambert (from Joigny)[b]	Banished
	Thevena, daughter of Claude Perissod (from Faucigny), wife of Gonin Genod (from Chambéry, *habitant*)	Executed
	Clauda, daughter of François de Lullier (from Faucigny), wife of Claude Chabel (pin maker, citizen)[c]	
	Antoine Tondu, aunt of Thierry Tondu (executioner)[c]	
	Guillaume, wife of Gonin de Soubz[c]	Banished
	Gonin de Soubz[c]	Banished
	Claude, son of Jehan Roussier (from Conflans, *bourgeois*)[c]	Banished
	Clemence, daughter of Pierre Lanqua (from Nantua), widow of Claude Durandel (from Lyon)	Banished
	Pernette, daughter of Louis de la Nouva (from Faucigny), widow of Ami Ruffy[c]	Executed
	Benoiste, daughter of Jehan de la Croix (from Macon), widow of Benoist Febvre[b, c]	Banished
	Ayma (alias Reniez), daughter of Rene Mauris (carpenter, *bourgeois*), wife of Andrew Boveyron (carpenter, *bourgeois*)[b]	Banished
	Janne, daughter of Antoine Bosson (from Arve), widow of Michel Mossu (*bourgeois*)[b]	Banished
	Rose, daughter of Louis Hostellier, wife of Amy Gros (citizen)[b]	Banished
	Jaqueme, daughter of Jean Lecher (from Gailliard), wife of Bernard Richard (*habitant*, carpenter, from Pressiez)[b, c]	Banished
	Jannine, daughter of Jean de Montoz (alias Recogniez, mason, *habitant*)[b]	Banished
	Ayma, wife of Martin le Maire (washerwoman)[b, c]	
	Clauda, daughter of Louis Mevaux (from Jussy), widow of Jehan Burnet (labourer)[b]	Banished
	Didier, son of Jean Marchand (from Gex, waggoner, *habitant*), aged forty[c]	Acquitted

Table 11 (*cont.*)

Arrested	Name[a]	Sentence
	Marthye, wife of Jaques Voultier (shoemaker)[c]	
	Mother of Marthye [*Voultier*][c]	
	Claudine, wife of Jean Clemencin (pin maker)	
	Pernon, daughter of Louis Chasse and Merma (from Bellerive), wife of Claude Besson (from Compeys)	Banished
	Claude, daughter of André Molliet (from Cluses), widow of (1) François Bene, (2) Jean Pensier[c]	Executed
	Clauda, wife of Henri Pellisson (from Perron)	
July	*Françoise*, daughter of Roz Collavin (from Faucigny)[b, c]	Banished
October–	*Thevena*, daughter of Tyvent Jean Couturier (from Ternier)	Executed
December	*Jeanne*, daughter of Gonet du Puys (from Landissy), aged twenty-eight	Executed
	Guillet, (citizen), son of Jean Vouchier (alias Label)	Acquitted
	Mauris, son of Aubert Molat (from Sala, labourer)[c]	Banished
	Jeanne, widow of Barthelemy Blanchon	Banished
	Martine Blanc, (from Crache), widow of François Mathieu (*habitant*)[b]	Banished
	Jeanne, daughter of Pierre Rey (Faucigny), wife of François Rosset (Faucigny)	Banished
	Pierre, son of Jean Guernoz (from Gex, labourer, *habitant*) aged sixtyd	Execute
	Robella, wife of Pierre Guernoz	Executed
	Jeanne, daughter of Pierre Guernoz and Robella, aged sixteen	Executed
	Alex, widow of Pierre Armand (spur maker)[b]	

Notes

[a] Those named in **bold** were involved in the 1545 conspiracy; those in *italics* were accused of witchcraft, those underlined were tortured.

[b] Mentioned in the sixteenth-century 'roll of witches and plague spreaders' preserved in AEG, PC2: 1331 [1571].

[c] Accused of using grease to commit evil (and to kill) but not explicitly to spread plague or not accused of contact with any grease.

driven into a frantic and frenetic investigation of plague spreading lends credence to their prosecutions in 1568. At every point, both in the outbreaks of these years and in those of earlier decades, the magistrates consistently demonstrated reluctance to find people to blame and punish for the presence (and return) of pestilence. When one considers the trials of those who resembled plague spreaders as well as the availability of torture one is surprised by the number of cases that ended in acquittal or were never actively pursued. The restraint of the city's leaders in 1569–70 contrasts with their actions in 1571.

As one can see immediately from Tables 10 and 11, the 1571 prosecutions are very confusing indeed. Some people are prosecuted as plague spreaders and witches, some only as plague spreaders, others solely as witches. The bulk of the executions (as in 1545) follow the opening trials and, as the process continues, more and more defendants are banished or acquitted. In marked contrast with 1530 and 1545, torture plays a significant role in these cases. As with the cases prosecuted in 1568 there are links between those arrested in 1571 and the events of 1545. What is most clear is that, in 1571, plague spreading and witchcraft are melding much more strongly into an interconnected activity. Increasingly, the judges seem to be assuming that, while not all witches may conspire to spread plague, there is every reason to suspect that a plague spreader will have consorted with Satan.

The initial case of 1571, against Martine Grandchamp, opened on 6 January.[79] Its continuation until the end of May ensured that this case linked up with the major prosecutions begun in that month. However, the case was interesting in making almost no mention of grease or plague. She was accused of various thefts and causing illnesses relating to cows and infants but without any association with pestilence. Her only previous brush with the law and the Consistory had been in the 1530s, when she had been prosecuted for dissolute dancing (the *virolet*).[80] Despite confrontations with witnesses, she denied she had ever gone to a Sabbath.[81] It was not until she was tortured that she confessed to a sexual relationship with the Devil (named *Robin*) and to having kissed his backside.[82] Thus, although there is a clear connection between this case and subsequent ones there is no obvious link with plague spreading.

Anyone hoping to identify a catalyst for the 1571 prosecutions might consider the case of Tevena Bonivard (see Table 9), who had been arrested in the final week of 1570.[83] Her case certainly spans the period of greatest activity for the courts in 1571 and, more important, she is actually identified as a *cureuse*. Her trial intimately links her with later cases.[84] In addition, she specifically accuses Robella Guernoz and Prudence Vesin.[85] Various people testified that she was rumoured to be a witch and involved in a number of suspicious deaths.[86] However, the confusing aspect of this trial, as with that of Grandchamp above, is that while witchcraft is clearly present there is no explicit reference to plague spreading. Moreover, there are no details on an oath-taking ceremony and an accompanying conspiracy. Thus, to the extent that these cases seem to have sparked the investigations of 1571, the initial motivation seems to have been the discovery of witchcraft. The result is that, from the outset, the cases prosecuted in 1571 differ dramatically and fundamentally from the cases of 1530, 1545 and even 1567–70. Witchcraft was an additional and rare aspect in the earlier cases but in 1571 it was key to the entire judicial process.[87]

As the public health situation deteriorated in a city reeling under its fifth consecutive year of plague, the damn finally burst in May and June with the mass arrest and prosecution of over sixty individuals.[88] The first two cases (against Christofle Mothey and Mya Bouloz) were crucial in setting the tone of those to follow.[89] Both were *cureuses* and Bouloz was linked with the events of 1545. Although Mothey was put to the *strappado* the day after her arrest, a 'box of grease' had already entered the discussions.[90] She denied receiving any *graisse* from Ayma Baud (see Table 10) and refuted the testimony of another witness that she had attended a synagogue.[91] The

introduction of these two defendants complicates the picture provided by the surviving dossier. Bedal is otherwise unknown, except as one of the names appearing
on the list of 'others suspected and examined because of depositions and lesser
charges'.[92] Baud is also tried but, although she appears in Mothey's trial on 12 May,
her dossier does not begin until 18 May – almost a full week later.[93] This may imply
that the trials which appear to have started at various times in May (and, perhaps,
even June) could relate to arrests that occurred at about the same time in early May.

What is also clear is that Baud's trial begins the process by which all the cases of
1571 are woven together into a massive tapestry of investigation, interrogation,
torture and punishment. She is variously confronted by Tevena Rey (first questioned on 22 December 1570), Françoise Favre (14 May 1571), Claude des Bois (16
May), Pernon Roch (23 May) and Marie Renyn (22 May).[94] The sentence and
summation emphatically declare that she was more than sufficiently (along with
nine others) convicted of 'having conjured the Devil to ruin and destroy this city'
and that they used grease 'greatly to increase the mortality in this city'. Despite at
least ten applications of the *strappado* she maintained her innocence. However, the
multitude of accusations (extracted by torture) that placed her at various synagogues
at Longemale and the Bourg-de-Four (in the heart of Geneva) allowed the judges
to convict.

If there were any lingering doubts in the minds of the judges that there was a
serious problem afoot, the case of Mya Bouloz would have dispelled them. She had
been arrested and banished as a plague spreader in 1545.[95] She readily admitted her
previous prosecution but it was not until she was tortured on 17 May that she confessed to any guilty then or in 1571.[96] What is most interesting in this case is that
the Devil does not play a part in her torture-induced confessions about the events
of 1545. She details the oath of 1545 as 'to murder the people [and] not to denounce
one another on pain of three straps'. In all she gives an accurate recitation of the
1545 conspiracy, including the names of the other conspirators.[97] However, when
she confesses to her more recent activities, she admits to attending satanic gatherings and to having renounced God and taken Satan as her master.[98] The single point
at which the two events seem bizarrely to blend is that she claims that Satan was
named Fiollet (as was, of course, one of the leaders of the 1545 conspiracy).[99]

The basic difference between the trials of 1530 and 1545 as opposed to these is
the interest expressed by the judges in witchcraft. For the most part, the court made
little if any attempt to identify the earlier conspirators as witches. Some confessed
to witchcraft but this element remained peripheral to the investigations and prosecutions in the earlier examples of plague spreading. However, in 1571, the courts
seem more interested in asking the defendant in front of them about their demonic
activities. Plague spreading, when it enters the trials, plays a secondary (though not
peripheral) role. This may relate to the way in which the trials, as a group, began.
In 1530 and 1545, the initial cases related to plague spreading. Convinced that they
were facing a serious conspiracy of a purely natural, yet dangerous, variety, the
courts focused on the identification of additional conspirators. In 1571, during a
major plague outbreak, the cases began with the arrest of a number of suspected

witches. Many of these witches confessed to spreading plague. The question that must arise is whether the plague spreading of 1571 was simply an example of demonic activity under the direction of Satan or a conspiracy by plague workers to make more money. That is, does one see in 1571 plague spreaders but no conspiracy to spread plague (as in 1530 and 1545)?

Françoise Favre used *graisse* given her by Satan to sicken and kill some people (and animals) but not specifically to spread plague. She did confess, under torture, that she and others had danced about at the Sabbaths singing, 'We will be rich.'[100] The 'poisonous grease' given to Claude des Bois by the Devil was specifically designed 'to grease the houses to the end that the mortality would continue'. The box of grease found under her bed had been given her by a woman, not a demon, and was for no other purpose than anointing her leg.[101] Significantly, when she eventually gave way to torture and confessed, she said that she and other women had made her grease.[102] She insisted, despite repeated applications of torture, that 'she was not of the coven'.[103]

The case of Henrietta Fais is even more confusing and disturbing. She explicitly links the grease and 'horn of powder' given her by Satan with the spreading of plague. As the sentence against her said, 'she had, in execution of his commands, spread the plague in various houses of the city by means of the grease that he had given her also she had used it to kill many people on whom she had applied it'.[104] She admits to possessing the grease (which seems to have been placed in evidence before her) without even the threat of torture. More worrying than her confession to demonic contacts were the depositions from Jaqueme (wife of Claude Allemande, citizen, merchant), Charlotte (wife of Gabriel Patru) and Jean (son of Guillet Collomb from Troinex). They all swore that they had heard her say that she had seen Satan in a garden belonging to M. Collomb over a year before.[105]

This case emphasises the problems and challenges presented by these prosecutions. There is no clear reason to think that the three witnesses were lying. Hence, one could reasonably conclude that Fais actually thought she had seen the Devil. She seems to have had grease in her possession and made no attempt to explain its presence away. As far as it goes, her testimony fits most of the stereotypes one associates with witches except for the important element of external corroboration (circumstantial evidence) provided by the grease and the depositions. More important for this study, her confession does not fit the pattern of plague spreading seen in the previous outbreaks. She does not appear to have been a *cureuse*, she was not part of a conspiracy bound by an oath, she was not under the direction of any trained medical practitioners and (finally) the court seems more interested in her experiences at the synagogue than in what she did with her greases and powders. Once again, the case suggests that a seismic shift has occurred, opening a fundamental gulf between plague spreading (as an individual Satan-led activity) in 1571 and the phenomenon (conspiratorial and natural) as seen before.

Indeed, the visual image of plague workers meeting together to take an oath and make grease contrasts starkly with the picture presented in the 1571 cases. In the earlier cases, the conspirators usually met in or near the pest house, concocted the grease, took an oath and later gathered to share out the spoils of their activities. The best example is the 'conspiratorial' tableau portrayed in the investigative summation against Marie Renyn:

> while she was disinfecting, the Devil entered the said house [where she was cleaning] in the form of a man around the hour of midnight. Using the same form of words as he used to entice the others he addressed himself to the said Marie exhorting her to give herself to him and to take him as her master. At this, giving way to the entreaties of her accomplices, she renounced God and her baptism, and having kissed the Devil as a sign of homage, he gave her 'the mark' and some grease like that subsequently found in a house where she and her aforesaid accomplice (since executed) had cleaned. When the Devil had made it and given it them, she greased with it in many and diverse places in this city (e.g. in the Main Street).[106]

This 'conspiracy' could hardly be less like those before.

The closest one gets to similarities with the earlier outbreaks are the court's attempts to insinuate that the ringleaders of this new conspiracy were Jehan de Laon and Claude de Meyriez.[107] Even here the pattern is inconsistent with the earlier conspiracies. These men are not medical practitioners – indeed, no trained medics seem to have been implicated in 1571. De Laon, a lace maker, and De Meyriez, a needle maker, may have served as Satan's chief minions but they were certainly not capable of devising a poisonous substance from medicaments and then directing a conspiracy of the city's plague staff. Moreover, De Meyriez's status almost saved him, as numerous Genevans came forward to attest that he was *un homme de bien*. The minister, Trembley, however, testified to his dissolute life and, especially, his penchant for dancing the *virolet*.[108]

Most of the remaining cases from 1571 add little to the discussion.[109] The court continues to show an interest in extraneous information. For example, Ayme Baud admitted that she had been before the Consistory for 'anticipating her wedding with her fiancé'.[110] Janne Novel confessed that her father had been executed as a witch at St-Cerges.[111] She also referred, *à la* 1530, to a greased handkerchief.[112] Claude Molliet was convicted of the double crime of *sorcellerie & empoysonnement*.[113] Despite accusations of plague spreading in Satigny, Guillet Vouchier (a citizen) was eventually released on licence, perhaps confirming that in some cases (especially those late in a period of mass prosecution) status had some value.[114] Also, one is again reminded of the partial nature of the records in the trial of Thevena Perissod, who was arrested and banished in 1569 for greasing, although no dossier survives.[115]

Moreover, in common with earlier periods of mass arrests, an investigation and even the use of torture did not necessarily produce a confession or a conviction. For example, Thivent Commona and his wife, Jaquema Longenoz, despite being suspected of involvement with many of the other defendants as well as in direct accusations made against them, were banished only for theft.[116] The trials also followed the earlier patterns in producing some suicides. Georgea de Langin jumped out of a prison window.[117] Despite this individual tragedy and the horrific number of executions, it is worth noting the large number of prosecutions that ended in banishment (i.e. 'not proven' verdicts) even at the height of the prosecutions.[118]

The stereotypical aspects of the phenomenon changed in the course of the 1567–71 outbreak and remained thereafter. Plague spreaders were now seen as individuals (usually involved in witchcraft) who spread plague in a rather haphazard manner to enrich themselves personally. The conspiratorial nature of the behaviour ceases to be a prominent feature. Likewise, the important role of medical practitioners in the activity also disappeared. In 1530 and 1545, plague spreading was done by a group of plague workers under the specific guidance of medical practitioners (especially barber-surgeons). They bound themselves in a pact by means of an oath and then concocted the grease from natural components much as any medicinal ointment would have been made. Armed with the grease, the plotters were instructed by the ringleaders to target specific homes of the wealthy. Although the grease was seen and caused distress to both magistrates and citizens, in reality the conspiracies were uncovered only by accident: the dropping of a handkerchief in 1535, the report from Thonon in 1545.

The cases just examined from the later outbreak in 1567–71 and, especially, the mass prosecutions of 1571 present an altogether different picture. The primary focus of the magisterial investigations is witchcraft – plague and plague spreading is almost incidental. There are no clear ringleaders and medical practitioners do not enter into the events. To the extent that there is any pact it is not among individuals *per se* but between the individuals (as individuals) and Satan.[119] The *graisse* is supernatural in origin and is used (along with various powders) to kill animals and people. Death by plague is not integral to the activity. Indeed, it is increasingly obvious that 'greasing' is no longer necessarily synonymous with 'plague spreading'. Although the perpetrators at times seem interested in making money, more often revenge or sheer malice is advanced as a motive. Indeed, the magistrates do not recognise a motivation that is purely socio-economic as they did in 1530 and 1545. It remains to be seen which variety of plague spreading – a medical conspiracy or individual witchcraft – is the more prominent after 1571 and outwith Geneva.

While areas other than Geneva must await the discussion of the next chapter, it seems clear that later examples of greasing in Geneva were of the latter (and later) variety. In 1573, Françoise du Chesne was executed for witchcraft and greasing.[120] A few years later, Samuel Granjean, a teenager, was prosecuted for the dangerous joke of applying grease to the city's public latrines. He admitted he had heard about the behaviour but had not seen the executions of 1571 (when he was about seven years old).[121] Decades later, in 1598, the Lieutenant investigated accusations against a poor beggar boy accused of greasing a fountain in Plainpalais. He was being told by twelve-year old François Martin that the unnamed boy had admitted to having greased that (and other) fountains, using a plume to apply the grease.[122]

The concerned reaction to the greasy fountain of 1598 may relate to the presence of plague in the city and its environs in the last few years of the sixteenth century. Plague raged closer and closer to Geneva in 1596 and was certainly present

in the city by July, when a girl who had died after eleven weeks of illness was categorically ruled to have died of plague.[123] The death of a foreigner in late May was
not proved to have been plague-related, though it was strongly suspected.[124] An
embassy from Lyon was taken to the pest house to verify the presence of the disease
as well as the appropriateness of Geneva's responses to it.[125] However, as in previous outbreaks, the reality was that the enforcement of plague regulations proved to
be well nigh impossible.[126] The pestilence continued into the next year with the
death of Pernette (daughter of Martin Jeanpierre).[127] A month later, the syndic
Chapeaurouge reported the death of an eight-year-old girl.[128] Although a significant outbreak, the Senate's minutes give no sense that this outbreak was on the same
scale of those in previous decades.[129]

In the same year that the beggar boy was spreading grease on the city's fountains,
the plague continued in and around Geneva. Savoyard soldiers were infected, as
were citizens in Annecy and Syon (because of Spanish troops).[130] The city was also
struck by the disease and, yet again, the regulations proved unenforceable.[131] Those
violating quarantine were threatened with a twenty-five-écu fine.[132] The mortality was sufficient to require the opening of a plague pit ('deeper than the height of
a man') and the Newgate during sermons to allow for the removal of the dead.[133]
The disposal of corpses was still a problem in midwinter, though the epidemic
seems not to have recurred.[134]

The last outbreak to produce any evidence at all of greasing was 1614–15.[135]
From the very beginning of 1614, the government was chronicling (and trying to
avoid) the inexorable advance of pestilence. Vevey and Thonon were afflicted and
embargoed.[136] As the outbreak worsened, Savoy also blockaded Thonon, while
Vaud, Collogny, Burgundy, Ternier, Chablais, Lausanne and Morges all succumbed.[137] The Senate noted the presence of the disease in the city on 11 June.[138]
However, its late arrival seems to have militated against its impact. Nevertheless, the
magistracy took the danger of a recurrence the next year seriously by clearing the
city of nearly 450 people. A close examination of the individuals named in the
Registres du Conseil suggests that the city was expelling young female domestics.
They were to return to their rural families.[139] It also established a permanent watch
to patrol the streets as well as the walls and gates.[140] The goods and finances of
Geneva's medical provision in its various hospitals were inventoried.[141]

The preparations were prescient, as the pestilence struck the entire region yet
again. Cossonay, Morges, Lyon, Nyon, Vaud, Jussy, Chambéry, Gex, Celigny,
Peney, Bourdigny, Savoy, Piedmont, Malagny and Cartigny were reported as
infected.[142] Delegates arrived from these areas to report on the situation in their
home towns and to assess the situation in Geneva.[143] There were also the constant
problems of the disposal of the dead and the enforcement of quarantine and embargoes.[144] There was particular concern that the dead were being buried secretly at
night in the streets.[145] The threat of depopulation because of flight was also a
problem on a scale not encountered before and resulted in the eventual fining of
over 175 individuals at the end of the outbreak.[146]

The city also experienced difficulty in finding plague workers, paying them (see

Appendix 6) and, then, regulating their behaviour. Simon Tuffé was hired as 'inspector of corpses' to identify the cause of death.[147] Unfortunately, the Senate was forced to prosecute him for failing to do his work after complaints from the citizenry.[148] There were also frequent accusations against the gravediggers. A number were arrested for demanding the keys to chests and safes in the houses of the dead and then stealing the valuables inside. The Senate resolved to put a stop to the behaviour.[149] Others of their profession refused to bury any dead Italians and had to be ordered to bury all without prejudice.[150] Also, in an echo of problems of previous outbreaks, those disinfecting were a frequent cause of concern and complaint. The initial attempts to place the onus of disinfecting upon the householders failed, and cleaners had to be hired.[151] The State tried to find 'some honourable cleaners' (*marrons gens de bien*).[152] Regulations were delineated on the best places to wash infected linen and the Senate had guards posted to stop the cleaners from washing linen in the city's fountains at night.[153] The workers were also accused of pilfering from the homes they were disinfecting (as in previous outbreaks) and suspicions were raised about workers from Piedmont and Savoy, though those from Cartigny were considered trustworthy.[154] Indeed, the complaints were widespread.[155]

These general difficulties were as nothing compared with the reappearance of greasing and plague spreading. Sergeant Benjamin Pepin reported to the Senate that various doors had been found with grease on them the previous night.[156] An investigation was undertaken to discover whether witchcraft or poison had caused plague at the house of Gideon Fleurnois.[157] Louise Luttier was acquitted and Romaine Bureau (wife of George Barda) was banished for sorcery.[158] A fortnight after Pepin's original report even more doors and gates were found greased and the Senate ordered four men to be posted in each *dizinier* 'to patrol at night to entrap the greasers' (*engraisseurs*)'.[159] Some gravediggers were also suspected of spreading grease.[160] However, these complaints never take the form of a general concern about a conspiracy or even a large coven of witches. Rather they appear to be similar to the concern about the presence of grease seen in the early years of longer outbreaks *before* the mass prosecutions.[161] Indeed, they appeared to be but one concern among many, as the prosecution of Charles de Pierre for 'predicting' the death of someone who died days later from plague showed.[162] There were no mass arrests (though about a dozen suspected witches were investigated), no conspiracy and no coven.[163]

The city's last plague outbreak (1635–40) followed the patterns seen in 1614–15 and earlier. As the plague approached from Germany in 1635 basic quarantine and embargo regulations were put into effect with regard to external areas and, eventually, within the city as well.[164] The Senate even took the precaution of 'fumigating' letters arriving from Germany.[165] The following year Geneva had to send a delegation to convince the authorities at Gex that the city was not beset by plague and therefore should not be embargoed.[166] Eventually, though, Geneva succumbed in mid-July.[167] The outbreak was more severe in 1637 but even in that year there was no sense of panic and, more important, no mention of greasing.[168] Not only was the pestilence worse in the city but it was more widespread in the environs.[169] The sole problem with plague workers also occurred in 1637 when Daniel Marchand was banished one year for theft and faulty cleaning as a *cureur*.[170]

The three following years of plague produced little of note. In 1638 a major charge of poisoning was brought against Pernette (daughter of Pierre Pontex from Choulley, wife of Jean Rigaud). She was eventually executed. The case is interesting for having expanded eventually to include Susanne Goudel and Susanne de la Rue, both of whom were banished for their part in the crime. However, the case was never given anything but a natural interpretation and, despite torture for Pierre Pontex, never led to any wider investigation.[171] A single case against Simonde Maget (widow of Thibaud Morance) for plague spreading and witchcraft ended when she was banished, being 'left to God's judgement'.[172] The only other if fascinating aspect of this year's plague was the decision to bury the Duc de Rohan in a side chapel of St-Pierre Cathedral after his death from plague. Such a burial in a Calvinist temple was somewhat contentious, as one may imagine. After all, Calvin himself was buried secretly at night in an unmarked grave.[173] The final two years of plague passed with little comment beyond the impact of the disease and embargoes on trade and the danger posed by quarantine breakers and beggars.[174]

The most that one can say about greasing in the post-1571 outbreaks is that it seems to have survived as a folk memory. People were certainly aware of plague spreading, as were the magistrates. However, the behaviour had altered to the point where even youths were able to joke about greasing and engage in it for a laugh. Despite the personal and organic connection between the conspirators of 1530, 1545 and 1571 the phenomenon had altered from a conspiracy involving a well organised group of individuals under the direction of medical practitioners into an activity engaged in by a disparate group linked individually with, and supposedly controlled by, Satan and supernatural demonic powers. The small cadre of conspiratorial plague spreaders of 1530 had blossomed, in 1545, into a large plot. By 1571, plague spreading had ceased to be a 'conspiracy' in any sense and had simply become one aspect of a wider, more stereotypical malicious use of poisonous grease by witches. Thereafter, greasing increasingly ceased to have any firm or consistent link with plague at all.

NOTES

1 AEG, PC1: 1458 (20 January–3 February 1568). Being a *natif* implies that his family was so poor that they had never attained any civic status despite his having been born in the city.

2 AEG, PC1: 1458 (20, 23 January 1568).

3 AEG, PC1: 1458 (23 January 1568). The fats were *meschantes graisses . . . porceau*. He eventually accused a number of people in Geneva and elsewhere: Jaquema Porrier, Pierre Remanet (Gex), Claude Guenand (Petit-Sacconex), Louise Grolier (Bourgignon, sister of the wife of Michaud Marnanda), de la Combe (wife of Grand Gonet in Mirabel), Jean

de Geneve (called Bourdignin), Claude de Matignin, Jeanne (wife of Claude de Matignin), Jeanne Bristeust, Blaise Combet (from Vizignin), Jean Conte, Ayme Griense, Louise Grolier, Jean de Chalex.

4 AEG, PC1: 1458 (24 January 1568).

5 AEG, PC1: 1458 (28 January 1568).

6 AEG, PC1: 1458 (3 February 1568). Not only did oath breaking amount to sedition but the law had long held a special disgust for poisoners as well, arguing that 'the laws of man consider someone who kills by poison to be worse than one who kills with a sword'. F. Collard, 'Horrendum Scelus: recherches sur le statut juridique du crime d'empoisonnement au Moyen Age', Revue historique 122 (1998): 737–63, especially 744.

7 AEG, PC1: 1457 (28 January–14 August 1568).

8 AEG, PC1: 1457 (12 August 1568).

9 AEG, PC1: 1479 (11–29 June 1568), Antoine, son of Jean de Bassat, from Cusiez in the mandement of Annecy, a carpenter.

10 AEG, PC1: 1479 (n.d., start of dossier). The other three witnesses were Mermet Roz, citizen; Jehanne, the wife of François Villars (a surgeon); and Janin Grangier. Villars said the confirmation of her assessment of him as an evil man was that 'he made the evil eye' ('il faisoit l'avugle') – he pretended to have a disability of sight.

11 AEG, PC1: 1479 (11 June 1568).

12 AEG, PC1: 1479 (12 June 1568).

13 This service was no minor burden on the city. In the period 13 October 1538–11 October 1536, over 10,000 poor foreigners passed through its doors. See B. Lescaze, Sauver l'âme, nourrir le corps (Geneva, 1985), p. 24. Such institutions could be immense. Cf. the Ospedale Maggiore, founded in 1456 by Francesco Sforza, the largest of Milan's twelve hospitals, which alone had 1,200 beds. J. D. Alsop, 'Some Notes on Seventeenth-Century Continental Hospitals', British Library Journal 7: 1 (1981): 70–5, especially 71. Cf. R. A. Mentzer, 'Organizational Endeavour and Charitable Impulse in Sixteenth Century France: the Case of Protestant Nîmes', French History 5: 1 (1991): 1–29.

14 Denying demons existed would be seen as an heretical view, while confessing that they did would invite the questioner to ask how one knew.

15 As he had not varied his testimony presumably he could be tortured because of the number of people testifying against him. AEG, PC1: 1479 (14 June 1568).

16 AEG, PC1: 1485 (17 August 1568).

17 AEG, PC1: 1485 (28 August 1568). She also mentioned poisonous powders to kill animals.

18 AEG, PC1: 1485 (30 August 1568).

19 AEG, PC1: 1485 (9 August 1568).

20 AEG, PC1: 1485 (17 August 1568).

21 This may recall, while not being identical to, the verge blanche that plague workers were expected to carry.

22 AEG, PC1: 1485 (17 August 1568).

23 AEG, PC1: 1485 (28 August 1568). She also mentioned poisonous powders to animals.

24 AEG, PC1: 1485 (30 August 1568).

25 The sentence also harks back to 1545 in ordering her right hand to be cut off before she was burned at Plainpalais.

26 On 'families of witches' (i.e. organic links) see E. le Roy Ladurie, Jasmin's Witch, trans. B. Pearce (Aldershot, 1987), p. 23, and R. Briggs, Witches and Neighbours: The Social and Cultural Context of European Witchcraft (London, 1996), pp. 24–5.

27 AEG, PC1: 1307 (6 November – 14 December 1568). It appears that she was also the widow of Pierre Tomberel, a deceased citizen (see 12 November 1568).

28 AEG, PC1: 1307 (6 November 1568): Pierre Fontana (an *habitant*), Pierre Muten (a citizen and seamster).

29 AEG, PC1: 1307 (6 November 1568): Gonin de Brue, Claude (wife of Ayme Pya), Jehanne (wife of François Matte from Choulier), Collette (wife of Claude Guillet), Claude de Jussel (the younger).

30 AEG, PC1: 1307 (6 November 1568): George (wife of Pierre Foudral), Claude Veillet (shoemaker and *habitant*), François Fusiere (widow of Thomas Bron), Legier Joly (citizen)

31 Her brother-in-law, François, was a senator in 1568.

32 AEG, PC1: 1307 (6 November 1568).

33 Such a prediction would sound like divining or that she might be involved in maintaining the plague until then.

34 AEG, PC1: 1307 (12 November 1568). Germain Colladon was the city's chief legal adviser and a member of the Conseil des Soixante, the highest post open to a naturalised citizen. Although he accepted, as did most, the traditional views on demonology and witchcraft, there were some who took another position. See J. L. Pearl, 'French Catholic Demonologists and their Enemies in the late Sixteenth and early Seventeenth Centuries', *Church History* 52 (1983): 457–67.

35 AEG, PC1: 1307 (17, 22 November 1568). Other depositions came from Marie Tabuis (widow of Philippe Delestra), François (wife of Claude Servand, again), Jehan Pictet (carpenter, *bourgeois*), Claude (widow of Jean Legier, carpenter).

36 AEG, PC1 1307 (22 November 1568).

37 AEG, PC1: 1307 (22 November 1568).

38 AEG, PC1: 1307 (22 November 1568).

39 AEG, PC1: 1307 (4 December 1568). The other depositions came from Nicolas Bully (surgeon, from Grange), Hugine Deroches (again), Guigne de la Place (an *habitant*), Guillaume Vouchier (a citizen), Philiberte (wife of Volayse le Marque), Claude (daughter of Ayme Pyz, chambermaid for Jaques Mermod's widow), Janne (wife of Ponsse Loutier, hatter), Jacob de la Rue (a citizen, his sister was Mermod's widow), Claude (wife of Seraphim Martel), Humbert le Sec (an *habitant*), Claude (wife of Thomas Fiollet), Guillaume Voisin (an *habitant*).

40 AEG, PC1: 1307 (6 December 1568).

41 AEG, PC1: 1307 (9 December 1568).

42 AEG, PC1: 1307 (9 December 1568).

43 See Mya Vellu (PC1: 1509), Pernon Bernard (PC2: 1309), Claude Nicolas (PC2: 1308).

44 AEG, PC1: 1307 (9 December 1568).

45 AEG, PC1: 1307 (n.d., but probably 13 December 1568).

46 AEG, PC1: 1307 (n.d., but almost certainly 14 December 1568).

47 AEG, PC2: 1308 (27 November–16 December 1568).

48 AEG, PC2: 1308 ([15] December 1568). The mildness of the outbreaks of 1567 and 1568 is obvious in that the 1540s epidemic is still being referred to as 'the time of the great plague'.

49 AEG, PC2: 1308 (10 December 1568).

50 AEG, PC1: 1509 (11 December 1568 – 28 December 1569 [actually 1568]). Geneva's notaries counted 26 December as the first day of the new year.

51 AEG, PC1: 1509 (21 December 1568).

52 AEG, PC1: 1509 (22 December 1568).

53 AEG, PC1: 1509 (23 December 1568). François Lengard said it looked like the ointment applied to her three buboes by Noblet on the instructions of Jehan Prenost (the
chief barber-surgeon at the pest house). However, she was not certain.

54 AEG, PC1: 1509 (12–28 December 1568). Although it is unclear what happened to the
people prosecuted in this dossier she certainly seems to have escaped punishment.

55 AEG, PC1: 1509 (17–20 December 1568). See Textor, *Pestilance*, p. 124, for a recipe and
G. Ungerer, 'George Baker: Translator of Aparicio de Zubia's Pamphlet on the *Oleum
Magistrale*', *Medical History* 30 (1986): 203–11.

56 AEG, PC1: 1509 (17–28 December 1568).

57 AEG, PC1: 1509 [28 December 1568].

58 AEG, PC2: 1309 (13–20 December 1568).

59 AEG, PC2: 1309 (*c.* 19 December 1568).

60 AEG, PC2: 1309 (13 December 1568): Antoina Desfosses, widow of Claude-Louis
Magnin; Petremand Pelloux, François Clerc (citizen). There were also depositions from
Marguerite (wife of Jaques Girod) and Clauda (daughter of Michel Varrachin).

61 AEG, PC2: 1309 (15 December 1568).

62 AEG, PC2: 1309 (14, 15 December 1568).

63 AEG, PC1: 1520 (31 January–7 February 1569).

64 The grease was seen by Bastien Didier (*bourgeois*), Claude (son of Joachim de la Mer),
Janne (wife of Jehan Molin), Andre Moureau (joiner and *habitant*) and Andre Arnault
(shoemaker, *habitant*) and Jaques (son of Andre Arnault).

65 AEG, PC2: 1311 (1 February 1569).

66 AEG, PC1: 1520 (31 August–5 September 1569).

67 AEG, PC1: 1520 (1 September 1569).

68 AEG, PC1: 1556 (10–21 October 1569).

69 AEG, PC1: 1565 (8 December 1569–12 January 1570).

70 AEG, PC1: 1585 (8–22 March 1570).

71 AEG, PC1: 1585 (11 March 1570).

72 AEG, PC1: 1585 (22 March 1570).

73 AEG, PC1: 1585 (n.d.).

74 AEG, PC1: 1586 (8–27 March 1570).

75 AEG, PC1: 1587 (27 March 1570).

76 AEG, PC2: 1326 (24 July 1570).

77 AEG, PC1: 1603 (24–27 July 1570).

78 AEG, PC2: 1324 (13 March–16 September 1570): Jaquema Justin (13 March), Catherine
(19 May), Pernette (6 August), Jaques Bastian (16 September).

79 AEG, PC1: 1625 (6 January–30 May 1571).

80 AEG, PC1: 1625 (6 January 1571). Cf. the role of the Catholic clerical court, the
Inquisition, in H. Kamen, *Inquisition and Society in Spain* (London, 1985). The dance
involved spinning very quickly, thereby making the skirt rise up. The Genevan
Consistory was composed of all the ministers of the republic (approximately twelve to
fifteen) who were paid employees of the state and twelve 'elders' who were drawn from
the three councils, including a syndic – and, thus, magistrates. The Consistory was not
entirely removed from the administration of plague regulations. For example, Monter
noted that, in 1569, the Consistory excommunicated nine people for failing adequately
to supervise their servants, thus increasing the chance of the disease spreading. 'The
Consistory of Geneva, 1559–1569', *Bibliothèque d'humanisme et renaissance* 138 (1976):
469–84, especially 483.

81 AEG, PC1: 1625 (18, 25 May 1571): Tevena Rey and a person called Pernon.

82 AEG, PC1: 1625 (26 May 1571).

83 AEG, PC1: 1660 (22 December 1570–18 July 1571).

84 AEG, PC1: 1660 (18 May 1571). Her dossier preserves extracts from cases against Prudence Utin, Robella Guernoz and Pernette Donzel.

85 AEG, PC1: 1660 (7 July 1571). She also implicates some who are unidentifiable: Claudaz Morello, Corbaz, Quiberta (wife of Jaques Quibert), Dardaigne, Genon (sister of Corbaz).

86 AEG, PC1: 1660 (22 December 1570): Claude, widow of Guillaume Vellu; Didier, widow of Nicod Chaumont (mason); Andre, son of Nicod Chaumont; (18 May 1571): François-Louis Guerin (merchant, *bourgeois*); (9 July 1571): François Varro, widow of Jean Chiccand.

87 The extremely brief dossier relating to Mathieu Roy focuses mostly on his role as a thief and embezzler as well as his past criminal activities in Savoy (whence he was banished) and Satigny (where some accomplices were being held). He is associated with witch-craft but not with plague spreading.

88 It was also in these months that the city received reports (from a Mon. Faulcon and from Lausanne) about plague spreading elsewhere. Lausanne said that the women it had arrested 'were going to enrich themselves greatly while disinfecting [*marronnant*]'. AEG, PH 1907, nos. 4 (Faulcon, 24 May 1571), 6 (Lausanne, 27 June 1571).

89 AEG, PC1: 1649 (10 May–18 June 1571). The dossier preserves sixteen separate cases of witchcraft and plague spreading (greasing).

90 AEG, PC1: 1649 (11 May 1571).

91 AEG, PC1: 1649 (12, 14 May 1571). Mya Bedal was the accuser.

92 AEG, PC2: 1331. This dossier lists individuals under a number of headings: 'those who were charged and accused of having been seen at a demonic synagogue by some of those executed', 'those charged on the basis of depositions', 'others suspected and examined because of depositions and lesser charges', 'others banished for the same reasons', 'those accused by those executed, with the names of their accusers'. Finally, there are those accused by Claude Dexert (alias Ravial) who had been executed on 14 November 1567, and his wife, Genon, who had hanged herself the same month in her prison cell. These latter seem to have played no part in the 1571 cases.

93 AEG, PC1: 1647. This dossier contains eight separate cases. That of Baud has docu-mentation dated 18 May–29 June 1571. There is a more general question about the sur-vival of dossiers, which some would suggest is rarer than might otherwise be thought. See Lescaze, 'Crimes', pp. 49–51.

94 AEG, PC1: 1649. The confrontations took place on 17, 19, 24 and 26 (Roch and Tenyn) May, respectively.

95 See AEG, PC1: 400.

96 AEG, PC1: 1649 (17 May 1571).

97 AEG, PC1: 1646 (19 May 1571).

98 AEG, PC1: 1649 (19 May 1571).

99 Genon de Coing (PC1: 1649, 14–22 May 1571) confessed to being a *cureuse* in 1545 but she had not been prosecuted then and she maintained that she did not know anyone named Fiollet (whether man or demon). Ayma Rollet, widow of Antoine Besson, was also connected, through marriage, with 1545 (see Table 4).

100 AEG, PC1: 1649 (14–21 May 1571, especially 18 May). With specific reference to plague spreading see the conflation in J. Grevin, *Deux livres des venins* (Antwerp: C.

Plantin, 1568), p. 12, and his *De Venenis libro duo* (Antwerp: C. Plantin, 1571), p. 9. Grevin refers the reader to Pliny, book 25, for similar accounts of witchcraft and plague spreading in the classical world.

101 AEG, PC1: 1649 (16–28 May 1571, especially 19 May). Before confessing to being a witch, she admitted (under torture) that she was a thief and a fornicator. The cause of the increasing conflation may lie in an earlier legal conflation of poisoning (*veneficium*) with diabolical acts (*maleficium*) in the late antique period. See Collard, '*Scelus*', pp. 753–4.

102 AEG, PC1: 1649 (23 May 1571). As she also said it was given her by Satan one can suppose either that he gave them a recipe or that torture had made her confused.

103 AEG, PC1: 1649 (24 May 1571).

104 AEG, PC1: 1649 (21–30 May 1571, the sentence).

105 AEG, PC1: 1649 (21 May 1571).

106 AEG, PC1: 1649 (22–6 May 1571, the summation).

107 AEG, PC1: 1649 (De Laon: 28 May–14 June; 30 May–18 June 1571).

108 AEG, PC1: 1649 (30 May, 6 June 1571). The other cases preserved in this dossier (against Pernon Roch, Prudence Utin, Elisabeth Bousier, Ayme Rollet, Pernette Curt, Mamade Chappuis and Louise Farquet) are a similar blend of witchcraft, Sabbath-going and plague spreading *à la* Tenyn above.

109 See AEG, PC2: 1335, containing depositions in five cases: Pierre Berchod and his wife (7 June 1571), Antoine Tondu (14 June), Ayme le Maire (22 June), Marthye Voultier and her mother (25 June), Alex Faucheron (4 December). Also PC2: 1338 (25–9 June 1571), involving Clauda Pellisson, Claudine Clemencin and Guillaume [Tissot, see also PC2: 1337, 20 June 1571]. Also, PC1: 1671 (19 October–21 November 1571), Thevena Couturier. PC1: 1673 (7–20 November 1571), Jeanne du Puy. PC1: 1672 (Jeanne Blanchon, 12 November 1571; Matine Mathieu, 19–23 November; Mauris Molat, 8–21 November). PC1: 1683 (26 November–21 December 1571), Pierre Guernoz, his wife (Robella), and his daughter (Jeanne).

110 AEG, PC1: 1647 (18 May–29 June 1571).

111 AEG, PC1: 1647 (18 May–19 June 1571).

112 AEG, PC1: 1647 (8 June 1571). The dossier also contains the cases of Jaquema Cartier, Clauda Bosson, Guillauma Tissot, Françoise Guaydon, Serma Cousturier and Laurence Esperon.

113 AEG, PC1: 1661 (26 June–17 July).

114 AEG, PC1: 1658 (5–13 November 1571). Cases against Didier Marchand and Jeanne Rey are also found here. The banishment of Françoise Collavin in July may also evidence a flagging in official enthusiasm for continued prosecutions and, especially, executions (PC1: 1663, 13–17 July 1571).

115 AEG, PC1: 1653 (7–20 June 1571). The file also contains the cases of Clauda Voula (27 May–13 June 1571), Pernon Calabri (2–12 June), Vincente Rogier (30 May–2 July), Clauda de Lallier (13–19 June) and Pernette de la Nouva (15 June–3 July).

116 AEG, PC1: 1652 (1–26 June 1571).

117 She may have been convinced that she had little chance of escaping the pyre, with her judicial and familial history. She had gone into banishment with her husband on the order of the Senate (see PC1: 752, August 1547), her mother had been executed as a witch, and her father (along with Cristin Graveur) had been attacked by Burgundian peasants calling them *bouteurs de peste* and *engraisseurs* (see PC2: 1271, 29 September 156?).

118 For example, the nineteen trials (AEG, PC1: 1650) of Petremande Boquet (15 May–8 June 1571), Janne Curlat (2–12 June), Jehanne Richard (2 June–10 July), Guillaume Cusin (28 May–26 June), Ayme d'Aynault (5–8 June), Gonin de Soubz & his wife, Guillaume (14–26 June), Humbert Tardif and his wife, Jehanne Jaquemoz (3 June–5 July), Claude Rousier (14–22 June), Janne Bosson (19–22 June), Rose Hostellier (20–6 June), Jaqueme Lecher (20 June–3 July), Clauda Mevaux (22 June–16 August), Pernon Chasse (25 June–12 September), Benoiste de la Croix (18 June–9 July), Clemence Lanqua (14 June–10 July), Jannine de Montoz (20 June–5 July), Ayma Mauris (18 June–10 July).

119 As J. B. Russell noted, 'it was the idea of a pact that seized the minds of the scholastics and the inquisitors most firmly' (p. 18), in *Witchcraft in the Middle Ages*. The Genevan fixation on the oath-taking ceremonies associated with plague spreading is undoubtedly an echo of this.

120 AEG, PC2: 1369 (4–11 November): alias Cousillon, daughter of Pierre, from Chablouz, in the parish of Lullin, wife of Thivent de Cimitiere, from Valiery.

121 AEG, PC2: 1531 (16–18 July 1578).

122 AEG, PC2: 1876 (11 July 1598). Testimony was also provided by François's mother, Pernette (aged forty) though not his father, Girard.

123 AEG, RC 91, fol. 132v (12 July 1596). The plague probably made its appearance at some point between discussions (fol. 40: 8 February) about a forthcoming trade fair and its arrival in Chambéry, La Roche and Savoy (fol. 96: 17 May).

124 AEG, RC 91, fol. 105 (31 May 1596).

125 AEG, RC 91, fol. 141v (26 July 1596).

126 AEG, RC 91, fols 207–207v (1 November 1596), 246 (24 December), 248 (28 December).

127 AEG, RC 92, fol. 11v (17 January 1597).

128 AEG, RC 92, fol. 32 (28 February 1597).

129 There are scant references to the disease in the minutes. See AEG, RC 92, fols 67 (30 April 1597), 76v (20 May), 122 (13 September), 134 (4 October).

130 AEG, RC 93, fols 56v (1 April 1598), 62v (10 April). On 4 July 1597 Savoy had consulted Geneva about the outbreak, requesting that arrangements be made for mutually acceptable health certificates, AEG, PH 2208.

131 AEG, RC 93, fols 78 (2 May 1598), 100v (21 June), 108v–109 (21 July).

132 AEG, RC 93, fol. 109v (14 July 1598).

133 AEG, RC 93, fols 109v (14 July 1598), 150v (20 September).

134 AEG, RC 94, fol. 15v (29 January 1599). Thus the outbreak lasted only two years.

135 The final plague outbreak in Geneva lacked any appearance of the phenomenon. See L. Gautier, 'La dernière peste de Genève', *MDG* 23 (1888–94): 1–61.

136 AEG, RC 112, fols 10v (7 January 1614), 14 (11 January), 25 (19 January), 25v (19 January).

137 AEG, RC 112, fols 40 (2 February 1614), 44–44v (11 February), 59v (26 February), 70–70v (15 March), 108 (25 April), 147v (6 June), 148–148v (6 June), 152 (10 June).

138 AEG, RC 112, fol. 153.

139 AEG, RC 112, fols 228v–236 (17 August 1614).

140 AEG, RC 113, fol. 26v (19 November 1614).

141 AEG, RC 113, fols 36–40 (6 August 1614).

142 AEG, RC 114, fols 12v (7 January 1615), 40 (13 February), 77 (31 March), 78 (1 April), 78 (3 April), 79 (4 April), 89v (7 April), 174–174v (29 July), 180 (7 August), 188 (16

August), 209 (31 August), 220 (8 September), 239v (25 September), 284 (24 October). Letters were exchanged in 1616 with Lausanne, Morges and Vevey about the return of good health. PH 2522 (8 June–6 July). Cf. A. Corbaz, *Un coin de terre genevoise* (Geneva, 1916), for details of Geneva's rural lands and crime.

143 AEG, RC 114, fols 195–195v (22 August 1615, Senator l'Anglois from Chambéry), 210 (1 September, Lyonnais silk merchants wanted their goods released). Plague control, as well as diplomacy and economic trade, required an amazing amount of travel by rulers of small states. See Naphy, 'Liberty', 384–5 as well as Naphy, 'Diplomacy', pp. 189–219 (*passim*), and I. Bátori, 'Daily Life and Culture of an Urban Elite: the Imperial City of Nördlingen in the Fifteenth and Sixteenth Century', *History of European Ideas* 11 (1989): 621–7, especially 623.

144 AEG, RC 114, fols 77 (31 March), 184v–185 (14 August), 191v (20 August), 196 (20 August), 215 (4 September), 232 (18 September), 235v (20 September), 280–280v (23 October).

145 AEG, RC 114, fol. 196v (23 August 1615). Two people who died suddenly after the sermon were ordered to be buried quickly in the alley where they had died, fol. 189 (18 August). Also, see the disputes surrounding the funeral of a girl on 10 October 1615 (PC2: 2089).

146 AEG, RC 114, fols 197 (23 August 1615), 339–345v (9 December; the named individuals were fined three to 150 écus).

147 AEG, RC 114, fol. 189v (18 August 1615). For the table see fols 260v–261v (7 October 1615).

148 AEG, RC 114, fol. 195v (22 August 1615); PC2: 2086 (21–2 August 1615). Pierre Benoit (citizen, apothecary) was prosecuted after the outbreak when he caused anxiety by making an incorrect diagnosis of plague. AEG, PC1: 2346 (11–14 January 1617).

149 AEG, RC 114, fols 202 (27 August 1615), 204 (28 August); PC2: 2087 (27 August 1615).

150 AEG, RC 114, fol. 232 (18 September 1615).

151 AEG, RC 114, fol. 196 (20 August 1615): people were told to buy their medicaments from three specified apothecaries and that, if necessary, the state would cover the cost.

152 AEG, RC 114, fol. 235v (20 September 1615). Despite Geneva's previous experiences with cleaners, a contemporary medical work made no attempt to underplay the importance of fumigation and disinfecting, M. Chandelle, *Petit Traicte et familiar de la peste* (Geneva: E. Gamonet, 1615), pp. 7–9, 62–6.

153 AEG, RC 114, fols 237 (22 September 1615), 243v (26 September), 246v–247 (29 September).

154 AEG, RC 114, fols 248v–249 (30 September 1615), 276v–277 (20 October), 285v (24 October). For example, Louis, an *habitant* (son of Pierre Porret), aged thirty-two, had his goods inventoried to find stolen property. PC1: 2302 (18–22 December 1615).

155 AEG, RC 114, fols 292 (18 October 1615), 314v (15 November), 323 (24 November).

156 AEG, RC 114, fol. 186v (15 August 1615).

157 AEG, RC 114, fol. 189v (18 August 1615).

158 AEG, RC 114, fol. 201 (26 August 1615).

159 AEG, RC 114, fol. 204 (28 August 1615). The guard was strengthened two weeks later, fol. 220v (8 September).

160 AEG, RC 114, fol. 213 (3 September 1615).

161 For example, in 1543–44, 1568–70.

162 AEG, PC2: 2090 (20 October 1615).

163 AEG, RC 114, fols 206v (29 August 1615), 210v–211 (1 September 1615).

164 AEG, RC 134, pp. 258 (4 September 1635), 261 (9 September), 364–7 (23 November). City-wide regulations were promulgated on 24 November, pp. 367–8. Plague was noted in Zurich, St-Gall, Burgundy, Gex and Vaud. Why plague ends is still a mystery, though some theories have been advanced, e.g A. B. Appleby, 'The Disappearance of Plague: A Continuing Puzzle', *Economic History Review* 33: 2 (1981): 161–73.

165 AEG, RC 134, p. 267 (9 September 1635). As recommended by physicians. Alvarus, *Petit recueil*, pl. 43.

166 AEG, RC 134, p. 214 (9 July 1636). A similar report was prepared in Onex about the outbreak there to reassure Geneva, pp. 323 (22 November), 324 bis–sex (n.d. but inserted at 23 November). In 1637, Gailliard and Ternier sent a similar committee of investigation (RC 136, p. 239).

167 AEG, RC 135, pp. 220 (20 July 1636), 228 (29 July).

168 AEG, RC 136, fols 33–33v (28 January 1637, those fleeing were fined), 71 (8 March, Jean Siccard fined twenty-five écus for fleeing), 83–84 (20 March, Jean Patri fined eighty-six florins for entering the city from an infected area, Savoy), 116–117 (24 April, St-Jullien's regulations were examined), 117–120 (24 April, Genevan regulations were promulgated on the advice of Jean Sarrasin, secretary of state), 120–121 (25 April, more regulations were decreed); pp. 301 (28 July, quarantine rules were not being obeyed), 303–304 (31 July, foreign beggars were expelled).

169 AEG, RC 136, fols 22, 27v (18, 25 January 1637, Lyon), 83 (20 March, Gailliard and Ternier), 84–84v (21 March, Collogny, Nyon, Vaud).

170 AEG, PC1: 3028 (27–31 January 1637).

171 AEG, RC 137, pp. 129 (27 February 1638), 137–8 (3 March), 139–40 (5 March), 145 (9 March).

172 AEG, PC1: 2944 (24–8 July 1633).

173 AEG, RC 137, p. 439 (18 June 1638).

174 AEG, RC 138, pp. 420 (21 June 1639), 588–9 (30 August), 597 (3 September); RC 139, fols 30 (24 February 1640), 70v (15 May).

CHAPTER SIX

SPREADING THE PHENOMENON

Poor woman, you are so unwell. If you give yourself to me, I will make you rich

Just as plague was not confined to Geneva, the behaviour of plague spreading was also more widely diffused. The previous chapters have hinted at this, with comments on trials in Thonon and Brig as well as the extensive correspondence between Geneva and its neighbours. The French-speaking areas now in Switzerland (Vaud, Jura, Lausanne and Neuchâtel) also saw examples of plague spreaders. In the lands of the Duchy of Savoy (present-day Piedmont in Italy and the French *départements* of Savoye and Haute-Savoye) aspects of plague-spreading trials have been found in the archives of Chambéry, Annecy and Turin. Other places in France, especially those in regular contact with Geneva, such as Lyon, Bourg-en-Bresse and Dijon, were not unaware of the problem. Finally, the *untori* trials in Milan in 1630 have been made famous by Alessandro Manzoni's fictional *I promessi sposi* and his historical account, *La storia della colonna infame*. Though never 'endemic' to these other locales, as it appears to have been in Geneva, plague spreading was a feature of plague outbreaks and, as in Milan, could occur elsewhere in as spectacular a form as in Geneva. Nor was plague spreading solely a sixteenth-century activity. In addition to the spectacular trials of seventeenth-century Milan, Geneva suffered later sporadic cases after its three major periods of plague spreading (1530, 1545–46, 1568–72). An examination of this wider context is essential for developing a fuller understanding of these conspiracies to profit during plague outbreaks by sustaining the disease and targeting the rich.

Geneva's closest neighbour both geographically, politically and religiously had also once been a prince-bishopric. Unlike Geneva, however, Lausanne had not been able to shake off the embrace of the Bernese army of liberation. It gained its independence from Savoy and saw the establishment of Protestantism but remained a city-state very much under the control of Berne. As the second largest (after Geneva) French-speaking town in the lands dominated by the Swiss (i.e. Berne), Lausanne and Geneva were bound to be close. Lausanne was often the place where Geneva's magistrates encountered and dealt with the leaders of Berne (their military protector). It would be surprising if behaviour as widespread in Geneva as plague spreading were not found in Lausanne. Nevertheless, although there were plague spreaders in Lausanne, the few references surviving in the records would seem to imply, as we shall see, that there were substantial differences either between the behaviour itself or in the way the authorities understood it.

The earliest records relating to plague in Lausanne confirm that the greatest danger facing the population was not from conspiratorial plague spreaders but from individuals refusing to obey the regulations relating to quarantine. The most frequent problem was the movement of infected people through the streets – a complaint often raised in Geneva by the Senate and the magistrates responsible for enforcing the rules. On 24 May 1519, various ordinances were decreed in Lausanne forbidding the infected from leaving their homes. Those suffering from plague were to remain confined to their houses. The people who had been dwelling in these houses when the first person was afflicted were also expected to stay indoors. Any visiting, whether by officials, neighbours or relatives, was to be done by talking to people at the window. In this way, food could be passed to them by baskets let down on ropes and some conversational contact maintained.[1] Another problem faced by the city officials was the disposal of waste and refuse from such houses. They were quick to forbid the throwing of infected items out of windows into the street.[2] This concern over possibly contagious items most closely recalls the use of 'poisoned' handkerchiefs by some Geneva plague spreaders, especially in 1530.

Lausanne also faced the problem of identifying plague when it appeared. A diagnosis involved a substantial alteration in traditional activities and practices. On the communal level, the declaration of a plague death usually meant that a whole range of regulations and ordinances controlling and circumscribing markets, trade and individual freedoms came into effect. For individuals themselves, the notification that plague was present in a house could lead to the confinement of its inhabitants inside the building or their relocation to the pest house. A plague death also produced a marked, and agonising, change of custom. Plague corpses were rarely allowed burial in the parish cemetery; they were most often buried outside the town walls. Also, the funerals of plague victims were frequently restricted as to the time of day they could be held (usually at dusk or at night), the number of mourners (as few as possible) and the amount of ceremony allowed (the bare minimum). Once an epidemic had been declared the social standing of medical practitioners rose dramatically. Finally, sudden death from disease not only left families bereft but frequently left the state burdened with orphans, the elderly, destitute widows and the infirm.[3] All these aspects of plague are hinted at in Lausanne's records.[4] Lausanne was also forced to hire and maintain a number of poor people as well as trained medical men to staff its Plague Hospital (St-Roch) and to care for the afflicted.[5]

The picture of plague spreading that emerges from the references surviving in Lausanne is considerably more complex, and scanty, than in Geneva. There are only a handful of cases that relate to criminal activity under cover of plague. In 1548, Louis Guyuchet (from Thonon) along with Magnin and Berthod Ranni admitted that they had been robbing homes when they went to collect the corpses of plague victims.[6] However, the only clutch of cases relating specifically to plague spreading come from 1571–72, when much of the western Alpine region was struck by a severe plague and Geneva experienced its greatest outbreak. In 1571, the Lausanne authorities began an investigation of a certain woman named Guigonne whom they had arrested for 'greasing'. She had previously worked as a *cureuse* in Geneva and it may be that the case was prompted by information coming from Geneva. Indeed, most of the depositions came from Genevans or related to events there. Magdalene, the wife of Henry de Bellies, an Italian *habitant* of Geneva, said that the accused had been suspected of causing some deaths in the house where she had lived. Jean-Pierre Clerc and his son Paul, both silk workers, said that Jean-Pierre's wife and a daughter had died after the appearance of 'white grease' on the door of the house where they lived (which was owned by a leading Genevan, Louis Franc). They testified that they believed Guigonne had put the grease there, and on other houses as well. Further testimony was provided by Gabrielle (widow of Pierre Domenge), Christophle de Lussine (from Sentue) and Pierre Cobeiran (a merchant *habitant* of Geneva). The best construction that can be put on the case is that Guigonne had fled to Lausanne, where she had had previous contacts, having been married there. As Lausanne was frequented by Genevans, it may be that she had been recognised and denounced entirely without any actual information having been received from Geneva.[7]

Unfortunately, there are two serious problems in examining this case of plague spreading in Lausanne. First, the case clearly relates to events in Geneva. Second, there are not enough details to garner any specific information on Guigonne's actions. Three interrelated cases relating to 1573 are more specific to Lausanne and highlight the idiosyncrasies of plague spreading in Lausanne to the extent that they can be reconstructed. On 11 February 1573, Pernon, the daughter of Claude Ferra, a native of Lausanne without civic status (*natif*), called La Futier, was interrogated. The dossier does not name the actual charge against her, so it is impossible to identify how the authorities categorised her actions. She denounced, as accomplices, Antoina Borchet (called La Belaz) and Guillauma Floret and said that 'the Devil had given the accomplices some money and some grease that would kill people with plague'. The grease was in a box and applied by paper (to keep from direct contact) on Satan's command 'to the handles of the doors throughout the city'. She specifically mentioned having contaminated the door of George Groz's house.[8] At some point during the same year, the courts investigated Jaquema, the daughter of Tyvent Burtin, widow of François Guerra. She was also a *natif* of Lausanne. Antoina Bochet, La Belaz, had given her grease to her. It was in a small box and, she said, was made from, among other things, a serpent's head.[9] She had used this grease to contaminate specific houses as she moved through Lausanne in her capacity as a *marron*, or plague worker.[10] Finally, a related case was prosecuted in 1582. Clauda Baulx, from Romanel, the widow of Antoine Baleyson, was being questioned about her activities as a witch. Among other things, she confessed that about nine years before (*c.* 1573) she had been given some grease by Satan to put on the 'handles of the house of Dedegres in which Pierre Vert lived with the intention that anyone touching [the grease] should die of plague'.[11]

What is immediately clear is that, in Lausanne at least, plague spreading was almost wholly conflated with witchcraft. The conflation is even more advanced than in Geneva in 1571 and sets the Lausanne cases apart from the Genevan ones of 1530 and 1545. Except for those accused in 1573, the accused were acting as individuals. Even in 1573, there is no evidence to suggest a well organised conspiracy, nor is there any structure to the behaviour under the direction of trained medical men such as barber-surgeons. These plague workers seem to have acted on their own. To the extent that they were being directed, their 'ringleader' was Satan. In addition, although Jaquema Burtin discussed the grease as a quite natural (and potentially poisonous) compound, the testimony from the other cases gives no details of its manufacture. In Geneva (until 1571), the plague-spreading grease was made by humans under the direction of barber-surgeons. There, the grease was a natural and poisonous medicament. The Lausanne grease, although also designed to kill by infecting with plague, was of supernatural origin.

In fact, the use of grease and *poussets* or *pucets* is a regular feature of witchcraft trials preserved in Lausanne.[12] It is worth discussing a few of these cases in some detail, as the information they contain shows a highly fluid understanding of witchcraft activity in an area that should have had a fairly stereotypical view of the crime. The 'standard' elements of witchcraft had appeared in Lausanne trials at least by the middle of the fifteenth century and were apparent thereafter providing evidence that the 'model' was known.[13] Nevertheless, just as plague spreading in Lausanne followed its own unique path, so Lausanne witches were unwilling to conform to the stereotype. When one recalls the use or threat of torture one would quite reasonably expect them to confess the 'approved' and recognised pattern.

On 1 October 1524, Claude Rolier from Tercelin was prosecuted as a witch.[14] He had used the *pusset* given him by the Devil to kill lots of beasts. Satan had styled himself by various names, for example, Beelzebub and Raphael. Two decades later, Antoine (called Fasiolaz), the widow of Jean de Burgundy from Beauregard, confessed to a number of thefts. She also said that about 1534 she had given herself to Satan. She recounted the traditional aspects of the demonic pact: Sabbath attendance, kissing Satan's backside, renouncing God and getting money that later turned to leaves.[15] She had transported herself to the meetings by rubbing a special ointment on a white stick and saying 'Go, depart for the Devil, go.' She confessed that she had been given a lethal *pucet* by her accomplice Colette Pellietta that she had used it to kill a fair number of pigs and a few people (mostly women) with whom she had argued.[16] A decade after this trial, Bernard du Crest from St-Croix admitted to a string of thefts as well as contact with Satan (named Robin). His fellow thieves had enticed him into a demonic pact by saying that 'if you want us to become rich we should find a good master who will give us money so that we will never again be poor'. He had used the compounds given him ('boettes de pusset et de la gresse') to kill men and beasts.[17] In 1553, Jordan Roglier (from the same Tercelin that had produced Claude Rolier above) was prosecuted for sorcery and for using demonic grease to poison some food.[18]

These isolated cases simply served as foretastes of a more serious outbreak of witchcraft employing supernatural grease in 1576. A number of cases survive from that year. As a group, they are fairly similar. Two mention that the witches chanted 'Let everyone die' at their Sabbaths.[19] They all mention that they had been given grease by the Devil to kill both men and beasts.[20] Two cases noted that the grease was green and that they used a black stick to spread it on things and beasts.[21] Other cases corroborate these details and, for the most part, simply conform to the stereotypical confessions one expects to find in witchcraft prosecutions of the period.[22]

Although it is tempting to complete the conflation of plague spreading and witchcraft, they are not identical activities. Some witches used grease that they said would kill people by spreading plague. Others employed grease that was lethal in a general sense and used extensively against animals as well as humans. In most cases, this latter grease was applied directly to animals or food. One case exists where the grease was put on door handles in the manner of plague spreading without any mention of plague.[23] However, not every case of witchcraft involved grease. For example, Peronette (called Possidance), the daughter of André de Porta, widow of Louis Sonner, from Rolle, was prosecuted for witchcraft and poisoning. In this case, she was actually accused of two distinct crimes: witchcraft and attempted murder.[24] The same day, Pierre Mather (called Fournier), from Rolle, a bourgeois of Lausanne, was tried for witchcraft. Both De Porta and Mather mention Colette Pellieta, who had given a *pousset* to Antoine, the widow of Jean de Burgundy but do not confess to having received or used any themselves. Also, a few years before the 1576 trials, Madeleine de Monthey from Cressy had been executed for perjury, theft and *malefices* (witchcraft).[25] Finally, the mere mention of activities associated with consorting with Satan did not necessarily lead the judges to suppose a demonic pact lying behind the activity under investigation. That is, activities such as poisoning or sexual deviance were capable of being 'natural' crimes entirely bereft of any demonic associations.[26]

At first glance, it would appear that the phenomenon of plague spreading in Lausanne differed markedly from that in Geneva. In a general sense, that is true. However, as we have seen, by the 1570s even Geneva's authorities were finding that accused plague spreaders were often guilty of witchcraft and that suspected witches were very likely to be spreading plague. In Geneva, the two activities remained almost wholly distinct, as the plague spreaders were bound as conspirators solely to one another (albeit some were also separately charged with having made a demonic pact). Also, the Genevan plague spreaders, by and large, continued to discuss the grease as a natural compound made by themselves under the direction of barber-surgeons. The conflation of the two crimes into a single activity associated with the demonic pact is almost complete elsewhere. However, it would be dangerous to assert this categorically, as the number of surviving cases is small and a similar small selection of cases from the large quantity extant in Geneva could produce the same result. What can be said is that in Lausanne plague spreading seems not to have been seen as a well organised conspiracy revolving around the workers in the pest house under the direction of medical professionals and was normally (if not always) closely associated with witchcraft.

The information from Neuchâtel is even patchier but just as tantalising. Even more so than in Lausanne, grease appears to have been intimately connected with witchcraft. While this may support the classification of plague spreading as a type of witchcraft à la Monter, it actually does the opposite. What is clear from Lausanne, and even more so from Neuchâtel, is that the use of grease by witches was regarded as normal. If this connection is so strong the Genevan refusal to classify plague spreading as a type of witchcraft and to pursue lines of enquiry (and torture) for information on Sabbaths, etc., is even more striking. Also, the few accusations of plague spreading from Lausanne fit the stereotypical witch pattern but not the pattern of plague spreading encountered in Geneva. In other words, the information from Lausanne, augmented by the following details from Neuchâtel, may be evidence of suspected witches who confessed to using the grease to spread plague. That is, the fame of the Genevan plague spreaders may have meant the behaviour was being amalgamated into the stereotype of witchcraft as it existed in the French-speaking Protestant areas of the western Alps. In Geneva, the 'stereotype' of plague spreading was so well developed by the 1570s that it was able to resist the complete conflation of the two crimes.

One thing is clear: the frequency of plague in the western Alps and, indeed, generally across Switzerland, gave plenty of opportunities for plague spreading to occur. The plague that struck Geneva in 1530 was part of a general epidemic (and famine) that afflicted much of the Swiss Confederacy in 1530–31.[27] The catastrophic plague that struck Geneva in the 1540s was also part of a wider outbreak. In 1539–41, Basle reported plague and this seems to have developed into a much wider epidemic across Switzerland until spring 1547.[28] Although Geneva was spared any plague in the 1550s and 1560s, the Swiss were not. Undoubtedly, Geneva would have been greatly troubled to have plague so close: the death of 30,000 in the lands of Berne during 1563 must have been especially distressing and worrying.[29] Eventually, this plague was able to breach Geneva's defences in the late 1560s and was probably exacerbated by the wet spring and summer of 1570 that produced a widespread famine.[30] The last two decades of the sixteenth century saw plague in Switzerland about every five years.[31] In Geneva, the first three decades of the next century saw fewer plagues.[32] However, the decade from 1629 to 1639 was not only a decade of almost continuous plague (with Geneva's last major outbreak in this period) but also a decade noted for famine and a disease that killed both men and animals (1639, perhaps an anthrax outbreak).[33]

One might expect the records of Neuchâtel to discuss the impact of the epidemic on numerous occasions throughout this period, especially in the sixteenth century. A few comments will suffice to show that the situation in the city conformed to that found elsewhere in the area. The plague that struck Geneva in 1530 and occasioned the first appearance of conspiratorial plague spreading also struck Neuchâtel. Antoine Aubert, vicar of the city, administered the last rites to Guillauma Guyot as she died of plague. He also witnessed her will, which her brother had to write, as no notary was willing to get close enough to take it down. The city ordered that her body should be examined for signs of disease and the reluctance of the notaries investigated 'openly in the public thoroughfare'. A few months later, Aubert witnessed another will, along with Guillaume Clotuz, who was in charge of 'those infected by the plague'. Despite the severity of the situation, the city noted that a traditional local festival (the Bénichon) would be celebrated and that a troop of soldiers would be sent to aid Geneva. Presumably this was to help in its liberation from Savoy and was all the more daring considering the presence of plague in that troubled city.[34]

Not only was it a gamble to send valuable soldiers to a plague-ridden city but Neuchâtel was still struggling with the impact of Protestantism, which was causing considerable local friction and conflict. Antoine Jacetet, from Cressy (of infamy in Lausanne, see above), had been prosecuted in his village by the local officials for working on Good Friday because 'for time beyond memory and according to the rules of our ancestors it has been our good custom to cease all work in honour of the passion of our Lord on Holy Friday before the [divine] service'. The chatelaine of Landeron, Pierre Varrollier, acting on behalf of the temporal lord (Jeanne de Ochberg, Duchess of Longueville, Countess of Neuchâtel), ruled that he did not have to pay the nine sols fine.[35] Nor were personal shouting matches unknown, as between Hugo Virrichauls (from St-Claire) a clerk, notary and judge, and Antoine Bersot, a monk living in Cressy, over the ending of the Mass in the area. A similar shouting match erupted in a tavern when a priest, Louis Glanne from Cressy, interrupted the Grace being said by a Protestant preacher (Antoine Thomasin from Cornauld).[36]

These few cases have been mentioned for a number of reasons. First, they show how volatile the religious situation was in the western Alps and the strength of feeling over alterations to the faith. Also, the regular appearance of Cressy as a place of confessional fighting is interesting. Thus far, there has been frequent comment on the willingness (or not) of localities to conflate plague spreading and witchcraft. It is also possible, in this present context, to note that it may have been possible for the authorities, especially in Geneva, to take an entirely different tack. It is extremely interesting that a conspiracy to poison, and one targeted at the socially – and therefore politically – prominent never led to the suspicion that these conspirators might have a motive other than profit. One might have thought that someone could have suspected that they were working for a foreign power. Indeed, since many of Geneva's plague spreaders came from areas still strongly Catholic and, in cases, under French (later Savoyard) control, it is truly amazing that they were never accused of a religious motivation for their activities. In Lausanne, the tendency (and the apparent drift in judicial thought in Geneva) was to associate the perpetrators with an even greater enemy, Satan.

From the surviving records, the most important period for the appearance of grease would appear to be the last dozen years of the sixteenth century. We do know that there was plague, as noted above, in the decades before c. 1585–1600 but these have left no records of plague spreading. We do know that a treatise on plague was written by Antoine Royet, who left Lyon in 1564 at the request of the officials of Neuchâtel. Since both places had plague, his move can hardly be seen as self-serving. He devoted a chapter to the 'means of cleaning the houses, clothes, linen and other possessions of plague sufferers'.[37] It must never be forgotten that the work of the poor fumigators and cleaners, mostly females, was under the supervision and direction of medical practitioners and they had, by virtue of his advice, access to and the use of various powders and cleaners – some dangerous and poisonous. We do know, as in Lausanne and Geneva, that Neuchâtel had to provide itself with men to control the medical response to the plague. The records mention Daniel Huguenon, Petremand Huguenauld, Collet Hingely and Henry Brisel as hospitalers during the period 1583–99.[38] Money was a constant problem for communities facing the enormous extra burden of caring for so many afflicted as well as the drop in income and taxes from the near suspension of the economy and mass unemployment.[39] There was the normal trauma occasioned by so many deaths, travail that lasted well beyond the disappearance of any disease as small societies were forced to deal with the aftermath of the demise of many healthy, able-bodied citizens.[40]

In this fraught and difficult environment, grease did make an appearance. However, even more than in the Lausanne records, the Neuchâtel references to the nefarious use of grease are wholly and inextricably connected with witchcraft.[41] Unlike Lausanne (and Geneva) such use never extended to a specific connection of the grease with plague although in many ways the cases extant in Neuchâtel contain many features in common with those in Lausanne and Geneva. Although a handful of trials specifically mention grease, many of the surviving witchcraft cases focus on the Sabbath and contact with Satan (variously named Violet, Muguet, Manuguet, Jacoben, Perroquet – and frequently dressed in green or yellow with big, round cow-like feet).[42] The (green) grease or *pousset* was used to kill men and beasts.[43] When mention was made of a means of application it was by a 'white stick'.[44] The witches using the grease were not part of any conspiracy and, apart from one mention of door locks and handles, the grease was normally applied or given directly to the intended victim.[45] Plague, despite numerous outbreaks in the same period, never enters into the evidence.[46] The closest one gets to a motive being admitted in the cases comes from an accused witch, Laurenette (daughter of Gerber de Fenin), who said that when she had been in the forest one day gathering wood she had fallen under the heavy burden and burst into tears, at which point a man in black had appeared before her and said, 'You poor woman, you are very unwell. If you will give yourself to me I will make you rich.'[47]

Although the records of the ancient duchy of Savoy are almost as limited and even more scattered (in Annecy, Chambéry and Turin) than those of French-speaking Switzerland – the Suisse Romande – they provide a picture of plague spreading more in keeping with the pattern encountered in Geneva. The close connection with Geneva is at once understandable and surprising. Prior to the revolution in the 1530s, Geneva had been the largest city in the duchy (although it was technically an imperial free city its overlord, the prince-bishop, was a vassal and relative of the Dukes of Savoy). After the 1530s, until the restoration of the duchy in the latter half of the sixteenth century, the 'capital' of Savoy was located at Chambéry under French control. Thereafter, it moved to Turin. In either case, Protestant Geneva maintained a wary but intimate relationship with Catholic Savoy.[48]

This relationship also involved interaction during times of plague. Important as the disease was in concentrating minds, and disrupting trade, it was not wholly able to triumph over the demands of finance. While the willingness of the conspirators to use plague for gain is the best example, others abound. For example, in the midst of the 1545 outbreak, Marie Escoffier and her son François were locked in a property dispute with Pierre Ruffy (secretary to Geneva's Senate) before the (French) Senate in Chambéry. This included a complaint from Humbert Tronchon, officer of Geneva and Ruffy's messenger, that he had been kept cooling his heels for five days in Chambéry after making the lengthy trip from Geneva on foot. Considering the fact that plague had been raging in Geneva since 1542, he was lucky to have been admitted at all.[49] Although this vignette highlights the ability of people and states to continue normal activities despite plague (or revolution or Reformation), plague was also able to play an interesting if unwitting role in a negative sense.

In the 1570s, while plague was yet again pulsating (to use a sixteenth-century Genevan expression) in the republic, the newly restored Duke of Savoy was trying to finalise the return of much of the southern shores of Lake Geneva from the Swiss to his control (and Catholicism). These important negotiations were being conducted with the Swiss (Bernese), the French and the duke without the participation of Geneva. However, the little city was not forgotten. Berne repeatedly complained about the Savoyard military blockade of the city and its trade. The duke replied, on 12 March 1570, that it was 'because plague had begun in the city for quite a while'. Despite this innocent assertion, other letters make it clear that this was simply a convenient excuse for concentrating the minds of the Genevans on the need to support the Treaty of Lausanne rather than pressing the Bernese into being recalcitrant.[50] The tactic worked and Savoy regained lands including villages and towns such as Thonon, Chamonix and Evian.[51]

Despite these barriers to co-operation, communication and trade, the reality was that Protestant Genevans lived cheek-by-jowl with Catholic Savoyards, to the discomfort of both. Savoy constantly faced the problem of its subjects crossing the border to hear (and, perhaps as confessional tourists, enjoy) Protestant sermons.[52] Geneva had the same problem but its position was further complicated by the fact that the period of Swiss suzerainty had allowed many of its citizens the chance to purchase land and estates in an area that was eventually both foreign and Catholic. They could not have been pleased to hear about two prominent Genevan citizens, Claude François Revilliod and George Plongeon (Sieur de Bellerive), contesting a property dispute who were happy to appeal to Charles Emmanuel, Duke of Savoy, especially as Revilliod was relying heavily on the testimony of a local Catholic priest to support his charge of grievous bodily assault by Plongeon.[53]

Complex as the confessional and political situation was in the western alps, one must never forget that plague (and perhaps money) was a great leveller. The reality was that most states, regardless of their political, religious, economic or military circumstances, chose to deal with plague not only in a similar manner but also in a co-operative way with their neighbours (and, at times, enemies). Savoy's records show the same concern evident in Geneva. For example, the plague outbreak of

1578 placed an extreme financial and bureaucratic burden on the state, which needed to employ numerous hospital workers and care for the afflicted. The records of the hospital in the Marche suburb contain eighty-one pages of charitable donations to the poor plague sufferers. It also gives some idea of the sums involved in the work of the fumigators and cleaners. The cleaning of eighteen houses in January 1578 cost over 460 florins. In that summer, thirteen *cureurs* and *cureuses* were paid a total of nearly 2,000 florins (over 150 florins per cleaner). The same group earned another 560 florins (forty-three florins each) in the autumn. Over 1,000 dead were listed and over 250 dwellings had to be cleaned.[54] In 1630, a similar reckoning put the cost of cleaning infected houses at 8,109 florins (one house cost 800 florins alone), while the cost of maintaining the afflicted in the pest house and cabins (contained in a list of over sixty folios) came to over 7,300 florins.[55] Communities, in addition to these burdens, had to put an end to the violation of quarantine regulations, limit movement from other afflicted areas and hire as many workers as possible: Chamonix imposed fines of £500 (and others assigned arbitrarily by the magistrates) for 'frequenting places and people suspected of infection while the contagion continues here'.[56]

Not only did the towns and villages of Savoy behave as and co-operate with Geneva but they also learned from events in the city. For example, in 1530, the duke received a letter from someone conversant with the latest developments in Geneva:

> my most awesome Lord, I must also advise you that the syndics of Geneva have arrested the priests of the pest house as well as the *hospitalier* (who is from Fribourg) with his wife and children and, also, Michel Caddo as well as many others of Geneva who have been spreading plague in the houses, as they have confessed. Also they have plotted the spreading [of the plague] in all your lands especially at St-Jullien, Villas and Gailliard.[57]

Having long known of the phenomenon in Geneva, it is hardly surprising that on 20 April 1577 Chambéry published a plague ordinance that noted:

> because the said contagion spreads in many places by means of 'greasers' and plague spreaders, and such 'greasings' take place at night, for this reason, we ordain that in the said towns and villages there will be inhibitions and prohibitions against all people, regardless of the social status they have, going along the streets at night, after 8.00 p.m. or the sounding of the 'Retreat' without a light. The penalty for contravening these regulations will be, in the first instance, a £50 fine, £100 the second time and, on the third occasion, three applications of the *strappado* and other arbitrary penalties [decided by the magistrates].[58]

This regulation (and its subsequent reprintings) would have been as valid in Geneva as any part of Savoy.

The Savoyard familiarity with, and obvious fear of, conspiratorial plague spreading would, one might expect, have led to prosecutions for the crime. If it did, no records survive, with the exception of a single example from May 1600. Francesco Duco was arrested for having 'greased' (*onto*) the doors of some houses in

Montagna. Also, he had placed the grease on the Hospedale del Santo Sudario and the Hostaria del Angelo. The grease (ointment, unguent) came from Fortuna di Bordinato, a barber-surgeon. He had passed along both the grease and the means of making it to people from Montagna to Turin such as Claudio Rosset, Claudio Fiollet and Giovanni di Pongeti (a barber from Monteliano), as well as Luis Vugliet, Claudio and Pierre Sublet (all three from Verona).[59]

Although the details from this case are very scant indeed, being gleaned not from the actual prosecutions but from a letter recounting the events for the benefit of the duke, it is possible to make some interesting comparisons with the phenomenon of plague spreading as it 'presented' in Geneva as opposed to other parts of the Suisse Romande. First, the writer of the letter seems to assume that the conspiracy was a purely natural event. The grease was produced by men and, as in Geneva, by those with medical training. There is no mention of a specific oath binding the partici-pants together but there was the implication that it was part of some widespread enterprise. The lack of any reference to witchcraft places this late example very much in the mould of the stereotypical plague spreader as it seems to have devel-oped in Geneva in the 1530s and 1540s. Despite some conflation with witchcraft in the 1560s and 1570s, the pattern was still strong in Geneva at that time. What is noticeable by its absence is the involvement of any women. It may well be, though, that the writer was simply alerting the duke to the names of the key figures that had been arrested or implicated. While it would be dangerous indeed to draw any firm conclusions from a single case (as it would from the few in Lausanne and Neuchâtel) it is fascinating to see that there was not, in all places, an inexorable move to meld plague spreading into the more traditional and understandable mould of the witch.

It would also be dangerous to assume that the writer of this letter would not have been able to differentiate other types of conspiracy, murder or poisoning. One of the main features of the Genevan prosecutions was the careful, often quite subtle, differentiation by Geneva's magistrates between diverse yet very similar nefarious acts. Thus, everyone who endangered public health by spreading plague was not immediately classed as a plague-spreader conspirator. Some were simply seen and prosecuted as violators of the various quarantine regulations. That is, their crime was breaking the various plague rules rather than intentionally, whether singly or in conspiracy, trying to spread the contagion.[60]

The picture of plague and plague spreading that has survived in the records of other parts of France near to Geneva is almost wholly non-existent. At best, there are distant echoes attesting to the familiarity with plague spreading as a Genevan phenomenon or 'affliction'. Catholic France was unlikely to be surprised that Geneva was the source of such an evil, being, as it were, the fount from which flowed the infection of Lutheranism/Protestantism that truly terrified many of the region's rulers. Indeed, documents regularly refer to the new faith as an infection and a plague.[61] Geneva may have had its conspirators spreading a natural, medical ailment but for many of its neighbours in Catholic France the city's greatest danger was the effluence of a supernatural, spiritual disease. At Morbeau, Genevan travel-lers found themselves attacked by locals both as infected 'Lutherans' and potential plague spreaders. As stones (or worse) flew at them they heard the patois rallying-cry of the good folk of Morbeau: 'If you're not from Morbeau, get out.'[62]

Martin, in his work on Jesuits and plague, has preserved a number of stray references to the phenomenon as well as other forms of intentional plague spreading. Heinrich Blessem wrote that Protestants in Graz during an outbreak in 1575 accused the Jesuits of starting the plague by means of sorcery. In return, Henricus Vivarus noted that Catholics accused zealous Lutherans of starting the 1600 plague in Ljubljana (though, apparently, without the aid of the dark arts).[63] Two other reports of greasing come from Jesuits in Italy. Paolo Siciola reported rumours of *untori* (unguent/salve spreaders, greasers) in Milan during the plague of 1576–77 and again in Turin in 1577 and 1600.[64] Although these are cases of a variety of plague spreading it seems clear that they are actually of a different nature.[65] There is even a reference to similarly bizarre behaviour in a letter to Pepys about an outbreak in Southampton: 'the people are so wicked in that town that it is reported that they take their foul plasters from their sores and in the night throw them into the window of fresh [uninfected] houses'.[66] Closer to Geneva, though, the Jesuits noted a more familiar behaviour.

Oliver Manare and Emond Auger accused the Huguenots of Lyon in 1564 of being greasers of plague.[67] A similar account (without a specific confessional bias) survives from the great medical writer Ambroise Paré.

> Lastly, I judge it fit to admonish Magistrates that they have their eies and mindes attentive upon a murderous and impious kinde of bearers and nurse-keepers, which allured with a desire of gain (which whilest the plague reignes, they get abundantly) anoint the walls, doors, thresholds, knockers of gates and lockes with the filth and ointments taken from such as have the plague, that the plague within a while after seazing upon these also, the masters of them fly away, and the family dispersed, they may there reigne alone, and freely and without punishment carry thence what they please, oft-times strangling such as lye ready to dy, lest recovering, they might be their accusers. This I remember happened at Lyons, Anno Dom. 1565.[68]

Fifteen years later, another Jesuit (William Creichton) recorded the same charge but doubted its veracity.[69] The discussion of Lyon below will show that this was part of an aborted attempt to link the plagues of greasing and Lutheranism (both from Geneva) in the minds of Lyon's Catholics. Ultimately the project failed.

Two other nefarious acts need a brief mention in this context if only to show, yet again, the ability of people's actions to mix, and of judges to distinguish between, evil acts and conspiracies. During 1577, in Chambéry, Giovanni Battista Atanasio noted the arrest of twenty conspirators who were poisoning meat and fruit. An antidote known to their group protected them: twelve pulverised juniper berries were mixed with wine and two burnt nuts left to soak overnight in the mixture. In the morning, the wine was drunk and the nuts were eaten.[70] Finally, from the nineteenth century, in the colony of Martinique, there is a case relating to practitioners of 'white magic' being targeted by 'poisoning witches'.[71] Coming in the midst of various epidemics and diseases, the fear that food was being poisoned was all the more believable. Between 1831 and 1842, seventy-three people were denounced as poisoners and fifty-two prosecuted. Of the 126 eventually examined by the courts twenty-four were executed.[72] Perhaps one reason why magistrates and individuals were willing to believe in the complete naturalness of conspiracies to poison or kill with plague was that such behaviour was not as uncommon as one might expect. One need only recall that some muggers today use needles (possibly tainted with HIV) as weapons and that various societies have passed (or are considering) severe penalties against anyone knowingly spreading HIV through casual consensual sex.

One should not infer from the paucity of information on plague spreaders that little or nothing is known about plague in the areas of south-eastern France. Rather, for the purposes of this study and, especially, this chapter some of the other details are very interesting indeed. For example, one may recall that in the Suisse Romande the Devil who produced the poisonous grease was called Muguet or Manuguet, which is very similar to – through probably unconnected with – the patois used in Chalon-sur-Saône of those who worked with plague victims: *maulgognets, mailgognettes* (the equivalent patois term in Geneva and Savoy was *marron*).[73] These workers, along with the *saccards* (who dealt with the effects and corpses of the dead of plague) were an extremely costly burden on the town and were placed under the direction of the barber Guillaume Prevost, whom the city had to release from the prisons of Chatelet to work for them.[74] They were also required to wear yellow bonnets and carry long black sticks so that passers-by could identify them at a distance and avoid them.[75] We also know from Bourg-en-Bresse that the threat of pilfering exposed in the plague-spreading conspiracies was integral to plague outbreaks. The council there passed draconian rules (1523) punishing anyone looting a house abandoned by inmates in the pest house.[76] They also placed great stress on the role of an oath taken before the magistrates on a missal for ensuring the loyalty of their workers.[77]

Perhaps the most interesting survival and one that greatly illuminates the importance of the role of the cleaners comes from Provence (1721) in the aftermath of Western Europe's last plague outbreak, which swept away half the population of Marseille in 1720.[78] The 'General Ordinance for the General Cleaning of the Houses, Furniture and Effects of the Infected' was presented to the Provençale consuls on 27 February 1721 and gives a detailed explanation of the processes used to clean the houses. As the measures had not altered greatly (beyond becoming more complex) since their development in late fifteenth-century Italy they give a clear idea of what these workers were supposed to be doing for their employers and why it would have been so easy for them to pilfer or, worse, spread plague.

First, the workers were to be entirely covered in a costume of waxed linen, including gloves and glasses. This would ensure that the particles of plague adhering to the effects would 'slip off' their clothing. It is unlikely that Geneva's workers wore anything so complex, as this uniform appears to have been an innovation of the mid-seventeenth century. They should gather everything they can which is suspected of being infected into one room. They should then close and seal the windows, hallways and chimneys. Clothes' lines should then be strung across the room and the infected linen, carpets, etc., strung on them for a general airing. All the bed things (mattress, blankets, hangings, etc.) should be hung out of a window on iron hooks and the window then closed. The linen and cloths in the wardrobes and chests need not be removed but the doors and lids should stand open while the fumigation takes place. Mirrors, pictures and other 'precious furnishings that should not be smoked' should be covered with linen. Once everything is ready, the house should be cleaned from top to bottom and all refuse and dirt placed in a heap in the street and burned. The fumigator should then begin at the top of the house and set his 'perfumes' on fire in each room, making sure that they are burning properly before closing the door and moving to the next room, and thence to the lower floors and, finally, to the street to burn the heap of refuse. This fire will fumigate the items hanging on the hooks from the window. Four and a half pounds of incense should be used for large apartments, two-thirds for medium-size dwellings and half for small houses. The houses (and rooms) must then be left sealed for three days. After that, the windows and doors should be opened and everything aired 'to remove the bad smell of the incense' (as sulphur was a major ingredient, this would have been essential). Two days after the opening of the house, it would be safe to touch the goods inside. Someone should be responsible for overseeing the process throughout the city (in Geneva, as elsewhere, a magistrate or barber – and frequently both). A red cross on the door would have already marked every house that had been infected; once the process is complete the mark should be overpainted with a white cross (the 'all clear' symbol).[79]

Even if one eliminates the more *outré* aspects of this programme (e.g. the outlandish outfit), it is clear that the cleaners had unlimited and intimate access to people's houses and possessions. Moreover, they were responsible for going through their chests, drawers and wardrobes. They also set fires in the houses, undoubtedly raising the fear of accidental fire raising. In many places, as in Geneva, the linen was actually removed, especially from beds, and carried to washing places for a boil wash.[80] The hanging of infected cloth and the throwing of infected refuse into the streets threatened the welfare of neighbours. Finally, the workers were themselves 'coated' with the disease through their contact with infected goods, houses, sufferers and corpses. By the very nature of their work they were plague carriers and potentially unintentional plague spreaders. It would have taken little effort or credulity for them to become intentional, conspiratorial plague spreaders.

This was, in fact, what happened to these workers in Lyon and Milan in the late sixteenth and early seventeenth centuries. It is to these two great cities that we must turn for a final look at the phenomenon beyond Geneva. The obvious place to begin is Lyon. Lyon was not only Geneva's chief trading partner but also its greatest rival. The establishment of rival fairs there in the late fifteenth century had led to severe economic decline in Geneva, not reversed until the arrival of significant numbers of skilled religious refugees, especially those engaged in the printing trade, in the mid to late sixteenth century.[81] In addition, Lyon and Geneva were the bastions of two opposing religious camps. Save for a few years early in the French wars of religion, Lyon was a predominantly Catholic city. Thus two confessionally opposed cities were locked in an intimate economic embrace and, at the same time, both were on the front line of the political and military conflicts between imperial and Savoyard forces in Italy and the French and Swiss armies opposed to them.

The *Actes consulares* of Lyon's government are as excellent a source for the study of magisterial reactions to plague as the *Registres du Conseil* of Geneva.[82] A few examples will have to suffice to show the detail in the records, the extensive period covered and the similarity of actions to those found elsewhere before turning to a more specific examination of plague workers and plague spreading. Although almost wholly dependent upon the poor to provide them with plague workers, late medieval and early modern cities were also convinced that they were one of the most dangerous sources, or vectors, of the pestilence. In 1480, Lyon ordered the expulsion of the 'large number of impoverished beggars being dirty, dishonest, infected beggars who [like the plague] are swarming through [the city]'.[83] Public meetings (including religious services) were regularly suspended.[84] The situation in Lyon, though, was further complicated by the presence of the King in the city for much of the year.[85] The King forced the city to establish a specific pest house (the Hospital of St-Laurent) outside the city rather than using the general hospital on the Rhône Bridge. He also insisted that the streets should be cleaned of refuse during the outbreak of 1496–97 and that a city-wide survey should be undertaken to identify victims and their houses for cleaning and quarantine.[86] During the first major epidemic of the next century, in 1506, Lyon made desperate enquiries to find extra funds to meet the cost of the emergency. A total of £32 was raised in two months.[87] Basically, this pattern continued without serious alteration until the beginning of the seventeenth century. In 1598, Lyon was still using the Hospital of St-Laurent (by now over a century old).[88] By 1614, the St-Laurent as well as the smaller St-Thomas Hospital were 'empty and useless' and the city undertook a thorough and general rationalisation of all the buildings in the city used as hospices and hospitals.[89] It proved to be timely, as the following year saw the return of the plague and the reactivation of the 'accustomed office' (and system of regulations).[90] Lyon may have had a new building but, as in most places, the methods of dealing with plague were those developed in the late fifteenth century.

Accompanying this pattern (and eventually, tradition) of responses, the good consuls of Lyon turned to two classes of people to provide them with their plague workers: trained medical practitioners (mostly barber-surgeons) and the poor (as gravediggers, cleaners, fumigators and servants at the pest house). As early as 1453, the government had to offer generous and long-term financial inducements to persuade medical men to offer their services. A barber named Poncet and his colleague, Dr Conrad, were offered exemption from the *taille* (tax) if they would work with the afflicted free of charge.[91] While a cost-effective system, this was hardly a good idea, since it meant that these men had to maintain their private practice when no one would have wanted them circulating freely between plague sufferers and other ill people.[92] There was also the danger that the failure of the state to provide an adequate service would lead people to turn to the 'private sector'. In 1521, Lyon initially decided to expel private cleaners and fumigators but, later, attempted to regulate their activities by insisting that they had to wear a linen top embroidered with a red cross.[93] Thus was born state-regulated private medical care.

Within two years, this situation proved inadequate and the city decided to retain the services of two *marrons* who were to be given a uniform part yellow and part turquoise. Claude Bergeron, a magistrate, was put in charge of these workers.[94] Thus, at the same time as Geneva, Lyon made the move to a more 'nationalised' system funded and controlled directly by the state. The same outbreak that struck Geneva in 1530 was still raging in Lyon during 1533 when the magistracy decided to sign a contract with 'Jean Pierre de Siegnoribus, an *habitant*, [medical] practitioner, from Piedmont who is excellent at disinfecting places struck by the plague so that his talents may be used on this occasion'.[95] Lyon experienced a pestilence in the mid-1540s and hired yet more workers (e.g. Jehan Guillibert, barber) to care for the sick. They also followed his advice and insisted that the plague pit must be at least 7½ ft deep.[96] Moreover, despite being themselves infected, they still used the plague in Geneva as an excuse to stop travellers (and the trade in fresh fish) from entering the city.[97]

The 'Great Plague' that afflicted Provence in 1581–89 also ravaged Geneva and Lyon about the same time. A famous hermit, Brother Valerius des Fains, who lived near Aix-en-Provence, was known for his ability to clean and fumigate houses and the city decided to avail itself of his services. He and his workers were invited to the city and he was offered a house.[98] It appears that he came with a trained staff. This may, in part, have been in response to the criticisms being voiced by many leading citizens of the incompetence of the cleaners then being employed by the city.[99] Not only did the city enlist the hermit but it also hired Jaques Beyret, surgeon, for the extravagant sum of forty écus per month.[100] It also introduced price controls on meat, with a special discount for the afflicted.[101] A steady flow of drugs was guaranteed by strict controls on the barber-surgeons and apothecaries of the city.[102] The scale of the outbreak overwhelmed all these efforts (as in Geneva a few years before). The St-Laurent proved too small and even the use of cabins and the hospital's garden were insufficient.[103] Nor was the city able to supply enough workers for the demand and so it accepted the offer of the Carmelites to work with the infected.[104]

The parallels between the history of plague at Geneva and at Lyon are too similar, and the cities too closely connected, to expect that Lyon would never experience an outbreak of conspiratorial plague spreading. The situation in Lyon was complicated by the popular use of the term *marron*. It meant, as in Geneva, the plague workers (especially gravediggers) but it was also a common term equivalent to 'redneck', 'hick' or 'cracker'. As such it applied to outsiders (country bumpkins or any foreigner) and poor migrants (for example, from the Alpine valleys). The best example was the appearance of placards 'in large letters posted at the city crossroads' saying 'Expel the *marrons*, expel them, because if you don't firewood will get dearer; and you [*marrons*], keep away from Toulouse, because if you go there they'll burn you as they did De Molyna, the medical doctor'.[105] The government came to the conclusion that this was aimed at merchants from Spain who came to the fairs although (as it noted) 'they are not *marrons*'. It wanted the culprits found and punished quickly to avoid any disruption of the city's lucrative fairs.[106] In effect, a group of citizens (almost as conspirators) were attacking the perceived threat posed to the city by outsiders. This same nearly paranoid fear of conspiracies infected the magistracy itself in 1557, when they became convinced that there was a bearded Spaniard wandering about the countryside with a suitcase full of drugs (to poison all the rivers and waters of France) and incendiary 'apples' (to be lobbed into windows). His target was the King and the entire royal family. So concerned was the state that they contacted the Crown and sent a detailed report to Geneva asking the Protestant magistrates there to look out for him, as he had been rumoured to have stayed in the city at some point.[107]

These two examples, both ludicrous in their own way, serve as a salutary reminder that it was an age (not so far removed from our own) that believed in conspiracies. A further conspiracy at Lyon specifically involved both plague spreaders and Geneva. Near the end of the Great Plague (1586), the royal governor, Mandelot, 'having been warned about the plans and plots hatched in this city by those of the new opinion [Protestantism, supported by their co-religionists in Geneva]'. He called a general assembly of the populace to gather information and to discuss what was to be done. The plot was also aimed at Chalon-sur-Saône and Macon and they were to be advised of the threat. Since Geneva had no military and was, in any case, struggling to cope with the twin problems of recovering from the devastating plague of the decade before and the massive influx of refugees after the St Bartholomew's Day massacre, it is hard to see what realistic threat the city could pose. However, seen in the context of the conspiratorial scare of 1577, there is every reason to think that Lyon was frightened of a 'biological' attack. In the end, Mandelot concluded that the rumours were without foundation.[108]

The threat behind the panic of 1586 may well have been the possibility of plague spreading by Protestants. Two events suggest this possibility. First, two years later, Lyon was in close consultation with Chambéry about an accused plague spreader (greaser) whom it was holding. He had admitted to having spread the plague in Chambéry, where some of his fellow conspirators were held.[109] Thus, the possibility of a conspiracy to spread plague was probably never far from the minds of Lyon's magistracy. More important, in 1577, Claude de Rubys, one of the city's premier orators and a rabid anti-Protestant, had openly accused the city's Huguenots of conspiring to destroy the Catholics by giving them plague. This accusation seems to have been part of a development in his polemical thought. In 1567, only three years after the Protestants' control of the city, he delivered the annual address to the city government (and invited guests) to celebrate their recent election.[110] His speech was primarily a polemical assault on the Huguenots and a call to the Catholic magistracy to remain firm in its resolve against any resurgence of the new faith. The terminology he used in attacking the disgraced and defeated Protestants is interesting both for what it says of them and, in the light of his later comments, what it does not say.

He began, in the opening moments of his oration, by labelling the Protestants as 'seditious and rebellious disturbers of the public tranquillity'. He felt compelled to refer to these sad and troubling events because 'there is still a certain root remaining in this land'.[111] Although the theme of his talk was a refutation of the Protestant claim to freedom of conscience, he could not resist recalling Protestants' 'murders, sacrileges, pilferings and thefts . . . all [their] vices and sins'. Despite facing such a great evil, 'we have been able to purge and clean [*nettoyee*] our city of these lying impostors'.[112] Their 'plots and plans [*entreprinses*]' had failed.[113] Of course, it was essential to explain how a conspiracy so obviously evil had managed to succeed even for a moment. De Rubys's explanation was simple and reminiscent not only of the promises made to the plague spreaders by the barbers but also of those made to the witches by Satan: 'to some they promised honours [*grandeurs*], to others wealth [*richesses*] and to others freedom [*liberté*]'. And their chief source of aid? 'The city of Geneva (Geneva, I say, our too near neighbour) which stole, under the pretext of religion, due obedience from the Duke of Savoy and their Bishop, their true and natural sovereigns'.[114] Fortunately, the magistrates had (at last) acted to stop 'this poisonous plague [*peste venimeuse*] from coming any closer to us' from 'Geneva (Geneva, I say) that cauldron of all evil'.[115]

Already, in the first half of his speech, De Rubys was painting a picture of Protestantism. It was seditious in violating the natural loyalty that subjects owe their masters. In Geneva, this treason had cast off the Dukes of Savoy and the Prince Bishop. In France it was aimed against the King. All talk of the Gospel was simply a pretence to cover their true goals: the overthrow of Catholicism and socio-political revolution. Freedom of conscience, which they demanded for themselves but by force of arms denied to others, was merely a duplicitous pretext to gain the freedom to sin.[116] There was deceit, disloyalty and evil here. Metaphorically, Protestantism was a plague, a cancer, and Geneva was its font. 'Their evil conspiracy [*conspiration*]' was propagating by means of sermons 'full of poison [*venin*]'.[117]

By mid-oration (or, rather, mid-sermon) he was ready to deal with the 'thirteen months' of Protestant supremacy in Lyon during which the Catholics were persecuted and the Mass was suspended. He held before the magistrates' eyes the memory of 'the demolition of the grand and sumptuous churches, the violation of the monasteries, likewise the convents, the pollution of the altars and the cruel death of so many good citizens, faithful servants of God and their King'.[118] The Huguenots' 'evil plans and plots' had failed despite 'the vile acts of cruelty'.[119] The government was required to maintain 'your diligent and continual vigilance . . . against their detestable conspiracies and plots'.[120]

He then turned to address the Protestants, crying out (probably quite literally), 'Cease then, Cease, I say, you detestable impostors – Luther, Melanchthon, Beza, Viret – and all you who have also been infected, [cease] your sermons so full of sedition and discord.' He ordered them to stop trying to 'seduce [us], these traitors and rebels'.[121] He closed by reminding his listeners that 'by [personal] experience' they had become acquainted with 'their sermons, consistories, and all their inventions [designed] to overthrow the King and his Crown and to kill all of us miserably or, at least, to drive use from our houses along with our wives and children'.

He left his audience with only one option, to 'hold [the Protestants] as mortal and capital enemies'.[122]

While there is nothing extraordinary about this style of polemic in the French wars of religion, the reinterpretation De Rubys places on these events a decade later shows how he had developed his polemic and was attempting to reshape history as well as provide yet another stick with which to beat the Protestants. In 1577, he published an account of the plague that was then raging in Lyon.[123] However, much of his account relates to a retelling and recasting of the plague years of the 1560s, the period (coincidentally) when the Protestants posed their greatest threat to the city. The success of this (re)moulding of history may have borne fruit in the investigation begun by Mandelot in 1586 (in the midst of a plague) to examine the possibility of a Protestant plot against the city.

De Rubys began by explaining to his readers that plague had three major means of propagation. First, God used the pestilence to punish evil. Second, plague was the result of bad (miasmic) air. Finally, infected people and materials could spread it. At first glance, one would assume that what would follow would be a straightforward and fairly traditional discussion of the spread of plague. What actually follows is considerably more interesting. 'In our times, we have seen a phenomenon in many places . . . the greasers [engresseurs] who a few years ago were convicted and executed as a result of their own confession in the city of Chambéry and elsewhere'.[124] He then digressed to say that:

> I myself recall that in 1555 when I was a young student in Padua I saw hanged and strangled a Spanish doctor and some others who had been hired to clean the houses of [Padua], then afflicted with this disease, but who, instead of cleaning, had infected the houses with some plasters that this master doctor had prepared and given them.[125]

He is clearly speaking not only from personal experience but also of events in Chambéry that he assumes will be familiar to his readers.

At Lyon, as his readers were aware, fear of these conspirators had led to certain precautions. There had been a rumour of 'certain plague spreaders who were said to be going about at night'. The decision was taken 'to arrange a good night watch for the city and to place lamps and lanterns at the [city's] intersections'. The magistracy had also issued 'rigorous edicts and public proclamations against these plague spreaders, erected gibbets at every intersection and, by placards, these plague spreaders were assured that they would, if captured, be nailed to and hanged from the same gibbets [just like the placards]'.[126] Fortunately, God had arranged that the conspirators had been captured on the Rhône Bridge, which they had been greasing in preparation for the morning arrival of the poor washerwomen to wash the linen (of the wealthy).[127] Thus far, his account could relate to events in Geneva. However, although he mentioned Chambéry, he had been careful not to discuss any plague spreaders in Geneva.

He then turned his attention to the events of 1564. The Protestants had designed 'great and dissolute plots' to overthrow the Catholic authorities of the city, which was one of 'the most important keys' to the kingdom. They faced one significant obstacle to the realisation of their dream and that was the military garrison. The most effective means they could devise for overcoming the soldiers was biological warfare: 'they were helped to their goal by that great and memorable contagion of plague that was then in the city of Basle'. From that city they imported 'in bales of merchandise certain bandages infected by this contagion and these they smeared [semerent] throughout the city even to the house of the King and royal princes'.[128] Thus, he provided the events of 1564, already discussed in his oration, with a more sinister aspect. Not only were the Protestants spiritually infected with a theological plague but also they were using the physical disease to advance their cause.

When he turned to the events of 1577 of which he was writing, this polemic was overwhelmingly useful but considerably more difficult to maintain. Contact with Geneva was better controlled and local Protestantism a fading memory – thanks, in part, to the city's rather enthusiastic participation in the massacre of Protestants after the events of St Bartholomew's Day in Paris. Nevertheless, ever a resourceful orator, De Rubys turned to proving that, yet again, the Protestants were conspiring against the city with plague as one of their chief weapons. His greatest obstacle was explaining how Huguenot supporters had managed to infiltrate the city with infected substances. Of one thing he was sure, 'this city has no worse enemies than the Calvinists . . . [and] we can affirm with certainty [they are no less opposed to us now] than in 1564'.[129]

His explanation of the means by which this great hatred was expressed is worth quoting at length:

> They then [in 1564] made use of the plague in Basle and Germany, to infect this city, and now, in this present year [1577], they use the plague in Venice, Milan and Lombardy to the same end. In two or three houses in this city there are certain of their partisans [partisantz] called Grisons because their ancestors were natives of the mountains between Lombardy and Switzerland . . . But they have abandoned the faith of their birthplace as they have the place itself. Thus, under the pretext of importing some Italian silk (using the name, title and privilege granted to the Grison), they have truthfully introduced the contagion into this city by means of some plague spreaders who have, as if miraculously, by the grace of God, been discovered in the time, hours and place where they thought they were safest.[130]

His conclusion was that the Huguenots should be driven from the city and its environs for two major reasons. First, their very presence invited divine wrath. In effect, they could bring plague upon the city by their mere existence. Second, even without the intervention of God, they were likely to import the plague into the city themselves.[131]

Inventive as this polemic is, it is also interesting for a number of other reasons. It is clear that part of the presumed effectiveness of the accusations is the public's familiarity with the phenomenon. He makes no attempt to associate the activity with a demonic pact or the satanic production of the grease. Indeed, he uses the term 'greasers' although his story does not mention grease; the plague is spread by infected cloth (bandages). A number of other problems afflict the rhetoric. Most of the cases he advances have nothing to do with Protestantism. The Spanish doctor he saw executed in Padua in 1555 was certainly a Catholic. He makes no claim that the plague spreaders in Chambéry were religiously motivated. It was fortuitous that there was plague in Basle and Germany (both infected by Protestantism) in 1564, but in 1577 he had to find his disease in the more Catholic locales of Venice, Milan and Lombardy. The translation of the disease from these orthodox cities to Lyon by Protestants required the intervention of the merchants from the Grison, who had seemingly managed to keep their Protestantism a closely guarded secret. How they induced Catholics in northern Italy to hide plague in a consignment of silk is anyone's guess.

Indeed, the difficulty of reconciling his 'facts' with his interpretation is one of the things that lends verisimilitude to the details. A polemicist clever enough to devise this interpretation would certainly have developed more convincing events unless he knew he had to retain them because they were too widely known. Finally, the greatest problem he faces in convincing his audience is that he is unable to mention the Genevan plague spreaders. Unless he was going to suggest that the conspiracies of 1530 (before the Genevan Reformation and involving a priest), 1545 and 1570 were 'practice runs' for the methodology, any mention of Geneva would cause his thesis to implode. The speed and ease with which Mandelot and the city government in 1586 dismissed a possible Genevan-backed conspiracy may suggest that the inherent contradictions in the charge were apparent to everyone. The weakness of his interpretative model is that people were too familiar with the phe-nomenon. They knew the Genevan events well enough to think of them even when he refused to speak the name. He even avoids naming Geneva when talking about the supposed Huguenot conspirators. Everyone would have believed that the phenomenon of plague spreading came from Geneva, but they would not have accepted De Rubys's understanding of the role of Geneva (or Protestants) in its inception or development. His interpretation was clever and potentially devastat-ing but the (stereotypical) realities of plague spreading were simply too well known. The simplest and most believable explanation for the motivation of plague-spreading conspiracies remained that articulated by the accused in Geneva: profit.

We must turn at last to Milan to see to what extent the phenomenon of plague spreading there differed from or conformed to the diverse understandings we have seen elsewhere.[132] Milan was no less familiar with plague than any other city in medieval and early modern Western Europe. Nor was it unaware of events in neigh-bouring cities. One of the major concerns of the rulers of Milan was to prevent plague from gaining a foothold in the city, in particular, or Lombardy, in general. To this end, it was essential for Milan to keep abreast of the health situation of its neighbours, especially those along major trading routes. This interest finds repeated expression in the city's records, where there are frequent references to contact being prohibited with various towns and cities in France, Switzerland, Italy and even farther afield: Geneva, Lyon, Paris, the Grison, the Valais, Hungary, Croatia, Germany, Chambéry, Avignon, Vienna, Antwerp, Berne, Fribourg, England, Provence, Gascony, Languedoc. These prohibitions could be carefully targeted at even the smallest village (e.g. Martigny, Faucigny and Thonon) as well as regions (Vaud, Swiss areas around the St-Gottard Pass).[133] In addition to relying on information garnered from various sources, the health officials in Milan also relied on the use of health certificates to ensure that travellers and merchants presenting themselves (and their goods) at the city gates had not been in contact with any infected locales.[134]

Thus, one would expect Milan to have been aware of the plague-spreading conspiracies of Lyon and Geneva as well as the isolated cases and rumours of plague spreaders in Piedmont and the rest of the Suisse Romande. The plague of 1576–77, known as San Carlo's plague (an allusion to the tireless work with the afflicted by the city's bishop, later saint, Carlo Borromeo), left over 17,000 dead in the city (of some 100,000) and another 8,000 in the countryside.[135] This plague was the first major outbreak since the terrible plague of 1524 and was accompanied by a significant outbreak in Venice (1575–77). As was the tradition, one of the first acts of the government was to order that 'scroungers, beggars and vagabonds . . . must vacate the city in six days or face either two applications of the strap [strappado, corde] or a flogging'.[136] The obvious immediate threat, beyond travellers and the groups already mentioned, was the unintentional spreading of the contagion by infected citizens violating the ordinances.[137] Less likely was the concern the city expressed about the threat posed by Jews. Although most other countries in Western Europe had expelled their Jews in the course of the fifteenth century, Italy still had cities with significant Jewish communities. The city feared the rumour that Jewish merchants might be coming from Venice with infected clothing for sale. A number of local areas either prohibited the entry of Jews or expelled those already present.[138]

However, the city faced the greater threat of conspiratorial plague spreading. Milan's concern about the phenomenon dates from the earliest period of the phenomenon in Geneva. The Public Health Committee had offered a reward of 100 scudi to anyone offering information relating to 'two most evil men, moved by a diabolical spirit [diabolico spirito] who want to spread plague in this city' as early as 1545.[139] Fifteen years later, an Antonio da Treviso was hanged and quartered in Broletto for having used an ointment (unguent, grease) to spread plague in Milan.[140] In 1564, another decree remarked that in Piedmont (Turin) and Lombardy (Milan) 'certain men, sad [tristi], evil [nefandi] and inimical [nemici] to human nature are, by their unguents, powders and other diabolical means [arti diaboliche] trying to spread plague [here]'.[141] By the plague of 1576, the threat of plague spreaders had become a regular feature of outbreaks. The governor of the city, Ayamonte, on 27 August 1576 noted that concern about various Spanish soldiers included the accusation that they were 'using unguents [unguenti] to infect the city'.[142] The following month, on 11 September, he asked Senator Brugora, of the Health Committee, and the doctor Taboada to look into concern about the 'greasing' (ungendo) of doors in the city.[143] After investigations and the offer of a reward and immunity to anyone providing information on the plague spreaders, the authorities came to the conclusion that the conspirators were trying to prolong the plague in Milan so that they might 'become rich by robbing the dead'. This was not an entirely unlikely scenario even in the Milanese context, since, later, on 8 August 1577, the officials discovered a conspiracy of monks and health workers to reintroduce the plague into the city by means of infected articles.[144]

The next occurrence of plague spreading related to the famous plague outbreak of 1630, a full century after the first instance of plague spreading in Geneva. A number of sources survive relating to this plague-spreading conspiracy, the most important of which is the edited text of the trials themselves.[145] This outbreak also produced a significant number of contemporary accounts and analyses that touched upon the phenomenon of the plague spreaders, perhaps the most interesting and important of which was written by Frederico Borromeo.[146] There is also an extensive, if extremely idiosyncratic, treatment of the phenomenon by a modern author, Franco Cordero.[147] Finally, Manzoni has made the plague spreaders famous throughout Italy by his literary and historical discussions of them.[148]

The contemporary authors are unanimous in their association of the activity with the demonic. However, this statement needs some careful examination. Tadino mentions the 'unguent [unguento] . . . made by diabolical skill' as well as the role of 'diabolical skill' in the conspiracy.[149] Lampugnano, writing only four years after the events, makes similar comments. He mentions 'diabolical/demonic skills/arts [diaboliche arti]', 'these diabolic/demonic men' who had conspired to produce 'contagious powders and plague-bearing greases [polueri contagiose & unguenti pestiferi]'.[150] Unlike De Rubys at Lyon, he notes that the activity had occurred in Geneva (as mentioned by Martin del Rio) and, at about the same time (1536), in Milan where forty people had been arrested for 'making the same powders and greases for spreading the plague'.[151] He also cites other sources that mentioned the phenomenon at Lyon.[152] There is no doubt, therefore, that these authors are discussing what they perceive to be behaviour with a long tradition and identical to that uncovered in Geneva and Lyon.

Frederico Borromeo was just as clear in his discussions and explanations of the plague spreaders and their grease. His fourth chapter was entitled 'The deceitful work of the demons'. Although one then expects an account that stresses the Sabbath as well as the gift of the miraculous powders and unguents from Satan to the plague spreaders what actually follows is an account of how the greases and powders were made, using toads, serpents and plague secretions.[153] Nevertheless, while the grease and powders are man-made, the knowledge comes from the Devil. Borromeo mentions that all 'witches, sorceresses, sorcerers and other wizards have made a pact with the Devil' and this is where they gain the information necessary to make their poisons.[154] Clearly, he assumes that this activity is the result of some relationship or conspiracy involving the plague spreaders and Satan. They are guided and instructed by the Devil and believe they will succeed because he has made promises to them (as magicians and poisoners) that make them think they are immune and can kill at will.[155] When he discusses the actual methods by which these poisonous substances are disseminated, he follows the stereotypical patterns associated with witchcraft. The powders are placed in various foods and kill when consumed.[156] In his work, the conflation of plague spreaders with witches is almost complete. However, his conflation is not without its problems.

As with De Rubys, the interpretation he puts upon the phenomenon does not quite accord with the actual details mentioned. Borromeo discusses the production of the grease as a wholly natural phenomenon. There is nothing supernatural about the substance itself. It is not given to the conspirators, rather they make it. Satan's role in this is, presumably, to supply the recipe. Borromeo asserts that they have made a pact with the Devil but the details are not mentioned. There is no Sabbath, sodomy, frenzied dancing or any of the other stereotypes associated with the formation of a demonic pact by witches. Also, his work lumps together all those involved in demonic pacts and activities from witches (by which one presumes he means the stereotypical Sabbath-going woman) to alchemists, astrologers and magicians.[157] In his world a number of things have been conflated into the category of 'witchcraft' in addition to the plague spreaders. Or perhaps it would be better to say that he sees a continuum of activities derived in some way from a relationship with the Devil. All these groups of people are associated with a demonic pact because their 'skills derive from, or rely upon, the deceitful work of Satan'. In this interpretation, witchcraft, plague spreading, alchemy, etc., are all sub-categories of a larger group which one might call 'demonic/diabolical arts/sciences', rather than the main classification being called 'witchcraft' and the other phenomena the activities of bizarre varieties of witches.

The problem with assuming that Borromeo is discussing a form of 'witchcraft' rather than 'demonic science' can be seen if one looks at the area of heresy. The Milanese archives include a number of decrees relating to heresy. However, closer examination shows that they include under this heading both witchcraft and Protestantism. Clearly, the word can have both uses but the conjunction of the two in the same lines of decrees might lead one to assume that both are seen as the same thing. Clearly, in this area, heresy is the main category (or crime) which encompasses, among other things, two different crimes: witchcraft and 'Lutheranism'.[158] No one would ever conclude from this that early modern Catholics viewed Protestantism as a peculiar form of witchcraft.[159] They may well have considered it diabolical, sinful, illegal and under the spell of satanic lies but that is not the same as witchcraft. Even the mention of Lutheran synagogues (the same word used for witches' Sabbaths) does not imply a conflation of the two activities. Likewise, the use of *maleficium* and *veneficium* is problematic.[160] They can refer to a supernatural act as well as an 'evil deed' and 'poisoning'.

The issue devolves, yet again, to the possibility that the people dealing with plague spreading might be making subtle distinctions between various nefarious (in the sense of ungodly as well as evil) activities. As Cordero reminds the student of the Milanese plague spreaders, the plots (*crimino-satanici*) were variously imputed to the French, the Duke of Savoy, Philip IV, Gonzalo de Cordoba and papal emissaries.[161] It is clear that Borromeo and his contemporaries thought the plague spreaders were 'the worst possible criminals'.[162] That does not necessarily mean that they thought the plague spreaders were the same as witches who rubbed grease on a stick, mounted it and flew to a Sabbath with a cloven-hoofed Satan or could turn themselves into diverse kinds of animals. Many people had, or tried to have, contact with learning and power beyond the natural world. For some, that placed them in contact with the Devil and demonic knowledge. Two realms of super and supranatural reality existed. The priests and sacrament of Catholicism gave the people of Milan access to the godly realm. Plague spreaders, Protestants, alchemists, magicians and witches were 'plugged in' to the other source of power and knowledge.

The *untori* cases themselves (22 June 1630–18 December 1631) show behaviour that has much in common with Geneva. The head of the conspiracy was, as in Geneva, a medical practitioner, a barber-surgeon (Giovanni Giacomo Mora). Some of his co-conspirators were employed by the city to work with plague victims and the Health Committee (e.g. Guglielmo Piazza). The production of the grease involved fat rendered from corpses and the addition of secretions from plague victims. However, some significant differences are immediately apparent (see Table 12). First, the accused were all men. Second, the conspiracy involved relatively few people. Next, there was a close connection between the conspiracy and the mercenaries in the city, recalling the previous association of soldiers and plague spreaders.[163] Finally, a number of close relations (wives and sons) of the accused were questioned but never charged – something that would have been unlikely to happen in Geneva (see Appendix 7).

The supposed conspiracy came to the attention of the state when a woman reported seeing someone behaving in a suspicious manner at night and then grease was subsequently found at the spot.[164] The information concerning the individual involved was very detailed.[165] Also, torture entered the interrogation process on the very first day.[166] The piteous cries of Piazza as he was tortured are precisely documented and they certainly echo the pleas of the Genevan conspirators.[167] Also, at his second interrogation, and during his second session of torture, Piazza asked the question one normally associates with witchcraft trials, 'O, my Lord, what do you want me to say?'[168] Despite the plea none of the interrogations shows any signs of prompting by the magistrates. As far as Piazza knew he was being questioned about his activities in a certain street on a given night. At his third interrogation he confessed that 'a barber-surgeon had given him the grease . . . a barber named Giovanni Giacomo, I don't know his last name'.[169] The grease was yellow and relatively firm. The other details that followed were likewise unprompted. If Piazza was inventing a story for the benefit of his inquisitors and to avoid further torture, he was doing so without any specific guidance from the investigators beyond their continual command that 'he must tell the truth'.[170] Piazza said that he did not know what was in the grease but was sure that it was poisonous and was made from a human corpse.[171] All he would say by way of explanation was that he had been promised 'a good fistful of money'.[172]

The authorities then conducted a search of Mora's shop and house without telling him what they were seeking. Two finds interested them. The first was two containers full of 'human waste'; the second was a 'viscous material, yellow and white'. They threw it at the wall to see if it would stick. Mora insisted that it was

Table 12   Milan's plague spreaders: the accused

Name Sentence	
Baldassarre, son of Cesare Litta	
Benedetto, son of Attilio Lucino	Acquitted
Carlo Vedano (called il Tegnone, arrested at Ossona and brought to Milan)[a]	Acquitted
Carlo, son of Fabriccio Crivelli	Acquitted
Francesco (called il Saracco), son of Bernardo Grioni	Acquitted
Francesco Massaglia	
Gaspare, son of Gerolamo Migliavacca	Executed
Gerolamo Migliavacca (called il Foresaro)	Executed
Gerolamo, son of Giovanni Turconi, *banchiere*	Acquitted
Giancinto Maganza, son of a friar, vagabond, called il Romano	
Giovani Ermes, son of Franceso Lampugnani, prisoner	
Giovanni Battista, son of Dionigi Ferrari, Mora's servant	
Giovanni Battista, son of Giovanni Paolo Cinquevie	Acquitted
Giovanni Battista, son of Giulio Sanguinetti, *banchiere*	Acquitted
Giovanni Battista, son of Giuseppe Bazio (called l'Inspiritato)	
Giovanni Battista, son of Orazio de Strigella	
Giovanni Gaetano, son of Francesco de Padilla, from Pizzighettone (Piceleonis)[b]	Acquitted
Giovanni Giacomo, son of Cesare Mora, barber, native of Milan	Executed
Giovanni Stefano, son of Pietro Paolo Baruello, died of plague in prison	
Guglielmo, son of Dominico Piazza, *commissario*	Executed
Matteo, son of Santo del Furno, brother-in-law of Guglielmo Piazza	
Pietro (called il Vacazza) Corona	
Pietro Francesco Tentore (called il Levo)	
Pietro Gerolamo, son of Melchione Bertoni	Executed
Pietro Verdeno, from Saragozza, soldier	

Notes

[a] 'Io facevo scola da srimia ho moglie' (Hortensia, daughter of Pietro Francesco Fontana, *bombardiere*, known to Giovanni Gaetano de Padilla).

[b] Called 'imputato principale'.

smoglio (grease).[173] Both his son and wife were questioned. The court was trying to prove that he both knew and had had recent contact with Piazza. Mora had denied knowing any particular *commissario* other than three he knew and said that he did not know their names. Mora's son said he knew Piazza by sight but Mora's wife denied knowing him.[174] A doctor, Giovanni Battista Vertua, and an official, Vittore Bescapè, were unable to identify the *smoglio* or to guess at its use. They were fairly certain that it was not what Mora said it was.[175] He was also questioned about the ointment, which he said was a plague cure or preventative.[176] Finally, he was taken to be tortured on 30 June 1630.[177] When he finally confessed to making the grease he related an entirely natural process.[178] The next day, after saying an Ave Maria and praying before a crucifix, he retracted his confession.[179]

When, in the course of the investigation, the name of Gerolamo Migliavacca was mentioned as an acquaintance of the defendants, he too was arrested. His house was searched.[180] They also examined Matteo del Furno, Baldassarre Litta, and Stefano Baruelo. Again, these men were seen in the company of Mora and/or Piazza.[181] As in Geneva, the main thrust of the questioning was to get the accused to admit that they knew one another and that they had been in recent contact. Any deviation or variation in their answers or discrepancies between what they said and what other witnesses had related were grounds for suspicion that they were lying. Once the court became convinced that the defendants were perjuring themselves they felt able to proceed to torture to get them 'to confess, by their own mouths, the truth'.[182]

The investigation proceeded much as in Geneva. Once the first defendants had been executed the cases against the later defendants tended to evaporate. The Milanese authorities used torture much more quickly in the investigatory process than would have been the case in Geneva. However, they had witnesses who put Piazza at the place where the grease was found behaving in a very suspicious manner. In addition to which, he initially denied being near the spot. Legally, he had perjured himself at the first interrogation and, therefore, made himself eligible (if one can use that word) for judicial torture. Mora's eventual explanation, that he had intended not to kill anyone but only that they should become ill, would seem to imply that the motivation (as seen elsewhere) was to prolong the plague.[183] Even when he again admitted that the grease was meant to kill and that he had been commissioned by Padiglia (alias Gaetano) and Sanguinetti he said the motivation was profit.[184]

One important consideration must be raised in relation to the trials themselves. If the authorities thought they were dealing with demonic activity and witchcraft they certainly made no effort to reveal their suspicion. Before their execution at the beginning of August, Mora and Piazza were never asked about any contact with Satan, nor did they express anything along those lines. Indeed, the first mention of the Devil came in the initial testimony of Bazio. When he was asked whether he knew Gerolamo Miglivavacca he said that he did and 'hated him more than the Devil hates holy water'.[185] It was not until 12 August that the authorities began to refer to the executed Mora and Piazza as 'men criminal, diabolical and inimical to God'.[186] The single significant confession relating to a demonic pact and the role of the Devil in the activity comes from the interrogations of Stefano Baruello.[187] He was specifically asked whether he had made any pact with the Devil and was told if he had to renounce it and commend his soul to God; he renounced the pact and threw himself on the mercy of the Lord.[188] He asked for a priest and was exorcised, renouncing 'Gola Gilba', a Jewish name for Satan.[189] However, as often in the Genevan cases, the authorities quickly turned the discussion away from the supernatural back to the very natural confessing of details and the names of other conspirators. Indeed, the primary association of this behaviour with 'diabolical arts' comes not from the cases themselves but from the glosses and interpretations placed on the phenomenon by contemporary authors such as Borromeo.

What one finds in Milan is that the trials themselves evidence features very similar to those in Geneva during 1530 and the 1540s. The judges are overwhelmingly concerned with the details of the activity as well as the names of possible co-conspirators. When demonic pacts or other aspects of witchcraft enter the discussion they are usually treated as a distraction or an additional crime. They are certainly not perceived to be an integral part of the crime under investigation. Baruello was certainly the most forthcoming and loquacious of the defendants and, among other things, his testimony led the judges to believe that he was involved in a demonic pact and perhaps possessed. Although this temporarily diverted their investigation it did not divert it into a new direction. Very quickly they returned to the mundane and extremely natural pursuit of a wholly human, albeit diabolically evil, conspiracy.

It is important to recall in conclusion that the involvement of conspirators or medical practitioners in cases prosecuted during plague years did not immediately lead to the suspicion of any plague spreading. Individuals could spread plague by breaking the ordinances. They could poison.[190] They could conspire to murder.[191] Medical men could use their expertise for evil.[192] None of this led to a charge of intentionally conspiring to spread plague although each was a part of the pattern. Unlike witchcraft (where the presence of one activity, e.g. Sabbath-going, almost inevitably produced confessions under torture of the whole stereotypical paraphernalia) the very 'naturalness' of the plague-spreading conspiracies militated against an easy or speedy application of a patterned straitjacket to certain cases involving set groups of people or crimes. One hypothesis may well be that the complexity of the situation as well as the diabolical nature of the crime led authorities to cast about for a more comprehensible explanation of the phenomenon. Although not ideally suited to the task, the witchcraft stereotype was malleable and involved enough similar features to serve the purpose. In other words, the plague spreaders were diabolical and directed by Satan. Where possible, judges may have been inclined to suspect that the confessed plague spreader before them might have committed activities more suited to the normal witchcraft stereotype. Where they made the connection and asked the right questions, under torture, their suppositions were confirmed. However, they did not always ask such questions and, even when they did, they often made it clear in the summation and sentence that they viewed the activities as distinct crimes.

The evidence from places other than Geneva suggests that where a single plague spreader was arrested the conflation was complete: the defendant was a witch, and spreading grease, whether plague-bearing or not, was but one of the activities. When the authorities were confronted with large-scale examples of the phenomenon, they seem not to have assumed a clear connection. Some of the conspirators might, individually and separately, be witches but the conspiracy was not witchcraft. In these cases, the most frequent interpretation of the behaviour was that it was motivated by greed and malice. The acts of the conspirators, including the preparation of the grease, were a wholly natural activity, regardless of how they learned of the recipe. When alternative interpretations were advanced, they tended to sit uneasily with the facts presented by the revisionists themselves. For example,

De Rubys tries valiantly yet ultimately fails to convince in his assertion that plague spreading was simply some complex, subtle and devious plot of the Huguenots. Likewise, the various authors contemporary with the 1630 Milan plague clearly consider the plague spreaders to be in the same 'demonic' camp as witches (and, one might add, Protestants and alchemists) without making the events any less natural in methodology or base in motivation.

NOTES

1 AVL, B11, unfoliated but dated.
2 AVL, B11 (3? July 1520).
3 Though one should not overplay the plight of widows, for example. See M. W. Wood, 'Paltry Peddlers or Essential Merchants? Women in the Distributive Trades in Early Modern Nuremburg', *SCJ* 12: 2 (1981): 3–13. Likewise, one cannot dismiss the long-term psychological impact of death on this scale. See, for example, the comment by Elisabeth Charlotte (Duchesse d'Orléans) fifty years after the death of her eldest son that 'I thought I must go mad. This pain cannot be imagined by someone who had never had a child. It is as if one's heart were torn out of one's body,' in E. Forster, 'From the Patient's Point of View: Illness and health in the Letters of Lisolette von der Pfalz, 1652–1722', *Bulletin of the Society for the History of Medicine* 60: 3 (1986): 297–320, especially 307.
4 For example, see AVL, B31/2, fols 29v (1 July 1572), Pierre Langin, a *bourgeois*, had died of plague, leaving an orphan daughter 'of a minor age' as a ward of the state; 42v (16 September 1575), Jaques Levriere, a *bourgeois* and surgeon was consulted about the plague; 76v–77 (3 January 1581), official notification that Jaques Parains had indeed died of plague on St Martin's Day 1580.
5 See AVL, D734, Aultres livrées de froment pour les marrons et guytes des pestifferez (unfoliated but dated 1565) where grain was distributed to Estienne Flamant (barber-surgeon for plague sufferers); Louis Forjoz and Claude Molliat (servants at the St-Roch Hospital); Claude Langin, his wife, and Louis Hyverez ('marrons').
6 ACV, Bh10/2, fol. 19–22v (8 August 1548).
7 AVL, E45, fol. 398 (29 July 1571).
8 AVL, E45, fols 315–317v.
9 For the place of serpents (and their close cousin, dragons) in understanding plague see P. Horden, 'Disease, Dragons and Saints: the Management of Epidemics in the Dark Ages', in T. Ranger and P. Slack, eds, *Epidemics and Ideas* (Cambridge, 1992), pp. 45–76.
10 AVL, E45, fols 517–519v. No date survives but a later index dates it to 1573. However, the same hand (probably nineteenth-century) in that index, despite the lack of references to Satan, Sabbaths or witchcraft, also labels this trial as a case of 'sorcellerie'.
11 AVL, E45, fols 236–239v (10 August 1582).
12 *Pousset, pusset, poussat, poulsat* is a word from the Suisse Romande and Provence that means 'magical & poisonous powder given by Satan to witches to perform their evil acts'. Pierrehumbert, *Neuchatelois*, pp. 448–9. In Vaud it could also mean 'a powder derived from medicinal plants', while in Provence it meant 'dust, fine sand or grains of corn'. It derived from *pousse*, a word used for fine, wind-blown snow. In more standard French, *pousset* could mean either a particular illness afflicting sheep or 'granules of bronze (shot)'. Poisonous greases and powders were included in the paraphernalia of

plague spreaders, witches and other poisoners. They need not, by definition, be magical.

13 ACV, Ac29 (unfoliated but dated), contains two cases that mention most of the 'normative' elements of Satanic pacts. However, even these are 'abnormal' in that the two witches were both men. See 30 July 1438 and the case of Aymonet (called Cossandes), son of Jaques Mangetaz, who consorted with Satan (in the form of a 'black man') at Sabbath, where he kissed his backside and allowed himself to be sodomised. Also 3 April 1448, where Pierre Chavaz confessed to the details of a Sabbath that included sodomy (but only of women, not himself).

14 ACV, Bh10/2. Lausanne witchcraft cases involve an abnormally large number of men.

15 For other types of demonic activity see A. M. Walker and E. H. Dickerman, '"A Woman under the Influence": A Case of Alleged Possession in Sixteenth Century France', *SCJ* 22: 3 (1991): 535–54.

16 AVL, E45, fols 410–412v (13 September 1541).

17 AVL, E45, fols 404–408 (10 July 1551).

18 ACV, Bh10/3, pp. 313–28 (22 August 1553).

19 AVL, E45, fols 420–425 (n.d., but bound with the 1576 trials and sharing a number of internal similarities), 521–524v (25 February 1576). The first case is that of Ayma (called Chenallet), daughter of Jean Fattye, widow of François George; the second, Clara, daughter of Claude Clerc, wife of Thivent Martin. All were from Cressy.

20 Satan appeared to them as a small black or dark bluish-green man named Robert or Raphael.

21 AVL, E45, fols 479–486 (26 June 1576), 505–508 (25 February 1576). The first case is of François, son of Jean Bosson from Villard (living in Bussigny); the second, Guillauma, daughter of Louis Chappelle from Freney, near Brig, wife of François Tissot from (the infamous) Cressy. A similar case exists from 24 January 1581, where Marie, daughter of Pierre Rey, wife of Pierre Fontanna from Faucigny admitted to sorcery and 'greasing'. ACV, Bh10/3, fols 703–710. See also ACV, Bh10/1, fols 215–217v (24 February 1624), for a similar confession from a Pierre Blondez.

22 See also AVL, E45, fols 498–502 (3 March 1576), and ACV, Bh10/3, pp. 593–608 (1 March 1576), 625–632 (15 June 1576). These cases involve, respectively, Pernon Prochet, the widow of Pierre Verey from Cressy; Antoine, daughter of Claude de Cloz from St-Croix; and Antoine, son of Jean du Mont from Bussigny.

23 ACV, Bh10/2, fols 107–109v (10 December 1606), Pernette, daughter of Jaques François from Faucigny (in Savoy), admitted that she had contaminated the door of a certain merchant named Pierre. She did not know whether the grease had worked but her intention was that he would die.

24 AVL, E45, fols 392–393v (9 August 1530).

25 AVL, E45, fol. 196 (9 April 1572).

26 See, for example, the case of poisoning brought against Bartholomea Evrad, widow of François du Four from Escublans. She had tried to kill her son-in-law, Michel Avenna, using a variety of poisons, including serpent's head, to no effect (other than giving him headache and making him very ill). Her attempt to get her nephew to buy some arsenic from an apothecary when he returned with another substance (she refused to pay him), AVL, E45, fol. 577 (4 June 1550). Also, the case of sodomy prosecuted against Claude, son of Mermet Plagniez from Evian, and Pauloz Chopin on 7 February 1604 (ACV, Bh10/1, fol. 140–143). For more on sodomy see S. Cohn, 'Criminality and the State in Renaissance Florence, 1344–1466', *Journal of Social History* (1980): 211–33.

27 Boyve 2: 330. Witches were often accused of causing famines, see H. Lehmann, 'The Persecution of Witches as Restoration of Order: the Case of Germany, 1590s-1650s', *Central European History* 21: 2 (1988): 107–21. For a case study of the dramatic impact of famine see D. Sella, 'Coping with Famine: the changing Demography of an Italian Village in the 1590s', *SCJ* 22: 2 (1991): 185–97.

28 Boyve 2: 421, 467, 485. For an excellent study of another Swiss city see F. Hatje, *Leben und Sterben in Zeitalter der Pest. Basel in 15. bis 17. Jahrhundert* (Basle, 1992).

29 Boyve 2: 510 (Basle, 1550–53); 3: 115 (1563, 4,000 dead in Basle), 134 (1564, Berne); 148 (1565).

30 Boyve 3: 172.

31 In 1575, 1577, 1582 (1,200 died in Basle), 1587 (with another famine), 1593 (another 900 dead in Basle), 1594 (Neuchâtel was badly struck), 1595, 1599. Boyve 3: 208, 231, 265, 298, 322, 329–30, 338, 255. The continual plagues in Provence in 1581–89 (the worst of the fourteen outbreaks in the sixteenth century) were called the 'Great Plague' or 'the Seven Year Plague'. See René Bruni, *Le Pays d'Apt malade de la peste* (Aix-en-Provence, 1963), p. 21.

32 In 1608 (Neuchâtel), 1609 (6,400 died in Basle), 1610 (a 'large mortality' was noted), 1612. Boyve 3: 371, 378, 402, 404.

33 See Boyve 4: 13, 18, 33, 35, 39, 42. He notes that chroniclers said that 1630 saw 'villages reduced to desert and grass grew across the roads'. In 1635, so many clergy died that many pulpits were left vacant for want of suitable candidates. Accounts from 1638 said that 'plague had raged throughout [the Confederacy]' since 1629.

34 See Rémy Scheurer, 'Farel et les Neuchâtelois de juillet à septembre 1530', in P. Barthel, R. Scheurer and R. Stauffer, eds, *Actes du Colloque Guillaume Farel* (Neuchâtel, 1983), vol. 1, pp. 83–7 (especially p. 87).

35 AEN, AJLL, MJLL 5: fols 28, 40 (22 April 1534). By the 1540s the overlord was François d'Orléans, Duke of Longueville, Count of Neuchâtel (see AEN, AJLL, MJLL 7, unfoliated but dated 8 December 1544).

36 AEN, AJLL, MJLL 7 (? July 1540/41).

37 See Edouard Cornaz, 'Le Diacre Antoine Royet et son traité de la peste, publié en 1583', in *Musée Neuchatelois* (1901): 109–18, especially 111–15.

38 See, for example, the undated documents in AEN, AJN, MJN 4, fol. 21 (1583); 5, fol. 22 (1583–86); 6, fols 48–49, 92v (1587–92); 7, fols 59v–60 (1593–99).

39 See, AEN, AJN, MJN 6, fols 15, 115v (a dispute over the hospitals funds), 59 (a dispute between a doctor and an apothecary), 75 (a large bequest to the hospital and *malladiere* by David Chaillet, minister).

40 See, for example, the various legal appeals relating to the estates of plague dead accompanying the outbreak of 1567: AEN, AJN, MJN 2, fols 91 (23 January 1568), 92 (22 October 1567), 93 (22 January 1567), 96 (16 January 1567), 115 (22 January 1567). Plague's trauma was, in part, because of its propensity for killing men in their prime. For one possible explanation of this see S. R. Ell, 'Iron in two Seventeenth Century Plague Epidemics', *Journal of Interdisciplinary History* 15:3 (1985): 445–57.

41 Cf. F. Chabloz, *Les Sorcieres neuchâteloises* (Neuchâtel, 1868).

42 For examples of the latter see a large clutch of cases dating to 1583: AEN, AJN, PCN 241, 117 (Janne Berna from Cluse, 5 January), 123 (Pernon, daughter of Mechie de Brot, 16 January), 133 (Eslise le Ruyer, 19 January), 139 (Marie, daughter of Hugonin Breguet, 21 January), 151 (Jean Prendon, 1 February), 155 (Pernon, daughter of Jean Gerard, 22 February), 165 (Marguerite, daughter of Jean Junoud, 17 February).

43 For the colour see AEN, AJN, PCN 241, fol. 67 (Claude, daughter of Pierre Marinet from Ternier, wife of George Jaquin, 16 November 1593).

44 AEN, AJN, PCN 241, fol. 79 (Catherine, daughter of Pierre Pomez, widow of Pierre Mathiez, 13 March 1599).

45 AEN, AJN, PCN 241, fol. 147 (Madeleine Merlou, 1 February 1583).

46 See also AEN, PCN 241, fols 81 (Jaqua, daughter of Blaise du Bird, widow of Estienet Salla, 13 March 1599), 91 (Blaise Cartier, widow of Claude Lambert, a former resident of Neuchâtel, 23 October 1601), as well as the case of Margeren, wife of Guillaume Boucard from 31 July 1610, in A. Quiquerez, 'Les sorciers du Val-de-Ruz et de la Neuveville', *Musée Neuchatelois* (1867): 4–13, at 7.

47 Quiquerez, 'Les sorciers', 7.

48 For more on Savoy in this period with special reference to medical history see R. Devos and B. Grosperrin, eds, 'La Savoie de la Réforme à la Révolution française', in J. P. Laguay, *Histoire de la Savoie* (Rennes, 1985), especially vol. 3, pp. 126–31; E. Burnier, *Histoire du Sénat de Savoie et des autres compagnies judiciaires* (Paris, 1864–65), especially vol. 1, pp. 1329–630; the five articles in the *Revue savoisienne* by C. A. Ducis, 'Hôpital des pestiférés', 13: 7 (25 July 1872): 57–8, 'L'Hôpital morbeaux ou des pestiférées', 13: 8 (25 August 1872): 65–6, 'L'Hôpital morbeaux de la Culaz', 13: 9 (25 September 1872): 72–4, 'Henri de Savoie et Anne de Lorraine', 23: 5 (21 May 1882): 37–9, 'Charles-Emmanuel de Savoie, Duc de Genevois et de Nemours', 23: 7 (30 July 1882): 53–4; A. van Gennep, *La Savoie* (Voreppe, 1991).

49 ADS, PCSS, B-02647. The case was still being considered on 2 April 1547.

50 AST, Geneva, cat. 12, maz. 1, folder 1.

51 For more on the religious strife as well as the plague in this area see A. Zanotto, *Histoire de la Vallée d'Aoste* (Aoste, 1968).

52 For example, ADS, PCSS, B-01718 (1614 and 1620), for cases of people going to Jussy for sermons and baptisms.

53 ADS, PCSS, B-04304 (16 December 1621).

54 ADS, AMC, FF282.

55 ADS, AMC, FF285.

56 ADHS, ACCh, GG15 (1616). They closed their borders to people from Geneva, Gex, Vaud, Valais, Ternier and Gailliard unless they came with acceptable health certificates. They also hired Pierre, son of François Charles from Bonneville, to 'purify, clean, and nurse' as needed by the magistracy. For more on the region see A. Perrin, *Histoire de la Vallée et du Prieuré de Chamonix* (Chambéry, 1887).

57 AST, Geneva, cat. 12, maz. 2, folder 4 (probably 1530).

58 AST, PS, cat. 2a, maz. 1, folder 1. An identical ordinance was reprinted at Montfalcon on 10 June 1587, see ADS, AMC, FF282. For more on the situation in the immediate vicinity of Chambéry see A. Gros, *Histoire de Maurienne* (Chambéry, 1946), and F. Bernard, *Histoire de Montmélian* (Chambéry, 1956).

59 AST, PS, cat. 2, maz. 1, folder 5 bis.

60 For example, on 18 August 1632, a senior plague official was prosecuted for neglecting his duty to see that houses, etc., were cleaned and, instead, extorting money from the afflicted to spare them the more exacting duties of the ordinances. ADS, PCSS, B-00912. On 16 March 1642, Bernard Mourouz was arrested at Thonon for failing to have his shop properly cleaned although he had removed himself to a plague cabin. ADS, PCSS, B-01789.

61 For example, ADA, Ms112 (sixteenth-century), p. 53, refers to 'many men infected by

the Lutheran sect'. Also ADA, Ms97–23 (January 1567), mentions the 'Lutheran plague'.

62 'Ch'té po de Marbeu, faudra t' n'allo.' See ADA, T509: Nelly Pobel-Prost, *Délinquant et Criminalité dans la Baronnie de Marboz aux XVIIe et XVIIIe siècles* (Mém. d'histoire moderne), p. 78.

63 A. Lynn Martin, *Plague? Jesuit Accounts of Epidemic Disease in the Sixteenth Century* (Kirksville, MO, 1996), p. 10.

64 Martin, *Plague?*, pp. 110–11.

65 Despite the renown of the phenomenon having spread far and wide see J. du Chesne, *Pestis Alexicacus* (Leipzig: T. Schurerus & B. Voigt, 1609), pp. 126–8.

66 Taylor, 'Hampshire', p. 117.

67 Cf. the report to England on the plague spreaders in Lyon during 1564 noted in N. L. Jones, *The Birth of the Elizabethan Age* (Oxford, 1993), p. 191 (and n. 1 on p. 279: British Library Add. 35831, fol. 188). I am grateful to Professor A. Pettegree for this reference.

68 A. Paré, *The Collected Works*, trans. Thomas Johnson (facsimile reprint, of London: Cotes & Young, 1634; New York, 1968), p. 830. Also, A. Paré, *Opera Chirurgica,* lib. XXI, *De peste* (Frankfurt: J. Feyrabend, 1594), p. 617: 'Denique monitos magistratus pervilem ut intentos oculos animosque habeant in parricidale quoddam et impium vespilonum genus, qui lucir quod grassante peste longe maximum faciunt cupiditate amplius illecti, parietes, ianuas, limina, serrasque aedium sanie et unguentis hominum peste laborantium oblinunt', and A. Paré, *Les Oeuures* (Paris: G. Buon, 1579): 'C'est qu'ils doiuçt auoir l'œil sur certaines larrons, meurtriers & empoisonneurs, plus qu'inhumains, qui gressent & barboüillent les parois & portes des bonnes maisons, de la sanie des charbons & bosses, & autres excrements des pestiferez, à fin de les infecter, pour puis apres auoir moyen d'entrer dedâs, piller & desrober, voire estrangler les pauures malades en leur lict: ce qui esté faict à Lyon l'an 1565. O Dieu, que tels galands meritent grande punition exemplaire! Que laisse à la discretion desdits Magistrats, qui ont charge de la police.' All three versions are quite distinct though, collectively, they present a fascinatingly detailed rendition of the phenomenon.

69 Martin, *Plague?*, p. 10.

70 Martin, *Plague?*, p. 111.

71 Even in the early modern period there was a more complex understanding of magic than one might presume in assuming that all magic derived from demonic contact. See S. M. Buhler, 'Marsilio Ficino's *De Stella Magorum* and Renaissance Views of the Magi', *Renaissance Quarterly* 43 (1990): 348–71. A. Macfarlane says, 'witchcraft is predominantly the pursuit of harmful ends by implicit/internal means. Sorcery combines harmful ends with explicit means. White magic pursues beneficial ends by explicit means,' in his 'Definitions of Witchcraft', in M. Marwick, ed., *Witchcraft and Sorcery* (London, 1982), pp. 44–7, especially p. 46. In the same volume (pp. 23–8), E. E. Evans-Pritchard ('Sorcery and Native Opinion') warns against casual confusion of the terms.

72 Philippe Delisle, 'Aux sources de l'univers magico-religieux martiniquais : esclavage et phobie des sorciers', *Cahiers d'histoire*, 41: 1 (1996): 61–76, especially 63–4.

73 Cf. P. Ladame, 'Les mandragores ou diables familiers à Genéve, au XVIe et au XVIIe siècle', *MDG* 23 (1888–94): 237–81.

74 ACC, Br1/639: Michel Canat de Chizy, *Deux ans de peste à Chalon-sur-Saône* (Chalon: J. Dejussieu, 1879), pp., 13, 15–16, 21–2. The workers were paid the lucrative amount of four to six écus per month (pp. 22–3) and the cost of cleaning houses and effects was the largest expense faced by the city during the plague (p. 27). See also ACC, G4267:

Henri Bon, *Essai historique sur les épidémies en Bourgogne* (Dijon: P. Berthier, n.d.), pp. 44, 47, 50, 57.

75 Bon, *Bourgogne*, pp. 48–9, recalling the jaunty colours frequently noted for Satan in the sorcery cases of the Suisse Romande.

76 Eugene Dubois, *Histoire des hospices de Bourg* (Bourg, 1932), p. 41.

77 Dubois, *Bourg*, p. 54.

78 W. G. Naphy and A. Spicer, *The Black Death and the History of Plagues, 1345–1730* (Stroud, 2000), pp. 129–50.

79 Bruni, *Apt*, pp. 142–4. See Hovel, *Traicte*, p. 10, and Fabri, *Les Contrepoissons*, fols 69–69v, for fumigation recipes. See Gourmelen, *Advertisement*, p. 17, on the separate fumigation of intersections.

80 Gourmelen, *Advertisement*, pp. 36–7, recommends washing in 'clean running water'.

81 Granting fairs to Lyon was certainly aimed at hurting Geneva's economic clout but may also have been designed to take part in the economic recovery of France after the Black Death and the Hundred Years' War. See P. T. Hoffman, 'Land Rent and Agricultural Productivity: The Paris Basin, 1450–1789', *Journal of Economic History* 51: 4 (1991): 771–805.

82 For more on Lyon see R. Gascon, *Grand Commerce et vie urbaine au XVIe siècle: Lyon et ses marchands* (Paris, 1971), two volumes; P. T. Hoffman, *Church and Community in the Diocese of Lyon, 1500–1789* (New Haven CT, 1984); M. Lucenet, *Lyon malade de la peste* (Palaiseau, 1981).

83 AML, BB17, fol. 60 (11 May 1480).

84 See AML, BB22, fol. 22 (16 September 1494).

85 During the years before the final establishment of the Crown at Paris, Lyon was the second capital of the realm and, often, the King was more in Lyon than in Paris.

86 AML, BB24, fols 7–8v (9 July 1496), 48v (29 September 1496), 119v (13 September 1497). A smaller St-Thomas Hospital was also opened.

87 AML, BB25, fols 50 (18 August 1506), 58 (22 September 1506).

88 AML, BB135, fols 55–56 (5 April 1598).

89 AML, BB150, pp. 53–6 (6 February 1614).

90 AML, BB151, fols 92v–93v (7 September 1615).

91 AML, BB6, fol. 73v (15 April 1453).

92 For a very good account of the place of the surgeon in the life of a patient see R. Jütte, 'Ageing and Body Image in the Sixteenth Century: Hermann Weinsberg's (1518–97) Perception of the Ageing Body', *European History Quarterly* 18: 3 (1988): 259–90.

93 AML, BB39, fols 136v–37 (30 August 1521).

94 AML, BB41, fol. 136v (7 August 1523).

95 AML, BB52, fol. 139v (8 May 1533).

96 AML, BB63, fols 42v–43v (22 October 1544), 65 (27 November 1544). The city's masons were told to lengthen and deepen the trench they had already dug in the cemetery of St-Nizier.

97 AML, BB61, fol. 81–81v (7 June 1543).

98 AML, BB117, fols 77v (4 March 1586), 181 (3 July 1586). A year later, the records noted that plague was also in Piedmont and Chambéry (i.e. Savoy) and that 'poor and dissolute' refugees might spread the disease to Lyon. BB118, fol. 155–155v (28 July 1587).

99 AML, BB117, fol. 74 (25 February 1586).

100 AML, BB117, fol. 79v (5 March 1586). Wealthy as Lyon was, this seems an extreme figure (480 écus per annum versus Calvin's annual salary of 100 écus) and it may be that

the scribe meant to write 40 écus per annum (with extra 'danger pay'), which seems more reasonable.

101 AML, BB117, fols 61v–62v (16 February 1586).

102 AML, BB117, fol. 82–82v (6 March 1586).

103 AML, BB117, fols 64v (19 February 1586), 85 (12 March 1586). Over 1,200 infected people were quarantined at or near the St-Laurent, fols 218v–219 (9 September 1586).

104 AML, BB117, fol. 85v (12 March 1586). An accompanying dearth of grain only worsened the situation, see fol. 103 (29 March 1586).

105 On the tense confessional situation there see J. Davies, 'Persecution and Protestantism: Toulouse, 1562–1575', *History Journal* 22: 1 (1979): 31–51.

106 AML, BB28, fol. 323 (8 December 1512). At the end of the decade the city used the appearance of plague as an excuse to rid the city of 'all *marrons*, rascals, and gypsies who are going about the streets and the churches'. BB37, fol. 297v (5 September 1519).

107 AML, BB79, fol. 208 (15 July 1557) and AEG, PH 1618 (15 July, 11 August 1557). Geneva took the report seriously and instigated an investigation. Cf. the plot by a former Fugger steward to poison the Prince Bishop of Würzburg in Roper, *Oedipus*, p. 130.

108 AML, BB117, fols 173v (25 June 1586), 175 (26 June 1586).

109 AML, BB121, fol. 196v (22 September 1588).

110 ADR, fonds Galle, D51: Claude de Rubys, *Oraison prononcee a Lyon a la creation des conseilliers et eschevins . . . 21 de Decembre 1567* (Lyon: Michel Jove, 1568). On polemic see M. U. Chrisman, 'From Polemic to Propaganda: the Development of Mass Persuasion in the late Sixteenth Century', *ARG* 73 (1982): 175–96.

111 Rubys, *Oraison*, fol. 1v. For more on the socio-cultural context in Lyon see N. Z. Davis, 'The Sacred and the Body Social in Sixteenth Century Lyon', *P&P* 90 (1981): 40–90, and her 'The Reasons of Misrule: Youth Groups and *Charivaris* in Sixteenth Century France', *P&P* 50 (1971): 41–75. On pre-Protestant heresy in Lyon see G. Audisio, 'How to Detect a Clandestine Minority: The Example of the Waldenses', *SCJ* 21: 2 (1990): 205–16.

112 Rubys, *Oraison*, fol. 3.

113 Rubys, *Oraison*, fol. 3v.

114 Rubys, *Oraison*, fol. 4.

115 Rubys, *Oraison*, fol. 4v.

116 Sin, especially satanic and heretical was a threat to the very existence of a state, a point that featured prominently in sermons and speeches of the time. P. Zumthor, 'The Great Game of Rhetoric', *New Literary History* 12: 493–508.

117 Rubys, *Oraison*, fol. 5.

118 Rubys, *Oraison*, fol. 5v.

119 Rubys, *Oraison*, fol. 6.

120 Rubys, *Oraison*, fol. 6v.

121 Rubys, *Oraison*, fol. 8.

122 Rubys, *Oraison*, fol. 8v.

123 BML, Côté 354 363, Claude de Rubys, *Discours sur la contagion de la peste qui esté ceste present annee en la ville de Lyon* (Lyon: J. d'Ogerolles, 1577).

124 Rubys, *Peste*, pp. 8–9.

125 Rubys, *Peste*, p. 9.

126 Rubys, *Peste*, p. 19.

127 Rubys, *Peste*, p. 29.

128 Rubys, *Peste*, pp. 31–2.

129 Rubys, *Peste*, p. 33.

130 Rubys, *Peste*, pp. 33–4. For more on plague and the Grisons see R. Seiler, *Zur Ikonographie der religiösen Pestdenkmäler des Kantons Graubünden* (Zürich, 1985).

131 Rubys, *Peste*, pp. 43–4.

132 For more on Milan, see E. S. Welch, *Art and Authority in Renaissance Milan* (New Haven CT, 1995).

133 See ASM, Sanità, p.a., cart. 278, folder 2 (1543–1630).

134 Two excellent examples survive of printed versions of these certificates issued in Geneva from 19 June 1670. The first certifies that Jaques Bonjon (aged sixty, medium height, bearded), Christofle Bonjon (aged forty-seven, medium height, bearded), and their two mules had, on the date given, left 'this our city, exempt (thanks be to God) of any danger or suspicion of a contagious malady'. A similar certificate was given the same day to Silvestre Bogere (aged seventeen, short, beardless), Charles Antoine Piaffa (aged eighteen, blond, short), and Estinne Bonjon (aged eighteen, short), who 'said they were going to Italy'. ASM, Sanità, p.a. 278, folder 4. There is also a printed example from Salzburg which has blanks for height, hair colour, eye colour and clothing. An example of the mobility of people comes from the criminal investigation of a 'wandering scholar' who had visited most of the regions in and around the western Alps, see ASM, Miscellanea storica, cart. 71 (19 March 1553).

135 *Aspetti dell' società lombarda in età spagnola,* Archivio di stato di Milano (Como, 1985), p. 57; Leonida Besozzi, *Le magistrature cittadine milanesi e la peste del 1576–1577* (Bologna, 1988), p. 11.

136 Besozzi, *Le magistrature*, p. 21. Three 'straps' was the more common threat (and probably explains the plague spreaders' oath to resist three applications of the *corde*. See ASM, Miscellanea storico, cart. 67 (1548).

137 Giovan Battista Capra was put in charge of a guard of 'honourable and notable' men to make sure the quarantine rules were being obeyed. Marcello Rincio, a doctor, replaced his deceased colleague, Cesare Landriani, in the task of identifying those suspected of plague. Besozzi, *Le magistrature*, pp. 22, 26.

138 Besozzi, *Le magistrature* pp, 23–4.

139 ASM, Sanità, p.a., cart. 279. In Milan this was a permanent magisterial body while the Genevan committee was an *ad hoc* sub-committee of the Senate.

140 Besozzi, *Le magistrature*, p. 42.

141 ASM, Sanità, p.a., cart. 3.

142 Besozzi, *Le magistrature*, p. 43; see also Joseph Ripamonti, *Chronistae urbis Mediolani de Peste quae fuit anno 1630* (Milan: C. Bassanu, 1641), p. 118, who mentions this earlier occurrence of the phenomenon in his account of the better-known events of the seventeenth century.

143 Besozzi, *Le magistrature*, p. 43.

144 Besozzi, *Le magistrature*, p. 44. Despite these unrelated conspiracies, Besozzi concludes by saying that 'the psychois of the 'greasers' . . . [is like a] tasteless joke and an episode of communal delinquency'.

145 *Processo*. See also ASM, Sanità, p.a., cart. 278, folders 2 and 5, and Biblioteca ASM, Acquisto no. 3 (Processo degli untori). Another published source with some details is the previously mentioned *Aspetti dell' società lombarda* (Decree against the plague spreaders, 7 August 1630).

146 Frederico Borromeo, *La peste di Milano (de pestilentia)*, Armando Torno, ed. (Milan,

1987). See also Agostino Lampugnano, *La pestilenza seguita in Milano l'anno 1630* (Milan: Carlo Ferrandi, 1634), and Alessandro Tadino, *Raguaglio dell'origine et giornali successi della gran Peste* (Milan: F. Ghisolfi, 1648). Borromeo's account, rather than the cases themselves, formed the basis of Manzoni's work. See L. von Pastor, *History of the Popes from the Close of the Middle Ages* (London, 1891–1941), vol. 29 (of thirty-five), p. 367 n. 10.

147 Franco Cordero, *La fabbrica della peste* (Rome, 1985).
148 In his fictional *I promessi sposi* and his more historiographical *La storia della Colonna infame.*
149 Tadino, *Raguaglio*, pp. 114–15.
150 Lampugnano, *La pestilenza*, p. 43.
151 Lampugnano, *La pestilenza*, pp. 56–7 (Del Rio, lib. 2, cap. 50).
152 Lampugnano, *La pestilenza*, p. 69 (Droet, *Conseil de peste*, cap. 10).
153 Borromeo, *La peste*, p. 53.
154 Borromeo, *La peste*, pp. 55, 60, 63 (where he mentions 'astrologers, alchemists and sorcerers').
155 Borromeo, *La peste*, pp. 57–8.
156 Borromeo, *La peste*, pp. 58–9.
157 Borromeo is widely out of step with his contemporaries in viewing these practitioners as supernatural, let alone demonic. Although aspects of their work had supernatural, connotations or applications, most viewed their efforts as benign and beneficial. For specific details see M Biagioli, 'The Social Status of Italian Mathematicians, 1450–1600', *History of Science* 27 (1989): 41–95; R. S. Westman, 'The Astronomer's Role in the Sixteenth Century: A Preliminary Study', *History of Science* 28 (1980): 105–47; B. T. Moran, 'Christoph Rothmann, the Copernican Theory, and Institutional and Technical Influences on the Criticism of Aristotelian Cosmology', *SCJ* 13: 3 (1982): 85–108. A thorough understanding of the relationship between the natural and supernatural can be found in S. Clark, *Thinking with Demons* (Oxford, 1999). For an early modern discussion of the entire subject see the excellent P. G. Maxwell-Stuart, ed. and trans., *Martín de Rio : Investigations into Magic* (Manchester, 2000).
158 Cf. L. Rothkrug, 'Holy Shrines, Religious Dissonance and Satan in the Origins of the German Reformation', *Historical Reflections* 14: 2 (1987): 143–286.
159 See ASM, Culto, p.a., 2105, folder 1, fols 3v, 9v, 11, 13–18 (especially 14v); folder 7, 30 August 1550 ('di lutherana h[e]r[e]sia . . . pullullana . . . che se faceano synagoghe . . . tale pestifero error . . . questa lutherana insolça') as well as 25 August 1550 (the examination of some Portuguese as 'false Christians', i.e. *conversos*). In Bologna, where there were also rumours of plague spreaders in 1630, the connection was even more confusing where the plague was spread by 'the plague-bearing poisons of the Devil', 'the Lutherans' and 'witches'. See Alessandro Pastore, 'Note su criminalità e giustizia in tempo di peste: Bologna e Ginevra fra '500 e '600', in A. Pastore, ed., *Città italiene del '500 tra Riforma e Controriforma* (Lucca, 1988), pp. 31–43, especially pp. 32–3.
160 ASM, Autografi, cart. 215, folder 35 (3 June 1550, the use of 'malfattore et complici' for murderers) and Fondo di Religione, 3623, 6 November 1634 ('maleficiati' is used for the consequences of various diseases). However, see H. de Marsilia, *Grassea insignis commentarius* (Lyon: Bonhome, 1543), fols 6v–8, 10v, where both *venenum* and *maleficium* are decidedly natural (in this case, in connection with homicide). See also L. de Bruyn, *Woman and the Devil in Sixteenth Century Literature* (Tisbury, 1979), p. 108, and her categories of *sagae/lamiae* (witches), *magi infames* (black magic practitioners) and *venifici* (adepts at poisoning), as well as Wier's assumption that poison is a skill natural

(rather than supernatural) to a witch: 'porro feminas ab initio ad veneficium fuisse pro-cliviores viris, gravissimi testantur authores'.

161 Cordero, *La fabbrica*, p. 7.

162 Borromeo, *La peste*, p. 60.

163 See above pp. 45, 53.

164 *Processi*, pp. 184–6.

165 For example, *Processi*, p. 189: 'era grande di statura vestito tutto di nero come ho detto con un'ongarina longa sino al ginnochio, ma non lo potei comprendere in faccia, perché aveva il capello tirato in giù sopra la faccia'.

166 Piazza was tortured the day he was arrested seemingly because his account of events and his actions did not exactly tally with that of the other witnesses. *Processi*, p. 192.

167 Cf. *Processi*, p. 192: 'ah per amor di Dio vostra signoria mi facci lasciar giù. Ah s. Carlo [the irony was probably lost on the participants], ah per amor di Dio vostra signoria me facci lasciar giù.'

168 *Processi*, p. 197.

169 *Processi*, p. 198.

170 *Processi*, pp. 198–9.

171 *Processi*, p. 199: 'detto onto fosse velenato, e potesse nocere alli corpi umani'.

172 *Processi*, p. 217.

173 *Processi*, p. 203.

174 *Processi*, pp. 207–8.

175 *Processi*, pp. 213–14.

176 *Processi*, p. 222: 'oglio d'oliva, olio laurino, oglio di sasso, cera nova, polvere di rosma-rino, polve di salvia, e polvere di quei bacchi di ginepro, et un poco d'acetto forte'.

177 *Processi*, pp. 232–5. He eventually said, 'tell me what you want me to say and I will say it'.

178 *Processi*, p. 234. Later (e.g. pp. 252–3), Piazza mentions the use of secretions from dead plague victims as an ingredient.

179 *Processi*, p. 236.

180 *Processi*, pp. 219–21.

181 *Processi*, pp. 225–6, 228, 242.

182 For example, *Processi*, pp. 228–30.

183 *Processi*, p. 238.

184 *Processi*, p. 270–1.

185 *Processi*, p. 325.

186 *Processi*, p. 343.

187 *Processi*, pp. 363–84.

188 *Processi*, p. 374.

189 *Processi*, p. 375 and the note on pp. 570–1.

190 For example, Louise de Pavy, wife of the lawyer Jean Claude Reymond, was arrested for poisoning some wine. ADS, PCSS, B-01663 (30 July 1627). On poison and women see A. Blamires, K. Pratt and C. W. Marx, eds, *Woman Defamed and Woman Defended: An Anthology of Medieval Texts* (Oxford, 1992), pp. 100, 157.

191 Ollivero Capello was the victim of a 'homicide bestial and premeditated' by Marc'Antonio and Gio'Antonio Cotto and their accomplices. AST, MC, maz. 2, no. 3 (21 October 1567).

192 See AST, MC, maz. 2, no. 1 (30 October 1553–24 October 1555) for a murder plot involving a barber-surgeon. See the rumoured death by poisoning of Isabelle

d'Armagnac at the hand of a doctor from Toulouse. R. C. Famiglietti, *Tales of the Marriage Bed from Medieval France* (Providence RI, 1992), p. 17. On poison see D. Potter, 'Marriage and Cruelty among the Protestant Nobility in Sixteenth Century France: Diane de Barbançon and Jean de Rohan, 1561–67', *European History Quarterly* 20: 1 (1990): 1–38.

CONCLUSION

$\mathbf{A}$t the beginning of this volume, a number of issues were raised. The major question to answer was the extent to which plague spreading and witchcraft could be safely and accurately amalgamated into a single activity. The primary conclusion of this study is that the conflation is much too simplistic. It is essential to see the behaviour as twofold. First, there is plague spreading as part of a conspiracy. Second, there are plague spreaders who are, for the most part, acting quite independently of one another. Another binary feature is the *graisse* used. In the conspiratorial version, the grease is a concoction devised by men largely drawn from the medical profession. The type of plague spreading conflated with witchcraft relies either on ointments actually supplied by Satan or produced to his recipe. Plague-spreading conspirators targeted their conspiracy and grease against the wealthy in the hope of gain both by thieving and by maintaining their plague jobs. The second variety of plague spreader seems to target people more haphazardly or primarily for personal reasons of grievance and ire or, in an even more dramatic departure from the primary model, to kill animals. The grease is used not to spread plague but to kill people or animals out of malice or spite, as frequently seen in Lausanne. Finally, in the trials of the conspirators the courts accept an interpretation of motive based on natural greed without Satan and without the supernatural. In cases of individual plague spreading, the motivation is understood to be demonic and diabolical malice.

If one supposes, therefore, that there are two fairly distinct types of plague spreading, how is one to place them in relation to witchcraft? Individual plague spreading, as seen most prominently in Geneva during 1571, most closely fits Monter's definition of behaviour by individuals 'technically in league with the Devil although lacking most of the ordinary paraphernalia of witchcraft'.[1] However, these cases are actually much closer to witchcraft than this implies. Most of the accused plague spreaders of 1571 also confessed to Sabbath attendance and consorting with Satan. In that sense, spreading grease was just one of the demonic things they did. Indeed, one might more accurately call them grease spreaders, since many of the trials do not explicitly link their *graisse* with plague. While a technicality, it is worth bearing in mind. The conspirators of 1530 and 1545, on the other hand, were not accused of, nor did they confess to, being in league with the Devil.

They did not attend Sabbaths. Indeed, one cannot really suggest that in any sense they were witches. If one were to do so it would be to do a great injustice to those magistrates who sat through the trials of both 1545 and 1571. These same justices found the defendants guilty of plague spreading in 1545 and yet in 1571 convicted a new group of defendants for *both* greasing and witchcraft. In a very important way these judges – and indeed some of the accused – with their organic and personal links with the previous events were drawing a distinction.

This leaves two possible interpretations. First, the conspiracies of 1530 and 1545 (as well as the *conspiracies* elsewhere) are so fundamentally different from the individual acts involving grease found at other times and in other places as to require them to be seen as similar yet wholly separate phenomena. The second approach would be to say that a bizarre and horrific activity when repeated consistently (as in Geneva) was eventually forced into a mould more amenable and comprehensible to the judges and magistrates. Thus, Geneva's magistrates responded over time much as the inquisitors did when confronted with the Friulian *benandanti*. At first they had little idea how to react to or interpret the behaviour they were facing. Eventually, they mentally altered it so that it could be absorbed into an existing pattern. In time, this élite-developed interpretation permeated down through society to the extent that even the *benandanti* began increasingly to see themselves in the same way despite all the mental contradictions it entailed. In such a schema, the Genevan conspirators eventually gave way to individuals governed by Satan rather than barber-surgeons. The state, unhappy with a socio-economic motive based on simple greed, reinterpreted the activity as yet another manifestation of a known evil, witchcraft. Eventually, the very real and natural conspiracy of plague workers under the direction of a medical practitioner gave way to individual witches being guided by that great practitioner of duplicity, the Devil.

There is little doubt that something had altered in the minds of the judges. This second interpretative model has some validity. However, certain caveats remain. The evidence from the trials themselves does not support a slow evolution over time. Rather, between 1545 and 1571 something dramatic must have changed. Indeed, the cases in 1568–70 differ quite radically from those of 1571. Also, the evidence from other locales, especially Milan and Lyon, suggests that at the same time (and later) the conspiratorial model with a natural, greed-driven motivation was still enjoying widespread currency.

It may be possible to suggest a more discreet and subtle view. Perhaps the answer lies at the very start of each mass of prosecutions. In 1530 and 1545 in Geneva, as well as later in Milan and Lyon, the authorities were convinced that they had stumbled on a conspiracy located within their plague staff. This basic assumption that the conspiracy was centred on the misuse of medical knowledge and was an attempt to exploit the prevailing health crisis for gain drove the entirety of the cases. The judges did not seek to find evidence of witchcraft because they did not think they were prosecuting witches. Their primary motivation was discovering the names of the conspirators and identifying which houses and (rich) individuals had been targeted. As a counterpoint to this, if the beginning of a mass prosecution was the discovery of a witch (or a few witches), the emphasis shifted fundamentally. Those who were then arrested were closely questioned about witchcraft because the judges assumed that they were dealing with a group of witches. In the first type of mass trial, the oath-taking ceremony and the purely natural production and distribution of *graisse* was the focus of interrogation because it provided the easiest and simplest means of identifying the majority of remaining conspirators. In trials sparked off by the arrest of a witch, the investigation quickly focused on the Sabbath (where grease was also dispersed) as the ideal point for query, since the details of the Sabbath would produce the maximum number of names of other witches.

One must also consider the impact of misogyny and patriarchal structures in these cases. In cases of individual greasing where the emphasis is clearly on witchcraft the pattern evidenced is more obviously like that of other witchcraft prosecutions. For example, most of the people prosecuted in 1571 were female and the males arrested tended to be of a lower social level. For the most part, all were rural inhabitants not native to Geneva. However, in Geneva (in 1530 and 1545), Lyon and Milan, conspiracies to spread plague via pestiferous grease were of a different character. In these, medical men of a reasonable social status directed and co-ordinated the activities of the mostly female conspirators. To the extent that one can find male domination of the female it lies within the conspiracies themselves rather then being part of the dynamic between court and criminal. The male ringleaders abused their female co-conspirators, they used them for sex, they beat them, and they even paid them less. In turn, the state executed the men in greater proportion than the accused female conspirators.

Indeed, one cannot propose a simple interpretation based on social status, either. Citizens were arrested and executed as well as foreigners and *bourgeois*. Admittedly, poor foreigners predominated but then they were overly represented among plague workers in the first place. If one is to attempt to find some deeper psychological explanation for the trials one might best consider the fraught relationship between the invalid and the carer. In times of plague the magistracy, normally independent, always proud, was forced to rely almost wholly upon poor foreigners. As a group, the élite would naturally have distrusted the carers they now found indispensable. Indeed, were it not for the severity of any given plague outbreak the very people who now secured the state's most important institution, the pest house, would have been expelled from the town. At the best of times, in the most advantageous of situations, it would be natural if some level of resentment were to develop towards a carer on the part of someone normally quite independent but now incapacitated. Plague outbreaks were not the best of times and the existing relationship between citizen magistrates and poor foreigners was not the best circumstance. It is not surprising that the magistracy as well as the wider population might be inclined to think the worst of the plague workers.

Nor, one should hasten not to forget, is it inconceivable that plague workers normally destitute might be tempted to steal from the homes of the infected while they were cleaning them. Any more than one should be surprised to learn that gravediggers might just rob a corpse of its valuables. These workers were struggling with an appalling situation, surrounded by death, near death, and fear of death. That they may have become desensitised to those around them is understandable. That they might chose to take advantage of a situation in which they might die at any moment is not beyond the bounds of probability. Even that they might try to make the best – and most – out of a bad situation is not impossible.

Although one can reasonably conclude that much of the testimony extracted under torture in 1571 is not credible, in the sense that people simply did not sit astride a stick, chant a few words and fly off to a Sabbath meal with Satan, then kiss his backside by way of farewell. However, the events as presented in the conspiracy cases are much more believable. There is nothing supernatural about taking an oath to commit a crime – even murder. Rendering a human foot, while nasty, is not supernatural. Adding plague pus to human fat, revolting as it sounds, is perfectly plausible. All the more when one remembers the desensitising nature of the work being undertaken, day in and day out, by the conspirators. No, the problem with accepting the reality of a conspiracy to spread plague rests on unwillingness to believe that people are capable of such evil. Indeed, part of the desire to dismiss the possibility that anyone could have thought that they themselves were a witch, willing and able to use magic to harm, rests with the same instinct.

However, in an age that has seen two world wars where poison gas was used on the battlefields and in death camps as well as biological and nuclear weapons in the Sino-Pacific theatre during the Second World War, we may be more inclined to credit the possibility that such a conspiracy actually happened. Is a conspiracy to spread plague by pest house workers for gain any less believable than the mugger using an HIV-infected hypodermic needle to rob someone? If entire nations can create, stockpile and contemplate the use of nerve gases and biological weapons based on anthrax, can one not consider that the authorities of Geneva, Lyon, Milan and elsewhere may just have been confronted with conspirators who actually thought they had a means of using plague to their benefit?

Obviously, one can easily dismiss the documentation as the production of a panic-stricken élite desperately striving to identify scapegoats to explain a present calamity. Of course, such a view leads one inevitably to conclude that few if any historical records have any reliability. On the other hand, if one gives even a moment's credence to these dossiers then certain features leap forward. First, even without the application of torture, the evidence admitted would lead one to believe that many of the defendants were trying hard to prevaricate. Also, many trials produced information, independent of one another, that served to validate that discovered in the other. This is no minor point. Information uncovered in Thonon, Syon and Geneva in 1545 was consistent and could not have been the result of collusion or 'leading questions' from the bench. Finally, and most important, not only were pots of grease found in the possession of many of the accused but it was found on the doors, door handles and locks of houses in various cities. While one may decide that the citizens simply imagined the grease, it seems a particularly facile way of dealing with the testimony in the depositions. If they could imagine grease out of thin air then others would certainly have been able to imagine that they could make plague-bearing grease or fly to a Sabbath. Concluding that late medieval and early modern society was one giant exercise in mass hallucination and hysteria, while hubristically reassuring to modern readers, is surely ludicrous. Failing that, one must admit the possibility that some individuals, under the leadership of a few medical practitioners, actually thought they could manipulate a plague outbreak to their benefit.

The overall conclusions from this study are hardly surprising. Destitute and desperate people placed in horrific and desensitising circumstances are capable of extremely bizarre and even evil behaviour. Groups of individuals may well have conspired to spread plague. In time, this nefarious behaviour became part and parcel of another evil activity, witchcraft. In the process, it lost much of what made it distinctive – conspiracy, the leadership of surgeons, and the motivation of simple greed. Nevertheless, it seems wrong to consider conspiracies to spread plague only as a type of witchcraft. However, individuals using grease to cause murder and mayhem fall more clearly into the traditional stereotype of the early modern witch. From the perspective of the court, the judges faced an extremely bizarre and frightening type of behaviour. For the most part, they met it with an amazing level of sophistication and care. One looks hard to find any evidence of panic or scapegoating. From the point of view of the defendants the situation is more complex. One cannot be sure that they were guilty of anything or that the motives ascribed to them were accurate or simply plausible to the court. Finally, while one cannot say with certainty that the information in these trials contains enough objective truth to convict, there is certainly enough circumstantial evidence to suggest a 'not proven' verdict.

NOTE

1 Monter, *Witchcraft*, p. 47.

APPENDIX ONE

HOUSEHOLDS INFECTED WITH
PLAGUE, 1542–46

Person/Household	Details	Date
Villager in Champel	Dead of plague	23 October 1542
Jean de Cortelles	Dead of plague	29 October 1542
Rose Inn	Infected, to be cleaned	3 November 1542
Claude Malbuisson	One woman infected	3 November 1542
Oddet Chenellet	One woman infected	3 November 1542
Magestray house	Infected	13 November 1542
Heustace Vincent, herald	Infected	25 January 1543
Wife of Tyvent Furjod	Suspected of plague	27 April 1543
François Boulat	Plague-carrying	27 April 1543
Croset, the butcher	House infected	17 May 1543
Michel Varro	One girl infected	21 May 1543
Richard Garnesse	Possibly plague-carrying	21 May 1543
Pierre Blanchet, minister	Dead of plague	1 June 1543
Jean Pernet (or Rojon), barber	Dead of plague	2 June 1543
Joly Cler	House infected	18 June 1543
Pierre de Veyrer	Infected	26 June 1543
Jean Bertier	Infected	15 July 1543
Estienne de la Maisonneuve	Infected	19 July 1543
Buguyet	Husband and wife dead of plague	3 September 1543
Guillaume Marchant	Dead of plague, estate left to Plague Hospital	23 October 1543
Antoine Bronges	Entire family dead of plague	23 October 1543
Canestran, labourer	Wife dead of plague	26 October 1543
Tyvent Laurent	Infected	11 December 1543
Unnamed debtor	Dead of plague, goods sold	21 December 1543
Jean Collomb	Girl dead of plague	30 August 1544
Jean Fiollet	Possible plague illness	6 October 1544
François Bel	Wife dead of plague	6 October 1544
Pierre Compagnion	Dead of plague	23 October 1544
George Malliet	House infected	15 September 1545
Christophle Surjod	Dead of plague, estate left to city	6 November 1544
Pierre Roph (or Taborin)	Quarantine violations	4 December 1544
Foreigner at Madeleine	Unknown illness, banished	13 January 1545

[202]

Person/Household	Details	Date
François Charnet	Father's house infected	27 January 1545
Claudaz Mossier (or Peytavin)	Infected with plague	12 March 1545
Two houses in St-Gervaix	Infected with plague	18 March 1545
Claude Savoye	Woman dead of plague	20 March 1545
Michel Varro	House 'greased'	20 March 1545
Two debtors in prison	Dead of plague	24 March 1545
Ayme Revilliod	Infected house	23 April 1545
Jean Vollan (or Gentil)	Husband and children dead	24 April 1545
Bastien Bessonet	Possible plague death	24 April 1545
City prisons	Infected by plague	24 April 1545
Humbert Richard	Widow infected by plague	27 April 1545
Plague Hospital	forty infected	11 May 1545
Plague Hospital	Minister and barber infected	11 May 1545
Humbert Viennesin	Infected with plague	21 May 1545
Claude Choudens	Dead of plague	10 November 1545
Jean Ferron	Possible plague death	26 July 1546
Roz Porral	Wife infected	27 September 1546
Jean Magnin, labourer	Infected by plague	15 October 1546

APPENDIX TWO

GENEVAN MEDICAL
PRACTITIONERS, 1536–46

Aubert, Henry	*Apothecaire*
Begney, Guillaume	*Apothecaire*
Canal, Mathieu	*Apothecaire*
De la Montaigne, Jean	*Apothecaire*
De la Pallud, Jean	*Apothecaire*
De la Rive, Girardin	*Apothecaire*
De Mara, Stephanis	*Apothecaire*
De Martereto, Antonius	*Apothecaire*
De Verruffis, Gaspard	*Apothecaire de l'hospital*
Dupan, Amblard	*Apothecaire*
Dupan, Claude	*Apothecaire*
Forjod, Bartholome	*Apothecaire*
Gervais, Amy	*Apothecaire*
Pierre, Bernardin	*Apothecaire*
Prieur, Burnet	*Apothecaire*
Varoz, Michel	*Apothecaire*
Voisin, Michel	*Apothecaire*
Vulliens, François	*Apothecaire*
Vulliermoz, Henri	*Apothecaire*
Fiollet, Jean	*Barbier et enterreur*
Fiollet, Pierre	*Barbier*
Blanc, Jaques	*Barbier*
Cheyserier, Jaques	*Barbier*
Conners, Claude	*Barbier*
Grangier, Jean	*Barbier*
Guilliard, Robert	*Barbier*
Moche, Claude	*Barbier-cirugien*
Pantray, François	*Barbier* (from Beauregard)
Pernost, Guillaume	*Barbier* (from Burgundy)
Ranier, Jaques	*Barbier-Cirugien*
Tallien, Bernard	*Barbier and enterreur* (from Dijon)
Villiard, Guillaume	*Barbier,* d. 13 May 1545 from plague
Von Zurich, Hans	*Barbier* (not hired; no French)
Charles, Alexander	*Cirugien*

Compagnion, Pierre	*Cirugien* (from Lyon), d. 23 October 1544 of plague
De Barberiis, François	*Cirugien* (from Salluce)
De Cortelles, Jean	*Cirugien*
De Nantua, Bastien	*Cirugien*
De Soye, Charles	*Cirugien*
De Vallence, Pierre	*Cirugien*
Frans, Villiet	*Cirugien* (from Zeeland)
Permet, Jean	*Cirugien*
Pernet, Jean (or Rojon)	*Cirugien* (from Neuchâtel), d. 2 June 1543 of plague
Fabri, Jaques	*Docteur*
Beljaquet, Louis	*Medicin*
Chappuis, François	*Medicin*
Imbert, Pierre	*Medicin* (from Dauphiné)

ACCUSED *ENGRAISSEURS*, 1543–46

Name	Alias(es)	Personnel details	Trial result
Basseta, Pernon	Basseta		Executed
Beguin, Clauda			
Bellefille, Rene		*Hospitalier*, father Louis, from Turenne, minister	Drawn with hot irons, quartered
Berchet, Collette		Father Tyvent Perrua, from Gex, *habitant*	
Berchod, Jean			Banished
Besson, Antoine	Urban		
Bonet, Pernon			Freed
Bossiez, Pernette		Father of Pierre	Banished
Boulat, François		Arrested for 'unintentionally' plague spreading, then rearrested for conspiracy, son of Jean, from Faucigny	Executed
Boulat, Mya	Buandiere	Widow of Pierre Gradel	Banished
Bourgeois, Petremand		Father Jean, arrested for buying poison (to murder his father)	Executed
Bourgonvilla, ?			
Burlat, Thivena (or Clauda)			Banished
Chabbod, Bertholomea	L'Allemandaz	Father Ayme	
Chappuis, Bernard		From Ville-le-Grand, shoemaker	Banished
Chappuis, Louise		*Habitant*	Executed
Charroton, ?		Husband Rollet Charroton	Banished

Name	Alias(es)	Personnel details	Trial result
Cherbonier, Pernon	Pernon Grand Claudaz	Father Gonin, widow of Jean Dunant,	
Chevallier, André			Banished
Collomb, Jeanne	Cugniet, Grand-Jeanne	From Bernex, Father Pierre, husband Humbert Fassonet, *habitant*	Banished
Coquet, Guilliema	Guichoda	Father Pierre, from Artas, *habitant*	Freed
Croysonet, Pernon	Marcaz	*Cureuse*, Father Martoz, from Chancy, *habitant*	
Dallinge, Bernard		Arrested at Thonon	
De Beaufort, Roseta		Husband Jean Pillitier (from Jussy), *habitant*	
Delacrispina, ?			Freed
Delafontana, Robella	Pirquaz	Father Jean, *habitant*	
Delarpaz, George			Freed
Depellis, Clauda	La Curtaz	Father Jaques	
Dorsier, Pernette	Paultaz	Father Monet, widow of François Dunant, *habitant*	Banished
Du Marteray, ?	Sept-Diables	Husband Antoine du Marterey	
Dunant, ?		Husband Louis Dunant	
Dunant, Louis	Semenaz		
Fiollet, Jean		From Usenens, barber, *habitant*	
Folliex, Clauda	Clauda La Ville, Clauda Ville-le-Grand	Father Humbert, from Ville-le-Grand	
Furjod, Tyvent		*Guidon*	Released
Galliard, Laurence		Father François Galliard, from La Roche, returned and convicted of theft	Banished, executed
Gay, Martina	La Freneysan	Father Jean, *habitant*, *cureuse*, Husband Jaques Bechod	
Girard, Genon		Father Jean, from Compesiere	
Granjean, Pernon			
Guex, Pernon		Father Amied, widow of Boniface Thorel	

Name	Alias(es)	Personnel details	Trial result
Guex, Thibaude		Husband Jean de Grisseney (alias Bonbillier), Father Claude	Executed
Guilliod, Antoina	La Guilloda	Father Reynon, from Montoux, husband Regnier, *hospitaliere*	Drawn with hot irons, quartered
Lentille, Jean	Dunant	*Habitant*, gravedigger	Died of injuries from torture, body burned
Margot, Clauda		Father Antoine, from Martigny, arrested for buying poison (to murder Jean Bourgeois)	Executed
Mermilliod, Christobla	La Christoblaz	Father Jean-Jaques, from Faucigny, *Cureuse*	
Monier, Bernada	Mugniez	From Lausanne, Father Jean	Suicide, body executed
Mossier, Clauda	Peytavin	Father Pierre, husband François Granjaques (or Granjean), executioner	
Mourys, Jaquema	Mauris	Father Claude, widow of Gaspard Sernier	
Mugneratz, Pernon			Banished
Muthilliod, Jeanne		Father Guillaume, from Dauphiné, widow of Raymond Verna, baker, *habitant*	
Ormond, Henreta		Father Jacques	
Palmier, Jean	Le Mouroz Tissot		
Pelloux, Tivena	Gervaise	Father Gonin, from Contamine, Husband Gervais Galliens (from Faucigny)	
Petitjean, ?		Arrested at Brig	Executed
Petitjean, ?		Widow of Petitjean (executed at Brig)	Banished
Pouthex, Henry			

Name	Alias(es)	Personnel details	Trial result
Regnaud, Michel			Admonished
Reveu, Genon	Bistyn, Bescuyn		Executed
Rey, Thassia			Freed
Roph, Pierre			
Tallien, ?		Husband Bernard Tallien, poisoned bread, has two children	Banished
Tallien, Bernard		*Barbier*, fornicator, blasphemer, thief	Banished
Tissier, Jean		From St-Martel in Bourbonois, gravedigger, weaver	
Villars, Bernarda		Father Jaques, from Nyon, husband Humbert Garliat	Banished

MAGISTERIAL PARTICIPATION, 1545–46 TRIALS

Name[a]	No. of defendants seen	No. of days attended
Ameaux, Pierre	12+	20+
Aubert, Henry	12+	20+
Balard, Jean	1	1
Beguin, François	3	2
Beljaquet, Louis	1	1
Beney, Guillaume	12+	20+
Bernard, Louis	12+	20+
Bonna, Pierre	12+	20+
Buttin, Pierre	12+	20+
Chappuis, François	1	1
Chautemps, Jean (procureur)	12+	20+
Chiccand, Antoine	12+	20+
Coquet, Jean	9	20+
Corne, Amblard	2	2
Coste, Pierre	12+	20+
Curtet, Jean-Ami (syndic[b])	12+	20+
Cusin, Jean	12+	20+
Darlod, Domaine (syndic)	12+	20+
Delestra, Claude	12+	20+
Desarts, Ami	1	1
Desarts, Jean (syndic)	12+	20+
Desfosses, Pierre (treasurer)	12+	16
Dorsière, Pierre	4	3
Dupan, Claude	12+	20+
Falquet, Petremand	1	1
Gerbel, Antoine (syndic)	12+	20+
Gervais, Ami	12+	18
Jesse, Pierre-Jean	1	1
Lambert, Jean	12+	20+
Malagniod, Pierre	11	20+
Malbuet, Jean	3	4
Malbuisson, Jean	12+	20+
Marchand, Jean	2	2

Name[a]	No. of defendants seen	No. of days attended
Mercier, Bartholomy	2	1
Monet, Roz	12+	10
Morel, Michel (syndic)	12+	20+
Pensabin, Jean	12+	20+
Pernet, Jean	1	1
Perret, Guillaume	2	1
Perrin, Ami (syndic)	12+	20+
Philippin, Jean (syndic)	3	4
Roset, Claude	12+	20+
Somareta, Pierre	1	1
Textor, Benoît	1	1
Tissot, Pierre (syndic)	9	11
Verna, Pierre	12+	20+

Notes

[a] Those named in **bold** attended the 1530 trials. Of the forty-five magistrates attending the 1530 trials, seven (16%) were present in 1545–46. Of the forty-six magistrates attending the 1530 the seven with experience of the 1530 trials represent 15%.

[b] As the trial spanned an electoral divide there were eight possible syndics in attendance.

INDIVIDUALS ACCUSED OF WITCHCRAFT, 1543–46

Name	Alias(es)	Personnel details	Trial result
Claude Vulliemoz	Grangiez		
Katherine		Wife of Antoine du Fossal, from Gex	Beaten, re-banished
Rolette		Widow of Pierre Pilliciez, from Baleyson	Re-banished
Pernette Dorsier		Daughter of Monet, widow of François Dunant	Banished
Louis Verchiere		From Satigny	
Andreaz		Widow of Pierre Juget, from Peney	
Morys	Mauris	Wife of Borgeaulx, from Satigny	Executed
Aymed Darvex		Confessed to being a witch for six years and and having renounced God and paid homage to Satan, legal opinion divided	Banished
Henry du Gerdil		From Peney	Fined, released
Claude Malliez		From Satigny	
Lyonardaz		Widow of Claude Donne (from Bourdigny), from Peney	Banished, beaten, re-banished
Tevenaz Paris		From Peney	Banished
Unnamed woman		Mother of Henry Juget	Died in custody
Bastien de Nantua	Le Bon Herige	Barber-surgeon	Banished
Charles de Soye		Barber-surgeon, diviner	Freed
Unnamed woman		Widow of Jean Pasteur of Vandoeuvres, amulet use	

APPENDIX SIX

GENEVA'S PLAGUE WORKERS, 1614–15

Pest house staff	Wage
Jean Gervais, minister	100 florins
Claude Bottillier, Gervais' servant	30 florins
Des Cousins, controller	112 6s
Pierre Baussan, scribe	30 florins
Isaac Chappuis, commissioner	48 florins
Jean Verpillier, fumigator of the Health Committee's chamber	15 florins
Abram Manget, fumigator of the Health Committee's chamber	15 florins
Guillaume Constantin, surgeon	405 florins
Michel du Bois, from Lyon, surgeon	425 florins
George Michel (and his wife), surgeon	200 florins
Abram Tabuis, visitor of corpses	30 florins
Jacques Picard, messenger	30 florins
Crochat, messenger	30 florins
Claude Marchant, messenger	30 florins
Guillaume Constantin's valet, messenger	30 florins
Servants for the afflicted	
Jean Bonnefoy	48 florins
Nicolas Desmoulins	48 florins
Widow Mecod	30 florins
Guillauma Mercier	30 florins
Antoine Thomas, registration clerk	14 florins
François Favre	30 florins
Jean du Perril	30 florins
Cleaners	
Frederich Deschamps	30 florins
Pierre Chastry	28 florins
Pierre Destra	28 florins
De l'Hondeus	28 florins
André Bachelard	28 florins
François Jolle	30 florins
Bertholome de Bellerive	28 florins

Pest house staff	Wage
George Venier	100 florins
Daniel Blanc	30 florins
Umbert Clerc	30 florins
Michel Graffez	30 florins
Nicolas Humbert	28 florins
Henry Corne	28 florins
Elizabeth Meillet	28 florins
Michel de Baptista	48 florins
Gravediggers	
François Donques	48 florins
Claude Destra	48 florins
Nicolas Bonnet	48 florins
Thyven Berchet	48 florins
Pierre Bordier	48 florins
Pierre Bron	48 florins
Bernardin Mondet	48 florins
Jacob Matthey	48 florins
Laurent Milland	48 florins
Total	**2,714 florins 6s**

APPENDIX SEVEN

MILAN'S PLAGUE SPREADERS: THE WITNESSES

Agostino, son of Giovanni Battista Stropini

Alvaro, son of Gabriele de Toledo, *capitano della porta del castello*

Ambrogio Bivio (called il Brusotto)

Ambrogio, son of Giuseppe Giramo

Andrea del Monte, from Magenta

Andrea Mereghitti, from Magenta

Angela, daughter of Gerolamo Bono

Antonia Costa, wife of Giovanni Pietro Porrada (from Magenta)

Antonio (called il Tame or Tamè), son of Bartolomeo Costa, *ortolano*

Antonio Leva

Antonio Levi, from Ossona

Antonio Paliardi, servant of De Padillo

Antonio, son of Giacomo Tomasi

Antonio, son of Giovanni Rachetta

Antonio, son of Vincenzo Mazzoletti, servant at the Sei Ladri Inn

Arcangelo Leva

Archileo Carcano, *fisico collegiato*

Archileo, son of Bartolomeo Carcano, *fisico collegiato*

Ascanio, son of Camillo Canobio

Baldassarre Reina, *console* of Ossona

Bartolomeo da san Pietro

Battista, son of Giovanni Giacomo Robiati

Benedetto Lucini

Benedetto, son of Giovanni Fattoni, servant of De Padilla

Bernardino, son of Bartolomeo Cassini, servant of De Padilla

Bernardo, son of Giovanni Pinova, servant at the Sei Ladri Inn

Bladassarre Bonesi, from Magenta

Bonone Pelizzoli

Brigida, daughter of Pomponio Glussiana, wife of Gaspare Migliavacca

Camillo Mazia, jailer

Camillo, son of Giulio Cesare Plato

Carlo (called il Tentorino), son of Francesco Bigatti, prisoner

Carlo Antonio, son of Francesco Pelizzoni

Carlo Rosati

Carlo, son of Cesare Scaranno, *jurisconsult*

Carlo, son of Ercole Tonelli

Carlo, son of Fabrizio Crivelli, prisoner

Carlo, son of Michele Martignoni

Caterina, daughter of Giovanni Battista Trocazzani, widow of Alessandro Rosa

Caterina, daughter of Melciore Bertoni, wife of Giovanni Stefano Baruello

Caterina, daughter of Sebastiano Baretta, widow of Giovanni Cusini

Catherine, Trocazzani, widow of Allesandro Rosa

Cesare Regna

Clara, daughter of Carlo Aretti, widow of Francesco Cinquanta

Clara, daughter of Giovanni Giacomo Brippis, wife of Giovanni Giacomo Mora

Cristoforo, son of Giovanni Battista Rosada, from Ossona

Cristoforo Barbai

Domenica Fulvi, wife of Giovanni Domenico

Domenico Turati, from Magenta

Domenico, son of Fabrizio Furio

Eustachio Romano, *segretario*

Felice, daughter of Gerolamo, Crippa (host)

Filippo Boisio

Frabricio Painelli, *baricello*

Francesca Casale, wife of Simon Frangilossi

Francesco Alemani, from Ossona

Francesco Gerolamo Giusto, *avvocato*

Francesco Medici, from Magenta

Francesco Portalupi, from Ossona

Francesco Stoppi

Francesco, son of Andrea Buffalo, from Alessandria, servant of De Padillo

Francesco, son of Fernando Gariboldi

Francesco, son of Gerolamo Pasquarelli, from Loreto, former servant of De Padillo, now of the Duke of Lerma

Francesco, son of Giovanni Battista Baratello, advocate

Francesco, son of Giovanni Battista Galli

Francesco, son of Giovanni Battista Rippa

Francesco, son of Giovanni Battista Ugazio, prisoner

Francesco, son of Giovanni Giacomo Massaia

Francesco, son of Giovanni Pietro Baretta

Francesco, son of Luigi de Vargos, governor of the castle

Francesco, son of Vincenzo Mazzoletti, frequents the Sei Ladri Inn

Gaspare Brizia, *pizzicagnolo*, from Ossona

Gerolamo Turati, from Magenta

Gerolamo, son of Antonio Mendozio

Gerolamo, son of Gerolamo Suarez, domestic of De Padilla

Gerolamo, son of Marco Antonio Insula,[a] *banchiere*

Geroloma, daughter of Giovanni Battista Salvatici, widow of Gerolamo Crippa (called il Cuoco)

Giacomina Andrioni, *lavandaia*

Giacomo, son of Domenico Scotti, prisoner

Giovani Ermes, son of Franceso Lampugnani, prisoner

Giovanni (called Bulone), son of Giacomo Bote

Giovanni Ambrogio, son of Guglielmo Roderio

Giovanni Andrea, son of Francesco Ciprando, *abate*

Giovanni Battista Cislago (Piazza's lawyer)

Giovanni Battista Vertua, *fisico*

Giovanni Battista, son of Antonio Dotti, Mora's neighbour

Giovanni Battista, son of Antonio Prina, barber

Giovanni Battista, son of Francesco Velati, *banchiere*

Giovanni Carlo, son of Antonio Speroni, Mora's neighbour

Giovanni Fernando, son of Giovanni Fernando de Mazuella, soldier in De Padilla's company

Giovanni Paolo Annoni, *baricello del lazzaretto*

Giovanni Paolo, son of Gaspare Casati

Giovanni Pietro Bocali, from Barco

Giovanni Pietro Porrada

Giovanni Pietro Rovida

Giovanni Pietro, son of Giovanni Gattista Migliavacce, cousin of Gerolamo (executed)

Giovanni Stefano Baruello, *mestatore*

Giovanni, son of Achille Vermigli, *cavalerizzo*

Giovanni, son of Roderico de Castagnida, *cancelliere* of the castle

Guglielmo, son of Giovanni Piccoli, Mora's neighbour

Lucia, daughter of Gerolamo Maineri

Marc Antonio, son of Giovanni Maria Zamarini, Mora's neighbour

Margherita Arpizanelli, *lavandaia*

Margherita, daughter of Giorgio Ciechetti, servant

of Giovanni Stefano Baruello

Margherita, daughter of Giovanni Albertini, wife of Gerolamo Migliavacca

Matteo (called Pesco), son of Romerio Volpi

Maurilia, daughter of Giovanni Paolo Pissina, wife of Matteo Furno

Mauro (Mora's lawyer)

Melchion, son of Simone de los Reies, from Segovia, *habitant* of Como

Melchione Garavaglia, from Ossona, *convocatio d'ufficia*

Melchione, son of Giovanni Battista Taurello

Michele, son of Giovanni Bertolini, servant at the Sei Ladri Inn

Nazario Castiglioni, sagrestano di Sant'Alessandr

Orsola Bianchi, wife of Ludovico Vigoni

Ortensia, daughter of Giovanni Andrea Castiglioni, wife of Alessandro Tradati

Ottavia, daughter of Giovanni Persici, wife of Gerolamo, Bono

Ottavio, son of Alberto Suario

Panfilio, son of Michele Rubuleno

Paolo Andrea Barberi

Paolo Gerolamo Castiglioi, *coadiutore nell'ufficio del capitano di giustizia*

Paolo Gerolamo, son of Bartolomea Cittadino

Paolo Gerolamo, son of Giovanni Giacomo Mora, barber

Paolo Gerolamo, son of Giuseppe Castoldi

Pietro Martire, son of Ambrogio Pulicelli

Pompeo, son of Bernardo Quarantino, advocate

Sebastiano Testa, jailer

Stefano, son of Giovanni Ambrogio Buzzi, *tintore*

Tommaso Grillo

Tommaso, *giudice collaterale dell'ufficio*

Tommaso, son of Giovanni Bertolini, servant at the Sei Ladri Inn

Vittore, son of Francesco Bescape, *fisico*

Notes
[a] Secretary in the office of Signor Giulio Sanduinetti.

BIBLIOGRAPHY

Primary sources, manuscript

ANNECY

Archives départmentales de la Haute-Savoie
Archives communales de Chamonix
   GG15 (Health Regulations)

BOURG-EN-BRESSE

Archives départmentales de l'Ain
   Ms 97–23 (Archives de Turin, correspondence, 1528–67)
   Ms 112 (Recueil de pièces concernant les ducs de Savoie)

CHAMBÉRY

Archives départmentales de Savoie
Procédures criminelles du Senat de Savoie
   B-01663, B-01718, B-01789, B-02647, B-04304, B-00912
Archives municipales de Chambéry
   FF282 (949), FF285 (952)

GENEVA

Archives d'État de Genève
Pièces historiques, 1299, 1304, 1310, 1335, 1345, 1347, 1357, 1358, 1618, 1873bis, 1765, 1767,
   1768, 1780, 1781, 1793, 1811, 1843, 1844, 1845, 1850, 1852, 1853, 1861, 1864, 1871,
   1877, 1907, 1921, 2208, 2522
Procés criminels, série 1: 388, 389, 391, 392, 393, 394, 396, 397, 398, 400, 401, 402, 403,
   407, 631, 752, 1307, 1309, 1457, 1458, 1479, 1485, 1509, 1516, 1520, 1556, 1565, 1585,
   1586, 1587, 1603, 1625, 1649, 1660, 1647, 1649, 1650, 1652, 1653, 1658, 1661, 1663,
   1671, 1672, 1673, 1683, 2302, 2346, 2944, 3028

Procés criminels, série 2: 221, 222, 223, 224, 225, 226, 229, 626, 627, 628, 629, 646, 679, 685, 703bis, 709, 720, 1271, 1307, 1308, 1309, 1311, 1324, 1326, 1331, 1335, 1337, 1338, 1369, 1531, 1876, 2086, 2087, 2089, 2090,

Registres de Consistoire, vol. 3

Registres du Conseil vols., 35–41 (1542–47), 62–7 (1567–72), 91–4 (1596–99), 112–14 (1613–15), 134–9 (1635–40)

LAUSANNE

Archives cantonalles de Vaud
  Ac29 (Sorcery)
  Bh10/1, 2, 3 (Sorcery)
Archives de la ville de Lausanne
  E45 (Registre de Cour criminelle, 1482–1618)

LYON

Archives municipales de Lyon
BB (Archives communales antérieures à 1790), vols.: 6 (1451–55), 17 (1482–83), 22 (1494–96), 24 (1498–1501), 25 (1511–12), 28 (1511–12), 37 (1517–20), 39 (1519–22), 41 (1523–24), 52 (1531–34), 61 (1542–44), 63 (1544–46), 79 (1556–57), 117 (1586), 121 (1588), 135 (1598), 150 (1614), 151 (1615)

MILAN

Archivio di Stato di Milano
Sanità, p.a., cart. 3, 278 (folder 2, 4, 5), 279
Miscellanea storica, cart. 67, 71
Acquisto no. 3 (Processo degli untori)
Culto, p.a., 2105, folder 1, 7
Autografi, cart. 215, folder 35

NEUCHÂTEL

Archives de l'État de Neuchâtel
Archives judiciaires de Neuchâtel
  Manuels de justice de Neuchâtel 2 (1566–70), 4 (1583), 6 (1587–92)
  Procédures criminelles de Neuchâtel 241 (1535–1667)
Archives judiciaires de Le Landeron
  Manuels judiciaires de Le Landeron 5 (1532–37), 7 (1537–47)

TURIN

Archivio di Stato di Torino
Materie criminali, inv. 132, mazzo 2: no. 1, 3

Geneva, inv. 11, categoria 12: mazzo 1 (folder 1), 2 (folder 4)
Pubblica Sanità inv. 74, categoria 2a, mazzo 1: folder 1, 5bis

Primary sources, published

Alvarus, M. E., *Petit recueil des remedes pour se preserver, guerir, & nettoyer en temps de peste* (Toulouse: R. Colomiez, 1628)

——*Sommaire des remedes tant preservatifs que curatifs de la peste* (Toulouse: widow of I. Colomiez, 1628)

Anon., *Aspetti dell' società lombarda in età spagnola, Archivio di stato di Milano* (Como, 1985)

——*Errores Gazariorum* (1450), in J. Hansen, *Quellen und Untersuchungen zur Geschichte des Hexenwahns und der Hexenverfolgung im Mittelalter* (Heidelsheim, 1963): 118–22

Aubert, J., *Traite contenant les causes, la curation, & preservation de la peste* (Lausanne: J. le Preux, 1571)

Barthel, P., Scheurer, R. and Stauffer, R., and eds, *Actes du Colloque Guillaume Farel* (Neuchâtel, 1983)

Bon, Henri, *Essai historique sur les épidémies en Bourgogne* (Dijon: P. Berthier, n.d.). ACC, G4267

Borromeo, Frederico, *La Peste di Milano (De pestilentia)*, ed. Armando Torno (Milan, 1987)

Beza, Theodore, *Epistularum theologicarum Theodori Bezae* (Geneva: Eustathium Vignon, 1575)

Chandelle, M., *Petit traicte et familiar de la peste* (Geneva: E. Gamonet, 1615)

Chesne, J. du, *Pestis Alexicacus* (Leipzig: T. Schurerus & B. Voigt, 1609)

Fabri, C., *Les Contrepoissons et experiences certaines contre la peste* (Paris: N. Chesneau, 1580)

Farinelli, G. and Paccagnini, E., eds, *Processi agli Untori* (Milan, 1988)

Gourmelen, E., *Advertisement et conseil a messieurs de Paris* (Paris: N. Chesneau, 1581, first published in 1567)

Grevin, J., *De Venenis libro duo* (Antwerp: C. Plantin, 1571)

——*Deux livres des venins* (Antwerp: C. Plantin, 1568)

Hovel, N., *Traicte de la Peste* (Paris: G. de Pré, 1573)

Lampugnano, Agostino, *La pestilenza seguita in Milano l'anno 1630* (Milan: Carlo Ferrandi, 1634)

Marsilia, H. de, *Grassea insignis commentarius* (Lyon: Bonhome, 1543)

Paré, A., *Les Oeuures* (Paris: G. Buon, 1579)

——*Opera Chirurgica XXI, De peste* (Frankfurt: J. Feyrabend, 1594)

——*The Collected Works*, trans. Thomas Johnson (facsimile reprint of London: Cotes & Young, 1634; New York, 1968)

Pobel-Prost, Nelly, *Délinquant et Criminalité dans la Baronnie de Marboz aux XVIIe et XVIIIe siècles* (Mém. d'histoire moderne), ADA, T509

Ripamonti, Joseph, *Chronistae urbis Mediolani de peste quae fuit anno 1630* (Milan: C. Bassanu, 1641)

Rivoire, E., van Berchem, V. *et al.*, eds, *Registres du Conseil de Genève* (Geneva: Kündig, 1900–40), thirteen volumes

Rubys, Claude de, *Discours sur la contagion de la peste qui esté ceste present annee en la ville de Lyon* (Lyon: J. d'Ogerolles, 1577). BML, Côté 354 363

——*Oraison prononcee a Lyon a la creation des conseilliers et eschevins . . . 21 de Decembre 1567* (Lyon: Michel Jove, 1568). ADR, fonds Galle, D51

Sarrasin, J. A., *De peste commentarius* (Lyon: L. Cloquemin, 1572)

Tadino, Alessandro, *Raguaglio dell'origine et giornali successi della gran Peste* (Milan: F. Ghisolfi, 1648)

Textor, Benoit, *De la maniere à preserver de la Pestilance* (Lyon: Tournes & Gazeau, 1551)

Secondary sources

Ahokas, J., 'Essai d'un glossaire genévois d'après les registres du Conseil de la ville de 1409 à 1536', *Mémoires de la Société néophilologique de Helsinki* 22 (1959): 228–41

Alsop, J. D., 'Some Notes on Seventeenth Century Continental Hospitals', *British Library Journal* 7: 1 (1981): 70–5

Anon., 'The plague plots of Geneva', *British Medical Journal: Nova et Vetera* 2 (1907): 99–100

Appleby, A. B., 'Epidemics and Famine in the Little Ice Age', *Journal of Interdisciplinary History* 10: 4 (1980): 643–63

——'The Disappearance of Plague: a Continuing Puzzle', *Economic History Review* 33: 2, pp. (1981)

Arrizabalaga, J., Henderson, J., and French, R. K., *The Great Pox: The French Disease in Renaissance Europe* (New Haven CT, 1997)

Astarita, T., *Village Justice: Community, Family and Popular Culture in Early Modern Italy* (Baltimore MD, 1999)

Audisio, G., 'How to detect a Clandestine Minority: The Example of the Waldenses', *SCJ* 21: 2 (1990): 205–16

Babel, A., *Histoire économique de Genève des origines au début du XVIe siècle* (Geneva, 1963)

Baldwin, M. R., 'Toads and Plague: Amulet Theory in Seventeenth Century Medicine', *Bulletin of the Society for the History of Medicine* 67: 2 (1993): 227–47

Barker, R., 'The Local Study of Plague', *Local Historian* 14 (1980–81): 332–46

Baroja, J. C., 'Witchcraft amongst the German and Slavonic Peoples', in M. Marwick, ed., *Witchcraft and Sorcery* (London, 1982), pp. 98–100

Barolsky, P., 'Cellini, Vasari and the Marvels of Malady', *SCJ* 24: 1 (1993): 41–5

Barstow, A. L., *Witchcraze: A new History of the European Witch Hunts* (San Francisco, 1994)

Basing, P. and Rhodes, D. E., 'English Plague Regulations and Italian Models: Printed and Manuscript Items in the Yelverton Collection', *British Library Journal* 23 (1997): 60–7

Bátori, I., 'Daily Life and Culture of an Urban Elite: The Imperial City of Nördlingen in the Fifteenth and Sixteenth Century', *History of European Ideas* 11 (1989): 621–7

Bergier, J. F., 'Marchands italiens à Genève au debut du XVIe siècle (1480–1540), in *Studi in onore di Armando Sapori* (Milan, 1957), pp. 889–91

——*Genève et l'économie européenne de la Renaissance* (Geneva, 1963)

——'Salaires des pasteurs de Genève au XVIe siècle', in *Mélanges d'histoire du XVIe siècle offerts à Henri Meylan*, Bibliothèque historique vaudoise 43 (Lausanne, 1970)

Bernard, F., *Histoire de Montmélian* (Chambéry, 1956)

Besozzi, L., *Le magistrature cittadine milanesi e la peste del 1576–1577* (Bologna, 1988)

Biagioli, M., 'The Social Status of Italian Mathematicians, 1450–1600', *History of Science* 27 (1989): 41–95

Blamires, A., Pratt, K. and Marx, C. W., eds, *Woman Defamed and Woman Defended: An Anthology of Medieval Texts* (Oxford, 1992)

Bowsky, W. M., 'The Impact of the Black Death upon Sienese Government and Society', *Speculum* 39: 1 (1964): 1–34

Boyve, J., *Annales historiques du comté de Neuchâtel et Valangin* (Neuchâtel, 1854–58), five volumes

Briggs, R., 'Women as Victims? Witches, Judges and the Community', *French History* 5: 4 (1991): 438–50

——*Witches and Neighbours: The Social and Cultural Context of European Witchcraft* (London, 1996)

Brockliss, L. W. B., and Jones, C., *The Medical World of Early Modern France* (Oxford, 1997)

Brodman, J. W., *Charity and Welfare: Hospitals and the Poor in Medieval Catalonia* (Philadelphia, 1998)

Brody, S. N., *The Disease of the Soul: Leprosy in Medieval Literature* (Ithaca NY, 1974)

Brucker, G. A., 'Bureaucracy and Social Welfare in the Renaissance: A Florentine Case Study', *Journal of Modern History* 55: 1 (1983): 1–21

——*Renaissance Florence: Society, Culture, and Religion* (Goldbach, 1994)

Bruni, R., *Le Pays d'Apt malade de la peste* (Aix-en-Provence, 1963)

Bruyn, L. de, *Woman and the Devil in Sixteenth Century Literature* (Tisbury, 1979)

Buhler, S. M., 'Marsilio Ficino's *De Stella Magorum* and Renaissance Views of the Magi', *Renaissance Quarterly* 43 (1990): 348–71

Burgy, F. M., *Les Semeurs de peste : procès d'engraisseurs à Genéve, 1545* (Mémoire de licence, 1982; AEG, Manuscrit historique, 252/241)

Burnier, E., *Histoire du Sénat de Savoie et des autres compagnies judiciaires* (Paris, 1864–65), two volumes

Carmichael, A. G., *Plague and the Poor in Renaissance Florence* (Cambridge, 1986)

——'Contagion Theory and Contagion Practice in Fifteenth-Century Milan', *Renaissance Quarterly* 64: 2 (1991): 213–56

Chabloz, F., *Les Sorcières neuchâteloises* (Neuchâtel, 1868)

Chaponnière, J. J. and Sordet L., 'Les hôpitaux de Genève avant la Réformation', *MDG*, 3 (Geneva, 1844): 165–471

Chevalier, L., *Recherches sur la réception du droit romain en Savoie* (Annecy, 1953)

Chizy, M. C. de, *Deux ans de peste à Chalon-sur-Saône* (Chalon, 1879)

Chrisman, M. U., 'From Polemic to Propaganda: The Development of Mass Persuasion in the late Sixteenth Century', *ARG* 73 (1982): 175–96

Cipolla, C. M., *Faith, Reason, and the Plague: A Tuscan Study of the Seventeenth Century* (Brighton, 1979)

——*Fighting the Plague in Seventeenth Century Italy* (Madison WI, 1981)

Clark, G., 'London's First Evacuees: A Population Study of Nursing Children', *Local Historian* 19 (1989): 100–6

Clark, S., 'The "Gendering" of Witchcraft in French Demonology: Misogyny or Polarity?' *French History* 5: 4 (1991): 426–37

——*Thinking with Demons* (Oxford, 1999).

Cohn, S., 'Criminality and the State in Renaissance Florence, 1344–1466', *Journal of Social History* (1980): 211–33

Collard, F., '*Horrendum Scelus:* recherches sur le statut juridique du crime d'empoisonnement au Moyen Age', *Revue historique* 122 (1998): 737–63

Conrad, L. I., 'Epidemic Disease in Formal and Popular Thought in early Islamic Society', in T. Ranger and P. Slack, eds, *Epidemics and Ideas* (Cambridge, 1992), pp. 77–99

Cook, H. J., 'The Society of Chemical Physicians, the New Philosophy, and the Restoration Court', *Bulletin of the Society of the History of Medicine* 61 (1987): 61–77

——Policing the Health of London: the College of Physicians and the early Stuart Monarchy', *Social History of Medicine* 2: 1 (1989): 1–34

Corbaz, A., *Un coin de terre genévoise* (Geneva, 1916)

Cordero, F., *La fabbrica della peste* (Rome, 1985)

Cornaz, E., 'Le diacre Antoine Royet et son traité de la peste, publié en 1583', *Musée Neuchatelois* (1901): 109–18

Cox, E. L., *The Green Count of Savoy: Amadeus VI and Transalpine Savoy in the Fourteenth Century* (Princeton NJ, 1967)

Crouzet, D., *Les Guerriers de Dieu* (Champ Vallon, 1990), two volumes

Cuvillier, J. P., 'Economic Change, Taxation and Social Mobility in German Towns in the late Middle Ages', *Journal of European Economic History* 15: 3 (1986): 535–48

D'Amico, J. F., 'Beatus Rhenanus, Tertullian and the Reformation: A Humanist's Critique of Scholasticism', *ARG* 71 (1980): 37–63

Davies, J., 'Persecution and Protestantism: Toulouse, 1562–75', *History Journal* 22: 1 (1979): 31–51

Davis, N. Z., 'The Reasons of Misrule: Youth Groups and *Charivaris* in Sixteenth Century France', *P&P* 50 (1971): 41–75

——'The Sacred and the Body Social in Sixteenth Century Lyon', *P&P* 90 (1981): 40–90

Debus, A. G., *The French Paracelsians* (Cambridge, 1991)

Derwa, M., 'L'influence de l'ésprit irénique sur le contenu doctrinal de la pensée de Castellion', *Revue belge de philologie et d'histoire* 58: 2 (1980): 355–81

Desan, P., 'Nationalism and History in France during the Renaissance', *Rinascimento* 24: 261–88

Devos, R. and Grosperrin, B., 'La Savoie de la Réforme à la Révolution française', in J. P. Laguay, ed., *Histoire de la Savoie* (Rennes, 1985), three volumes

Dobbie, B. M. W., 'An Attempt to estimate the True Rate of Maternal Mortality, Sixteenth to Eighteenth Centuries', *Medical History* 26 (1982): 79–90

Dobson, M. J., *Contours of Death and Disease in Early Modern England* (Cambridge, 1997)

Dols, M. W., *Medieval Islamic Medicine* (London, 1984)

Doumergue, E., *Jean Calvin* (Geneva, 1899), seven volumes.

Dubois, E., *Histoire des hospices de Bourg* (Bourg, 1932)

Dubois, H., 'Peste noire et viticulture en Bourgogne et en Chablais', in *Mélanges offerts à Edouard Perroy* (Paris, n.d.), pp. 428–38 [ACC, G4267]

Dubrow, H., 'Paracelsian Medicine in *Volpone*', *Durham University Journal* 77: 2 (1985): 175–7

Ducis, C. A., 'Hôpital des pestiférés', *Revue Savoisienne* 13: 7 (25 July 1872): 57–8

——'L'Hôpital morbeaux ou des pestiférées', *Revue Savoisienne* 13: 8 (25 August 1872): 65–6

——'L'Hôpital morbeaux de la Culaz', *Revue Savoisienne* 13: 9 (25 September 1872): 72–4

——'Henri de Savoie et Anne de Lorraine', *Revue Savoisienne* 23: 5 (21 May 1882): 37–9

——'Charles-Emmanuel de Savoie, Duc de Genevois et de Némours', *Revue Savoisienne* 23: 7 (30 July 1882): 53–4

Dunant, É., *Les Relations politiques de Genève avec Berne et les Suisses* (Geneva, 1894)

Duval, C., 'Procès de sorciers à Viry : bailliage de Ternier de 1534–48', *Bulletin de l'Institut national genevois* 24 (1882): 297–515

Eamon, W., 'Science and Popular Culture in Sixteenth Century Italy: The "Professors of Secrets" and their Books', *SCJ* 16: 4 (1985): 471–85

Edgerton, S. Y., 'Icons of Justice', *P&P* 89 (1980): 23–38

Ell, S. R., 'Iron in two Seventeenth Century Plague Epidemics', *Journal of Interdisciplinary History* 15:3 (1985): 445–57

Evans-Pritchard, E. E., 'Sorcery and Native Opinion', in M. Marwick, ed., *Witchcraft and Sorcery* (London, 1982), 23–8

Famiglietti, R. C., *Tales of the Marriage Bed from Medieval France* (Providence RI, 1992)

Favrat, L., ed., *Glossaire du patois de la Suisse romande* (Lausanne, 1866)

Fleischer, M. P., '"Are Women Human?" The Debate of 1595 between Valens Acidalius and Simon Gediccus', *SCJ* 12: 2 (1981): 107–20

Forster, E., 'From the Patient's Point of View: Illness and health in the Letters of Lisolette von der Pfalz (1652–1722)', *Bulletin of the Society for the History of Medicine* 60: 3 (1986): 297–320

Fortune, R. F., 'Sorcerers of Dobu', in M. Marwick, ed., *Witchcraft and Sorcery* (London, 1982), pp. 102–7

French, R. K., *Medicine from the Black Death to the French Disease* (Aldershot, 1998)

Friedrichs, C. R., *Urban Politics in early modern Europe* (London, 2000)

Gascon, R., *Grand commerce et vie urbaine au XVIe siècle : Lyon et ses marchands* (Paris, 1971), two volumes

Gautier, J. A., *Familles genevoises d'origine italienne* (Bari, 1893)

——*Histoire de Genève* (Geneva, 1896), nine volumes

Gautier, L., 'La dernière peste de Genève', *MDG* 23 (1888–94): 1–61

Gennep, A. van, *La Savoie* (Voreppe, 1991)

Gentilcore, D., *Healers and Healing in Early Modern Italy* (Manchester, 1998)

Ginzburg, C., *Night Battles* (London, 1992)

Goldberg, P. J. P., 'Mortality and Economic Change in the Diocese of York, 1390–1514', *Northern History* 29 (1988): 38–55

Gonthier, J. F., 'La peste à Annecy en 1629–30', *Revue savoisienne* 37 (1896): 170–2

Gordon, B. and Marshall, P., eds *Place of the Dead: Death and Remembrance in Late Medieval and Early Modern Europe* (Cambridge, 2000)

Gottfried, R. S., 'English Medical Practitioners, 1340–1530', *Bulletin of Medical History* 58 (1984): 164–82

Grell, O. P., 'Plague in Elizabethan and Stuart London: The Dutch Response', *Medical History* 34 (1990): 424–39

——'Conflicting Duties: Plague and the Obligations of Early Modern Physicians towards Patients and Commonwealth in England and the Netherlands', *Clio Medica* 24 (1993): 131–52

Gros, A., *Histoire de Maurienne* (Chambéry, 1946)

Hall, W. G., 'A Country General Practitioner at work in Somerset, 1686–1706: John Westover of Wedmore', *Local Historian* 20 (1990): 173–86

Hallman, B. M., 'Italian "Natural Superiority" and the Lutheran Question, 1517–46', *ARG* 71 (1980): 134–48

Hardin, J., 'Johann Christoph Ettner: Physician, Novelist, and Alchemist', *Daphnis* 19: 1 (1990): 135–59

Harlay, D., 'The Beginnings of the Tobacco Controversy: Puritanism, James I, and the Royal Physicians', *Bulletin of Medical History* 67 (1993): 28–50

Hatje, F., *Leben und Sterben in Zeitalter der Pest. Basel in 15. bis 17. Jahrhundert* (Basle, 1992)

Headley, J. M., 'Gattinara, Erasmus, and the Imperial Configurations of Humanism', *ARG* 71 (1980): 64–98

Henderson, J., 'The Parish and the Poor in Florence at the Time of the Black Death: The Case of S. Frediano', *Continuity and Change* 3: 2 (1988): 247–72

Herlihy, D. and Cohn, S., *The Black Death and the Transformation of the West* (Cambridge, 1997)

Hillman, D. and Mazzio, C., eds, *The Body in Parts: Fantasies of Corporeality in early modern Europe* (New York, 1997)

Hochstadt, S., 'Migration in Pre-industrial Germany', *Central European History* 16: 3 (1983): 195–224

Hoffman, M., 'Faith and Piety in Erasmus' Thought', *SCJ* 20: 2 (1989): 241–58

Hoffman, P. T., *Church and Community in the Diocese of Lyon, 1500–1789* (New Haven CT, 1984)

——'Land Rent and Agricultural Productivity: The Paris Basin, 1450–1789', *Journal of Economic History* 51: 4 (1991): 771–805

Hopkins, D. R., *Princes and Peasants: Smallpox in History* (Chicago, 1983)

Horden, P., 'Disease, Dragons and Saints: The Management of Epidemics in the Dark Ages', in T. Ranger and P. Slack, eds, *Epidemics and Ideas* (Cambridge, 1992), pp. 45–76

Hughes, D. O., 'Distinguishing Signs: Ear-rings, Jews and Franciscan Rhetoric in the Italian Renaissance City', *P&P* 112 (1986): 3–59

Hults, L. C., 'Baldung's *Bewitched Groom* Revisited: Artistic Temperament, Fantasy and the "Dream of Reason"', *SCJ* 15: 3 (1984): 259–79

——'Baldung and the Witches of Freiburg: The Evidence of Images', *Journal of Interdisciplinary History* 18: 2 (1987): 249–76

Innes, W. C., *Social Concern in Calvin's Geneva* (Allison Park PA, 1983)

Jones, N. L., *The Birth of the Elizabethan Age* (Oxford, 1993)

Joubert, L., *Popular Errors*, trans. G. D. de Rocher (London, 1989)

Jütte, R., 'Ageing and Body Image in the Sixteenth Century: Hermann Weinsberg's (1518–97) Perception of the Ageing Body', *European History Quarterly* 18: 3 (1988): 259–90

——*Poverty and Deviance in Early Modern Europe* (Cambridge, 1994)

Kamen, H., *Inquisition and Society in Spain* (London, 1985)

Karant-Nunn, S. C., 'Continuity and Change: Some Effects of the Reformation on the Women of Zwickau', *SCJ* 13: 2 (1982): 17–41

Keefer, M. H., 'Agrippa's Dilemma: Hermetic "Rebirth" and the Ambivalence of *De Vanitate* and *De Occulta Philosophia*', *Renaissance Quarterly* 41 (1988): 614–53

Kelly, J., 'Early Feminist Theory and the *Querelle des Femmes*, 1400–1789', *Signs* 8: 1 (1982): 4–28

Kempshall, M. S., *The Common Good in late medieval Political Thought* (Oxford, 1999)

Kingdon, R. M., 'The First Calvinist Divorce', in R. A. Mentzer, ed., *Sin and the Calvinists: Morals, Control and the Consistory in the Reformed Tradition* (Kirksville MO, 1994), pp. 1–14

Klaits, J., *Servants of Satan: The Age of the Witch Hunts* (Bloomington IN, 1985)

Koslofsky, C. M., *The Reformation of the Dead: Death and Ritual in Early Modern Europe, 1450–1700* (Basingstoke, 2000)

Kroon, M. de, 'Martin Bucer and the Problem of Tolerance', *SCJ* 19: 2 (1988): 157–68

Küpfer, E., *Morges dans le passé : la période bernoise* (Lausanne, 1944)

Ladame, P., 'Les Mandragores ou diables familiers à Genéve au XVIe et au XVIIe siècle', *MDG* 23 (1888–94): 237–81

Ladurie, E. le Roy, *Jasmin's Witch*, trans. B. Pearce (Aldershot, 1987)

Langbein, J. H., *Prosecuting Crime in the Renaissance* (Cambridge MA, 1974)

——*Torture and the Law of Proof* (Chicago, 1977)

Lavorel, J. M., *Cluses et le Faucigny* (Annecy, 1888)

Law, J. E., *Venice and the Veneto in the Early Renaissance* (Aldershot, 1994)

Lescaze, B., 'Crimes et criminels à Genève en 1572', in *Pour une histoire qualitative: études offertes à Sven Stelling-Michaud* (Geneva, 1975), pp. 45–71

——*Sauver l'âme, nourrir le corps* (Geneva, 1985)

Letonnelier, G., 'Mesures prises pour éviter la peste, à Annecy, en 1503', *Revue savoisienne* 52 (1911): 44–8

Levack, B. P., *The Witch Hunt in early modern Europe* (Harlow, 1987)

Lindemann, M., *Medicine and Society in Early Modern Europe* (Cambridge, 1999)

Lingo, A. K., 'Empirics and Charlatans in Early Modern France: The Genesis of the Classification of the "Other" in Medical Practice', *Journal of Social History* 19 (1986): 583–604

Lucenet, M., *Lyon malade de la peste* (Palaiseau, 1981)

Macfarlane, A., 'Definitions of Witchcraft', in M. Marwick, ed., *Witchcraft and Sorcery* (London, 1982), pp. 44–7

Mack, A., *In Time of Plague: The History and Social Consequences of lethal Epidemic Disease* (New York, 1991)

Martensen, R. L., '"Habit of Reason": Anatomy and Anglicanism in Restoration England', *Bulletin of the Society for the History of Medicine* 66: 4 (1992): 511–35

Martin, A. L., *Plague? Jesuit Accounts of Epidemic Disease in the Sixteenth Century* (Kirksville MO, 1996)

Martin, R., *Witchcraft and the Inquisition in Venice, 1550–1650* (Oxford, 1989)

Mathers, C. J., 'Family Partnerships and International Trade in Early Modern Europe: Merchants from Burgos in England and France, 1470–1575', *Business History Review* 62 (1988): 367–97

Maxcey, C. E., 'Why do good? Dietenberger's Reply to Luther', *ARG* 75 (1984): 93–112

Maxwell-Stuart, P. G., ed. and trans., *Martín del Rio: Investigations into Magic* (Manchester, 2000).

Mayer, C. A., *Clémont Marot* (Paris, 1972)

McIntosh, M. K., 'Local Responses to the Poor in Late Medieval and Tudor England', *Continuity and Change* 3: 2 (1988): 209–45

Mentzer, R. A., 'Organizational Endeavour and Charitable Impulse in Sixteenth Century France: The Case of Protestant Nîmes', *French History* 5: 1 (1991): 1–29

Messerli, M., *Le Médecin vaudois à travers les âges* (Lausanne, 1929)

Middleton, W. E. K., 'An Unpublished Letter from Marcello Malpighi', *Bulletin of the Society for the History of Medicine* 59 (1985): 105–8

Midelfort, H. C. E., *Witch Hunting in South-western Germany, 1562–1684: The Social and Intellectual Foundations* (Stanford CA, 1972)

Monter, E. W., 'Inflation and Witchcraft: The Case of Jean Bodin', in T. K. Rabb and J. E. Seigel, eds, *Action and Conviction in Early Modern Europe* (Princeton NJ, 1969), pp. 371–89

——'Witchcraft in Geneva, 1537–1662', *Journal of Modern History* 43: 2 (1971): 179–204

——*Witchcraft in France and Switzerland: The Borderlands during the Reform* (Ithaca NY, 1976)

——'The Consistory of Geneva, 1559–69', *Bibliothèque d'humanisme et renaissance* 138 (1976): 469–84)

——*Ritual, Myth and Magic in Early Modern Europe* (Columbus OH, 1983)

Moran, B. T., 'Christoph Rothmann, the Copernican Theory, and Institutional and Technical Influences on the Criticism of Aristotelian Cosmology', *SCJ* 13: 3 (1982): 85–108

Moran, J. A. H., 'Clerical Recruitment in the Diocese of York, 1340–1530: Data and Commentary', *Journal of Ecclesiastical History* 34: 1 (1983): 19–54

Murphy, T. D., 'The Transformation of Traditional Medical Culture under the Old Regime', *Historical Reflections* 16 (1989): 307–50

Murray, J., 'Agnolo Firenzuola on Female Sexuality and Women's Equality', *SCJ* 22: 2 (1991): 199–213

Naphy, W. G. and Spicer, A., *The Black Death and the History of Plagues, 1345–1730* (Stroud, 2000)

Naphy, W. G., 'The Renovation of the Ministry in Calvin's Geneva', in A. Pettegree, ed., *The Reformation of the Parishes: The Ministry and the Reformation in Town and Country* (Manchester, 1993), pp. 113–32

——*Calvin and the Consolidation of the Genevan Reformation* (Manchester, 1994)

——'Calvin's Letters: Reflections on their Usefulness in studying Genevan History', *ARG*, 86 (1995): 78–86

——'The Reformation and the Evolution of Geneva's Schools' in B. Kümin, ed., *Reformations Old and New: Essays on the Socio-economic Impact of Religious Change, c. 1470–1630* (Aldershot, 1996), pp. 185–202

——'The Price of Liberty: Genevan Security and Defence Spending, 1535–55', *War in History* 5: 4 (1998): 379–99

——'Genevan Diplomacy and Foreign Policy, *c.* 1535–60: Balancing on the Edge of the Confederacy', in W. Kaiser, C. Sieber-Lehmann and C. Windler, eds, *Eidgenössische «Grenzfälle»: Mülhausen und Genf/En marge de la Confédération: Mulhouse et Genève* (Basle, 2000), pp. 189–219

Neuschel, K. B., *Word of Honor: Interpreting Noble Culture in Sixteenth Century France* (London, 1989)

Olivier, E., *Médecine et santé dans le Pays de Vaud*, Bibliothèque historique vaudoise 29 (Lausanne, 1962)

Olson, J. E., *Calvin and Social Welfare: Deacons and the Bourse Française* (Selinsgrove, PA, 1989)

Park, K. and Daston, L. J., 'Unnatural Conceptions: The Study of Monsters in Sixteenth and Seventeenth Century France and England', *P&P* 92 (1981): 20–54

Pastor, L. von, *History of the Popes from the Close of the Middle Ages* (London, 1891–1941), thirty-five volumes

Pastore, A., 'Note su criminalità e giustizia in tempo di peste: Bologna e Ginevra fra '500 e '600', in A. Pastore, ed., *Città italiane del '500 tra Riforma e Controriforma* (Lucca, 1988), pp. 31–43

Pearl, J. L., 'French Catholic Demonologists and their Enemies in the late Sixteenth and early Seventeenth Centuries', *Church History* 52 (1983): 457–67

Pelling, M., 'Healing the Sick Poor: Social Policy and Disability in Norwich, 1550–1640', *Medical History* 29 (1985): 115–37

——*The Common Lot: Sickness, Medical Occupations and the Urban Poor in Early Modern England* (London, 1998)

Perkins, W., *Midwifery and Medicine in Early Modern France: Louise Bourgeois* (Exeter, 1996)

Perrin, A., *Histoire de la Vallée et du Prieuré de Chamonix* (Chambéry, 1887)

Pfister, O., *Das Christentum und die Angst* (Zürich, 1944)

——*Calvins Eingreifen in die Hexer- und Hexenprozesse von Peney 1545 nach seiner Bedeutungen für Geschichte und Gegenwart* (Zürich, 1947)

Philippe D., 'Aux sources de l'univers magico-religieux martiniquais: esclavage et phobie des sorciers', *Cahiers d'Histoire* 41: 1 (1996): 61–76

Piaget, A, 'Une lettre de Benoît Tixier aux Quatre Ministraux', *Musée Neuchatelois* (1920): 134–5

Picot, J., *Histoire de Genève* (Geneva, 1811), three volumes

Pictet de Sergey, A. J. P., *Genève, origine et développement de cette république* (Geneva, 1847), two volumes

Pierrehumbert, W., ed., *Dictionnaire historique du parler Neuchâtelois et Suisse romande* (Neuchâtel, 1926)

Platt, C., *King Death: The Black Death and its Aftermath in Late Medieval England* (London, 1996)

Pomata, G., *Contracting a Cure: Patients, Healers, and the Law in Early Modern Bologna* (Baltimore MD, 1998)

Potter, D., 'Marriage and Cruelty among the Protestant Nobility in Sixteenth Century France: Diane de Barbançon and Jean de Rohan, 1561–67', *European History Quarterly* 20: 1 (1990): 1–38

Pullan, B., 'Support and Redeem: Charity and Poor Relief in Italian Cities from the Fourteenth to the Seventeenth Century', *Continuity and Change* 3: 2 (1988): 177–208

——*Poverty and Charity: Europe, Italy and Venice, 1400–1700* (Aldershot, 1994)

Purkiss, D., *The Witch in History* (London, 1996)

Quiquerez, A., 'Les sorciers du Val-de-Ruz et de la Neuveville', *Musée Neuchatelois* (1867): 4–13

Remer, G., 'Rhetoric and the Erasmian Defence of Religious Toleration', *History of Political Thought* 10: 3 (1989): 377–403

Roberts, A., 'The Plague in England', *History Today* 30: 29–34

Roget, A., *Les Suisses et Genève* (Geneva, 1864), four volumes

Roper, L., 'Will and Honour: Sex, Words and Power in Augsburg Criminal Trials', *Radical History Review* 43 (1989): 45–71

——*Oedipus and the Devil: Witchcraft, Sexuality and Religion in Early Modern Europe* (London, 1994)

Rothkrug, L., 'Holy Shrines, Religious Dissonance and Satan in the Origins of the German Reformation', *Historical Reflections* 14: 2 (1987): 143–286

Rowan, S., 'Imperial Taxes and German Politics in the Fifteenth Century: An Outline', *Central European History* 13: 3 (1980): 203–18

Rublack, U., *The Crimes of Women in Early Modern Germany* (Oxford, 1999)

Rushton, P., 'Lunatics and Idiots: Mental Disability, the Community, and the Poor Law in North-east England, 1600–1800', *Medical History* 32 (1988): 34–50

Russell, J. B., *Witchcraft in the Middle Ages* (London, 1972)

Russell, P. A., 'Syphilis: God's Scourge or Nature's Vengeance?' *ARG* 80 (1989): 286–306

Schapera, I., 'Sorcery and Witchcraft in Bechuanaland [Botswana]', in M. Marwick, ed., *Witchcraft and Sorcery* (London, 1982), pp. 108–18

Schatzmiller, J., *Jews, Medicine, and Medieval Society* (Berkeley CA, 1994)

Scheurer, R., 'Farel et les Neuchâtelois de juillet à septembre 1530', in P. Barthel, R. Scheurer and R. Stauffer, eds, *Actes du Colloque Guillaume Farel* (Neuchâtel, 1983), vol. 1 (of two), pp. 83–7.

Seiler, R., *Zur Ikonographie der religiösen Pestdenkmäler des Kantons Graubünden* (Zürich, 1985)

Sella, D., 'Coping with Famine: The changing Demography of an Italian Village in the 1590s', *SCJ* 22: 2 (1991): 185–97

Siraisi, N. G., *Medieval and Renaissance Medicine: An Introduction to Knowledge and Practice* (Chicago, 1990)

——'Girolamo Cardano and the Art of Medical Narrative', *Journal of the History of Ideas* 52: 4 (1991): 581–602

Slack, P., *The Impact of Plague on Tudor and Stuart England* (Oxford, 1990)

Spon, J., *Histoire de Genève* (Geneva: Fabri & Barrillot, 1730; reprinted Geneva, 1976), two volumes

Steel, D., 'Plague Writing: From Boccaccio to Camus', *Journal of European Studies* 11 (1981): 88–110

Stromer, W. von, 'Commercial Policy and Economic Conjuncture in Nuremberg at the close of the Middle Ages: a Model of Economic Policy', *Journal of European Economic History* 10: 1 (1981): 119–29

Stuart, K., *Defiled Trades and Social Outcasts: Honor and Ritual Pollution in Early Modern Germany* (Cambridge, 1999)

Taylor, J., 'Plague in the Towns of Hampshire: The Epidemic of 1665–66', *Southern History* 6 (1984): 104–22

Terpstra, N., 'Piety and Punishment: The Lay *Conforteria* and Civic Justice in Sixteenth Century Bologna', *SCJ* 22: 4 (1991): 679–94

Thomas, K., *Religion and the Decline of Magic: Studies in Popular Beliefs in Sixteenth and Seventeenth Century England* (London, 1971)

Thorndike, L., *A History of Magic and Experimental Science* (New York, 1923–58), eight volumes

Thourel, A., *Histoire de Genève* (Geneva, 1833), three volumes

Traister, B. H., '"Matrix and the Pain Thereof": a Sixteenth Century Gynaecological Essay', *Medical History* 35 (1991): 436–51

Trevor-Roper, H., *The European Witch Craze of the sixteenth and seventeenth Centuries* (London, 1969)

Turchetti, M., 'Religious Concord and Political Tolerance in Sixteenth Century and Seventeenth Century France', *SCJ* 22: 1 (1991): 15–25

——'Une question mal posée: Érasme et la tolérance. L'idée de *sygkatabasis*', *Bibliothèque d'humanisme et renaissance* 53 (2001): 379–95

Ungerer, G., 'George Baker: Translator of Aparicio de Zubia's Pamphlet on the *Oleum Magistrale*', *Medical History* 30 (1986): 203–11

Vaucher, P., *Luttes de Genève contre la Savoie (1517–1530)* (Geneva, 1889)

Vaullet, A., *Histoire de la ville De la Roche* (Annecy, 1874)

Walker, A. M., and Dickerman, E. H., '"A Woman under the Influence": a Case of Alleged Possession in Sixteenth-Century France', *SCJ* 22: 3 (Fall, 1991): 535–54

Wear, A., *Healers and Healing in Early Modern England* (Aldershot, 1998)

Weaver, F. E., 'Women and Religion in Early Modern France', *Catholic Historical Review* 67: 1 (1981): 50–9

Weissman, R. F. E. 'Brothers and Strangers: Confraternal Charity in Renaissance Florence', *Historical Reflections* 15: 1 (1988): 27–45

Welch, E. S., *Art and Authority in Renaissance Milan* (New Haven CT, 1995)

Wensky, M., 'Women's Guilds in Cologne in the Later Middle Ages', *Journal of European Economic History* 11: 3 (1982): 631–50

Westman, R. S., 'The Astronomer's Role in the Sixteenth Century: A Preliminary Study', *History of Science* 28 (1980): 105–47

White, R., 'Castellio against Calvin: The Turk in the Toleration Controversy of the Sixteenth Century', *Bibliothèque d'humanisme et renaissance* 46 (1984): 573–86

Wiesner, M. E., 'Wandervogels and Women: Journeymen's Concepts of Masculinity in Early Modern Germany', *Journal of Social History* 24: 4 (1991): 767–82

Wood, M. W., 'Paltry Peddlers or Essential Merchants? Women in the Distributive Trades in Early Modern Nuremberg', *SCJ* 12: 2 (1981): 3–13

Wright, W. J., 'A Closer Look at House Poor Relief through the Common Chest and Indigence in Sixteenth Century Hesse', *ARG* 70 (1979): 225–37

Zanotto, A., *Histoire de la vallée d'Aoste* (Aoste, 1968)

Zguta, R., 'The One-day Votive Church: A Religious Response to the Black Death in Early Russia', *Slavic Review* 40: 3 (1981): 423–32

Ziegler, P., *The Black Death* (London, 1997)

Zika, C., 'Hosts, Processions and Pilgrimages: Controlling the Sacred in Fifteenth Century Germany', *P&P* 118 (1988): 25–64

Zumthor, P., 'The Great Game of Rhetoric', *New Literary History* 12: 493–508

INDEX

Note: page numbers in **bold** refer to main entries.